$85.00

HISTORICAL DICTIONARIES OF
RELIGIONS, PHILOSOPHIES, AND MOVEMENTS

Jon Woronoff, Series Editor

1. *Buddhism*, by Charles S. Prebish, 1993
2. *Mormonism*, by Davis Bitton, 1994. *Out of print. See no. 32.*
3. *Ecumenical Christianity*, by Ans Joachim van der Bent, 1994
4. *Terrorism*, by Sean Anderson and Stephen Sloan, 1995. *Out of print. See no. 41.*
5. *Sikhism*, by W. H. McLeod, 1995. *Out of print. See no. 59.*
6. *Feminism*, by Janet K. Boles and Diane Long Hoeveler, 1995. *Out of print. See no. 52.*
7. *Olympic Movement*, by Ian Buchanan and Bill Mallon, 1995. *Out of print. See no. 39.*
8. *Methodism*, by Charles Yrigoyen Jr. and Susan E. Warrick, 1996. *Out of print. See no. 57.*
9. *Orthodox Church*, by Michael Prokurat, Alexander Golitzin, and Michael D. Peterson, 1996
10. *Organized Labor*, by James C. Docherty, 1996. *Out of print. See no. 50.*
11. *Civil Rights Movement*, by Ralph E. Luker, 1997
12. *Catholicism*, by William J. Collinge, 1997
13. *Hinduism*, by Bruce M. Sullivan, 1997
14. *North American Environmentalism*, by Edward R. Wells and Alan M. Schwartz, 1997
15. *Welfare State*, by Bent Greve, 1998. *Out of print. See no. 63.*
16. *Socialism*, by James C. Docherty, 1997. *Out of print. See no. 73.*
17. *Bahá'í Faith*, by Hugh C. Adamson and Philip Hainsworth, 1998. *Out of print. See no. 71.*
18. *Taoism*, by Julian F. Pas in cooperation with Man Kam Leung, 1998
19. *Judaism*, by Norman Solomon, 1998. *Out of print. See no. 69.*
20. *Green Movement*, by Elim Papadakis, 1998. *Out of print. See no. 80.*
21. *Nietzscheanism*, by Carol Diethe, 1999. *Out of print. See no. 75.*

Historical Dictionary of Hume's Philosophy

Kenneth R. Merrill

Historical Dictionaries of Religions,
Philosophies, and Movements, No. 86

The Scarecrow Press, Inc.
Lanham, Maryland • Toronto • Plymouth, UK
2008

SCARECROW PRESS, INC.

Published in the United States of America
by Scarecrow Press, Inc.
A wholly owned subsidary of
The Rowman & Littlefield Publishing Group, Inc.
4501 Forbes Boulevard, Suite 200, Lanham, Maryland 20706
www.scarecrowpress.com

Estover Road
Plymouth PL6 7PY
United Kingdom

British Library Cataloguing in Publication Information Available

Library of Congress Cataloging-in-Publication Data

Merrill, Kenneth R. (Kenneth Rogers), 1932–
   Historical dictionary of Hume's philosophy / Kenneth R. Merrill.
     p. cm. — (Historical dictionaries of religions, philosophies, and movements)
   Includes bibliographical references.
   ISBN-13: 978-0-8108-5361-4 (hardcover : alk. paper)
   ISBN-10: 0-8108-5361-2 (hardcover : alk. paper)
   eISBN-13: 978-0-8108-6253-1
   eISBN-10: 0-8108-6253-0
   1. Hume, David, 1711–1776—Dictionaries. I. Title.
  B1451.M47 2008
  192—dc22   2008006708

For Vanita

Contents

Editor's Foreword

David Hume is among the top contenders for the greatest philosopher—certainly one of the very best in the 18th century to write in English, although few of his contemporaries recognized his true stature. For the last century or so, his reputation has been on the rise. Indeed, it is little short of amazing that Hume's ideas should continue to exert such lively influence not only on philosophy but also religion, politics, economics, and perspectives on human nature. Of course there are detractors, but his genius shines brightly after nearly three centuries, and his views are still relevant and important today.

Studying Hume is clearly rewarding, but as with the study of any great philosopher it can sometimes be difficult—thus a handy guide such as this *Historical Dictionary of Hume's Philosophy*. It describes Hume the man, his thought, and his times and presents his major writings, concepts, and arguments, as well as the views of other philosophers who influenced him or were influenced by him. While it focuses mainly on Hume the philosopher, this dictionary does not neglect Hume the historian, essayist, economist, and diplomat. On the contrary, it shows that Hume's thought cannot be neatly divided into the philosophical and non-philosophical.

This book was written by Kenneth R. Merrill, emeritus professor of philosophy and former department chair at the University of Oklahoma, where he taught for well over four decades. He has been keenly interested in Hume ever since his doctoral work at Northwestern University, and he has lectured and written extensively on Hume and other 17th- and 18th-century philosophers. Here he provides a broad framework for integrating and understanding the profound and wide-ranging work of a truly great thinker.

Jon Woronoff
Series Editor

Preface

It is hardly necessary today to make a case for Hume's stature as a philosopher. He is, indeed, widely regarded as the greatest philosopher ever to write in the English language. It was not always so. In his own day and for most of the 19th century, Hume was seen by many as merely a negative, destructive skeptic—undoubtedly very clever, but not to be taken seriously as a philosopher. (A notable exception was the great German philosopher Immanuel Kant, who deplored the misreading of Hume's intentions and credited Hume with waking him, Kant, from his "dogmatic slumber.") Early in the 20th century, the Scottish philosopher Norman Kemp Smith argued that Hume's "skepticism" was in fact a variety of naturalism, which is directed mainly against rationalist philosophical theories and not against commonsense notions of causation, the external world, morality, and the like. Hume scholars have criticized many of Kemp Smith's specific claims, but no one doubts the key role he played in changing the way Hume is interpreted. It is a pleasure to note that Hume scholarship is flourishing today, as it has been for the past several decades. Even critics who find Hume's arguments unconvincing are generally willing to concede that his philosophy is eminently worthy of careful attention.

Hume was not just a great philosopher; he was also a great stylist. So it is surprising—even dismaying—to find that he seems to provide no clear, definitive answers to any number of important questions that he raises. Even when we allow for readers who ignore context or read carelessly (or both), and for what Hume calls "merely verbal disputes," there remain differences of opinion among able and thorough scholars about Hume's real position on several key issues. I have tried throughout this book to be faithful to Hume's own texts in describing his views. Since I provide copious references to those texts, readers may judge for themselves how well I have succeeded. For what I take to be obvious reasons, I avoid scholarly disputes about Hume. I do note from time to time that disputes exist about this or that issue, but I have sought to be evenhanded when I characterize differences of opinion among Hume scholars.

Evenhandedness is one thing; *completeness* is a different matter. Essentially, completeness is impossible. I have had to make countless decisions about what to include and what to omit—often with a pang of regret about the exclusions. Many decisions were obvious, especially about entries in the dictionary proper, but not all of them. I had no precise set of criteria for deciding, but I was guided in large measure by the character of the book. It is a *dictionary*, which means that even the longer entries are too short to include blow-by-blow accounts of scholarly disagreements. Such differences of opinion are sometimes noted, and readers may consult the bibliography for details. Moreover, it is a *historical* dictionary, which means that thinkers such as Ralph Cudworth, George Campbell, and Richard Price—not household names even in philosophical households—get an entry because they were important to Hume, because they help readers to understand Hume, or because they were part of the background against which Hume wrote. Several better-known philosophers—Descartes, Francis Hutcheson, and Kant, for example—also get entries for the same reasons. There are historical notes scattered throughout, calling attention to affinities, debts, antagonisms, etc.

This book is intended mainly for the non-specialist, but it should be a useful compendium for readers of all sorts. It is not intended to be (and in any case could not be) a substitute for reading Hume's own writings, but it should help readers—especially those new to Hume—to see the general shape of Hume's philosophy and thus understand his writings better. And it deals with a great many details of that philosophy.

Although the entries in the dictionary are as self-contained as feasible, it is obviously impossible to make them absolutely so. The aim—a difficult one to realize—has been to strike a balance between making entries self-contained and keeping repetition within practical bounds. Some entries come closer to the ideal than others. Many entries refer readers to related topics (some of them indicated by **boldface** type), which help to make the entry in question fuller and easier to understand. However, readers will find it useful to go through the introduction, basically a sketch of Hume's philosophy that appears before the dictionary proper, as a way of setting particular topics in a larger context. Further, it would be advisable for readers to look at a few basic topics in the dictionary as a background for more specific topics. I will mention a half-dozen or so.

Hume is an *empiricist*, which is to say that he seeks to base all aspects of his philosophy on experience. For Hume, experience gets cashed out primarily in terms of perceptions, especially in the more narrowly philosophical parts of his system (which constitute the major focus of this book). Accordingly, it would be helpful for readers to study the entries EXPERIENCE and PERCEPTIONS before going to other entries. The same advice applies to the entry RELATIONS OF IDEAS AND MATTERS OF FACT, which describes the two fundamental kinds of knowledge in Hume's epistemology, and to the entry CAUSE/ CAUSATION, which concerns the most important relation (by far, as Hume holds) in our knowledge of matters of fact. A few entries are of a general philosophical sort and not focused on Hume—e.g., COMMON SENSE, EMPIRICISM AND RATIONALISM, ETHICS, KNOWL- EDGE, and MIND.

It is a pleasure to express my thanks to my colleagues Ray Elugardo, James Hawthorne, and Zev Trachtenberg for sharing their expertise with me on several topics. I am especially indebted to Monte Cook, who made (literally) scores of helpful suggestions about substance and expo- sition. Hugh Benson, the chair of my department, has been unfailingly supportive of my work on this book. The series editor, Jon Woronoff, has been patient with my unmet deadlines and helpful in myriad ways. My thanks to him. I have learned more than I could ever calculate from the scores of Hume-o-philes whose works I have read or with whom I have talked about Hume. Thanks.

Finally, I dedicate this book to my wife, Vanita, in love and grati- tude.

Abbreviations and References

The most frequently cited of Hume's works are abbreviated as follows:

THN. *A Treatise of Human Nature.* Two different editions of this work (both published by Oxford University Press) are widely used nowadays: the 1978 Selby-Bigge/Nidditch edition and the 2000 Norton edition. To accommodate both sets of users, citations are made to both editions. The older one is cited first, by page number only. The newer edition is cited next, by book, part, section, and paragraph number, separated by periods, in that order. The two citations are separated by a semicolon. Thus, the notation "THN, 23; 1.1.7.13" refers to page 23 of the Selby-Bigge/Nidditch edition and to book 1, part 1, section 7, paragraph 13 of the Norton edition. Exceptions: The introduction and the abstract are not divided into parts. Consequently, citations to them in the Norton edition are to page and paragraph numbers; e.g., "5.8" means page 5, paragraph 8, and "413.25" means page 413, paragraph 25. Citations to the Selby-Bigge/Nidditch edition are not affected; i.e., they are given by page number only.

EHU. *An Enquiry Concerning Human Understanding.*

EPM. *An Enquiry Concerning the Principles of Morals.* As with the *Treatise*, there are two widely used editions of the two *Enquiries* (again, both published by Oxford). One: In the 1975 Selby-Bigge/Nidditch edition (the same editors as for THN), both *Enquiries* are printed in a single volume. Two: *An Enquiry Concerning the Principles of Morals*, edited by Tom L. Beauchamp, was published in 1998, and *An Enquiry Concerning Human Understanding*, also edited by Beauchamp, followed a year later. Citations to the Selby-Bigge/Nidditch edition are given first and are by page number only. Citations to the Beauchamp editions are by page number followed by a period and a paragraph number. The two citations are separated by a semicolon. Thus, "EPM, 218;

108.15" refers to page 218 of the Selby-Bigge/Nidditch edition and to page 108, paragraph 15 of the Beauchamp edition. Exactly the same form is used for citations to EHU.

Dialogues. *Dialogues Concerning Natural Religion*. Citations are to the Norman Kemp Smith edition, which is probably the most widely used of the several that are available.

NHR. *The Natural History of Religion*. Citations are to the H. E. Root edition, published by Stanford University Press.

Essays. *Essays Moral, Political, and Literary*. Citations are to the volume edited by Eugene F. Miller, published by Liberty*Classics*.

A Letter. *A Letter from a Gentleman to His Friend in Edinburgh*. The 1967 Edinburgh University Press version of this letter is out of print. However, it is reprinted as part of the Hackett Publishing Company edition of *An Enquiry Concerning Human Understanding*, edited by Eric Steinberg, which is the one I cite and is readily available.

History. *The History of England*. References are to the Liberty*Classics* edition.

Other abbreviations and references are as follows:

John Locke's *An Essay Concerning Human Understanding* (Peter H. Nidditch, editor) is cited as *Essay* followed by page and section numbers. Thus, "528.§9" refers to page 528, section 9.

The phrases *Old Style* and *New Style* (abbreviated O.S. and N.S.), used with dates, refer to the Julian calendar and the Gregorian calendar respectively. The more accurate Gregorian calendar was promulgated by Pope Gregory XIII in 1582 but was not adopted by Britain until 1752. Accordingly, Hume was born Old Style but died New Style.

Chronology

1603 Elizabeth I, Queen of England and the last Tudor monarch, dies. James I (who was already James VI of Scotland) accedes to the throne of England as the first Stuart monarch.

1625 James I dies and is succeeded by his eldest surviving son, who becomes Charles I.

1642–49 English civil war.

1649 Charles I is beheaded. The English Parliament abolishes the monarchy.

1649–60 Interregnum: years of the Commonwealth and the Protectorate.

1660 The monarchy is restored with the accession of Charles II, eldest surviving son of Charles I.

1685 Charles II dies. James II, younger son of Charles I and brother of Charles II, accedes to the throne.

1688 James II is deposed in the Glorious Revolution.

1689 William of Orange (William III) and Mary (William's wife and James II's daughter) are proclaimed king and queen by Parliament.

1689 John Locke's *An Essay Concerning Human Understanding* is published.

1690 Locke's *Two Treatises of Government* is published.

1694 Queen Mary dies.

1701 James II dies.

1701   The Act of Settlement establishes the line of succession to the English throne.

1702   William III dies.

1702   Anne, daughter of James II, accedes to the throne.

1707   The Act of Union, ratified by the English and Scottish Parliaments, makes England and Scotland one kingdom. The Scottish Parliament abolishes itself.

1710   George Berkeley's *A Treatise Concerning the Principles of Human Knowledge* is published.

1710   The Scottish philosopher Thomas Reid is born in Strachan, Aberdeenshire, Scotland, on 26 April (O.S.), exactly one year before Hume.

1711   David Hume is born on 26 April (O.S.) in Edinburgh, Scotland.

1712   The philosopher Jean-Jacques Rousseau is born in Geneva.

1713   George Berkeley's *Three Dialogues between Hylas and Philonous* is published.

1714   Dying without an heir, Queen Anne becomes the last Stuart monarch.

1714   Under terms of the Act of Settlement, the German Elector of Hanover, a great-grandson of James I, becomes George I, the first of the Hanoverian British monarchs.

1715   Jacobites mount an unsuccessful uprising (known as *the '15*), intended to restore the Stuart monarchy.

1723   Hume enrolls at the University of Edinburgh.

1724   The German philosopher Immanuel Kant is born.

1727   George I dies. His son accedes to the throne as George II.

1734–37   Hume sojourns in France, where he composes *A Treatise of Human Nature*.

1739   Books 1 and 2 of Hume's *A Treatise of Human Nature* are published.

1740 Book 3 of the *Treatise* is published.

1741–42 Hume's *Essays, Moral and Political*, Volumes 1 and 2, are published.

1745 Jacobites mount their most substantial uprising (known as *the '45*), marching as far south as Derby in north central England.

1745 Hume fails to secure appointment to the chair of ethics and pneumatical philosophy at the University of Edinburgh.

1746 Remnants of the Jacobite force of 1745 are hunted down and routed by the English army at Culloden Moor, near Inverness in northwest Scotland.

1748 Hume's *Philosophical Essays Concerning Human Understanding* is published. (The title was changed in 1756 to *An Enquiry Concerning Human Understanding*.)

1751 Hume's *An Enquiry Concerning the Principles of Morals* is published.

1751 Hume fails to secure appointment to the chair of logic at Glasgow University.

1752 Hume's *Political Discourses* is published.

1752–57 Hume serves as Keeper of the Advocates' Library in Edinburgh, with access to 30,000 volumes.

1754–62 Hume's *The History of England* is published in six volumes, which appear in reverse chronological order.

1757 Hume's *The Natural History of Religion* is published.

1760 George II dies. His grandson accedes to the throne as George III.

1762 The complete *History* is published in six quarto volumes, in the correct chronological order.

1763 *History* is published in eight octavo volumes.

1776 The American colonies declare their independence of Britain on 4 July (N.S.).

1776   David Hume dies on 25 August (N.S.), at the age of 65 years and four months.

1777   *The Life of David Hume, Esq., Written by Himself* is published.

1779   Hume's *Dialogues Concerning Natural Religion* is published, thanks to the efforts of his nephew, also named David.

Introduction

David Hume is a great philosopher. He is also an excellent writer. Happy the philosopher who is both, for the two kinds of excellence do not always go together. Plato is the paradigm case of the philosopher-writer: a truly great philosopher, regarded by many as the greatest who ever lived, and a writer worthy of the philosopher. Aristotle, Plato's student and chief rival for "best ever," will never be mistaken for a great writer. **Immanuel Kant**, perhaps the greatest philosopher since Aristotle, is not a good writer (some estimates are more harsh—"wretchedly bad," for example). On the other hand, the Irishman **George Berkeley** may well be the best stylist ever to write philosophy in English, but he is not Hume's equal as a philosopher. Hume may not be the greatest philosopher since Plato, or the best writer of philosophy; but who in the last 500 years outshines him in combining philosophical genius and stylistic gift?

It is worth pausing to note that Hume wrote in English, which means that English-speaking readers do not need a translator to tell them what he said. This is a significant advantage. Very few students of the history of philosophy are sufficiently fluent in Greek, Latin, French, Dutch, German, or whatever to read Plato, Thomas Aquinas, **René Descartes**, Benedict Spinoza, Kant, or whomever in the original languages. With these authors, if a passage seems unclear, we must first try to tell whether the translation is accurate—which is to say that we encounter an additional barrier to understanding. If, on the other hand, Hume's meaning is unclear, readers fluent in English can deal with his own words rather than the English equivalent (more or less) of words in some other language. And such readers can savor Hume's writing—its cadences, diction, use of figures of speech, etc.—firsthand.

Hume was a many-sided genius, as the title of a book of essays about Hume reminds us. Some of the sides are better known than others.

Every student of the history of philosophy knows that Hume forced us to rethink what we thought we knew about causation and morality and religion, among other things. On the other hand, very few of those students know that James Madison, the "father" of the U.S. Constitution and the fourth U.S. president, drew heavily from Hume's *Essays*—especially his "Idea of a Perfect Commonwealth"—to combat the widespread belief that a large country could not sustain a republican form of government. Hume's writings also exerted a strong influence on the Scottish philosopher-economist Adam Smith, whose *Wealth of Nations* [short title] is probably the most famous work in economics ever published. Hume wrote a multi-volume history of England and upwards of 50 essays about political, moral, and literary subjects. And, as suggested above, he wrote extensively about philosophy in the more restrictive sense (metaphysics, epistemology, ethics), though Hume himself saw no sharp separation between the various disciplines devoted to the study of human nature.

Indeed, Hume wrote about most of the things that people have found to be important or interesting (or, of course, both), and he did so (for the most part anyway) in an engaging style. The qualifier *for the most part anyway* is required to make a place for Hume's youthful masterpiece, *A Treatise of Human Nature*, which is a work of unmistakable philosophical genius but is not written in an engaging style.

Hume notes (in section 1 of EHU) that humans are active and social beings no less than reasonable beings, and that the most perfect character is one that strikes a balance between the extremes of the mere philosopher and the ignorant doer. In like fashion, he contrasts two species of philosophy: "the easy and obvious" vs. "the accurate and abstruse." And, as with character, Hume does not want to discard either sort of inquiry *tout court*. The ideal is to "unite the boundaries of the different species of philosophy, by reconciling profound inquiry with clearness, and truth with novelty." Reasoning in "this easy manner" should have the salutary effect of subverting a kind of abstruse philosophy that shelters superstition, absurdity, and error (EHU, 16; 95.17). Except for THN, Hume's philosophical writings are reasonably successful in realizing his goal of combining precision with readability. Although THN does not compare with the two *Enquiries* or the *Dialogues* for style, it is still the gold standard for Hume's philosophical views, in the opinion of many Hume scholars (and, to be fair, it is not *badly* written).

Hume's professed aim in philosophy is straightforward and (perhaps misleadingly) simple: to construct a map of human nature ("mental geography," as Hume himself calls it) by a careful study of how people actually live, think, feel, and judge. This project comprises a positive side (drawing the map, as it were) and a negative side (criticizing inaccurate maps). As an empiricist, Hume must subject his claims to the test of experience. This means that he rejects any preconceived program that would substitute abstract a priori reasoning for actual observations. In Hume's view, we cannot deduce facts about the external world or about human beings from putative self-evident principles and definitions. Hume says, in effect, "Don't tell me how things *must* be. Tell me, on the basis of empirically accessible evidence, how things actually *are*."

Hume's stance sets him in direct opposition to rationalist philosophers such as Descartes, Spinoza, and Leibniz, who try to do exactly what Hume says no one can do. And it helps us to understand the skeptical side of Hume's philosophy, which is directed primarily against rationalist theories about human nature, knowledge, morality, and the world. These theories purport to demonstrate that our beliefs about the external world, other people, causation, moral obligation, etc. rest on rationally unshakable foundations. Hume argues that our basic beliefs have no such rational basis, but he never says that these beliefs are false or that we ought not hold them. Instead, he offers explanations of how we acquire them and why we cannot give them up. By way of a survey of his life and times and a discussion of the outlines of his thought, this introduction invites readers to meet, or renew acquaintance with, the man and the philosopher David Hume.[1] It provides a useful background for the dictionary proper, which covers myriad details about Hume's writings. Unlike the dictionary itself, the introduction does not have to observe alphabetical order but can offer a narrative account of relevant facts about Hume and his world.

A SKETCH OF HUME'S LIFE

The philosopher David Hume was born in Edinburgh, Scotland, on 26 April (O.S.) 1711, the son of Joseph Home [*sic*] and Catherine Falconer. The family name was written *Home, Hume*, and several other ways, but all were pronounced *Hume* (rhymes with *plume*). Catherine, David's mother, was the daughter of Sir David Falconer, Lord President of the Court of Session, and his wife, Mary. After Sir David died, Mary was courted by the widower John Home, who brought to the marriage five children from a previous union—among them Joseph, the oldest son, who was to become the father of the famous philosopher. With Mary's seven little Falconers (including Catherine), the household became home to 12 children. So, the bride (Catherine Falconer) and groom (Joseph Home) at their January 1708 wedding were also step-sister and step-brother (but not related by blood). Within three years, three children were born: John (the primary heir), Catherine, and David.

As the firstborn son of the elder John Home (David's paternal grandfather), Joseph inherited the Home family estate at Ninewells when his father died in 1696. Thus, Joseph was only 15 years old when he became (nominally at least) the laird of the estate. Ninewells, named for the springs that flow from a hillside into the Whiteadder (or Whitewater) River, lies on the outskirts of Chirnside village, which is nine miles west of Berwick (pronounced, with customary British disdain for phonetics, *Ber-ik*). Several generations of Ninewell Homes (or Humes) had divided time between the family estate and Edinburgh (30 miles or so to the west), passing the winter at their "house" (i.e., apartment) in the Scottish capital. When Joseph died in 1713, at the young age of 33, that town-and-country arrangement proved too costly for the widow Catherine, left to care for three children less than five years old. As David observes in *My Own Life,* his mother and father both came from well-connected families; but they were not rich. And as the younger son, David inherited only a small patrimony; under the laws of primogeniture, John, the elder son, got the lion's share of the family fortune. The widow Catherine Home never remarried, presumably by choice (David describes his mother as "a woman of singular Merit" and as "young and handsome"), opting instead to devote herself "entirely to the rearing and educating of her Children."

Very little is known of Hume's life in the decade between the death of his father and his matriculation, at the same time as his brother (early 1723), in the University of Edinburgh. He must have had some instruction at home, inasmuch as he could not have enrolled in the University without knowing how to read and write English and, almost certainly, some Latin. Tutors, often young clergymen, typically served several households, an arrangement dictated by financial necessity. Hume says that he was "seized very early with a passion for Literature," quite possibly as early as his pre-University studies. At the University, the young David—not quite 12 years old when he entered—applied himself to a variety of subjects: the traditional (Latin, logic, metaphysics), but also the modern (**Samuel Pufendorf**, **Francis Bacon**, and the "new philosophy" of **John Locke** and **Isaac Newton**). The influence of Locke and Newton on Hume's thought was profound and permanent, and also pretty obvious.

Among ancient writers, **Cicero** was an early favorite of Hume's and exerted an important and lasting influence. Indeed, while his family supposed that David was reading legal writings, he was "secretly devouring" Cicero and Virgil. Given both his temperament (his "Studious disposition, . . . Sobriety, and . . . Industry") and the legal career pursued by several earlier Ninewell Humes, he seemed a natural for the Law. But in fact, he tells us in *My Own Life*, he found himself possessed of "an unsurmountable Aversion to everything but the pursuits of Philosophy and general Learning." Like many of Hume's sweeping statements, this one is likely to mislead if taken literally. Although he did eventually turn away from the study of law, he acquired a decent level of competence in legal matters (Mossner points out that Hume served as judge-advocate to a military expedition in 1746 and that he executed various sorts of legal documents throughout his life).

When Hume left the University of Edinburgh in either 1725 or 1726 (it is not certain which), at 14 or 15 years of age, he knew that he wanted to be a "man of Letters," but had little idea how he might realize his dream. He had decided against a career in law, and his loss of at least a significant part of his religious beliefs rendered him unfit for the clergy. One studies law or theology or medicine in order to become a lawyer or a minister or a physician—which is to say that the studies have only instrumental value, as a means of attaining some other end. A man of letters, on the contrary, studies literature (poetry, essays, drama, novels, etc.) or philosophy as something having intrinsic value, not merely as means to some extrinsic goal. But how can a man of modest means combine the demands of a money-making profession with the leisure required for such a life? Lawyers and physicians and clergymen are paid for their services. But a man of letters? Through a good many years of his life, Hume had no reliable and continuing answer to that question.

In 1729, after three years of intense thought and unremitting study, Hume found himself carried into a "new Scene of Thought," in which learning about human nature is the key to all knowledge. This discovery was the first intimation of the "science of human nature" that Hume elaborated in great detail in *A Treatise of Human Nature*, published in 1739 (Books 1 and 2) and 1740 (Book 3). Not surprisingly, the years of unflagging work exacted a price. In *My Own Life*, Hume says laconically that his health was "a little broken by [his] ardent Application." "A little broken" understates his physical and emotional suffering almost to the point of absurdity, as Hume himself makes clear in a long, detailed letter written in 1734. Obviously, he had to get out of the study and into "a more Active Scene of Life," which he found in southwest England, as a clerk in a Bristol business establishment. That arrangement was short-lived: David quarreled with the proprietor and either quit or was fired after only a few months. But the brief respite from the rigors of study proved to be the therapy he needed. With his physical and mental vigor restored, he was soon on his way to France.

The years 1734–1737 were pivotal in Hume's life: He "discovered" France, and he wrote *A Treatise of Human Nature* while sojourning in the country he came to love (albeit with an occasional tinge of ambivalence). He went first to Paris, where he introduced himself to the Chevalier (Michael Edward) Ramsay, a Scottish expatriate and the cousin of Hume's childhood friend Michael Ramsay. A convert to Roman Catholicism, the Chevalier Ramsay had made quite a name for himself in France; and though he found Hume unduly self-confident and was later highly critical of Hume's philosophy, he was extraordinarily gracious and helpful to the young David. Paris was, of course, much too expensive for Hume's meager resources; so he went to Rheims (or Reims), about 100 miles northeast of Paris, bearing letters of introduction from the Chevalier Ramsay. But he found, after about a year, that he could not afford to live in Rheims either; and, it has been conjectured, he may have found that his active social life in Rheims left too little time for his work. His next move, the last he would make on this first journey to France, was to La Flèche, which lies southwest of Paris. The great French philosopher and mathematician **René Descartes** had spent eight or nine years as a student in the Jesuit school at La Flèche (130 years or so before Hume's arrival in the town). Despite profound differences in philosophical and religious views, Hume and the local Jesuits conversed amicably. Hume was especially pleased to have access to the school's library. And he found the quiet and leisure to complete — or virtually complete — *A Treatise of Human Nature*, which had been his principal reason for going to France. In the late summer of 1737, the 26-year-old David Hume returned to England, precious manuscript in hand.

Hume seems to have believed that he could find a London publisher and wrap up the details for getting his *Treatise* before the world in the space of a month or so — an illusion springing from his youth and inexperience. As a writer who had published nothing, Hume should have known that he would not be courted by the men of Fleet Street. To make matters worse, he insisted on contractual terms (regarding subsequent editions and additional volumes, for example) that publishers would be loath to concede, especially to a stripling who held no trump cards.

Unlike many writers of the time, Hume never had, or sought, the patronage of a wealthy nobleman, whose backing would serve to ease the misgivings and lessen the risks of a publisher. As it turned out, the months of waiting produced some salutary effects. In particular, Hume was able to revise portions of the manuscript that seemed, to his less hurried judgment, to bear the marks of haste and enthusiasm. By far, the most important revision was the excision — *castration* is Hume's inelegant word for it — of a section dealing with miracles. (In 1748, a descendant of that deleted section was published as "Of Miracles" in *An Enquiry Concerning Human Understanding*.) Hume's motives in deciding to omit "Reasonings Concerning Miracles" are pretty obvious: He wanted to steer clear of gratuitous disputes, and he wished to avoid offending Bishop **Joseph Butler**, a writer whom he genuinely admired. Indeed, while he was in London, Hume tried unsuccessfully to see Butler (Butler was away from London when Hume called at his lodgings).

J. Y. T. Greig, the author of a biography about Hume, surmises that Hume's harsh attitude toward the churches and churchmen might have been softened if he had developed a friendship with Butler, who was strikingly different from most of the clergymen Hume knew. Greig describes Butler as "devout without bigotry, courteous and enlightened, gentle but acute" — precisely the sort of man who could have enlarged Hume's myopic vision of religion, especially since Hume was already favorably impressed by Butler's writings. Greig's conjecture is not implausible, but who knows? Hume did in fact enjoy the company of a number of open-minded Scottish ministers, a few of whom became his close friends; and these associations served to temper his antagonism to religion. But it must be admitted that none of them were in Butler's class intellectually.

In September 1738—one year after his return from France—Hume closed a deal with John Noon to publish book 1 ("Of the Understanding") and book 2 ("Of the Passions") of the *Treatise*. Those two books appeared in January 1739. Book 3 ("Of Morals") was brought out in November 1740, by a different publisher, Thomas Longman. After years of unremitting work and a full year of searching for a publisher, Hume was deeply disappointed by the reception his *Treatise* received. His lament (in *My Own Life*) is one of the most frequently quoted passages in all his writings: "Never literary Attempt was more unfortunate than my Treatise of human Nature. It fell *dead-born from the Press*; without reaching such distinction even to excite a Murmur among the Zealots." But he proceeds immediately to minimize its effect on him: ". . . being naturally of a cheerful and sanguine Temper, I very soon recovered the Blow, and prosecuted with great Ardour my Studies in the Country." There is some measure of hyperbole in both statements: The *Treatise* was not wholly ignored even at the time of its publication, and within a few years zealots went well beyond murmuring; and there is ample evidence that the ill-success of the *Treatise* rankled Hume the rest of his life, pushing him so far as to repudiate it (at least publicly). Hume's continuing unhappiness with the reception of his *Treatise* is noted by Thomas Edward Ritchie, the author of the first book-length biography of Hume; but it is pretty obvious in any case. This much, however, is plainly true: None of his contemporaries—with the possible qualified exception of the great German philosopher **Immanuel Kant**—recognized the high philosophical genius exhibited in the *Treatise*.

As a way of answering distorted or unfair reviews of the *Treatise* (and of promoting the book), Hume published anonymously (in March 1740) *An Abstract of a Book lately Published; Entituled, A Treatise of Human Nature, &c. Wherein the Chief Argument of that Book is farther Illustrated and Explained.* The *Treatise* itself appeared without Hume's name on the title page (it was not until 1748 that he published anything under his own name), but it soon became an open secret that he was the author. On the other hand, the author of the *Abstract* really was anonymous and remained so—at least "officially"—until 1938, when Hume's authorship was conclusively established.

The success of Hume's next venture into publishing, *Essays Moral and Political* (Vol. I, 1741; Vol. II, 1742), was a balm to his wounded sensibilities, as well as a modest source of much-needed income. That Joseph Butler recommended the *Essays* all around was an unexpected lagniappe that pleased the young author immensely. Hume spent a good part of the next few years at Ninewells, his ancestral home, with his mother, sister, and brother, John, the enterprising laird of the estate. During this time, David maintained an active social life, visiting friends and relatives in the vicinity and well beyond (Glasgow, for example).

In 1745 the chair of ethics and pneumatical (spiritual) philosophy at the University of Edinburgh became vacant through the resignation of its tenant. With the aid of some influential friends, Hume made a serious effort to secure the position for himself. He saw the appointment as an almost ideal answer to his problems with money and access to a good library—and so it would have been. It came as no surprise that Hume's enemies painted him as a heretic, skeptic, deist, atheist, etc., and, consequently, unfit to fill the post. But Hume was quite unprepared to learn of **Francis Hutcheson**'s opposition, since he and Hutcheson had been on friendly terms in their correspondence and in person; and he was stung by it. In Hutcheson's defense, it should be said that he knew Hume to be unqualified for the position *as it was described* (among other things, the holder of the chair was required to defend the truth of the Christian religion). Hume probably could not have carried the day even with Hutcheson's strong support and a fortiori was doomed without it. In a strange twist, Hutcheson himself was offered the position, but declined.

Hume's only other attempt to secure an academic appointment came six years later (1751), when he allowed his name to be put forward by his friends for the chair in Logic at Glasgow University—with the same disappointing result as before. But this time, David was less personally involved than in the 1745 fight in Edinburgh. In the earlier episode, he had published an anonymous pamphlet, *A Letter from a Gentleman to His Friend in Edinburgh . . .* , in which he replied to several accusations that had been lodged against him (one of the extremely infrequent violations of his own resolution "never to reply to any body"). By 1751, he had at least begun to realize that the battle lines in appointments of the sort in question were drawn at least as much on political as on religious grounds—even though his "irreligion" was cited as the decisive consideration. His two unsuccessful candidacies for a university position are evidence, incidentally, that the *Treatise* did *not* go unread. It was among the weapons used to scuttle his efforts to become a professor. And it is part of the reason Hume came to repudiate his first — and, in the opinion of many, his greatest — work.

Before a final decision was taken on the Edinburgh professorship, Hume left Scotland for England, in response to an unexpected invitation from the Marquis of Annandale to join him as companion and tutor. The Marquis had been favorably impressed by *Essays Political and Moral* and offered Hume £300 a year, plus £100 immediately for traveling expenses. Hume's very brief account of this adventure (in *My Own Life*) stresses the generous stipend, a windfall for the perpetually cash-strapped young philosopher. He gives only the slightest hint that the 25-year-old, enormously wealthy Marquis was also quite insane. After a few relatively quiet and pleasant months with David, the Marquis began to exhibit the behavior that eventually got him declared a lunatic: wild, rapid mood swings, from amiable to abusive, self-induced vomiting after eating, etc. He discharged and rehired Hume many times. With the Marchioness Annandale, the Marquis's mother, living in Scotland, the management of the family estate outside London was, for practical purposes, turned over to one Philip Vincent, a cousin of the Marquis and a Captain in the Royal Navy. According to someone who knew him well, Vincent was a "low, dirty, despicable fellow" — a description that Hume eventually found to be entirely accurate. Hume left the employ of Lord Annandale with more money (though he was still owed £75) and with a practical lesson about human cupidity and chicanery. During the same year (1745) Hume's mother, Catherine Home, died — a loss that left him desolate and, no doubt, feeling guilty for being absent in her time of great need.

The year 1745 is notable for another reason: The Rising of '45, the last and most extensive of the **Jacobite** Rebellions that were mounted as a means of restoring the Stuart descendants of James II to the British throne. David Hume had ties of friendship and even family to many Jacobites, but he was himself strongly opposed to the cause they espoused. Even so, he and his fellow Caledonians living in England were well advised to lie low rather than expose themselves to the mindless anti-Scot feeling rekindled by the Jacobite incursion into England.

After the unpleasant but financially profitable year in the company of the lunatic Lord Annandale and the charlatan Captain Vincent, Hume decided to return to Scotland by way of London. While in London, he met a distant relative of the Ninewells Humes, Lt. General James St. Clair, who took an immediate liking to David and offered him the position of private secretary on a military expedition. Not really wanting to go back to Scotland at the time, Hume accepted the offer. The expedition was originally supposed to sail to Canada, not later than 1 August 1746, for the purpose of capturing Quebec. Unfortunately, the people in charge of the undertaking were incompetent, indecisive, dilatory, and divided about how to accomplish their mission. After months of delay, winter was too close for them to brave the Atlantic for the frigid shores of North America. So, the expedition was diverted to the Brittany Coast of France—with vague orders, inadequate equipment, undermanned military units, with no intelligence about the strength or location of enemy troops or ordnance, with no maps of the territory to be invaded! Naturally, it ended ignominiously, and would have been even worse had the French army not been engaged in Flanders. But General St. Clair's military career was not seriously affected, and Hume came out of the fiasco with some additional assets. He saw firsthand the sorts of idiocy and self-serving maneuvers high-ranking officials are capable of, and he learned a bit about warfare from up close. He formed new friendships, many of which were lasting. And General St. Clair remembered David when he again needed a secretary to accompany him on a mission.

The second invitation from General St. Clair came in late 1747, after David had been in Scotland several months. He accepted the invitation, but reluctantly. St. Clair was being dispatched to Vienna and Turin to prod Britain's allies in the War of the Austrian Succession to live up to their agreements. This messy, confused conflict, which Britain participated in by proxy, had dragged on for seven years; and all parties were weary of it. As it turned out, the peace treaty of Aix-la-Chapelle ended the war and rendered St. Clair's mission pointless; but it was in many ways a useful adventure for Hume. The St. Clair party followed a leisurely route through Holland (which Hume describes as ugly—it was winter), Germany (several cities), Austria (in particular Vienna), and Italy. He rubbed elbows with royalty and nobility and observed something of the workings of diplomacy—useful experiences for the future historian (and, it should be noted, for the "cautious observer" of human life in its many and varied forms).

Before he departed for London, in early 1748, to join General St. Clair's diplomatic mission, Hume had finished revising the manuscript of *Philosophical Essays Concerning Human Understanding*, which was published in 1748. (In 1756, the title was changed to *An Enquiry Concerning Human Understanding*, as it has been known ever since.) Essentially a recasting of book 1 of THN, the book was the fruit of six years of frequently interrupted work. Besides being more "reader-friendly" than the corresponding portion of THN, the *Enquiry* (to use its more common title) is notable for its inclusion of "Of Miracles," which Hume had excised from the earlier work. It has a second provocative section, "Of a Particular Providence and of a Future State"—a curious title for a discussion that has little to do with a particular providence or a future state. The original title of that section—"Of the Practical Consequences of Natural Religion"—was more apt.

In the same year, 1748, a third edition of *Essays Moral and Political* was brought out (it contained three new essays and so was not *strictly* the third edition of the earlier work). Hume's refurbishing of the unfortunate *Treatise* continued with the publication, in 1751, of *An Enquiry Concerning the Principles of Morals*. Hume says (in *My Own Life*) that this book is "of all [his] writings, historical, philosophical, or literary, incomparably the best." This estimate has struck many (including this writer) as mistaken, and Hume himself concedes that he ought to leave such judgments to others. For all its merits, alas, Hume laments that the book "came unnoticed and unobserved into the World." In 1757 Hume completed his rewriting of the *Treatise* with the publication of a work that came to be known as *A Dissertation on the Passions*, which corresponds to part 2 ("Of the Passions") of THN. The *Dissertation* has never enjoyed the success of the two *Enquiries*. The decade of the 1750s saw Hume's literary fame (some of it unfavorable, to be sure) and his worldly fortune on the rise. He tells us that his *Political Discourses* (1752) was the only one of his works to be successful on its first publication; it was well received at home and abroad. His appointment, in 1752, as keeper of the advocates library provided little money but gave him access to 30,000 volumes—a godsend for the aspiring historian. From 1754 to 1762, the volumes of *The History of England* were published in reverse chronological order, beginning with the Stuart monarchies and proceeding back through the Tudors and ending with the Roman Conquest. The six volumes were published in the proper historical sequence, in 1762. Although the first two volumes (on the Stuarts and the Tudors) were roundly attacked (they seemed to offend all sides to the various controversies treated), the *History* proved to be popular beyond Hume's fondest expectations. His writings on metaphysics, epistemology, and ethics had established Hume's reputation as a philosopher of the first rank; but it was the first volume of his *History*, which covers the reigns of the Stuart monarchs James I and Charles I, that made him a truly *popular* author. Hume's 19th-century biographer John Hill Burton offers an obvious but apt explanation: ". . . the readers of metaphysics and ethics are a small number; while the readers of history, and especially of the history of their own country, are a community nearly as great as the number of those who can read their own language."[2] Hume began writing the *Dialogues Concerning Natural Religion* as early as 1750, and continued to revise it periodically until the year of his death. It was published posthumously, in 1779.

As suggested above, not all the attention paid to Hume's writings was welcome. His enemies had adduced the *Treatise* and, later, the first *Enquiry* as evidence of his unfitness for appointment to professorships at the University of Edinburgh and the University of Glasgow. Quite apart from those controversies, the essay "Of Miracles" provoked a spate of indignant responses, as did *The Natural History of Religion*, which was published in 1757 after much pushing and pulling about what to excise and what to leave in. It was Hume's unhappy lot—albeit a proof of his eminence—to be the object of countless attacks, some of them civil, but many "in the usual Style of Controversy." His equable disposition and natural cheerfulness notwithstanding, he was distressed and wounded by the constant barrage of denunciation directed at him, the more so because much of it came from his fellow Scots. To understate his feeling, it took some of the bloom off his triumphs.

To be fair and accurate, it must be admitted that some of the charges against Hume had a basis in fact. A good example may be found in the first edition of Volume I of the *History of England*, which covers the first two Stuart monarchs (some of the most offensive passages were omitted from subsequent editions). Even the generally sympathetic and admiring biographer J. Y. T. Greig argues that Hume's indiscriminate prejudice against all forms of Christianity leads him to sin against common justice in his treatment of the Reformers Martin Luther, John Calvin, John Knox, and their 17th-century successors. His treatment of Roman Catholicism is more openly hostile, but that did not bother most of his critics. And it must be remembered that among his critics were friends who loved David but found his views odious.

While Hume's reception in Britain was, at best, mixed, the case was very different in continental Europe, especially in France. The widely influential French philosopher Baron de Montesquieu was the first distinguished European writer to recognize Hume's excellence, but by no means the last. The French took notice (usually favorable) of Hume from the time his works began to appear in translation (in the early 1750s). When Hume returned to France in 1763 as personal secretary to the newly appointed ambassador (Lord Hertford), the Scottish philosopher, historian, and man of letters was received with great enthusiasm. The French admired him for his brilliance, of course, but they also found him a charming, agreeable guest at all manner of social functions. Most of them were ready to forgive his atrocious spoken French (imagine the Gallic *r* produced with a Scottish burr!); and, given the inveterate French dislike of the English, it did not hurt that he was a Scot, not an Englishman. The affection—even adulation—for Hume never abated during the 26 months of his stay in France. Supercilious Englishmen might sniff at the royal treatment accorded Hume, but to the French he was *le bon David*—a man whose awkward corpulence could not conceal a good, honest, amiable heart.

While he was in Paris, Hume maintained friendly relations with several of the so-called *philosophes*—intellectuals associated with the French Enlightenment and the publication of the massive *Encyclopédie*. Among the more famous men of this group, Hume knew Diderot, Baron d'Holbach, and D'Alembert (Hume's personal favorite). Hume never met Voltaire—the most famous of them all—but Voltaire expressed admiration for Hume's writings (and Hume himself) on numerous occasions. Hume's opinion of Voltaire was decidedly less positive. He regarded the other *philosophes* as altogether too dogmatic in their militant atheism and scarcely less so in metaphysics, economics, politics, etc. They were cocksure of themselves, arrogant, and given to ridiculing opponents—but not without some interesting ideas.

When Lord Hertford, the ambassador, returned to England on private business, Hume became the *chargé d'affaires* at the British embassy in Paris—a position he held for about four months, until the arrival of the new ambassador. A few months before he himself departed France for Britain, Hume was persuaded to invite the immensely gifted, but squirrelly, philosopher Jean-Jacques Rousseau to accompany him to England. He did this in the face of strong, repeated warnings from his friends among the *philosophes* that Rousseau was impossible to get along with, that he invariably quarreled with those who tried to help him—facts that they knew from personal experience as well as from many well-documented accounts.

From their arrival in London in January 1766, Hume found Rousseau finical about many things, but did not immediately discern the strain of pathological suspiciousness that would soon manifest itself in full-blown lunacy. After all, Rousseau had in fact been persecuted most of his life. Despite the many substantial proofs of Hume's friendship and goodwill, and the utter absence of any evidence to the contrary, Rousseau came to believe—sincerely, we must suppose—that Hume had intended all along to do him great harm.

Hume was at first stunned by the groundless calumny directed at him by Rousseau; then he was roused to indignation. He wrote a spirited but civil letter to Rousseau, in which he rebutted the false accusations leveled against him. But he wrote a second letter, this one to Baron d'Holbach in Paris, that gave vent to his anger at the "atrocious villain" he had once affectionately described as "this nice little man." The Baron lost no time in spreading the news all over Europe. (These two letters are very rare violations of Hume's resolution not to reply to criticism. But the "criticism" in this case was a vicious and utterly baseless assault on his character, not an attack on something he had written.) Later, Hume read Rousseau's lengthy, detailed, psychotic account of what Rousseau imagined to be the vast international conspiracy that had been hatched to humiliate him. Hume's strongly ambivalent feelings were aptly described by one of his correspondents, Lady Hervey: detestation for Rousseau's malevolence and compassion for his madness.

After the sad, painful business with Rousseau had played itself out, Hume returned to Scotland in the late summer of 1766, "not richer, but with much more money and a much larger Income by means of Lord Hertford's Friendship, than I left it" (*My Own Life*). But he was back in London in less than six months, this time as undersecretary of state to General Conway, Lord Hertford's brother. Hume accepted the appointment reluctantly, but he found that it had its rewards, among which was frequent contact with the social, political, and literary elite of Britain. In an ironic twist that he enjoyed to the hilt, Hume—the "great infidel"—was often the de facto dispenser of church patronage in Scotland. Just under a year later (in January 1768) General Conway resigned his office, thereby putting Hume out of work.

Hume hung around London for the better part of two years before returning to Edinburgh in August 1769. He left Scotland only once during the last seven years of his life, traveling to London and Bath in a vain attempt to find a cure for his final illness. For the most part, these years were pleasant for David, who, as the most famous writer in Scotland, never wanted for agreeable, brilliant company. To be sure, his philosophical and religious views were as uncongenial as ever to many people, even among his friends. But criticisms were usually couched in civil language, the most notable—and irritating—exception being **James Beattie**'s *An Essay on the Nature and Immutability of Truth*, which lampoons a distorted version of Hume. The book proved to be enormously popular, much to Hume's chagrin; but he kept to his rule of not replying to critics—not even to "that bigoted silly Fellow, Beattie." Hume's own major intellectual occupation during these years was revising his *Essays* and *History*, something he continued to do until he died.

By 1775, the symptoms of Hume's fatal illness—probably colon cancer with metastatic involvement of the liver—were too palpable and insistent (for example, losing 70 pounds of weight) to be passed off as inconsequential. He accepted the inevitable with courage and even humor, and he tried to continue living as he had done for most of his life. For example, in March and April 1776—four months before his death—he read Edward Gibbon's *Decline and Fall of the Roman Empire* and Adam Smith's *Wealth of Nations*, and wrote enthusiastic letters of congratulation to the authors. When he was no longer able to visit his friends, he received them hospitably in his own lodgings, very nearly to the last day of his life. He died on 25 August (N.S.) 1776, at just the time news of the American Declaration of Independence reached Britain—an event that Hume would have heartily endorsed.

Neither David Hume nor his sister, Catherine, ever married. In his early twenties, David was accused of being the father of a child conceived by a local woman named Agnes Galbraith, who had already given birth to two babies out of wedlock. David had left Scotland before Agnes lodged her charge and so had no chance to respond to it—a circumstance that made her claim less credible, inasmuch as she had had ample time to implicate him before his departure. The Presbytery considered the evidence and concluded that the accusation was "not proven"—a term of art consistent with either actual guilt or innocence. David's brother, John, married at the age of 42 and had eight children over the next 12 years, five of whom lived to adulthood. Of these, the second son, also named David (born 1757), is of special interest; for it was he who had the courage to ensure that his uncle's *Dialogues Concerning Natural Religion* be published (in 1779), after **Adam Smith** failed to honor Hume's dying entreaty.

David Hume was a philosopher of genius—no doubt about that. And it should be clear by now that he was a good and generous man. He describes himself in *My Own Life* like this: "I was . . . a man of mild Dispositions, of Command of Temper, of an open, social, and cheerful Humour, capable of Attachment, but little susceptible of Enmity, and of great Moderation in all my Passions." Despite many attacks on Hume's character, both during his life and after his death, we have abundant evidence that his self-appraisal is accurate. Adam Smith, perhaps Hume's closest friend, wrote to the publisher William Strahan a long and moving account of the final illness of "our late excellent friend, Mr. Hume" (a letter, incidentally, that triggered years of bitter denunciations of Smith by Hume's detractors). The final paragraph of the letter is a glowing eulogy upon Hume's "happily balanced" temper. Here is the last sentence: "Upon the whole, I have always considered him, both in his lifetime, and since his death, as approaching as nearly to the idea of a perfectly wise and virtuous man, as perhaps the nature of human frailty will admit."

Admirers of David Hume will concur in the estimate Greig offers of Smith's encomium: "Adam Smith knew his man."

HUME'S TIMES

The Political Landscape of England/Britain

Although the years of David Hume's life (1711–1776) lie wholly within the 18th century, we cannot begin to understand the world in which he lived without looking briefly at some events and conditions in the preceding two centuries, and especially the last 15 years or so of the 17th century. The long reign of Queen Elizabeth I (1558–1603) saw the emergence of England as a nation to be reckoned with. The defeat of the Spanish Armada in 1588 put an exclamation point after the English claim to equality (at least) with France and Spain. With that equality came, willy-nilly, what Hobbes describes as the *condition of war*, which comprises not merely actual fighting, but also "the known disposition thereto during all the time there is no assurance to the contrary" (*Leviathan*, part 1, chapter 13). And there was enough actual fighting to satisfy all but the most sanguinary appetites.

On her deathbed, the childless Elizabeth I named her successor: James VI of Scotland (the son of Mary Queen of Scots and Lord Darnley) became James I of England. As the first of seven (or eight, depending on how you count William and Mary) Stuart monarchs, James I symbolically — but not politically — united England and Scotland. Although the transition from Tudor to Stuart dynasty went quite smoothly, the reigns of James I and Charles I were marked by bitter factional struggles, culminating in the two English Civil Wars (1642–1649), the beheading of Charles I in 1649, and the abolition of the monarchy by Parliament. Following the 11-year Interregnum (comprising the Commonwealth and the Protectorates of Oliver Cromwell and his son Richard), the monarchy was restored in 1660 with the accession of Charles II, the eldest surviving son of Charles I. Charles II was shrewd enough to ride out the religious, political, economic, and constitutional infighting of the next 25 years, in no small part by keeping his Catholic sympathies under wraps. He died a natural death in 1685, succeeded by his younger brother, who became James II.

As if being an open Catholic was not a sufficient liability for the monarch of a Protestant nation, James II incurred non-sectarian wrath by his autocratic, officious reign, interfering with the conduct of the courts and local governments (among other self-subverting acts). In the Glorious Revolution of 1688, James II was deposed but was allowed to escape to France. His older daughter, Mary, and her husband, the Prince of Orange — both Protestants — returned from exile to become Queen Mary II and King William III, ruling jointly until Mary's death in 1694. William's reign ended with his death in 1702. (The terms *Tory* and *Whig* — as applied to English/British political factions — date from the last decade or so of the 17th century. Tories supported the Stuart succession through James II; Whigs opposed it. The meaning of the terms evolved over the years, as the prospect of a Stuart restoration became increasingly remote. Thus, Lord North in the 1770s was a Tory but assuredly *not* a Jacobite.)

In 1701, the year before William III died, Parliament passed the Act of Settlement, which prescribed the line of succession to the English throne in case both William and Princess Anne (the younger daughter of James II) should die without heirs. The act had the general effect of removing the male line of Stuarts from the succession — a provision that would not be put to any real test until 1714, the year of Queen Anne's death.

Princess Anne became Queen Anne, the last Stuart monarch, in 1702. The most important event of her reign was the Act of Union (1707), whereby the kingdoms of England and Scotland were officially joined into one nation, whose people would be represented by one Parliament (the one in London). By accepting the Act of Union, Scotland bound itself to honor the terms of the Act of Settlement — a consequence odious to the partisans of James II and his son. In return, Scotland expected England to accept it as an equal partner in matters political, religious, and economic (a forlorn expectation, for the most part, as it turned out). The War of the Spanish Succession began the year before Anne's coronation and persisted through almost all of her reign. The word *Byzantine* might have been coined to describe the maze of alliances, antagonisms, battles, accommodations, subterfuges, etc., etc., to be found in the course of that war; but at least one outcome is clear: Britain got most of the things it sought and came out smelling like a rose, clearly second to none among world powers. Among other concessions, France recognized the Hanoverian succession to the British throne enunciated in the Act of Settlement. (This did not keep France from making league with enemies of the Act; e.g., the **Jacobites**.)

As prescribed by terms of the Act of Settlement, Queen Anne's successor was George Louis, the great-grandson of James I and the Elector of Hanover, who was crowned as George I, the first British monarch of the house of Hanover. George I was not particularly likeable or admirable; he spent a lot of time away from Britain; and he never bothered to learn English, the language of his subjects. Not surprisingly, he was not popular in Britain. But he was seen as a bulwark against the return of

Roman Catholic Stuarts, and for that reason was never in any real danger of being overthrown. Not that there were not some Britons—mainly the Jacobites—who devoutly sought his removal in favor of James Francis Edward Stuart, the son and rightful heir of James II (as they believed). Jacobite uprisings began in 1689 (just after the accession of William III), cropped up again in 1708 (just after the Act of Union), in 1715 (*the '15*, just after the accession of George I), and in 1719 (instigated by Spain for its own purposes). These efforts to enthrone James F. E. Stuart (later called *The Old Pretender*) failed abjectly. Twenty-five years later, Jacobites found a new standard-bearer in Charles Edward Stuart (*The Young Pretender*, also called *Bonnie Prince Charlie*), son of *The Old Pretender*.

The Rising of '45 produced a few Jacobite victories and, indeed, saw its army march from Scotland as far south as Derby, a hundred miles north of London. But the expected reinforcements from the French and English sympathizers never came, and Prince Charlie's forces retreated into Scotland, finally being hunted down and routed by the English army at Culloden Moor (near Inverness) in 1746. The bonnie prince managed, barely, to elude the English and make his way to France, and Stuart pretenders persisted into the 19th century; but, for practical purposes, Jacobite hopes were buried with the valiant, overmatched Scots at Culloden.

In the aftermath of the '45, many Jacobites and fellow travelers were treated harshly. A harrowing example: When the 400-member garrison left by Prince Charles in the northern English town of Carlisle was captured by an English force commanded by George II's son William Augustus, all the officers were hanged and the enlisted men exiled to the West Indies. (It is worth noting that David Hume had numerous Jacobite friends and relatives but never wavered in his opposition to Jacobitism. His *Political Essays* [1752] included "Of the Protestant Succession," in which he sets out the Jacobite argument for the Stuart succession and the opposing Whig argument evenhandedly, but concludes with a strong endorsement of the house of Hanover.)

During David Hume's lifetime, Britain became the British Empire, its dominion stretching from North America to India. Much of this success in acquiring colonies and eliminating competition from other powers lay in fashioning peace treaties to its advantage. But the first quarter-century of Hanoverian monarchies (that of George I and the first dozen or so years of George II's) was a time of (relative) peace with other nations. George I was frequently out of London, tending to business in Hanover and, consequently, had to rely on his ministers—most notably, Robert Walpole—to manage the affairs of the British state. Walpole gained a reputation for financial and political astuteness by taking bold measures to end the national nightmare that followed the collapse of the South Sea Company (popularly known as the *South Sea Bubble*), which had left thousands of investors with huge losses. He helped to abort a Jacobite plot (in 1722) to seize control of the government, and used the incident to deepen public distrust of the Tories, whom he indiscriminately lumped with the Jacobites. And it worked: Whig ascendancy over the Tories was not seriously challenged for almost five decades. Walpole managed to keep Britain out of war—sometimes in the face of opposition from his own party—until 1739, when Britain declared war on Spain. This conflict never amounted to much, but it led to involvement in the War of the Austrian Succession (described above in the section on Hume's life), which ended in a peace treaty favorable to Britain.

The Seven Years War (1756–1763), at least the part of it that pitted Britain against France, was mainly about the colonial rivalry between those two powers. Thanks in large part to the tenacity and military acumen of William Pitt the Elder, Britain bested France on land and sea (with the subsidized help of Prussia, an emerging power on the continent). The Treaty of Paris (1763) confirmed Britain's status as the greatest colonial power on earth. But it was on the verge of a stunning setback—the loss of the American colonies. Pitt offered numerous measures—none of which included independence for the colonies—that might well have averted the looming disaster, but to no avail. He warned George III and his Tory first minister, Lord North, that their harsh, repressive policies would drive the colonists to armed rebellion; but his prescient advice was rejected and he was vilified as seditious. Unlike Pitt, Hume would have welcomed the ultimate outcome: an independent nation in North America.

The Enlightenment

The term *Enlightenment* (German *Aufklärung*) is usefully elastic in at least two ways—the chronological and the doctrinal. Unlike *The Reign of Elizabeth I*, which denotes the years 1558 to 1603, *The Enlighten-ment* has no sharp temporal bounds. It may refer to the 18th century, or it may also include certain thinkers and movements from the 17th (e.g., **John Locke**, **Pierre Bayle**, and, even further back, Thomas Hobbes, René Descartes, and Francis Bacon). As this list of 17th-century precursors suggests, *Enlightenment* covers a range of thinkers who differed from one another on some important issues. For example, the most celebrated of the French *philosophes*—Voltaire—was a convinced deist (he described himself, misleadingly, as a *theist*); but several other well-known *philosophes* were atheists (of both the avowed and the closet variety). The English-born American deist Ethan Allen, author of *Reason the Only Oracle of Man*, scornfully dismisses those who believe that "wisdom, order and design" could be produced by "non-entity, chaos, confusion and old night" (i.e., atheists). And the three greatest philosophers of the 18th century—Hume, Rousseau, and Kant—are less sanguine than the *philosophes* about the power of reason to discover the truth about reality and morality. (The English-born American writer Thomas Paine published *The Age of Reason* in 1794, 10 years after Ethan Allen's book, which it closely resembles in doctrine. The phrase *Age of Reason* is often used as more or less synonymous with *Enlightenment*.)

If the thinkers of the Enlightenment quarreled among themselves on substantive matters, they were more nearly in agreement on what they opposed. They rejected appeals to authority to settle questions in politics, religion, science, you name it. The only appeal must be to the intrinsic reasonableness of the answer, where *reasonableness* is taken to include human experience and common sense as well as abstract ratiocination. As noted above, they differed about precisely where the pursuit of reasonableness would take us.

Implicit in the repudiation of external authority as a source of truth, is the affirmation of freedom. When the principle is stated positively (i.e., as the embracing of freedom), disagreements among its proponents become apparent very quickly. Does *freedom* mean merely the absence of restraints and constraints (what Isaiah Berlin calls *negative freedom*)? The first sentence of book 1 of Rousseau's *Social Contract* suggests that freedom is the natural state of human beings: "Man was born free, and everywhere he is in chains." A kindred spirit echoes in the rallying cry of the French Revolution: *liberté, égalité, fraternité.*

Against this notion, most writers of the period argue that meaningful freedom is an achievement of civil society. In the absence of restraints and securities imposed by lawful government, any (putative) freedom would expose a person to the arbitrary will of anyone stronger or more devious than he is. If *that* is freedom, who would want it? Of course, **Rousseau** acknowledges the necessity of civil government, even for the attainment of a secure sort of freedom; but his vision of a good citizen and a good society differs markedly from that of the typical *philosophe*. Indeed, although Rousseau is often numbered among the *philosophes* and was a contributor to the *Encyclopédie*, his thinking is often antithetical to — and not merely discernibly different from — that of the more "normal" *philosophe*.

The *Encyclopédie* is the most perfect embodiment of some central features of the Enlightenment. The following expanded (but still not complete) title offers a clue to the range and extent of this stupendous undertaking (35 volumes published between 1750 and 1780): *Encyclopédie, ou dictionnaire raisonné des sciences, des arts et des métiers, par une société de gens de letters. . . .* This encyclopedia was intended to be a compendium of human knowledge, comprising sciences, arts, and crafts — i.e., *philosophy* in the broad 18th-century sense. The philosophical (narrow sense) assumptions about the origins and limits of human knowledge come straight out of Locke's empiricism; the ideal of a *systematic* taxonomy of sciences owes something to Francis Bacon.

Thinkers of the age of reason champion reason as the sole reliable source of human knowledge, without worrying about nice distinctions between reason and sense, reason and imagination, etc. (as contrasted with Locke and Hume, for example, who do pay attention to such distinctions). For their purposes, it does not really matter that *reason* has no precise, univocal sense. It serves to mark off genuine knowledge (that obtained by the use of reason) from the counterfeit (that obtained, for example, by divine revelation). They also generally (and inconsistently) denounce "metaphysics," by which they understand the rationalistic systems of philosophers such as Descartes, Benedict Spinoza, and Gottfried Wilhelm Leibniz. They ignore or fail to notice that their own doctrines (often materialistic) are every whit as metaphysical as those of, say, Spinoza.

In political theory, the *philosophes* are broadly Lockean, as they are in theory of knowledge. Of necessity, their criticisms of absolutism and their endorsement of republicanism were oblique or muted. Voltaire learned the hard way how costly it could be to express opinions plainly and frankly: several visits to the Bastille and banishments from Paris (which were not, however, wholly without redeeming value). His two-year exile in England acquainted him firsthand with a level of freedom not known in France (in the *Encyclopédie*, the phrase *English liberty* is sometimes used for *political liberty*). For Voltaire and his comrades, freedom of thought and expression is a *sine qua non* of progress in human affairs of every description. They were not dogmatic about the specific *polity* required (monarchical or parliamentary), so long as citizens were governed by laws, not by the arbitrary decrees of the sovereign.

The beginnings of the Enlightenment lie outside France—in Britain, for example; but its most dramatic, full-blown flowering is found in France. Accordingly, most of this section is devoted to its French embodiment. But the ideas and attitudes of the Enlightenment crop up across Europe and (primarily after the Revolution) in North America. For example, the German philosopher Immanuel Kant published a brief essay entitled "What Is Enlightenment?" in which he identifies freedom as the crux of the matter—but freedom with a Kantian twist. Here is the first paragraph:

> Enlightenment is man's release from self-incurred tutelage. Tutelage is man's inability to make use of his understanding without direction from another. Self-incurred is this tutelage when its cause lies not in lack of reason but in lack of resolution and courage to use it without direction from another. *Sapere aude!* [Dare to be wise!] "Have courage to use your own reason!"—that is the motto of enlightenment.[3]

For our purposes, the Scottish Enlightenment deserves at least brief notice. Like the Enlightenment generally, the Scottish version has no sharp chronological boundaries; but it can be taken as extending from 1730 to 1790, more or less. (This dating follows the suggestion of the editors of *A Hotbed of Genius: The Scottish Enlightenment, 1730–1790*—an excellent brief study of the period.) David Hume and Adam Smith are the best known of the many men whose genius and hard work made their geographically remote land the intellectual and scientific equal of any on the planet during several decades of the 18th century. Of the many factors that made this flowering possible, the emergence of influential ecclesiastical moderates was of major importance. Indeed, some of the leading figures of the Enlightenment were also ministers of the Church of Scotland: Hugh Blair was a literary critic and became the first Professor of Rhetoric and Belles Lettres at Edinburgh University. Adam Ferguson was a historian and what would today be called a sociologist. William Robertson was a historian whose writings covered some of the same ground as Hume's *History*. He was a leader of the moderates and became principal of Edinburgh University. All three of these ministers were good friends of the "infidel" Hume, who needed their support on more than one occasion. Joseph Black was a physician who attended Hume in his last illness, but Black is better known as a chemist. It was he who discovered carbon dioxide (which he called *fixed air*, as distinguished from atmospheric air) and developed an accurate method of measuring heat, together with an instrument—the calorimeter—for doing the measuring. James Hutton is widely regarded as the father of modern geology. Going against the prevailing theory of *catastrophism* (i.e., that certain physical properties of the earth are best explained as the result of catastrophic events—a world-wide flood, for example), Hutton argued that these properties were the result of eons of ordinary physical processes that are still at work today (the theory of *uniformitarianism*). These seven men may be taken as representative of the scores of Scottish thinkers who advanced our understanding of the physical, social, and emotional world we inhabit.

The Age of Reason, especially on its philosophical side, had its critics even at the time (Rousseau comes to mind at once) and generated many more in the Romantic movement of the late 18th century and the first half of the 19th. Hume and Kant, the two greatest philosophers of the 18th century, narrowly circumscribe the lessons that reason can teach us about the world and ourselves. The English-American mathematician/logician/philosopher Alfred North Whitehead gives us an astute and eloquent summary of the triumphs and failures of the Age of Reason:

> *Les philosophes* were not philosophers. They were men of genius, clear-headed and acute, who applied the seventeenth-century group of scientific abstractions to the analysis of the unbounded universe. Their triumph, in respect to the circle of ideas mainly interesting to their contemporaries, was overwhelming. Whatever did not fit into their scheme was ignored, derided, disbelieved. Their hatred of Gothic architecture symbolises their lack of sympathy with dim perspectives. It was the age of reason, healthy,

manly, upstanding reason; but, of one-eyed reason, deficient in its vision of depth. We cannot overrate the debt of gratitude which we owe to these men. For a thousand years Europe had been a prey to intolerant, intolerable visionaries. The common sense of the eighteenth century, its grasp of the obvious facts of human suffering, and of the obvious demands of human nature, acted on the world like a bath of moral cleansing. Voltaire must have the credit, that he hated injustice, he hated cruelty, he hated senseless repression, and he hated hocus-pocus. Furthermore, when he saw them, he knew them. In these supreme virtues, he was typical of his century, on its better side. But if men cannot live on bread alone, still less can they do so on disinfectants.[4]

AN OUTLINE OF HUME'S PHILOSOPHY

General Outlook/Method

Hume announces his overall goal in the "Introduction" to his youthful masterpiece, *A Treatise of Human Nature*; namely, to discover the basic principles of the *science of man* (or of human nature). Without knowledge of these principles, we remain ignorant of "the only solid foundation for the other sciences" (THN, xvi; 4.7). That is because *every* science—even so formal and bloodless a discipline as mathematics—reflects the activity of the human mind. If this dependence holds for mathematics and the natural sciences (*natural philosophy*, to use Hume's phrase), it holds *a fortiori* for those inquiries in which human beings are the *objects* of study, as well as the subjects conducting the inquiry. It is with the second sort of inquiry—those sciences whose connection with human nature is obvious and avowed—that Hume is primarily concerned. This broad category comprises four basic sciences: Logic (what we would call *theory of knowledge* or *epistemology*), Morals, Criticism, and Politics. *Logic* seeks "to explain the principles and operations of our reasoning faculty, and the nature of our ideas" (THN, xv; 4.5). *Morals and criticism* "regard our tastes and sentiments" (ibid.). *Politics* "consider men as united in society, and dependent on each other" (ibid.).

Hume's approach to the science of human nature is adumbrated in the subtitle of THN: "Being an Attempt to introduce the experimental method into MORAL SUBJECTS." (Note that *experimental* here means *based on experience*, and that *moral subjects* are human beings and what they do, think, feel, etc.) Applying the experimental method to *natural* subjects led to the spectacular successes of **Isaac Newton**, Robert Boyle, et al.—a fact that emboldens Hume to hope for similar success in the science of human nature. Like the redoubtable Newton, Hume has no use for hypotheses, conjectures, or theories that take us beyond the limits of human experience. They should be rejected as "presumptuous and chimerical" (THN, xvii; 5.8). Neither "the ultimate original qualities of human nature" nor those of matter can be deduced from self-evident, free-standing metaphysical truths (contrary to the claims of rationalist philosophers such as **Descartes**, Spinoza, and Leibniz). Indeed, such ultimate and original qualities are not accessible to us by any means at all. The only solid foundation for any science that investigates matters of fact of any sort is experience and observation: ". . . we can give no reason for our most general and most refin'd principles, beside our experience of their reality . . ." (THN, xviii; 5.9). In a word, Hume is an *empiricist*.

The terms *rationalism* and *empiricism* are not exact and do not refer to mutually exclusive classes, but they do signify real and important differences, especially in method and general outlook. The Latin root of *rationalism*, ratio, means *reason*, a cognitive faculty that (according to rationalist philosophers) discovers truths independently of experience. Consider, for example, Euclid's demonstration that there are infinitely many prime numbers—a wonderfully clear and simple illustration of the power of abstract reason to establish a result that transcends any possible human experience. Empiricists would respond that Euclid's proof is about *numbers*, which are abstract entities, not about things in the real world. Empiricists, no less than rationalists, accept and applaud Euclid's demonstration; but they reject it (and any other instance of purely formal reasoning) as a model for philosophy or science.

The Greek root of *empiricism*, ἐμπειρία (empeiria)—means *experience*, which empiricist philosophers regard as the primary way to find out what the world is like. Can abstract reason tell us why bread will nourish a human being but not a tiger (one of Hume's own examples)? It cannot. That is something we discover by experience. The basis of Hume's objection to rationalist speculations is usefully summarized in his response to the **occasionalism** of the French Cartesian philosopher **Nicolas Malebranche**. Hume agrees with much of Malebranche's analysis of causation, but he rejects Malebranche's argument that God is the only real cause in the universe and that what we ordinarily take to be causes are in reality *occasions* for God to do the real causal work. Hume's estimate of that theory is well known: "We are got into fairy land, long ere we have reached the last steps of our theory." He goes on immediately to tell the reader *why* we have entered fairy land:

> *There* we have no reason to trust our common methods of argument, or to think that our usual analogies and probabilities have any authority. Our line is too short to fathom such immense abysses. And however we may flatter ourselves that we are guided, in every step which we take, by a kind of verisimilitude and experience, we may be assured that this fancied experience has no authority when we thus apply it to subjects that lie entirely out of the sphere of experience. (EHU, 72; 142.24; italics are in Hume's text)

Like John Locke more than half a century earlier (1690), Hume seeks to rein in our restless imagination. When we encounter conclusions "so extraordinary, and so remote from common life and experience" (ibid.), we may be sure that we have gone beyond the reach of our mental faculties. But such conclusions are the stock-in-trade of rationalist philosophers—or so the empiricists believe. By looking very briefly at the "Big Three" of modern rationalism—Descartes, Spinoza, and Leibniz—we can get some additional examples of doctrines the empiricists regard as baseless.

In his best-known work, the *Meditations*, Descartes begins by proposing to doubt all his previous beliefs that are not rationally certain—a class that contains most of his previous beliefs, since they were adopted uncritically. After rejecting the obvious candidates for certainty—e.g., those based on our sense perceptions ("seeing is believing")—he finds that he cannot doubt his own existence: Even to be deceived, he must exist. He further discovers that the key to the certainty he seeks is clarity and distinctness. Whatever I perceive very clearly and distinctly is true. Armed with this criterion, together with the causal axiom that whatever begins to exist must have a cause of existence, Descartes proceeds to prove the existence of an omnipotent, non-deceiving God, whose benevolence guarantees the truth of our clear and distinct ideas. Does Descartes really bring off this ambitious project? Hume offers some critical thoughts on Descartes' use of doubt as a philosophical tool and on God's role as guarantor of our clear and distinct ideas (EHU, 149–53; 199–202).

Spinoza's *Ethics* is probably the purest expression of the rationalist temper in philosophy. Spinoza develops his philosophical system *more geometrico*—in the manner of geometry—laying out axioms, definitions, and postulates as the foundation for demonstrating scores of propositions (or *theorems*) about God, the human mind, human bondage and freedom, and how we should live. God is defined as an absolutely infinite being; i.e., as a substance that comprises infinitely many attributes, each of which expresses an eternal and infinite essence. Such daunting statements actually make good sense within Spinoza's system, and his system is surely a work of genius. Hume's question would be: Why should we believe that any of it has any connection with the world we live in? Spinoza's whole project is carried out by *reason*, with ill-disguised contempt for any notions built on sense experience. It is hard to imagine an outlook more diametrically opposed to Hume's (but some commentators have suggested points of affinity between the two).

Leibniz's philosophy is full of excellent examples of rationalism at work; e.g., his theory that reality consists of substances called *monads*, which have no real contact with one another and are, accordingly, described as *windowless*. But his best-known claim is that the actual world is the best of all possible worlds. How does Leibniz know this? The demonstration is pretty straightforward. Of the infinitely many logically possible worlds (i.e., worlds that harbor no internal contradictions), God chooses the best. To choose anything else would be inconsistent with his perfection. The best of the possible worlds is the one that optimally combines the greatest number of beings with the simplest laws for governing those beings. Imagine two lines intersecting at a non-right angle, one line representing the number of beings and the other representing simplicity of laws: X. The point of intersection signifies the best possible combination of numbers and simplicity. Any variation on this combination—greater numbers of beings or simpler laws—would be less perfect than the one we have. Leibniz's reasoning about this matter is a wonderful example of how rationalists can reach conclusions without even the pretense of appealing to actual experience.

It should be obvious that rationalists see mathematics, with its clarity and precision, as the model for human knowledge. Descartes and Leibniz were great mathematicians as well as philosophers. Curiously, it is the non-mathematician Spinoza who exploited the method most resolutely. Generally, the empiricists take the natural sciences—physics and chemistry are prime examples, but physiology and medicine, too—as a more appropriate model for the sort of knowledge of matters of fact that human beings are capable of attaining. Mathematics has an interest of its own, and it may be useful when applied to the world of experience; but its role is strictly ancillary. It cannot, of itself, tell us anything about ourselves or the world we live in.

The natural sciences and the moral sciences are alike in having no access to trans-experiential reality (if such there be), but getting accurate data is harder for the moral sciences. A piece of copper, for example, cannot know that a physicist has predicted that it will melt at ca. 1800° Fahrenheit (ca. 982° Celsius). The prediction cannot possibly affect the outcome of the experiment. The case is, of course, different with people. If I learn of a prediction about what I will do in a certain situation, I may intentionally act so as to falsify the prediction. In the natural sciences, experiments are often (not always) repeatable. When human beings are involved, it is often impossible to re-create the conditions required for a repeat experiment. Suppose, for example, that I want to show that I could have made a different choice from the one I made five years ago; and I do so by putting myself in the same situation I was in five years ago. But the current situation is *not* the same. Not only have I changed in myriad ways; my motive now—to prove that I acted freely five years ago—is radically different from my motive then. (This is an adaptation of Hume's own example in "Of Liberty and Necessity.") And the limitation is perfectly general: If the objects of study are possessed of thought, feeling, and the capacity for reflection, there is no way of obviating all the concomitant difficulties. The best we can do is to observe how people actually behave in a variety of circumstances—"in company, in affairs [i.e., in public or private business], and in their pleasures" (THN, xix; 6.10).

From what has been said so far, it should be obvious that we cannot understand what Hume was doing—and, equally, what he saw himself as doing—if we forget that he was a historian, an economist, an essayist on a wide range of topics, and a diplomat, as well as a philosopher in the narrower sense. This is precisely what we would expect, given his conception of how the science of man is to be constructed: As a first step, find out all we can about individual and collective human behavior. Then try to discern what laws are at work in shaping that behavior. (There is a distinctly Baconian flavor to the procedure Hume describes.) It seems obvious that Hume's philosophical notions affect the way he *describes* human conduct, even in his (comparatively) non-philosophical writings (e.g., the *History*). But having noted that there is an important connection between Hume the philosopher and Hume the historian/ essayist, etc., we must note also that Hume himself wrote books focused pretty narrowly on *philosophical* issues (most notably, THN, EHU, and EPM), and that Hume is indisputably great as a *philosopher*, not as a historian or an essayist. Accordingly, in the overview that follows, more attention will be devoted to the philosophical side of Hume's system than to the historical, sociological, political side; and this is also true of the Dictionary proper.

Metaphysics/Epistemology (Theory of Knowledge)

At the beginning of his enormously influential *An Essay Concerning Human Understanding* (published in late 1689), John Locke tells his readers of a frustrating, stalemated discussion — or wrangle — that led to the writing of the book. At the root of the fruitless debate, he concluded, was the failure of the participants to consider the limits of the human mind, to determine the sorts of objects it can — or cannot — deal with. This examination must come first, on pain of inevitable confusion and obscurity. Thus motivated, Locke sets out in the *Essay* to discover the origin, the certainty, and the extent of human knowledge, as well as the grounds and degrees of belief, opinion, and assent.

With virtually no substantive changes, Locke's description of his motive and purpose in writing the *Essay* could have been adopted by Hume for his *Treatise* (and, later, the first *Enquiry*). Like Locke, Hume deplores the common practice of philosophers and theologians who venture into abstruse, highfalutin speculations, without ever bothering to ask whether the mind is fitted to undertake such flights into the Empyrean. It is the duty of philosophy to analyze the powers and limits of the mind, with an eye to cultivating a "true metaphysics" by which to subvert the "false and adulterate" — much as agents of the U.S. Treasury learn to spot *counterfeit* currency by becoming thoroughly familiar with *genuine* currency.

As a modest but secure starting point for the "accurate" philosophy he wants to lay out, Hume proposes a "mental geography, or delineation of the distinct parts and powers of the mind" (EHU, 13; 93.13). It is undeniable, Hume says, that the human mind is possessed of various distinguishable faculties and powers. This means that what we assert about the mind and its capacities is true or false, and, further, that ascertaining the truth or falsity of such assertions lies within "the compass of human understanding." It remains to be seen whether our inquiries can penetrate to the "secret springs and principles" that actuate the operations of the mind, but even a simple taxonomy of the mind represents a solid beginning.

No one can doubt that actually suffering a painful burn is quite different from *imagining* a painful burn or even *remembering* it. The same distinction holds across the board, whether we are talking about love or anger or seeing or hearing or tasting. All the **perceptions** of the mind (absolutely anything that we sense, think, feel, imagine, etc.) may be divided into two kinds (or species): **impressions** (our more lively perceptions) and **ideas** or thoughts (our less lively perceptions). Impressions may be subdivided into those of *sensation* and those of *reflection* (also called *secondary impressions*), and ideas may be classified as belonging to *memory* or *imagination*. Perceptions—both impressions and ideas—are either *simple* or *complex*, the simple being those that "admit of no distinction nor separation" (THN, 2; 1.1.1.2). Seeing a uniformly red disc would be an example of a simple impression of sensation.

Although we may suppose that we have "unbounded liberty" to think or imagine what never was on land or sea (monsters, golden mountains, etc.), we are in fact limited by the materials furnished to us by "our outward or inward sentiment" (what Locke calls *sensation* or *reflection*)—in a word, *perceptions*. The "creative power of the mind" in fact amounts to no more than "compounding, transposing, augmenting, or diminishing the materials afforded us by the senses and experience" (EHU, 19; 97.5). In THN, Hume enunciates the following "general proposition": "That all our simple ideas in their first appearance are deriv'd from simple impressions, which are correspondent to them, and which they exactly represent" (4; 1.1.1.7). *Nota bene*: The principle applies only to *simple* ideas and impressions. Hume regards the "general proposition" as a factual claim about human experience, not as an a priori self-evident truth; and he offers a couple of arguments for it. *See* PERCEPTIONS; also THN, 5; 1.1.1.8–9; and EHU, 19–20; 97–98.

Having shown that ideas depend on impressions, and not the other way around, Hume teases the reader by asserting that, under certain circumstances, a simple idea might arise without a corresponding antecedent impression. This intriguing, controversial suggestion is referred to as the **missing shade of blue**. Given the priority of impressions over ideas (the missing shade notwithstanding), Hume proposes a question for testing the significance of any term (or concept) that strikes us as suspect: *From what impression is that supposed idea derived?* Failing to find any such impression, we must conclude that the term has no (genuine) meaning.

As part of his polemic against the doctrine of **innate ideas**, John Locke likens the mind of the newborn to white paper, void of all characters (*tabula rasa*, in scholastic terminology). All the (apparently) multifarious *materials* of reason and knowledge come from experience; i.e., from Sensation (the outer sense) or Reflection (the internal sense). Hume agrees that "all the materials of thinking are derived either from our outward or inward sentiment" (EHU, 19; 97.5), though he disapproves of the way Locke handles the question of innateness (e.g., EHU, 22n. 1; 99.9n. 1).

Having shown that ideas (or thoughts) arise from impressions, Hume needs to explain the natural affinity or relation that certain ideas have to other ideas. He does this by introducing the principles of the **association of ideas**, the most general of which are *resemblance, contiguity in space or time*, and *cause and effect*. These three "principles of connexion" operate automatically—i.e., without conscious effort on our part—as a kind of "gentle force, which commonly prevails" (THN, 10; 1.1.4.1).

In THN, Hume distinguishes four additional **relations** (seven in all), as a starting point for his discussion of knowledge and probability. Fortunately for the reader, in EHU Hume needs only *two* categories to effect an exclusive and exhaustive classification of "all the objects of human reason or enquiry": **Relations of Ideas and Matters of Fact**. Every instance of genuine human knowledge falls into one or the other of these two classes, but never into both. Here is an analogy (but *only* an analogy) of Hume's taxonomy: Every natural number (a.k.a. whole number or integer) is either *odd* or *even*, but no natural number is both odd and even. Propositions expressing relations of ideas are known with certainty, but they tell us nothing about "real existence and matter of fact." For example, the proposition "All triangles have three sides" tells us what it *means* for an object to be a triangle, but it says nothing about whether a particular object is in fact a triangle, or even whether any triangle actually exists. On the other hand, propositions expressing matters of fact can never be known with certainty, but they do assert something about the real world. The proposition "It will rain tomorrow" (assuming that place and time are sufficiently clear from the context) may turn out to be false, but it asserts something about events in the world. Relations of ideas and matters of fact (or, more accurately, propositions expressing them) have mirror-image "virtues": Relations of ideas may be known with certainty, but they are factually empty; whereas matters of fact can never be known with certainty, but they have factual content.

Hume has acute and historically important things to say about relations of ideas, but he is mainly concerned with matters of fact. If we want to learn about matters of fact that lie "beyond the present testimony of our senses, or the records of our memory" (EHU, 26; 108.3), we must rely on the relation of cause and effect. Our belief that it will rain tomorrow is based on the connection between certain current conditions — e.g., the presence of clouds, wind currents of a particular description, barometric pressure, weather in adjacent areas, etc. — and another condition that usually follows the first set of conditions — rain, in this instance. The phrase *usually follows* indicates that we are not dealing with a definition or a merely conceptual connection; we are dealing with a real causal connection. Such connections cannot be discerned a priori but must be learned by experience. We know a priori that *triangular* logically entails *three-sided*, but we have no comparable knowledge of what, if anything, happens when a moving billiard ball strikes a stationary ball. That kind of knowledge comes only from experience; and even after we have repeatedly seen one ball move when struck by another, it is *Custom* or *Habit*—not reason—that induces us to expect the second ball to move when it is struck by the first. We cannot separate *bachelor* from *unmarried man*, but we can *always* mentally separate the *cause-event* from the *effect-event*. In Hume's own words, "The mind can never possibly find the effect in the supposed cause, by the most accurate scrutiny and examination" (EHU, 29; 111.9).

Granting that we discover causal connections only by experience, and never by reason, how do we know that the same connections will obtain in the future? What assurance can we have that the future will resemble the past? This question is referred to as the problem of **induction**, or the *Uniformity of Nature*, though Hume himself does not use those terms. Hume's answer to the question is that neither reason nor experience can assure us that causal associations we have discovered in the past will persist into the future. Notice carefully that Hume does *not* say that the future will *not* resemble the past or that we are *mistaken* to believe that it will. His point is about the *justification* of that belief. Hume's influence on subsequent discussions of causation and induction is hard to overstate. It is pervasive and profound.

Where reason and experience both fail us, nature takes over. Neither reason nor experience can provide a rational basis for believing in induction, but we cannot help believing in it (and would not survive long if we actually succeeded in doubting it). On the *assumption* that the past *is* a reliable guide to the future, we may rank beliefs as more or less justified. Setting aside our beliefs about relations of ideas (which are, so to speak, maximally justified), we may be more or less justified in our beliefs about matters of fact. Hume describes wise (i.e., prudent or reasonable) people as those who proportion their beliefs to the evidence, and this sort of *proportioning* rests on our estimates of probability. But Hume is interested not only in how we might try to *justify* our beliefs (i.e., show that they are true or probably true); he is also interested in the *nature* or *character* of **belief**, without regard to its truth or falsity—the *phenomenology* of belief, we may call it (Hume does not).

We all know firsthand the difference between two different sets of *propositional attitudes*: fantasy, reverie, imagination, wishful thinking, woolgathering, etc.—on the one hand—and genuine belief, on the other. We certainly know the difference between *hoping* that our car has enough gasoline to reach the next service station and *being confident* (i.e., *believing*) that it does. But it is not so easy to *say* precisely what that difference is. Hume locates the difference in certain immediately felt qualities of belief vs. fantasy, and in the role of belief in guiding conduct. Hume's description of belief anticipates some features of the account given by the American pragmatist Charles Sanders Peirce, who says that we believe something to the extent that we are prepared to act on it, should the occasion arise.

Ethics/Moral Philosophy

Human beings are profoundly, unavoidably, and more or less constantly concerned with moral issues—right and wrong, **virtue** and vice, duty, obligation, and the like. Accordingly, an account of morals must occupy a central place in any adequate science of human nature. And Hume lavishes on moral philosophy precisely the sort of attention and care its importance demands. In this brief sketch, we will touch upon several aspects of Hume's moral philosophy, taking special notice of three of its most important features: the reality of moral distinctions, the rejection of reason as the source of moral distinctions, and the criteria for distinguishing virtue from vice.

1. Hume sets out his ethical theory most fully and systematically in two places: in book 3 ("Of Morals") of THN, and in EPM. Hume himself describes EPM as merely a recasting of the earlier work in a simpler and more palatable form, with no significant doctrinal differences. There are obvious differences in style and emphasis and some changes in vocabulary (e.g., the distinction between "natural" and "artificial" virtues effectively disappears in EPM). It is a matter of dispute whether there are in fact substantive differences between the two accounts; but there is no doubt that both of them undertake two principal tasks: to show that our notions of virtue and vice are rooted in human nature and human experience, and to show that moral distinctions are not derived from **reason**, but from sentiment or passion.

2. It can hardly be overemphasized that although Hume rejects reason as the source of moral distinctions, he insists on the reality of such distinctions. They cannot be explained by education alone; they are rooted in "the original constitution of the mind" (EPM, 214; 105.3). Hume has little patience with those "disingenuous disputants" who pretend to believe that "all characters and actions [are] alike entitled to the affection and regard of everyone" (EPM, 169–70; 73.2). On that reckoning, Joseph Stalin and St. Francis of Assisi would be morally indistinguishable. No one really believes that. It is, if anything, even more certain that no one could *live* as an amoralist unless he or she were truly insane—or perhaps we should say *even if* he or she were truly insane.

In dismissing amoralism as a serious position, Hume adopts a *commonsense* stance. There is an instructive parallel (several of them, in fact) between Hume's theory of knowledge and his moral philosophy.

He rejects *rationalist theories* of causation (which claim that we have a priori intuitive knowledge of the principle of causation), but he never denies the reality of causal relations. Just as we do not acquire our basic beliefs about the external world—ordinary physical objects, other people, and the pervasiveness of causal relations—from reason, so we do not get our basic moral notions of good and evil, right and wrong, from reason. However, once we have acquired the notions of cause and of morality by non-rational means, we use reason to clarify the precise character of these concepts and thereby to determine the conditions for their proper application.

It is understandable that readers of Hume's writings on moral philosophy should be confused by what appear to be inconsistent claims about the *status* of moral categories and judgments. On the one hand, moral distinctions are said to consist in *feelings* of approval or disapproval—a subjectivist-looking position. Readers might be pardoned who conclude that Hume does in fact subvert the reality of moral distinctions, his own strenuous denial notwithstanding. Such persons must read on; there is more to the story. Morality is *born* in personal feeling or sentiment, but it has a public career (to borrow language from A. N. Whitehead). Feelings per se may be incurably private and lacking in truth-value (i.e., truth or falsity); but distinctively *moral* feelings must arise from what Hume calls "the general survey" (for example, at THN 499; 3.2.2.24). They must transcend our own private interests; they must be disinterested. Moral judgments (i.e., judgments flowing from or supervening upon or, in the view of some, identical with, moral feelings) are not merely private and void of truth-value. Moral judgments have an obdurate "logic" of their own. Perhaps most important, they must be applied evenhandedly: If I find a quality in my friend's character to be morally praiseworthy, then I must also find the same quality in my enemy's character to be morally praiseworthy—on pain of being inconsistent (and hypocritical). This is the objectivist side of Hume's ethical theory. If we read the "subjectivist" and the "objectivist" passages carefully and in context, we may conclude that they are not actually inconsistent but, rather, complementary parts of the overall theory. (Or so it may be argued. Some commentators emphasize one or the other of the two sides, while others maintain that Hume has no coherent ethical theory at all.)

To avoid misunderstanding, we should note that *objective* does not mean quite the same thing when applied to moral judgments as when applied to judgments about garden-variety matters of fact, although there is an overlap of meaning. When Hume is trying to show that reason alone cannot move us to act, he notes that we can easily ascertain "the distinct boundaries and offices of *reason* and of *taste.*" Reason "conveys the knowledge of truth and falsehood; [taste] gives the sentiment of beauty and deformity, vice and virtue" (EPM, 294; 163.21; italics are in Hume's text). Reason reveals objects as they really exist in nature, without addition or diminution. Taste, on the contrary, "has a productive faculty, and gilding or staining all natural objects with the colours, borrowed from internal sentiment, raises, in a manner, a new creation" (ibid.). It is worth noting that Hume says similar things about the way we acquire the notion of *necessary connexion* between cause and effect. Briefly, he locates necessary connection in the mind, not in the objects themselves. Fortunately for our survival, necessary connection plays no practical role in our recognition of particular causal relations. (That Hume actually denies real causal connections in nature is questioned by some Hume scholars, but he is clear that our only *acquaintance* with necessary connection is by way of *feelings.*)

Hume is here drawing a commonsense distinction that can be illustrated by the difference between merely perceiving a Clydesdale horse (its size, color, bodily conformation, etc.) and responding to (what we take to be) its magnificence and beauty. In this contrast, the size of the horse is objective in a way that its beauty is not. The horse has a real property of, say, standing six feet at the withers, whether anyone perceives it or not. The horse has no comparably real and independent property of being beautiful. However, our judgment that the horse is beautiful is not—or need not be—merely arbitrary or idiosyncratic or individual. It is a judgment that almost all persons familiar with horses would concur in—a judgment, we would say, that is elicited by qualities we perceive in the horse. It is significant that we correct, or revise, our aesthetic and moral judgments about beauty or virtue, just as we correct our perceptual judgments about shape, size, distance, etc. This would make no sense if moral and aesthetic judgments were merely expressions of arbitrary personal reactions. In that case, we might *change* our judgments, but we could not *correct* them. (*See*, e.g., THN, 582, 603; 3.3.1.16, 3.3.3.2.)

Moral judgments, then, are like aesthetic judgments in being rooted in sentiment or taste but also in not being reducible to intractably arbitrary and individual feelings. There are *standards* of taste and of morality that reflect fundamental and universal facts about human nature and, accordingly, may properly be described as *objective*. We regularly and routinely attribute moral and aesthetic properties to persons or things (*generous, selfish, wicked, virtuous, beautiful, ugly*, etc.).; we do not suppose that we are merely projecting our own inner feelings or sentiments onto things in the world. The main difference between aesthetic judgments and moral judgments is that moral judgments must be *disinterested*; i.e., our allocation of praise and blame must be evenhanded, must rise above self-interest.

3. Is morality discerned by reason or by sentiment/feeling? Many 18th-century writers (Hume among them) saw this dichotomy as exhausting the possible explanations of our capacity for distinguishing virtue from vice, good from evil. According to the ethical rationalist, moral distinctions are derived from reason, from judgments of truth and falsity; virtue consists essentially in conformity to reason (vice being negatively defined as contrariety to reason). As proponents of some such view, Hume mentions **Ralph Cudworth** (1617–1688), **Samuel Clarke** (1675–1729), **Nicolas Malebranche** (1638–1715) by name, and alludes to Baron de Montesquieu (1689–1755) and **William Wollaston** (1660–1724) without naming them. (*See* THN, 455–470; 3.1.1; EPM, 197n.1; 93.34n.12.) Hume rejects all such theories; he comes down emphatically against reason and, by default at least, for sentiment. (*See* section 1—"Moral Distinctions not deriv'd from Reason"—of book 3, part 1 of THN.)

Hume attacks **ethical rationalism** along several fronts, but most commentators agree that these numerous arguments are variants of two or three interconnected basic ones. First, morals arouse passions and induce us to act or forbear acting. On the contrary, reason by itself arouses no passions and never inclines us to do anything or to refrain from doing anything; it is impotent in this arena. That is because reason is concerned exclusively with **relations of ideas** (e.g., demonstrating theorems in mathematics) or **matters of fact** (e.g., discovering causal connections). Hume devotes some space and ingenuity to showing that in neither capacity can reason account for moral distinctions.

Further, Hume reminds us that reason has to do with truth and falsehood; i.e., with the agreement or disagreement of our judgments with real relations of ideas or with real matters of fact. Since our passions, volitions, and actions—the stuff of morality—are "original facts and realities, compleat in themselves, and [imply] no reference to other passions, volitions, and actions" (THN, 458; 3.1.1.9), they cannot agree or disagree with anything and, consequently, cannot be either true or false. That is to say, they cannot be either conformable to reason or contrary to reason. They can, however, be laudable or blameworthy—which is proof that being laudable or blameworthy is not the same as being reasonable or unreasonable.

To balance Hume's vigorous rejection of reason as the source of moral distinctions, we should add that reason is involved whenever we *say* or *assert* anything about our feelings of moral approval or disapproval. Even to apply the labels *laudable, blameworthy, virtuous, vicious*, etc., is to invoke concepts or abstract ideas, and this is plainly the work of reason. In his zeal to discredit rationalism, Hume sometimes lapses into hyperbolic or incautious claims; e.g., that reason is the slave of the passions. Though perhaps strictly and narrowly true, this assertion is liable to be misleading. By itself, reason can neither initiate nor prevent any action or volition; but it can indirectly affect our moral sentiments and judgments in profound ways (e.g., by showing that some object of desire is either non-existent or unobtainable). And reason performs crucial service in acquainting us with all the facts relevant to moral appraisal. Suppose, for example, that after strongly condemning Buford Coldiron for killing Hiram Bulstrode, we learn that, with no provocation whatever, Bulstrode had violently attacked Coldiron with a machette. Desperate to save his own life, Coldiron shot Bulstrode, with fatal results. With this additional fact in place (a fact certified by causal reason), we cease to condemn Buford Coldiron. He acted in self-defense, to which no moral or legal stigma is attached. (The names and events are, of course, wholly imaginary.)

Having shown (as he believes) that reason cannot be the source of moral distinctions, Hume tells us what *is* that source: "Moral distinctions [are] deriv'd from a moral sense" (the title of section 2 of THN, book 3, part 1). The term **moral sense** is liable to be misconstrued as referring to a special faculty by which we discern objective, peculiarly moral properties. That is not what Hume means. In EPM (published 11 years after THN), he speaks of "some internal sense or feeling" (173; 75.9) and of *sentiment*, without any substantive change in doctrine from THN.

4. Hume has a lot to say about virtue generally and about particular virtues, and he offers a definition of *virtue*: *"whatever mental action or quality gives to a spectator the pleasing sentiment of approbation*; and vice the contrary" (EPM, 289; 169.10; italics are in Hume's text). He specifies (in what amounts to a correlative definition of *virtue*) just what those approbation-evoking actions or qualities have in common; namely, they are useful or agreeable (or both) to the person himself or to others (or both) (EPM, 268; 145.1). The two definitions are complementary in that they speak of the *sentiment* of approbation and of the *qualities* that elicit the sentiment.

We find an action or sentiment or character virtuous because we feel a pleasure "of a particular kind" when we view it. It is worth reiterating that not just any sort of pleasure will do. The requisite kind of pleasure is produced by the "general survey"; i.e., by a disinterested or impartial viewing. Human beings are by their very nature—and not merely by nurture or inculcation—sympathetic creatures, able to share the pleasures and pains of others. We are capable of being altruistic in our attitudes and actions, though we are at least equally capable of being selfish. This means that Hume rejects the doctrine of **egoism** (not Hume's term)—the theory that all voluntary human actions are selfish (associated, most notably, with Thomas Hobbes, but also with **Bernard de Mandeville**). Indeed, Hume denounces "the selfish system of morals" with eloquent indignation (EPM, 295–97; 164–65). *See AN ENQUIRY CONCERNING THE PRINCIPLES OF MORALS.*

5. Hume scholars disagree about the most accurate general label for Hume's ethical theory: *subjectivist, projectionist, objectivist, realist, emotivist, utilitarian, naturalist.* Of course, Hume himself uses none of these tags; they did not exist in his time. Passages from THN and EPM may be cited that seem to lend support to each of these characterizations; but they cannot all be accurate descriptions of Hume's theory as a whole, since some are incompatible with others (e.g., *projectivist* and *realist*). Some critics see this as evidence of the incoherence of the theory. Defenders of Hume may point out that human moral phenomena (behavior and reflective thought) are too complex and pervasive to be faithfully represented by a single exclusive formula. The various labels may all be apt for describing *different facets* of Hume's moral philosophy—just as *andante, adagio*, and *vivace* may be properly applied to the different movements of a symphony

or concerto. (This debate among commentators about Hume's ethical theory parallels similar debates about his views on almost any topic he ever treated. No effort is made in this book—here or elsewhere—to settle these disputes.)

Philosophy of Religion

From an early age, Hume had no personal religious beliefs—certainly none of the traditional sort—and yet his interest in religion remained keen and virtually continuous his whole life. Just why this was so is a matter of conjecture, a fact that has not stopped a number of commentators from offering answers to the problem. Whatever the psychological roots of his preoccupation, Hume's contributions to the philosophy of religion are monumental: profound, wide-ranging, and enormously influential. The principal sources of Hume's views on religion are section 10 ("Of Miracles") and section 11 ("Of a particular Providence and of a future State") of EHU; *The Natural History of Religion*; and **Dialogues Concerning Natural Religion**. To these may be added four essays that have a more or less direct bearing on religious issues: "Of Superstition and Enthusiasm," "Of Suicide," "Of the Immortality of the Soul," and "The Platonist." It would be a mistake to suppose that the writings just mentioned, which are expressly about some aspects of religion, exhaust what Hume has to say on the subject. In fact, the whole tenor of his empiricist philosophy, with its emphasis on ordinary experience and its proscription of speculative flights of fancy, sets it in opposition to the tenets and practices of what Hume calls "popular religion." In this brief sketch, several facets of Hume's philosophy of religion will be highlighted.

1. Hume's attitude toward religion is negative, in varying degrees of explicitness and frankness. Because it is usually tied to superstition, Hume argues, religion is emotionally and practically more powerful than science or philosophy. "Generally speaking," Hume says, "the errors in religion are dangerous; those in philosophy only ridiculous" (THN, 272; 1.4.7.13). He argues that religion—especially the more fanatical, abstemious, and otherworldly sort—has a corrosive effect on the moral and social character of its adherents ("Bad influence of popular religions on morality" is the title of a chapter in *The Natural History of Religion*). The "monkish virtues," as Hume calls them—celibacy,

fasting, penance, mortification, self-denial, humility, silence, solitude, etc. — are in reality vices, not virtues at all. They do not make one a better person or a better citizen. On the contrary, they stultify normal human impulses, aspirations, and feelings: They "stupify the understanding and harden the heart, obscure the fancy and sour the temper" (EPM, 270; 146.3).

Later in EPM, Hume draws the same contrast between natural and artificial lives, but in less savage language: "They [i.e., people imbued with superstitious beliefs about otherworldly rewards and punishments] are in a different element from the rest of mankind; and the natural principles of their mind play not with the same regularity, as if left to themselves, free from the illusions of religious superstition or philosophical enthusiasm" (EPM, 343; 199.57). (To avoid the impression that Hume indulged in an indiscriminate broad-brush condemnation of all religious believers, we should note that he had several good friends among the Scottish clergy — some of whom publicly defended him against what they regarded as unfair attacks. Further, Hume seems to have held Bishop Joseph Butler, among other Christian philosophers, in genuine esteem. But it may be doubted that Hume ever traced any of the admirable qualities of these people to their religious convictions. Indeed, he seemed to think that they were good *in spite of* their religious beliefs.)

Hume's sundering of morality from religion obviously puts him at odds with those who see God as the only possible ground of morality. The 19th-century Russian novelist Fyodor Dostoevski expresses the latter view through his character Ivan Karamazov: "If God does not exist, then everything is permitted." The idea seems to be that morality must be imposed externally, that only the prospect of reward or punishment can induce people to behave morally. Hume takes the polar opposite position; namely, that morality is rooted in human nature and developed in the actual practices of society. What is permitted and what is forbidden arise naturally from the collective experience of the various groups that impose duties — positive and negative — on their members (the family, the state, the guild, the church, and so forth). Religion does, of course, exert an influence on morals (often, in Hume's opinion, a noxious one); but that is just a natural fact about human behavior and not a mandate from God.

2. When Hume wrote THN (in the 1730s), it was widely assumed that the existence of God was beyond question and that the miracles

described in the New Testament proved the divine origin of Christianity. Hume tries to subvert both assumptions.

a) First, Hume dismisses the traditional a priori arguments that claim to *demonstrate* the existence of God—the so-called *ontological* argument, and the *cosmological* argument for the necessity of a first uncaused cause. According to Hume, *no* matter of fact can be demonstrated. "Whatever *is* may *not be*. No negation of a fact can involve a contradiction. The non-existence of any being, without exception, is as clear and distinct an idea as its existence" (EHU, 164; 209.28; the italics are in Hume's text). These considerations apply to all matters of fact, even those we have no actual reason to doubt.

b) If we want to establish the existence of any being, we must do so by arguments from its cause or its effect; that is, arguments founded entirely on experience. The argument to (or from) **design** (sometimes called the *teleological* argument) meets this preliminary requirement. However, upon close examination, Hume finds that the design argument is far less persuasive than its proponents suppose, though it is not entirely without merit.

c) Even if the argument to/from design were as powerful as many believed it to be, the appeal to **miracles** as the chief evidence for a particular religion would be futile. In "Of Miracles" Hume tries to show that we can never have sufficient testimonial evidence for the occurrence of a miracle to overbalance its inherent improbability. Since a miracle is, by definition, the violation of a law of nature, the best we can hope for is a standoff in case the positive testimonial evidence were maximally strong. In fact, Hume contends, the case for miracles is incomparably weaker than that. In Hume's opinion, history affords no example of a purported miracle whose testimonial evidence came close to neutralizing—let alone defeating—the strong presumption against it.

3. In *The Natural History of Religion*, Hume distinguishes two questions about religion that demand answers: one about "its foundation in reason" and the other about "its origin in human nature" (NHR, 21). The first question—the one he is *not* dealing with in this work—is easy to answer: "The whole frame of nature bespeaks an intelligent author; and no rational enquirer can, after serious reflection, suspend his belief a moment with regard to the primary principles of genuine Theism and Religion" (ibid.). Given his criticisms of the argument from design, we

may suspect that Hume is here speaking ironically, or at least hyperbolically. But that is not his topic anyway. He seeks to locate the beginnings of religion in the constitution of the human mind and the world in which human beings live. That, he says, is a harder task.

Whether or not Hume really believes that the existence of "an intelligent author" of nature is too obvious for serious doubt, he contends that religion has its origins in the inability of human beings to control many natural events of life-and-death importance—famine, floods, pestilence, and the like—together with the fears and hopes that are inevitably produced by this impotence. The practitioners of the earliest religions evince no interest in explaining the order of nature, but rather in somehow placating the unseen powers operating within that order. Hume says that some societies seem not to have had any religion at all, while conceding that the presence of *some* religious belief is exceedingly widespread, both in time and geography. The primary religion of mankind, Hume argues, was polytheism (which he also calls *idolatry*), with monotheism a later development that regularly gave way to a renewed polytheism ("Flux and Reflux of Polytheism and Theism" is a chapter title). These facts—the occasional absence of religion altogether and the great diversity of particular religious beliefs—indicate that religious principles are not as deeply rooted in human nature as certain other plainly irresistible beliefs (e.g., in the existence of other people, external objects, and causation). Religious principles are, as Hume puts it, "secondary" and, as a consequence, subject to perversion by various accidents and causes.

Critics of NHR complain that Hume's account of the origin and nature of religious beliefs amounts to little more than armchair anthropology—inevitable, perhaps, in one who was born half a century too soon to make use of the findings of scientific anthropology. Less excusable—because not inevitable or unavoidable—is Hume's choosing examples and illustrations to fit his preconceived theories about religion. And not excusable at all is his practice of virtually ignoring the positive fruits of at least some varieties of religion, fruits that Hume knew both from history and from his own personal acquaintances. Without denying the justice of these strictures, we might say that NHR has the virtue of its defects: Though one-sided and biased, it is effective in forcing readers to acknowledge the darker side of the story of religion in human life.

Varia

Hume's writings cover a wide range of subjects: philosophy in the narrow sense, history, religion, economics, politics, literature, criticism, etc., etc. Most commentators now hold that we cannot properly understand Hume's treatment of the "standard" philosophical topics—knowledge, perception, causation, skepticism, and the like—without taking account of his views about topics falling outside the "standard" ambit. Although Hume himself contrasts "the easy and obvious philosophy" with "the accurate and abstruse" (EHU, 6; 88.3), he intends no invidious comparison. On the contrary, both ways of doing philosophy are commended. Human beings are born for action, but also for reflection; the ideal life would incorporate both sides of human nature. The same goes for writing style, and Hume's own writings exemplify both the easy and obvious and the accurate and abstruse ways of doing philosophy. Even his more narrowly philosophical works (e.g., THN, EHU, and EPM) are informed by his broad knowledge of history and literature. In that way he carries out his announced intention to found the science of human nature on a comprehensive examination of what people actually do "in company, in affairs, and in their pleasures" (THN, xix; 6.10). Such an examination must include what people actually did in times past and in other places; i.e., it must be rooted in history.

Hume is unique among great philosophers in being also a first-rate historian. If Hume uses his knowledge of history in developing his epistemology or his ethical theory, it is also true that he applies his philosophical principles to the study of history (or economics or literary criticism or aesthetics). As a historian, he seeks to show how events and movements are better understood as the consequences of human nature than as random (or divinely appointed) happenings. In his essay "The Populousness of Ancient Nations" Hume appeals to common sense sharpened by logic to refute the claim (widely believed in the 18th century) that the population of the ancient world was greater than that of Hume's own world. After considering Hume's marshaling of the evidence, a contemporary reader is apt to wonder how so implausible a view could ever have gained any currency. Hume also wrote about the role of money in economics (he is strongly anti-mercantilist), the balance of trade (do not worry about what may appear to be an unfavorable balance), and interest (he argues that interest rates are not a function of the amount of money in circulation), among other topics.

Although Hume never confuses moral judgments with artistic (or what we would call *aesthetic*) judgments, he holds that both sorts of judgment are founded on *taste* or *sentiment*, not on reason. This sounds like subjectivism and relativism, and the wide (or even *wild*) disparities in aesthetic tastes seem to confirm the maxim *de gustibus non disputandum est* [there is no disputing taste]. But, of course, we *do* dispute tastes more or less constantly. Further, some opinions about, say, painting or literature, would be (almost) universally rejected as silly; e.g., that Andy Warhol is a greater artist than Rembrandt or that Zane Grey is a better writer than Shakespeare. In a well-known and influential essay—"Of the Standard of Taste"—Hume develops a theory, based on actual human practice, that allows for non-arbitrary, objective standards in what he calls *criticism*, while preserving the affective origins of all aesthetic judgments. To be a discriminating critic, one must cultivate a certain delicacy of imagination, must have wide experience, and must avoid prejudice.

To the question "Is Hume an objectivist or subjectivist in aesthetics?" the correct answer is "Yes" (or, less coyly, "Both")—which is also the correct answer to the question "Is Hume an objectivist or subjectivist in ethics?"

NOTES

1. Works used in the sketch of Hume's life include the book-length biographies by Thomas Edward Ritchie, John Hill Burton, J. Y. T. Greig, and Ernest Campbell Mossner; also the two volumes of Hume's letters edited by Greig and the single volume of letters edited by Mossner and Raymond Klibansky. Hume's tantalizingly brief autobiography—*My Own Life*—is both bane and blessing. As the testament of the dying Hume (written four months before his death), it is irreplaceable. But it contains a few erroneous or ambiguous statements of fact and some misleading generalizations. Accordingly, it has been used generously but warily.

2. *Life and Correspondence of David Hume*, Vol. I, 399.

3. I. Kant, *On History*, 3; translated by Lewis White Beck.

4. Alfred North Whitehead, *Science and the Modern World* (New York: Macmillan, 1954), 86–87. This work was published originally in 1925.

Dictionary

– A –

ABSTRACT IDEAS. According to **John Locke**, one of the ways we come to have general ideas is by *abstraction*. For example, we can abstract the color *white* from our perception of milk and snow, and then apply the term to any other objects that have that property. We can use the same method (plus a couple more) to acquire ideas of more complicated things—triangles, dogs, horses, men, etc. Even small children learn the names for distinct colors, shapes, animals, etc., and are able to tell a red ball from a blue one and a dog from a cat. That is a matter of commonsense fact. The question that interests Hume is this: What sort of idea do we have when we refer to an abstract property (say, blue in general) or to an abstract set of properties (say, dog in general)?

Both **George Berkeley** and Hume criticize what they take to be Locke's answer to the question, and they both choose the same example from Locke. (Hume acknowledges his debt to Berkeley on this topic [THN, 17; 1.1.7.1; and EHU, 155n1; 203n32].) According to Locke, the *general idea of a triangle* is neither equilateral nor isosceles nor scalene, but "all and none of these at once." It is "something imperfect, that cannot exist; an *Idea* wherein some parts of several different and inconsistent *Ideas* are put together" (*Essay*, 596, §9). It is easy to ridicule Locke's example, as Berkeley and Hume do. Obviously, a triangle must be equilateral, isosceles, or scalene; and even more obviously, a triangle cannot be all three at once. The Lockean general idea of a triangle seems to be an absurdity squared. (It is a matter of scholarly debate whether Berkeley interprets Locke's doctrine accurately and fairly, but that question need not detain us.)

So far as Hume is concerned, Locke gives away the game when he admits that the general idea of a triangle refers to something that cannot exist. Hume's argument is straightforward: If I can form an idea of x, then it is possible for x to exist. It follows (by the logical argument-form known as *modus tollens*) that if x cannot exist, then I cannot form an idea of x. Since absolutely everything that actually exists is perfectly determinate and particular, we know (as Locke concedes) that a general triangle cannot possibly exist. This means that *all* our ideas are similarly particular and determinate. Just as we cannot draw a line in general (i.e., a line that has no particular length), so we cannot form the *idea* of such a line. For us to have an idea of a line and to have an idea of a line of some precise length are one and the same thing.

If we have no abstract ideas, how can we demonstrate geometrical theorems about *all* triangles or circles (as we certainly can)? Or, to take a more homely example, how can we decide to get a dog for a pet without knowing even what breed of dog, to say nothing of which particular dog (as we certainly can)? Language itself would be quite impossible if we did not have words that refer indifferently to any one of a class of objects. Hume's answer is that we invest a *particular* idea with a kind of *functional generality* by the use we make of the idea. He describes abstract ideas as being "*particular in their nature, but general in their representation*" (THN, 22; 1.1.7.10; italics are in Hume's text). These ideas are "really nothing but particular ones, consider'd in a certain light" (THN, 34; 1.2.3.5).

A particular idea acquires a legitimate, intelligible generality by being "attached to a general term, which recalls, upon occasion, other particular ones, that resemble, in certain circumstances, the idea, present to the mind" (EHU, 158n1; 205n34). Because these ideas are associated with general terms, they can represent a "vast variety" of objects that are alike in some respects but differ widely in others. The word *horse*, for example, calls to mind a particular horse of a certain color and size; but because *horse* is applied to animals of other colors and sizes, we can easily reason about them even when we do not literally have ideas of them in mind. Hume uses this line of argument to attack the claim that our ideas of space and time must be infinitely divisible (EHU, 155–58; 204–5).

We might say that although we do not in fact have any abstract ideas, we often treat a particular idea *as if* it were abstract. When we demonstrate, for example, that the area of *any* triangle—equilateral, isosceles, scalene, acute, obtuse, right, etc.—can be obtained by a single formula, we focus on certain properties and ignore, so to speak, those properties that are irrelevant to our purpose. This we do without ever having an abstract general idea. Consider a very simple case: When a geometry teacher uses a piece of chalk tied to a string to show students how to bisect a line, the students understand immediately that the technique can be applied to any line, whatever its length, color, etc. Hume emphasizes the role of custom and habit in effecting the transition from a particular idea to other ideas that resemble it in relevant ways.

Hume uses his theory of abstract ideas to explain what is called a *distinction of reason*, i.e., a distinction between two aspects of an object that cannot in reality be separated (color and shape, for example, or the length and breadth of a line). Hume concedes that this *seems* to be inconsistent with his doctrine that if two things can be distinguished or separated in thought, then they can (in principle anyway) exist separately. Or, to state the same doctrine in a logically equivalent form: If two things cannot exist separately, then they cannot be separated or distinguished in thought. What does Hume have in mind by a distinction that "implies neither a difference nor separation?" (THN, 25; 1.1.7.17). If it is properly understood, a distinction of **reason** fits that description.

When we see a globe of white marble, we perceive the color with a certain shape or form. We cannot actually perceive the color without some form (and vice versa), but we can notice the resemblance in shape between a globe of white marble and a globe of black marble; or we can notice the resemblance in color between a globe of white marble and a cube of white marble. In this way, "we find two separate resemblances [of color and shape], in what formerly seem'd, and really is, perfectly inseparable" (THN, 25; 1.1.7.18). Even though we cannot literally perceive or imagine a color that has no shape, we can "carry our eye" to one property (the color or the shape) and consider its relation to other objects of the same kind (white or black or globose or cubic). We may describe Hume's account of distinctions of reason as *phenomenological*, i.e., one that looks very carefully at actual human experience.

Hume's most sustained and direct discussion of abstract ideas is in THN, 17–25; 1.1.7; but he puts abstract ideas to work elsewhere—e.g., in explaining how we get the ideas of **space and time** (THN, 34–35; 1.2.3.5–7). He also invokes his doctrine of abstract ideas (and, more generally, of the priority of impressions to ideas) to refute the rationalist claim that only some superior faculty of the mind—pure intellect—can understand the "refin'd and spiritual" objects of mathematical reasoning (THN, 72; 1.3.1.7).

A historical note: Hume begins his discussion of abstract ideas by noting that "Dr. Berkeley" had disputed the received opinion about the nature of abstract or general ideas. Locke is not mentioned by name, but he is pretty clearly the main target of Hume's—and Berkeley's—criticism (as noted at the beginning of this entry). Hume introduces the correlative notion of a distinction of reason by complaining that it has been much discussed but little understood. It is indeed a topic of great interest for medieval philosophers such as John Duns Scotus (1266–1308), who draws *formal* distinctions among the attributes of God (omnipotence, omniscience, etc.) without denying God's absolute simplicity. Closer to Hume's own time, the French philosopher-mathematician **René Descartes** argues that there are three kinds of *distinction*: a *real* distinction, a *modal* distinction, and a *conceptual* distinction. The second and third of these—the *modal* and the *conceptual*—answer, more or less, to Hume's *distinction of reason*. Readers may judge for themselves whether Hume's explanation is an improvement over Descartes'. See Descartes' *Principles of Philosophy*, part 1, §60–62.

ARGUMENT FROM/TO DESIGN. *See* DESIGN, ARGUMENT FROM/TO.

ASSOCIATION (OR CONNEXION) OF IDEAS. The **imagination** can combine ideas in a virtually unlimited variety of ways. For example, it can join the head of a man with the body of a horse to form the mythological centaur. But many ideas exhibit natural affinities that require no conscious manipulation. Hume refers to these links as a "gentle force," which unites ideas that are related by *resem-*

blance, *contiguity in time or place*, or *causation*. A photograph of a person leads naturally to thoughts about the person in the photograph (resemblance). The mention of a place disposes us to think of other places in the same area; and when we remember an event, we are likely to think of other events that occurred at or about the same time (contiguity in space or time). When we recall burning ourselves, we immediately associate the incident with the accompanying pain (causation). The three principles of association (or connection) are not the only ones, but Hume contends that they are the only *general* ones. (See THN, 10–13; 1.1.4.1–7; EHU, section 3.) Hume holds that *impressions*—as against *ideas*—are associated only by *resemblance* (THN, 283; 2.1.4.3).

Hume is not the first thinker to appeal to the association of ideas to explain certain mental phenomena, but he claims to make more extensive use of the principles than any of his predecessors. Indeed, the principles are of "vast consequence" in the science of human nature, since they bind the parts of the universe together *so far as the universe is known to us*. In Hume's own words, "they are really *to us* the cement of the universe, and all the operations of the mind must, in great measure, depend on them" (THN, 662; 417.35; italics are in Hume's text).

– B –

BACON, FRANCIS (1561–1626). Born three years after the accession of Elizabeth I to the English throne and four years before Shakespeare, Francis Bacon achieved fame (and a degree of infamy) as an essayist, politician, and philosopher. Under James I, he was knighted, made Baron Verulam, Viscount St. Albans, and lord chancellor. He was convicted of taking a bribe and assessed a large fine and a prison sentence. Both the fine and the sentence were vacated, but his political life was over. (It has been duly noted that Sir Francis found *against* the man accused of offering the bribe.) For present purposes, it is Bacon's method for the advancement of knowledge that is of interest.

The negative side of Bacon's approach is at least as significant as the positive. Specifically, he inveighs against the Aristotelian obsession with syllogisms and, generally, against the appeal to a priori principles rather than careful examination of the facts. It is a simple and straightforward matter of formal logic to determine whether the conclusion of a syllogism follows necessarily from the premises. But the conclusion will be of scant value if its premises are founded on nothing more substantial than empty general truths and guesses about matters of fact—a description that Bacon applies wholesale to medieval philosophy and science. Apart from the inimical influence of medieval thought, Bacon recognizes that the human mind itself shelters prejudices and inclinations that militate against progress in science. He likens the mind to a mirror that is intrinsically capable of reflecting reality; but, to do so, the mirror must first be cleaned and resurfaced. (These impediments to knowledge are strikingly illustrated in what Bacon calls "idols" of the mind: Idols of the Tribe, Idols of the Cave, Idols of the Marketplace, and Idols of the Theater. Readers interested in what Bacon says about these idols should consult his *Novum Organum* [*New Organon*], which he intended to supplant Aristotle's *old* Organon.)

In the *Abstract* of THN, Hume lauds "My Lord Bacon" as "the father of experimental physicks [*sic*]" (646; 407.2). Whether or not such high praise is actually deserved, it indicates Hume's admiration for the inductive method recommended by Bacon. According to that method, we must begin our investigations with a generous number of particular observations, taking care to exclude those that do not fit the working hypothesis. We ascend step by step to more general principles (or "axioms"), in sharp contrast to the medieval practice of beginning with supposedly universal propositions or generalizing from meager or ill-chosen particulars. Bacon's own example has to do with the cause of heat, but it is too esoteric and byzantine to recount here. A simpler (but obviously anachronistic) case is the discovery of the cause of yellow fever by Walter Reed and his associates in the early years of the 20th century. Through a series of carefully controlled experiments, they showed beyond practical doubt that the disease is spread by the female aëdes mosquito. This knowledge made it possible for communities to prevent outbreaks of the disease (e.g., by destroying the habitat of the mosquitoes)—a happy instance of Bacon's famous dictum "knowledge is power."

Bacon's method has been criticized as simplistic and as weak on the role of imagination in framing hypotheses, and Bacon certainly had no inkling of the way mathematics would shape modern science. But he breathed a spirit of optimism into the scientific enterprise: By using the right method and ridding ourselves of prejudices, we can far surpass the boundaries of knowledge that our forebears deemed absolute. Hume exhibits a measure of that optimism in his conviction that the science of man can rival the natural sciences in exactness and scope. His expectations sound Baconian: "If, in examining several phaenomena, we find that they resolve themselves into one common principle, and can trace this principle into another, we shall at last arrive at those few simple principles, on which all the rest depend." But he adds this characteristic caveat: "And tho' we can never arrive at the ultimate principles, 'tis a satisfaction to go as far as our faculties will allow us" (THN, 646; 407.1).

BAYES'S THEOREM. Thomas Bayes (1702–1761) was an English non-conformist minister who is known chiefly for his paper "Essay towards solving a problem in the doctrine of chances," which was published posthumously in 1763 by his friend **Richard Price**. The work in that essay was the basis for a theorem (not explicitly formulated by Bayes) that bears his name: *Bayes's Theorem*. The theorem has been given several different formulations, but the basic idea is both simple and intuitively correct: The conditional probability of some hypothesis, given a particular piece of supporting evidence, is greater than the probability of the hypothesis itself (i.e., without the supporting evidence) to the degree that the evidence is unlikely in itself but likely given the hypothesis. A simple example will make the abstract statement clear. Let the hypothesis (h) be that you have won a multi-million dollar lottery (a hypothesis of *extremely* low probability), and let the evidence (e) be that the director of the lottery has officially notified you that you have won. The conditional probability of the hypothesis (that you have won the lottery), given the evidence (that you have been officially informed that you have won), is greater than the probability of the hypothesis by itself, to the extent that the evidence is improbable in itself but probable, given the hypothesis. In other words, it is improbable in the extreme that you would be informed that you have won the lottery; the odds against it are astronomical. On the other hand, it is highly probable that you would be informed that you had won the lottery, *given that* *you had in fact won it.* Here is a very simple formulation of the theorem:

$$P(h/e) = [P(h) \times P(e/h)] / P(e)$$

That is, the probability of *h*, given *e*, is equal to the probability of *h* times the probability of *e*, given *h*, divided by the probability of *e*.

The abstract side of the theorem is uncontroversial. Indeed, it can be demonstrated as a consequence of the standard set of axioms governing conditional probability. On the other hand, it is a matter of considerable dispute whether—and if so, precisely how—the theorem provides a rule for *revising* or *updating* the probability of a hypothesis if new evidence is added to the antecedent, or prior, evidence. It is, in other words, a point of contention whether Bayes's theorem is of much value for adjudicating substantive disagreements. For our purposes, the theorem is of interest because some scholars have used it in assessing Hume's arguments in "Of Miracles" (section 10 of EHU). It is easy to see why. The antecedent, or prior, probability of a miracle story's actually being true is so low that, as Hume puts it, we should believe the miracle story only if the falsity of the supporting evidence (*testimonial* evidence in this case) would be an even greater miracle than the one asserted in the story (EHU, 116; 174.13).

BAYLE, PIERRE (1647–1706). The French author of the massive *Dictionnaire historique et critique* (two volumes, 1695 and 1697) and other lesser works was a major influence on Hume's thinking, especially about **skepticism**. Bayle lived in a time of great religious and political turmoil and persecution—a circumstance that no doubt strengthened his belief in and advocacy of tolerance.

Bayle's own religious views are hard to make out, despite his professions of Christian faith. Is he being ironic? Quite sincere? What is not in doubt is his dialectical skill in drawing out the vexing problems in any important philosophical or theological opinion you can name. For example, in discussing the paradoxes of Zeno of Elea (according to which motion—and, indeed, any kind of change—is impossible), Bayle tries to show, by the most painstaking, patient, and thorough analysis, that *no* theory of space and time is coherent. And he does the same thing for the mind-body problem and any other philosophical issue he considers. The outcome is always the same, an intractable skepticism, which he accepts blandly and renders harmless by appealing to the revealed truths of his faith. These truths are also irrational, but that does not matter to Bayle.

Unlike Bayle, Hume *is* troubled by the skepticism growing out of the contradictions and paradoxes that he professes to discern in our beliefs. Hume seeks to *mitigate* the corrosive, disquieting effects of skepticism, mainly by appealing to natural human instincts and activities. (*See* PYRRHONISM.) Like Hume, the German philosopher/mathematician Leibniz was troubled by Bayle's omnivorous skepticism. He wrote his *Theodicy*, in part, as an answer to Bayle's contention that the problem of evil (how evil can exist in a world governed by an all-powerful, perfectly good God) makes it impossible to reconcile faith with **reason**.

Not all of Bayle's arguments are on target. Some of them are puzzling, or worse. For example, he says that the religious doctrine of God's creation of the world *ex nihilo* contradicts the principle that nothing comes out of nothing. But that is an obvious misunderstanding of the doctrine. *God* (who has always existed and always will) is the sufficient cause of whatever else exists. The doctrine may or may not be true, but it is plainly not contrary to the causal principle that whatever begins to exist must have a cause of existence. And some of his arguments make use of false premises. Such occasional lapses notwithstanding, Bayle's dissection of philosophical theories and his vast learning are generally impressive.

Hume's debt to Bayle is profound and pervasive. His efforts in THN to develop intelligible accounts of mathematics and space and time, and his canvassing of the varieties of skepticism—all these spring from his reading of Bayle.

BEATTIE, JAMES (1735–1803). Beattie was a Scottish poet and philosopher who defended common sense against such "enemies" as **René Descartes** and **Nicolas Malebranche**, but most especially his fellow Britons **George Berkeley** and David Hume. His criticisms were not without some philosophical bite; but where Hume was concerned, he sometimes descended into personal attack. Hume did not often respond publicly to his critics, but he privately described Beattie as "that bigoted silly Fellow." The great German philosopher **Immanuel Kant** mentions Beattie, along with **Thomas Reid**, as one who misunderstood Hume's point about **causation**. Beattie's principal philosophical work, *Essay on the Nature and Immutability of Truth, in Opposition to Sophistry and Scepticism*, was published in 1770 (six years before Hume died) and was widely celebrated as a crushing refutation of Hume's **skepticism** (or what Beattie took for skepticism anyway). It is regrettable that Beattie is often looked upon as a buffoon (for good reason) rather than as a philosopher who had some interesting things to say about skepticism.

BELIEF. We all know the difference between believing something and doubting it, and we know about the varying *degrees* of belief; but it is hard to say precisely what the difference is. In THN, Hume offers an unhelpful definition in the jargon of that word: A belief is "a lively idea related to or associated with a present impression" (96; 1.3.7.5). Several years later (in EHU, 48–49; 125), he concedes that it may be impossible to *define* belief precisely, but we can describe certain features of the sentiment. Hume sees no problem with beliefs whose objects are propositions expressing **relations of ideas**, dispatching the subject with three sentences in THN (95; 1.3.7.3). As either intuitively or demonstratively true, such propositions compel belief absolutely. They cannot be understood without being believed. Their opposites are, literally, inconceivable and, a fortiori, not susceptible of being believed. Accordingly, Hume devotes all his attention to beliefs about **matters of fact**, whose opposites are always conceivable even when the facts involved are *practically* beyond doubt.

Hume begins his treatment of belief by saying what belief *cannot* be. Although the raw materials of experience come exclusively by way of the internal and external senses (sensation and reflection), the mind is free to combine, compound, separate, and divide ideas in an almost endless variety of ways. We can imagine flying horses, talking pigs, golden mountains, centaurs, etc., etc. We can imagine that Abraham Lincoln wrested the death-dealing pistol from John Wilkes Booth and shot his would-be assailant. But we cannot *believe* any of those things; we cannot manipulate belief at will. This implies that belief cannot be some "peculiar idea" that we annex to the object of our belief; for otherwise we could *believe* anything we could *conceive*. Hume does not say so explicitly, but the best candidate for the required "peculiar idea" would be *a separate idea of **existence***;

but we have no such idea. (This argument is logically independent of Hume's own argument from the involuntariness of belief, which he regards as decisive.)

As a species of natural instinct, belief ensues when the mind is in certain circumstances; reason can neither induce nor prevent belief. In this respect, belief is like sense perception, wherein we are passive: ". . . *belief is more properly an act of the sensitive, than of the cogitative part of our natures*" (THN, 183; 1.4.1.8; italics are in Hume's text). Hume never alters the essentials of his account of belief (specifically, its involuntary character), but he allows that our understanding may indirectly affect belief by invoking general rules and our fund of past experiences. Whatever our senses may tell us, we know that an airplane flying at 20,000 feet is in fact much larger than it appears to us on the ground. (See THN, 631–32; 1.3.19.10–12.) We cannot choose what to believe, but we may to some degree control the circumstances in which it occurs and thereby exert some influence on it. Hume stresses the role of *education* as an artificial (and sometimes noxious) but extremely powerful cause of belief (see, e.g., THN, 116–17; 1.3.9.16–19).

When Hume comes to describe the nature of belief—to give the *phenomenology* of belief, so to speak—he points to the *manner* or *way* the object appears to the mind, or the way it *feels* to the mind. In the jargon of recent philosophy, Hume is concerned here with *propositional attitudes*—how we regard a proposition rather than *what* it asserts. Belief or assent is determined by the *vivacity* of the perceptions before the mind (THN, 86; 1.3.5.7). "[B]elief is nothing but a more vivid, lively, forcible, firm, steady conception of an object, than what the imagination alone is ever able to attain" (EHU, 49; 125.12). These terms—*vivid, lively, forcible, firm, steady*—refer to introspectible qualities of our experience. To these, Hume adds some very important characteristics of belief that are at once less readily open to mental inspection and more accessible to external observation: the superior influence of belief on our behavior and on our emotional state.

In linking belief to possible action, Hume anticipates the 19th-century Scottish philosopher Alexander Bain (1818–1903), who explains belief as a readiness to act, should the occasion arise. If a wealthy man professes to believe in the importance of giving money to charitable institutions, but never gives any himself despite frequent opportunities to do so, we are likely to conclude that he has no such belief. The old adage has it right: "Actions speak more loudly than words." Beliefs affect our emotions more deeply and enduringly than fantasies or dreams. The joy or sadness we feel in dreams, or daydreams, cannot survive our waking up. On the contrary, genuine beliefs (whether true or false) are the scaffolding of our emotional life. (The importance of readiness to act as a sign of belief is less obvious when the belief is about some theoretical matter; e.g., the metaphysical status of numbers or the Big Bang hypothesis.)

In looking for the ways our beliefs are influenced, Hume finds three relations that typically unite ideas that would otherwise be loose and discrete—*resemblance, contiguity in space and time*, and **causation** (*see* ASSOCIATION OF IDEAS). Of these three relations, *causation* is incomparably the most important for our knowledge of matters of fact. This means that Hume is mightily interested in discovering how we come to have the notion that some objects are connected by the relation of cause and effect.

BERKELEY, GEORGE (1685–1753). The Irishman Berkeley is the second of the empiricist triumvirate of **Locke**, Berkeley, and Hume. Berkeley lived in Newport, Rhode Island, from 1729 until 1731, and the city of Berkeley, California, is named after him. He was a clergyman, eventually becoming Bishop of Cloyne, Ireland, as well as an acute philosopher and an excellent stylist. Indeed, he is regarded by some as the best stylist ever to write philosophy in the English language, combining clarity, precision, and simplicity in a remarkable way. He published his most noteworthy philosophical works as a very young man: *A Treatise Concerning the Principles of Human Knowledge* (1710) and *Three Dialogues between Hylas and Philonous* (1713). This entry will concentrate on Berkeley's polemic against the philosophical notion of *matter* or *material substance*, and on his own view that ordinary physical objects exist only when they are perceived—a view that he defends as commonsensical.

What do we know about the material objects that we perceive? "We know nothing but particular qualities and perceptions. . . . [O]ur idea of any body, a peach, for instance, is only that of a particular taste, colour, figure, size, consistence, &c" (THN, 658; 414.28). Those sentences were written by Hume, but they express Berkeley's opinion faithfully. Some philosophers—materialists—hold that underlying, or supporting, the perceptible qualities (or *ideas*, as Berkeley usually calls them) of color, shape, texture, etc., is an unknown something the materialists call *matter* or *material substance* or *substratum*. This substance is not perceptible, or else it would be a color or a shape or some other sensible quality or some combination of such qualities. In other words, matter or material substance is *not* a garden-variety physical object—a ball or a tree or the sun or a lake or whatever. What, then, is the relation between perceptible qualities and this substance? Generally, two answers have been given: **perceptions** *represent* the substance, or perceptions are *caused* by the substance (which the perceptions may or may not represent).

Berkeley sees insoluble problems with either one of the answers. How can something invisible be *represented* by something visible, or something unextended be represented by something extended (and so on for the other perceptible qualities)? The obvious answer is "in no way." In the course of subverting the claim that ideas represent entities radically different from ideas, Berkeley offers an acute analysis of the doctrine of **primary and secondary qualities** (an analysis that Hume makes use of). Further, how can something imperceptible (material substance) be the *cause* of something perceptible? It seems that material substance (in the philosopher's sense, remember) can stand in no intelligible relation to what we can perceive. Even if we could make sense of the philosopher's material substance (we cannot), we could not find any work for it to do. It would be utterly useless for explaining anything at all.

Berkeley's own view is that the objects of ordinary experience exist only when they are perceived. This doctrine is often expressed in the Latin phrase *esse est percipi*, "to be is to be perceived." But this gives only half of Berkeley's ontology—the half comprising perceptible objects. The full phrase is *esse est percipi aut percipere*, to be is to be perceived *or* to perceive. Besides perceived or perceivable objects, there are the minds that perceive them—either finite minds or the infinite mind, God. So far as perceptible objects go, it is inconceivable that they should exist apart from being perceived. Ideas cannot be caused by something utterly different from themselves (material substance, for example), and ideas clearly cannot cause themselves. They exist only as the objects of minds or souls or selves. Since we (i.e., finite minds) are not the causes of most of the objects we perceive, and they must be caused by some active being, we are assured of the existence of an all-knowing mind—God. God also ensures the existence of objects when no one else is perceiving them. This doctrine occasioned an imaginary poetic exchange, as follows:

> There was a young man who said "God
> Must think it exceedingly odd
> If he finds that this tree
> Continues to be
> When there's no one about in the Quad."

The puzzlement elicited this reply:

> Dear Sir:
> Your astonishment's odd;
> I am always about in the Quad.
> And that's why the tree
> Will continue to be,
> Since observed by
> *Yours faithfully,*
> God.

Berkeley correctly anticipated that his *esse est percipi* doctrine would be derided as dissolving genuine physical objects into collections of ideas, and he offers arguments to counter such strictures. The 18th-century lexicographer and literary figure Dr. Samuel Johnson claimed to refute Berkeley by kicking a stone, but in fact merely advertised his complete misunderstanding of Berkeley's point: Kicking the stone and feeling its solidity is an ordinary, non-mysterious experience that has nothing to do with some putative non-perceivable, incomprehensible *material substance.*

Berkeley is at pains to dispel the suspicion that his doctrine flies in the face of **common sense** and reduces the accomplishments of science to illusion. It may sound strange, Berkeley concedes, to say that we eat ideas, but not at all strange—indeed, it is obviously true—to say that we eat things that we perceive (and only such things). As to science, Berkeley challenges the reader to name a single discovery of the incomparable Isaac Newton that in any way or to any degree depends on positing the existence of an unperceivable and inconceivable material substance. It is ironic, Berkeley argues, that those who accuse him of generating **skepticism** are themselves the actual skeptics, by placing real objects beyond the reach of human experience. John Locke, with his dualism of mind and permanently concealed material objects, is Berkeley's primary target, but his criticism applies to any doctrine that places an opaque barrier between the mind and the world.

Hume acknowledges that Berkeley intends his philosophy to be non-skeptical, but he contends that it is skeptical nonetheless. As evidence, Hume submits the following fact (or what he takes to be a fact): Berkeley's arguments *"admit of no answer and produce no conviction"* (EHU, 155n1; 203n23; italics are in Hume's text). Hume agrees with Berkeley that neither the senses nor **reason** can provide any basis for believing in the existence of objects that are independent of our perception of them and that continue to exist when we are not perceiving them. However, Hume holds that we cannot be argued out of believing in distinct, independent objects. In other words, he rejects Berkeley's claim that we cannot *really* believe in the existence of something that is both unperceivable and literally inconceivable. Hume says that we do believe in the distinct, independent existence of objects, but he concedes that we have no faintest inkling of how such objects differ from our perceptions. The best we can do is to say that our perceptions bear some incomprehensible relation to external objects—assuming that we do not simply identify the objects with our perceptions. *See also* RELIGION.

BLUE, MISSING SHADE OF. *See* MISSING SHADE OF BLUE.

BUTLER, JOSEPH (1692–1752). Butler was an English philosopher and cleric, Bishop of Bristol and later Bishop of Durham, and a powerful influence on 18th-century philosophical and theological thought. He was admired by Hume, and is still admired for the clarity, the analytical skill, and the keen psychological observations of his writings on ethics. His work in the philosophy of **religion** no longer commands the interest it did two centuries or so back, not because it is defective but because few philosophers today have any interest in Butler's kind of apologetics.

Butler's ethical theory is set out in *Fifteen Sermons Preached at the Rolls Chapel* (1726) and in an appendix ("A Dissertation of the Nature of Virtue") to his other major work, *The Analogy of Religion, Natural and Revealed, to the Constitution and Course of Nature* (1736). The word *sermons* should not mislead us: Butler seeks to show that human beings can discern the difference between virtue and vice without divine revelation (although some important truths cannot be known apart from revelation). In the "Preface" to the sermons (the first three of which are devoted to explaining what is meant by "the nature of man"), he notes that we may approach the study of morals in either of two ways—"from inquiring into the abstract relations of things" [the rationalist way] or "from a matter of fact, namely, what the particular nature of man is" [the empiricist way]. Butler opts for the second way (the matter-of-fact approach)— a commitment that leads Hume to praise "Dr. Butler" for "founding his accurate [disquisition] of human nature intirely [*sic*] upon experience" (THN, 646; 407.2). Unlike Hume, who rejects the rationalist approach completely, Butler holds that both ways lead to the same thing—namely, our obligation to practice virtue—and that they lend strength to each other.

Butler's refutation of the doctrine of **egoism**—that all voluntary human actions are motivated solely by self-love—affords an excellent example of his power of analysis and observation. It is also of interest because Hume undertakes a similar subverting of "the selfish system of morals" (in appendix 2 of EPM). Only a few points of Butler's subtle and detailed arguments can be indicated here. It is true, Butler says, that human beings have a general desire for their own happiness, which comes from—or *is*—self-love; but it is straightforwardly false that all motives can be reduced by "a philosophical chymistry" (Hume's phrase) to self-love. If we look at human nature honestly, without the distorting blinkers of some a priori theory, we see as much evidence that we were made for society and to do good to others as that we were made to look out for our own interests. In fact, self-love and benevolence, virtue and interest, are distinguishable but not opposed to one another. As Butler puts it in his most famous sentence, "Every thing is what it is, and not another thing."

Butler reminds us that human nature is a pretty complicated affair, and that is true in spades of human motivation. Particular appetites and desires require, for their satisfaction, particular objects that are suited to those appetites and desires. To say that we are motivated by self-love to eat or play cards or listen to Mozart is just as unhelpful and implausible as it sounds. It is no less implausible and simplistic to say that when we are generous or benevolent, it is always out of self-love. We are, normally, generous or benevolent because we find that sort of act intrinsically desirable and not because we expect some benefit. Both self-love and benevolence are rooted in human nature; neither can be reduced to the other; and self-love is no more contrary to benevolence than it is to "any other particular affection." Intelligent benevolence often produces more happiness than any amount of overtly selfish seeking of happiness (which is not to be identified with self-love). Philosophers such as **Thomas Hobbes** and **Bernard de Mandeville** are led to deny these commonsense facts by an excessive deference to some a priori hypothesis or theory that they have adopted.

It is worth noting that Butler does not try to equate benevolence with virtue or self-love with vice. Benevolence may evince weakness and so be blamable in some circumstances, and self-love "in its due degree" may be as morally good as any other affection. It is *conscience* that pronounces our actions and motives to be right or wrong in themselves and not merely as conducing to desirable or undesirable consequences.

In Butler's own lifetime, *The Analogy of Religion* was more celebrated than his *Sermons*. Butler wrote it, in part, as a response to a book published in 1730—*Christianity as Old as the Creation: Or, The Gospel a Republication of the Religion of Nature*—by Matthew Tindal, who called himself a "Christian deist" (a combination that Christians and deists alike tended to regard as an oxymoron). The title of the work, which came to be known as "the deist's Bible," accurately describes its central claim; namely, that what is true in Christianity can be known by **reason** alone, apart from revelation, and that what cannot be thus known is not true.

Butler's *Analogy* is directed to readers who, like the deists, share his belief that God is the Author of nature and a moral being as well. Further, they admit that there are many things about God's creation that we do not understand. Our knowledge of such matters is beset with difficulties and is only probable. If, as Butler argues, the difficulties that deists profess to discern in revealed religion are analogous to those encountered in our knowledge of natural laws and principles, then the deists should not reject religious claims as unworthy of serious attention. Butler's aim, then, is extremely modest. He does not pretend to prove that the doctrines of revealed religion are true, but only that deists ought to be open to the possibility that revelation may teach us truths that we could not acquire by unaided reason.

Hume concurs in the essentials of Butler's refutation of egoism (shorn of any theological trappings, as Hume would regard them). On the other hand, Hume rejects all demonstrations of the existence of God (and any other matter of fact) and finds significant problems with even the more modest analogical argument to (or from) design. He is particularly emphatic in divesting God (if such a being exists) of any moral qualities. Accordingly, Hume would not be among the readers to whom Butler addresses his *Analogy* (*see* DESIGN, ARGUMENT FROM/TO).

– C –

CAMPBELL, GEORGE (1719–1796). Campbell was a Scottish minister, theologian, and philosopher who described himself as Hume's "friendly adversary." And that he was. Hume was reading Campbell's newly published *The Philosophy of Rhetoric* when James Boswell called on Hume in early July 1776, less than two months before the great philosopher died. But it is Campbell's *A Dissertation on Miracles* (1762) that bears most directly on Hume, especially the famous/notorious essay "Of Miracles." Hume was able to read the manuscript of *A Dissertation* before it was published, thanks to the mediation of Hugh Blair, a friend of both men. Hume made a few brief substantive comments on Campbell's criticisms and complained that the use of inflammatory epithets (e.g., "infidel") was inappropriate in a philosophical work. Campbell agreed with the complaint and removed the offending language, a gracious gesture that helped to solidify the genuine respect that these two friendly adversaries felt for one another. But friendly or not, Campbell's criticisms of Hume on miracles are still pointed and vigorous—perhaps the most astute and wide-ranging to be found in the 18th century.

The nub of Hume's position in "Of Miracles" amounts to the claim that we can never be actually justified in accepting a miracle story on the basis of testimonial evidence, even though such a case is *theoretically* possible. Campbell's animadversions are directed at both the psycho-genetic question of how we come to credit testimony and the epistemic question of how we *ought* to assess testimony. Hume himself does not draw any clear distinction between the two kinds of questions — which is not to say that he does not, or would not, recognize the distinction. Below are a few of Campbell's criticisms.

1. Hume says that human beings learn by experience to credit testimony. If Hume were right on that score, Campbell points out, small children would be naturally skeptical and would, by degrees, become more credulous as they had more experience of the (usual) connection between testimony and truth. Of course, very nearly the opposite is in fact true: Children are by nature trusting and become skeptical only after they are told things that turn out to be false.

2. Contrary to what Hume says, testimony enjoys, and should enjoy, the strongest presumption of veracity until it is refuted by experience. Hume recognizes the necessity of accepting testimony, but his account of the nature and ground of testimonial evidence is fundamentally wrong.

3. Hume has his own stock of "natural" **beliefs** (not Hume's term) that do not admit of rational justification but are nonetheless absolutely essential to human life. Testimony is no less foundational than memory, which Hume accepts without question. We do, of course, check particular memory claims by experience; but it would be quite impossible to justify our general reliance on memory in that fashion: Without memory, there would *be* no experience. Moreover, our knowledge of the world owes vastly more to testimony than to individual memory. It is just arbitrary to confer on memory a fundamental status denied to testimony. Campbell points out what appear to be severe problems with Hume's account of how we come to accept testimony — i.e., by appealing to experience. If Hume means *individual* experience, then the claim is wildly implausible, even if not strictly and formally impossible. If Hume means something like *collective experience*, then he has straightforwardly begged the very question at issue; namely, why should we believe the testimony of other people? Some Hume scholars (e.g., Tony Pitson) have tried to

show that Hume's theory of testimony is neither improbable in the extreme nor circular (though admittedly Hume's exposition is not a model of perspicuity).

4. Hume proposes a *numerical computation* (Campbell's phrase) for deciding between two competing claims (or propositions or proposals); namely, subtract the weaker claim (i.e., the one with fewer "experiments" on its side) from the stronger one. The numerical *difference* between the two represents the degree of assurance one has in adopting the stronger claim over the weaker. Campbell argues that when we apply Hume's general method to conflicting testimonial evidence, we immediately encounter serious problems. The testimony of a single eyewitness, for example, may properly outweigh a thousand "contradictory experiments." Hume knows this, of course; but long before we have added the required qualifications, conditions, exceptions, and caveats, we have abandoned Hume's method of *balancing likelihoods* as a means of assessing testimonial evidence—or so Campbell contends. Whether or not Campbell's strictures are fatal, they raise pertinent, important questions. Some parts of Campbell's broadside anticipate the more formal examination undertaken by the American philosopher C. S. Peirce (who corrects some of Hume's purely mathematical errors).

The core of Hume's case against the credibility of miracle stories is that a miracle would violate the laws of nature—laws that have been established, Hume tells us, by "a firm and unalterable experience" (EHU, 114; 173.12). Otherwise stated, there is "a uniform experience against every miraculous event" (EHU, 115; 173.12). How does Hume know this? Mainly—indeed, almost entirely—by testimony. But Hume himself notes that history abounds with stories of miracles and prodigies, i.e., violations of the laws of nature. Campbell wants to know how Hume can seriously assert (a) that the laws of nature are established by absolutely uniform human experience and also (b) that untold numbers of people have claimed to be witnesses of miracles.

CAUSE/CAUSATION/CAUSE-EFFECT. This entry covers several aspects of Hume's theory of causation.

Hume's preoccupation with cause pervades his writings, but two sources are canonical for his "official" doctrine: part 3 ("Of knowledge and probability"), book 1 of THN, and sections 4, 5, 6, and 7 of EHU.

Hume's extensive treatment of cause (and the related issue of **Induction**)—especially its negative side—is his most distinctive contribution to philosophy. For Hume, the cause-effect relation is the most important source of knowledge of objects and events lying beyond immediate perception or memory. In fact, he says (e.g., in EHU, 26; 109.4) that it is the *only* means we have of knowing such objects or events. Though one sometimes reads or hears it said that Hume denies the existence of causation, such statements are either straightforwardly false or highly misleading ways of saying something true (e.g., that Hume criticizes certain *theories* of causation).

1. To say that *A causes B* is to say, at a minimum, that whenever *A* occurs, *B* occurs, too. We can couch this in terms of *conditions*: If *A* causes *B*, then *A* is a *sufficient* condition of *B*, and *B* is a *necessary* condition of *A*. So, knowing that *A* has occurred is enough (i.e., sufficient) for us to know that *B* has occurred; and knowing that *B* has *not* occurred assures us that *A* has not occurred either. That is, *B* is necessary—a *conditio sine qua non*—for *A*. Generally, the cause, *A*, is not a *necessary* condition of the effect, *B* (though Hume sometimes treats cause as also a necessary condition). Striking an ordinary hen egg forcefully with a hammer is sufficient to break the egg, but it is not necessary. Dropping the egg from a height of 10 feet onto a hard surface, or running over it with an automobile, will do the trick just as well as striking it with a hammer. (The account of causation just given, though formally correct, must be applied to Hume with care. As we shall see shortly, Hume insists that cause-effect relations are not discoverable a priori by the operation of **reason** alone; they are matters of fact that are discovered by **experience**. Accordingly, we must be careful in our use of *know* when we speak of *Hume's* doctrine of causation.)

2. Hume's concern with causation is principally *epistemic*, not *metaphysical*. That is, Hume is mainly interested in how we *know* causal relations, not whether causal relations really exist apart from our awareness of them. Not that Hume has no interest at all in the second issue; he just devotes most of his attention to the first one. (Whether Hume believes in real extra-mental causes has been the subject of lively debate over the past couple of decades. See the discussion of the *regularity* theory of cause later in this entry.)

3. Hume raises two logically distinct questions about our notion of cause: (a) How do we acquire our **belief** in causation? and (b) how, if at all, can we rationally justify that belief? We will take up the first question in the next section. Let us now consider the second one. That we acquire a belief by non-rational means does not, by itself, preclude our subsequently discovering a rational basis for the belief. An example should make the distinction clear. The 19th-century German organic chemist Friedrich Kekulé had been puzzling over the structure of the benzene molecule when he dreamed about a snake swallowing its own tail. When he awoke, he was struck by the thought that the shape of the tail-swallowing snake—a circle—was the same as that of the benzene molecule. His dream inspired the benzene-ring theory, which proved to be correct. Kekulé's belief had a non-rational origin but was confirmed scientifically.

We should be clear about what the Kekulé example shows and—perhaps more important—what it does not show. It shows that the origin of an **idea** and the confirmation of the idea are two distinct matters. Kekulé's dream was the inspiration for his benzene-ring theory, but the evidential value of the dream for the theory was close to zero. Hume would agree with this analysis but would insist that we have no free-standing rational justification for *any* beliefs about matters of fact—whether the belief be about a particular fact or be expressed in some theory about matters of fact (e.g., the structure of the benzene molecule). We have no a priori grounds for accepting Kekulé's theory; we have only the evidence provided by experience. The same holds true of all our causal judgments. Even after we get the concept of cause, we never find any basis other than experience— or, as Hume often puts it, *custom and habit*—for those judgments.

It is useful to compare our beliefs about *relations of ideas* with our beliefs about *matters of fact* (see EHU, 25; 108.1). We know that propositions expressing relations of ideas are true (or false, as the case may be) merely by paying attention to the ideas (concepts) involved. We know intuitively that a triangle has three sides, and we know demonstratively that the sum of the angles of a Euclidean triangle is 180 degrees. The contradictories of these propositions are inconceivable; so we do not have to consult experience about them. As Hume puts it, such propositions "are discoverable by the mere operation of thought, without dependence on what is anywhere existent in the universe" (EHU, 25; 108.1). On the other hand, our knowledge of matters of fact is never that certain, and is attained by different means. To say that some triangles have four sides is not even false; it is gibberish. By contrast, it may be false to say that an ordinary egg will not crack if I strike it forcefully with a hammer (and we would surely *expect* the assertion to be false); but it is not gibberish. It is just as intelligible as the (probably) true statement that the egg *will* break. The verdict is delivered by *experience, not* by reason. (Notice that Hume does not say that we can actually *believe* that an egg could survive a strong hammer blow intact—only that we can *conceive* or *imagine* it.)

In THN (79–80; 1.3.3.3), Hume offers a fuller explanation of why causal statements are always *contingent* (i.e., not *necessarily* true). That the idea of a cause is *distinct* from the idea of its effect is self-evident. Any two distinct ideas are *separable* from each other, and this means that we can conceive the one without the other. Recall the example in the preceding paragraph: Striking an egg with a hammer and the egg's cracking are two distinct events, and we may conceive the first event without the second. By contrast, the ideas of *triangle* and *three-sided* are not conceivable as separate. Hume applies this analysis both to particular causal judgments and to the general causal principle or maxim that whatever begins to exist must have a cause of existence (see the discussion of the causal maxim later in this entry).

4. To explain how we come to believe in particular cause-effect relations, Hume chooses an exceedingly simple example—one billiard ball striking another. For his purposes, he wants nothing exotic or out of the ordinary, and the billiard balls fill the bill perfectly. We know—or think we know—that the second ball will begin to move when the first ball rolls into it. But *how* do we know? Since the cause (the impact of the first ball against the second) and the effect (the movement of the second ball) are two distinct events, we could never discover the effect simply by analyzing the cause. (The German philosopher **Immanuel Kant** praises Hume for seeing that the cause-effect relation is not, in Kant's language, *analytic.*) If we consider the situation a priori (i.e., apart from experience), we may conceive "a hundred different events" that might follow from the first ball's striking the second: the two balls might come to complete

rest; the second ball might fly straight up into the air or do pirouettes or turn to powder or do anything else that does not involve a logical contradiction. It is *experience*—and experience alone—that tells us what happens when Ball$_1$ strikes Ball$_2$. That small children and even lower animals discern causal relations proves that we do not acquire the notion of cause from reason. We are dealing with a *matter of fact*, not a *relation of ideas*.

Long experience in a world full of cause-effect relations, Hume says, may lead us to believe that we can operate with reason alone, but that is an illusion. We can never know a priori that July in the Northern Hemisphere will be hotter than January. We believe that because of long experience, not because of abstract reasoning. (For a discussion of the problems surrounding predictions, *see* INDUCTION.)

5. What is Hume's conception of cause? As was noted earlier in this entry, to say that *A* causes *B* is to say (at least) that whenever *A* occurs, *B* also occurs. After observing that, considered a priori (i.e., apart from experience), any object may be the cause or the effect of any other object, Hume proposes some general rules by which we may know which objects really are causes of other objects (THN, 173–76; 1.3.15.1–12). He lists eight such rules, of which the first three may be considered (almost) *definitive* of cause (as he conceives it). These rules anticipate, to some extent, the methods developed by the English philosopher John Stuart Mill in the 19th century for identifying causal relations between events.

(a) The cause and effect must be contiguous in space and time. That is, there must be no gaps in time or space between the cause and the effect. This rule has the effect of excluding any so-called *action at a distance*. This means that if *A* causes *C*, and *A* and *C* are not spatio-temporally contiguous, there must be intermediate causes that are so related.

(b) The cause must occur before the effect, but without any gaps, as required by (a). Some philosophers (e.g., Aristotle) hold that cause and effect are simultaneous, but Hume has an ingenious argument to show that such a relation would annihilate time. Because *simultaneous with* is (with some esoteric exceptions) a *transitive* relation (not Hume's language), every item in any causal sequence of *any* length would occur at the same time if Aristotle et al. were right. "For if one cause were co-temporary with its effect, and this effect with *its* effect, and so on, 'tis plain there wou'd be no such thing as succession, and all objects must be co-existent" (THN, 76; 1.3.2.7).

(c) The cause and the effect must be constantly conjoined; i.e., neither one ever occurs without the other. "'Tis chiefly this quality, that constitutes the relation" (THN, 173; 1.3.15.5). Note that Hume uses *cause* here as both a sufficient and a necessary condition, as he does in the last five rules by which to judge of causes and effects. He sometimes speaks of "compleat" causes or "sole" causes, which means that Hume includes background conditions as part of the cause. For example, scratching a match on a rough surface will cause the match to light—but not if the match is wet or there is no oxygen present or if any one of a number of other presupposed conditions fails.

Hume is famous—or notorious—for giving two definitions of *cause*, which have generated a great deal of controversy. The first of the two definitions summarizes the three conditions just listed: "... *an object, followed by another, and where all the objects similar to the first are followed by objects similar to the second*" (EHU, 76; 146.29; italics are in Hume's text; cf. THN, 170; 1.3.14.35). Hume immediately adds this coda: "Or in other words *where, if the first object had not been, the second had never existed.*" But the "in other words" definition is not equivalent to the first one; it is a contrary-to-fact conditional, which states a necessary condition—a *sine qua non.* This suggests that the effects could not have been produced by a different cause—a claim that is usually not true. An automobile may fail to start because it has no fuel, but it may have plenty of fuel and fail to start because its battery is dead. It follows that lack of fuel is a sufficient condition of the automobile's not starting, but it is not a necessary condition of its not starting—not, that is, a *conditio sine qua non.* The second of Hume's two definitions (which brings in the reaction of the observer) will be considered below.

The three conditions given above are *almost* definitive of (Humean) cause, and they are the only ones listed by Hume as being useful in the detection of causes. But Hume concedes that the ordinary notion of cause contains another element—the *necessary connexion* between cause and effect. The first three conditions—i.e., spatio-temporal contiguity, temporal priority of the cause to the effect, and the constant conjunction of cause and effect—refer to empirically observable properties of events (see, e.g., THN, 168–69; 1.3.14.28). No mystery here. But what about *necessary connexion*? Where does *that* **idea** come from?

Hume considers the possible sources of our idea of a necessary connection between cause and effect. We have already seen that it cannot be the abstract, or a priori, analysis of cause or effect; each is distinct from the other and might, in principle, occur without the other. There is no single quality "which universally belongs to all beings" (THN, 75; 1.3.2.5) that would make them either causes or effects. This is manifestly true of the qualities revealed by our senses — shape, color, sound, odor, texture, or taste. They tell us nothing about cause and effect.

Perhaps we can find the source of our idea of causal power by introspection — e.g., by considering the connection between volition and the movement of our limbs. I decide to move my arm, and it moves. John Locke says that our clearest idea of active power comes precisely from this ability to initiate voluntary movements of parts of our body (as well as from our ability to initiate a train of ideas). Alas, Hume contends, we are no more conscious of the link between volitions and bodily motions than we are of the physical influence that produces motion in a billiard ball when it is struck by another ball. Indeed, we are, if possible, even more in the dark about volitions and bodily actions because we have no idea how two such disparate entities as mind and body could interact. We know that we can move our arm at will, but we have no impression of the means by which the operation is effected. Hume puts it this way: "One event follows another; but we never can observe any tie between them. They seem *conjoined*, but never *connected*" (EHU, 74; 144.26; italics are in Hume's text).

Hume's search for the source of our idea of necessary connection has, so far, come up empty. And yet we *do* have such an idea, and, according to Hume's own theory, it must have its source in some sort of impression. Since the idea cannot arise from an impression of sensation (seeing, hearing, etc.), it must be produced by an impression of reflection (or a *secondary* impression). (*See* PERCEPTIONS.) After we observe a constant conjunction between two similar objects or events (when one happens, the other always follows), we come to *expect* the second whenever the first occurs — though the repetition reveals nothing new about the objects or events themselves. The required impression of reflection is the propensity, or determination, of the mind, produced by custom or habit, to look for the second of the associated pair when the first appears. "This connexion . . . which we *feel* in the mind, this customary transition of the imagination from one object to its usual attendant, is the sentiment or impression from which we form the idea of power or necessary connexion" (EHU, 75; 145.28; italics are in Hume's text; cf. THN, 164–66; 1.3.14.19–22).

Whereas the first three components of the cause-effect relation — namely, spatio-temporal contiguity, priority of the cause to the effect, and constant conjunction — represent observable objective facts about the natural world, the fourth component — necessary connection — "exists in the mind, not in objects" (THN, 165; 1.3.14.22). With this explanation, Hume offers a second definition of *cause*: "*an object followed by another, and whose appearance always conveys the thought to that other*" (EHU, 77; 146.29; italics are in Hume's text; cf. THN, 170; 1.3.14.35). In Hume's terminology, the second definition considers cause as a *natural* relation; the first definition (given earlier in this entry) considers cause as a *philosophical* relation. (For an explanation of the terms, *see* RELATIONS.) When discussing necessity and its relation to human liberty or freedom, Hume says that the two senses of *necessity* (i.e., either "the constant conjunction of like objects" or "the inference of the understanding from one object to the other") are "indeed, at bottom the same" (EHU, 97; 160.27). This suggests that, strictly, Hume has given us just one definition of *cause*, which may be construed as philosophical or natural, depending on whether one focuses on the objects related (the *relata*) or on the mind that views the objects.

A historical note: Hume's doctrine of causation represents a considerable simplification over the Aristotelian account, which comprises four distinct kinds of causes: *material, formal, efficient*, and *final*. Hume recognizes only *efficient* causes, inasmuch as the other three do not satisfy his criteria for a real causal relation between objects or events. However, it should be pointed out that the Greek word αἰτία (*aitia*) is much broader than the English word *cause*, which is the usual translation. Thus, the difference is, in part (but only in part), a matter of words. It is also worth noting that Hume denies any difference between physical and psychological causation, or "moral and physical necessity," as he puts it. (*See* LIBERTY AND NECESSITY.) Almost a century before Hume, the French philosopher **René Descartes** (1596–1650) had banished final causes (i.e., causes that explain by referring to the *end* or *purpose* of the objects/events in question) from science, on the grounds that we do not know the purposes for which God created the world. We must stick to discovering *efficient* causes.

6. Following Hume's own example, we have so far devoted almost exclusive attention to the *epistemic* side of his theory of causation—i.e., to the question of what we *know* about the cause-effect relation. Scholars are pretty well agreed that Hume is agnostic about our ability to discern real causal connections by sense, imagination, or reason. Our knowledge of causal connections goes no deeper than noticing that certain objects or events go regularly with other objects or events—what Hume calls *constant conjunction*. The second billiard ball *always*, without fail, moves when it is struck by the first ball. Some commentators argue that this is *all* there is to Hume's doctrine of causation—regular sequences of objects/events and *nothing more*, the *regularity theory*. Others contend that Hume takes such regular sequences as *signs* of real objective causal connections, always conceding that the connections are hidden from our view. A considerable secondary literature has been generated by this debate between those who see Hume as a *causal realist* and those who see him as a (metaphysical) *regularity theorist*.

7. It is a general maxim in philosophy, Hume says, "that *whatever begins to exist, must have a cause of existence*" (THN, 78; 1.3.3.1; italics are in Hume's text). Although Hume actually believes that the maxim is true, he argues vigorously that it is neither intuitive nor demonstrable. Since the idea of the cause is separable from the idea of the effect, we may suppose one without the other. We may imagine an object to come into existence without any cause—something that we could not do if the relation between cause and effect were intuitive (as the relation in "3 is greater than 2") or demonstrable (as the relation in "the angles of a triangle are equal to two right angles"). The purported demonstrations of the causal maxim are all guilty of the fallacy of begging the question, i.e., of taking for granted the very point to be proved. Hume cites **Thomas Hobbes**, **John Locke**, and **Samuel Clarke** as famous philosophers who offer defective arguments for the rational certainty of the causal maxim. (Some critics

deny that Hobbes, Locke, and Clarke actually use the arguments Hume ascribes to them. That is a point worth noting, but one that we cannot explore.)

Two such arguments (attributed to Clarke and Locke, respectively) are that if an event could occur without a cause, it would (a) have to cause itself (which would require that it exist before it existed), or (b) it would be caused by *nothing*. But, as Hume reminds us, the question in dispute is *whether* a cause is always necessary, not *when* or *where* or *how* the cause operates.

An even less substantial argument begins from the premise that every effect presupposes a cause (which is true by definition) and draws the non sequitur conclusion that every *being* or every *event* must be preceded by a cause. That argument is fallacious in exactly the same way as this one: Every husband must have a wife; therefore, every man is married. The mistake lies in the question-begging description of a being or an event as an effect. (For Hume's arguments, see THN, book 1, part 3, section 3.)

As noted above, Hume never says, or even intimates, that he doubts the actual truth of the "general maxim in philosophy" about causation. He believes it; he is a thoroughgoing determinist. He denies only that we have any rational basis for the belief. *See* LIBERTY AND NECESSITY for a discussion of determinism and how, on Hume's view, it can be reconciled with human freedom.

A historical note: Hume was influenced by the writings of the French philosopher **Nicolas Malebranche**, especially about the problems of making sense of causation. Hume agrees with Malebranche that we can find no intelligible connection between ordinary objects or events that are said to be causally joined. However, he rejects Malebranche's doctrine of *occasionalism*, according to which what we call causes are actually *occasions* for God to do the real causal work. Hume's verdict on that theory is worth quoting: "We are got into fairy land, long ere we have reached the last steps of our theory . . ." (EHU, 72; 142.24). Nevertheless, it has been said (with self-conscious hyperbole, no doubt) that Hume is Malebranche without God.

CICERO. Marcus Tullius Cicero—also called *Tully*—was born in 106 B.C., in Arpinum, a provincial town some distance east of Rome. He was pursued and killed, on Mark Antony's orders, as he tried to flee Rome in 43 B.C. He was a contemporary of Julius Caesar, Pompey, Mark Antony, and Octavian (later Augustus) during the demise of the Roman Republic and the birth of the Roman Empire; and he played important roles—as orator, politician, and philosopher—during those turbulent, violent years. He is widely regarded as the greatest Roman orator, but not as a great philosopher. Hume's own estimate coincides with the general opinion: "The abstract philosophy of CICERO has lost its credit: The vehemence of his oratory is still the object of our admiration" (*Essays*, 243). Nonetheless, Hume cites Cicero as a non-superstitious philosopher of antiquity—no small virtue in Hume's eyes (*Essays*, 463n278).

Hume mentions Cicero as being among the authors he began reading as a young man, and Cicero's influence is evident (and frequently acknowledged) in most of Hume's writings. The form (and some of the substance) of Hume's posthumously published *Dialogues Concerning Natural Religion* is modeled on Cicero's *On the Nature of the Gods* (*De natura deodorum*). In his discussion of the causes of belief (specifically, *contiguity*), Hume quotes a longish passage from Cicero's *About the Ends of Goods and Evils* (*De finibus bonorum et malorum*), which notes the effect of physical proximity in enlivening our ideas of people who once inhabited the place. (Hume quotes the same passage in THN, 630; 1.3.8.5n21 and in EHU, 52n1; 128n9.) Hume refers to Cicero much more often when he is discussing moral or political or literary subjects. For example, in appendix 4 of EPM ("Of Some Verbal Disputes"), Hume quotes a passage from *The Orator* (*De oratore*) in which Cicero argues that we cannot draw a sharp line between virtues that benefit the public and those that benefit primarily the virtuous person himself/herself—though we find it useful to make approximate distinctions along those lines (EPM, 319n1; 181n72). It is worth noting that Hume himself proposes a fourfold division of the qualities comprised by personal merit or virtue: those that are *agreeable* to oneself or to others and those that are *useful* to oneself or to others (e.g., EPM, 268–70; 145–47). Appendix 4 reminds us that Hume does not intend his taxonomy to be taken as marking out mutually exclusive domains.

Readers may consult the indexes to the *Essays* and EPM to see how often Cicero is invoked on a variety of topics—virtue and vice, eloquence, courage, the state of nature, etc., etc. Even when Cicero is not mentioned explicitly, his influence is often discernible in Hume's own views. In a letter to **Francis Hutcheson**, the young Hume declares that he prefers to take his catalogue of virtues from Cicero's *Offices*, not from *The Whole Duty of Man*. (Note: The second work Hume refers to is attributed to the Oxford theologian Richard Allestree and was published about 1658. It should not be confused with **Samuel Pufendorf**'s *De officio hominis et civis*, which was freely—and curiously—translated into English as *The Whole Duty of Man According to the Law of Nature*.)

The essential philosophical difference between the two works lies in the attitude each recommends that we take toward nature, especially human nature. Cicero and the author of *The Whole Duty of Man* agree that certain passions—pride, for example—tend to arise naturally in certain circumstances. But whereas Cicero holds that we should try to live in accordance with our ingrained natural inclinations (with the help of our **reason**), *The Whole Duty of Man* urges us to resist many of them as delusive and sinful. Hume's own sympathies are clearly shown in his contemptuous treatment of what he calls "monkish virtues"—celibacy, fasting, penance, mortification, self-denial, humility, and the like—which he declares to be not virtues at all, but vices. Such "virtues" run directly counter to deeply rooted human sentiments and, indeed, can be maintained only by "the delusive glosses of superstition and false religion" (EPM, 270; 146.3).

Although Hume embraces many of Cicero's particular insights, he is less positive about the philosophical reasoning underlying those insights. To put it another way, Hume thinks that Cicero is almost always right in his conclusions but weak on the theoretical side. However, Hume follows Cicero in endorsing this fundamental philosophical principle: Human knowledge of matter of fact is incurably fallible, but extreme **skepticism** is not desirable and, indeed, is not possible. Nature quickly and decisively defeats such pretended suspension of **belief**. Belief is not a matter of choice. Given certain circumstances, we find ourselves believing, willy nilly. In such situations, we can no more avoid believing than we can avoid feeling gratitude when we receive benefits or resentment when we suffer injustice. "All these operations are a species of natural instincts, which no reasoning or process of the thought and understanding is able either to produce or prevent" (EHU, 46–47; 123.8). Hume's Ciceronian viewpoint rejects the extremes of rationalism and **Pyrrhonism** (immoderate or excessive skepticism) in epistemology and the extremes of asceticism and hedonism in ethics.

CLARKE, SAMUEL (1675–1729). Clarke was an English philosopher and theologian who developed a metaphysical-epistemological and ethical rationalism that comes close to being the perfect mirror image of Hume's own position. Clarke sets out the essentials of his metaphysics and ethics in his aptly titled Boyle lectures for 1704 and 1705: *A Demonstration of the Being and Attributes of God* and *A Discourse Concerning the Unchangeable Obligations of Natural Religion, and the Truth and Certainty of the Christian Revelation.* (The title of the second lecture makes it plain that, on Clarke's view, we can discern our fundamental moral obligations by **reason** alone, with no aid from revelation.) Clarke fell under the influence of Isaac Newton during his days at Cambridge and, much later, was Newton's surrogate in a series of letters exchanged with the great German philosopher/mathematician Wilhelm Gottfried Leibniz.

Hume is especially interested in a central thesis in Clarke's demonstration of the existence (or "being") of God; namely, that nothing comes from nothing (*ex nihilo nihil fit*) or, in Hume's own language, that "*whatever begins to exist, must have a cause of existence*" (THN, 78; 1.3.3.1; italics are in Hume's text). In criticizing the alleged necessity of that thesis, Hume mentions an argument by "Dr. *Clarke* and others" (THN, 80n2; 1.3.3.5n18; the italics are in Hume's text). The argument goes like this: Everything must have a **cause**, for otherwise a thing would have to cause itself, i.e., to exist before it existed—an obvious impossibility. Unfortunately for Dr. Clarke and others, the argument is plainly circular: It assumes as true the very point that is to be proved; namely, that everything must have some cause or other.

Without naming him, Hume seems clearly to have had Clarke in mind as a target when he refers to those "who affirm that virtue is nothing but a conformity to reason; that there are eternal fitnesses and unfitnesses of things, which are the same to every rational being that considers them; that the immutable measures of right and wrong impose an obligation, not only on human creatures, but also on the Deity himself" (THN, 456; 3.1.1.4). These philosophers suppose that we can distinguish between moral good and evil by reason alone, in stark opposition to Hume's repeated assertion that reason alone cannot supply that distinction. (For Hume's arguments against such claims, *see* ETHICAL RATIONALISM; see also the sketch of Hume's moral philosophy in the introduction to this book.) It is worth pointing out that Hume does not deny the importance of reason in moral evaluation. He denies only that reason by itself can enable us to make the requisite distinctions. *See also* RELIGION.

COMMON SENSE. To avoid misunderstanding, we should note at the outset that this entry has nothing to do with the ancient and medieval *sensus communis*, a supposed cognitive faculty that coordinates reports from the different senses—for example, the diverse perceptions of space afforded by seeing and touching. That concept had pretty well disappeared from philosophy by Hume's time. Hume in fact uses the locution *common sense* many times, always in its ordinary, non-technical meaning; and our concern here is with plain old common sense.

Commonsense beliefs or principles come at more than one level of universality and stubbornness. Hume describes foundational, Level-One (not Hume's terms) beliefs or principles as "permanent, irresistible, and universal" (THN, 225; 1.4.4.1)—e.g., the existence of the external world, the existence of other people, and the existence of causal connections. Principles of this sort are "the foundation of all our thoughts and actions, so that upon their removal human nature must immediately perish and go to ruin" (ibid.). Hume contrasts such genuinely unavoidable and indispensable principles with those that are "changeable, weak, and irregular"—e.g., the baseless conjectures and imaginings of all too many philosophers, both ancient and modern. (A note about terms: If we assume that we cannot believe something we have never thought about, it is perhaps slightly misleading to say that ordinary, unphilosophical people *believe* basic principles—not because they doubt the principles, but because they have never thought about them at all. But we can certainly say that ordinary people *evince* or *manifest* their beliefs by their actions and that they would affirm those beliefs if anyone ever asked them. So long as people act as if they believe in an independent, casually efficacious world, it does not much matter what words we use to describe their attitude. Accordingly, we shall continue to refer to these unshakable convictions as *beliefs*.)

As Hume suggests, rock-bottom commonsense beliefs—about the external world, other people, and causal relations, for example—represent the operation of instincts at the core of human nature itself. These beliefs do not arise from the operation of reason, nor are they in the least danger of being overturned by the operation of reason. We should note that although people in every place and in all times have believed in the external world and causal connections, they have differed widely—even wildly—in describing the details of that world and those causal connections.

At a less fundamental level, many well-founded commonsense beliefs are circumscribed both historically and geographically. They may have emerged with the growth of knowledge and technology and would, consequently, make no sense to persons lacking the requisite background. The way babies learn about the world—gravity, the persistence of objects, etc.—provides a kind of analogy with the way successive generations learn to accommodate facts, events, and principles unknown to their ancestors (think of airplanes, radios, telephones, computers, etc.). For all his undoubted intelligence, David Hume would draw a complete blank if he were to read the commonsense warning about keeping electrical appliances out of water. It is a matter of common sense to inhabitants of Manitoba, Canada, that one does not plant tomatoes outside during December, but not to inhabitants of New South Wales, Australia. At even more specialized levels, commonsense maxims (or matters of *common knowledge*, as they are sometimes called) abound in horse breeding, rocket science, cardiovascular surgery, poker playing, and scores of other more or less esoteric areas. Unlike truly universal and ineradicable commonsense principles, which we acquire without reflection or sophistication, higher-level commonsense beliefs demand a greater amount of acquired knowledge.

Common sense and *commonsensical* are, in most instances, "good" words; i.e., they generally convey a positive or approving attitude. Thomas Paine (1737–1809), perhaps the most successful pamphleteer in American history, gave the simple title *Common Sense* to his call for the North American colonists of 1776 to declare their independence from Britain, a title suggesting that the case for separation from the mother country was not esoteric or hard to follow. That case, Paine says, is based on simple facts, plain arguments, and common sense. One need not be learned or brilliant to understand the principle *taxation without representation is tyranny*—a principle that the British king, George III, and the British parliament persistently violated in their treatment of the colonists. Since the oppressors in London (king and parliament) adamantly refused to change their unjust policies, a prudent man—a man of *common sense*—was forced to abandon the route of peaceful petition and prepare for war. Such was Thomas Paine's commonsensical case for independence.

Some critics have accused Hume of seeking to subvert belief in such basic matters as the existence of the external world and causal relations. Even if that were Hume's intention (it is not), he is perfectly clear that no philosophical reasoning could induce people to abandon those beliefs. As Hume himself puts it, "*A Man must have lost all common Sense to doubt [them]*" (*A Letter*, 118; italics are in Hume's text). Whatever extreme skeptics may *say* about suspending all belief, their actions show that their doubts are not sustainable in reality. Hume puts his retort succinctly: "Nature [or common sense] is always too strong for principle [in this instance, skeptical argument]" (EHU, 160; 207.23). Notice that it is nature, or common sense—and not reason—that defeats skepticism.

Hume normally treats common sense as a weapon against superstition and unrestrained speculation. A reasonable skeptic rejects "abstruse, remote and refined arguments," but adheres to "common sense and the plain instincts of nature" (*Dialogues*, 154). Indeed, common sense and **experience** are natural allies of theory and speculation when we reason about trade or morals or politics or criticism. "To philosophise on such subjects is nothing essentially different from reasoning on common life . . ." (*Dialogues*, 134). On the other hand, when we allow our speculations to outstrip our cognitive powers and reliable evidence (as is the custom of some philosophers and theologians), we sever that alliance. Common sense and experience cannot perform their usual salutary role in so radically unfamiliar a world. It is as if we were in a foreign country, ignorant of the language, the laws, and the customs (*Dialogues*, 134–35).

It must be added that Hume does not reject what he calls "profound and abstract" philosophy as useless. On the contrary, he argues that such philosophy is "the only catholic remedy, fitted for all persons and all dispositions; and is alone able to subvert that abstruse philosophy and metaphysical jargon, which, being mixed up with popular superstition, renders it in a manner impenetrable to careless reasoners, and gives it the air of science and wisdom" (EHU, 12–13; 92.12). Nevertheless, Hume seeks to reconcile "profound enquiry with clearness, and truth with novelty" (EHU, 16; 95.17), to strike a balance between the easy and the difficult philosophy. (For Hume's lively and instructive discussion of the different species of philosophy, read section 1 of EHU.)

Historical notes: The Irish philosopher **George Berkeley** rejects the metaphysical notion of material substance (i.e., an unknowable, unperceivable something or other) but embraces the commonsense reality of perceivable objects (i.e., objects that are visible, audible, tangible, etc.). Accordingly, Dr. Samuel Johnson's famous stone-kicking "refutation" of Berkeley reflects only his elementary misunderstanding of Berkeley, not the triumph of common sense over nonsense. **Thomas Reid**, Hume's contemporary and a philosopher of genius in his own right, was the founder and greatest proponent of what came to be known as *Scottish Commonsense Philosophy*. Reid argues that Hume (who was much admired by Reid) demonstrated the inevitable skeptical consequences of the "ideal" theory, according to which the mind is never aware of real independent objects, but only of its own ideas or perceptions. The theory originated with the French philosopher **René Descartes** and was endorsed by **John Locke**, but it was Hume who unflinchingly showed the skeptical, anti-commonsense cul-de-sac to which it led—or so Reid contends. (Curiously, Reid does not regard Locke as a skeptic.) Reid develops a wide-ranging philosophical system that exhibits the rational basis of commonsense beliefs about the external world, the mind, and morality.

The English philosopher G. E. [George Edward] Moore (1873–1958) defends commonsense beliefs against various sorts of skepticism. In his well-known and influential essay "A Defense of Common Sense," Moore argues that he knows with certainty that some propositions—e.g., "There exists at present a living human body, which is *my* body"—are true. This means that any skeptical argument purporting to undermine that proposition would have to rest on premises that are, *at best*, no more certain than the proposition itself, and probably less certain. Bertrand Russell (1872–1970), an English philosopher and logician and a fellow Cantabrigian with G. E. Moore, tells of receiving a letter from a woman who professed to be a solipsist (i.e., one who believes that only she and her experiences are real) and to be puzzled why more people were not solipsists. One can only suppose (or at least hope) that Russell's correspondent was having a bit of fun by seeming to advocate an obviously self-stultifying position. (To whom could a solipsist write a letter?) The problem raised by Russell's correspondent is broadly logical (or conceptual), but any person of common sense could spot the nonsense at once. The letter-writing solipsist seems unwittingly to have provided an example of the form of humor known as the Irish bull; e.g., "Infertility is hereditary. If your parents had no children, you probably won't either."

We (i.e., human beings) are fortunate, Hume thinks, that we acquire basic commonsense beliefs with little or no reasoning or effort. In the normal course of events, we come to believe in an independent world inhabited by persons like ourselves. And a good thing, too! We would be in a hopelessly labile and dangerous predicament if we had to provide rationally compelling evidence for the existence of the external world and the stability of causal connections. Not to worry! "Nature has not left this to [our] choice, and has doubtless esteem'd it an affair of too great importance to be trusted to our uncertain reasonings and speculations" (THN, 187; 1.4.2.1). Some observers may interpret this salubrious arrangement as evidence of God's providential care; post-Darwin observers may see it as an evolutionary advantage, without any religious significance. For Hume, it is simply a fact—a very important fact—about how people are connected to their natural and social worlds. *See* NATURAL BELIEF.

COOPER, ANTHONY ASHLEY. *See* SHAFTESBURY.

CUDWORTH, RALPH (1617–1688). Cudworth was one of a group of philosophers and theologians referred to as the *Cambridge Platonists*—a label that signifies certain common sympathies (e.g., opposition to Calvinism and what they regarded as fanaticism) but not necessarily a common body of doctrines. They are uniformly innatists (i.e., they hold that the human mind or soul is invested with certain intellectual and moral notions that could not be derived from experience), and as such they are among the targets of **John Locke**'s extended polemic against the doctrine of **innate ideas**. This suggests, correctly, that they emphasize the role of **reason** in acquiring knowledge, against both empiricists (who stress experience) and fideists (who rely on revelation).

Cudworth was the equal (at least) of any of the other Cambridge Platonists as a systematic philosopher, and he was known to Hume. He published the first part of *The True Intellectual System of the Universe*, which is devoted to the refutation of atheism, in 1678. The other two parts were never published. However, two posthumously published pieces more or less carry out the plan of the original work: *A Treatise Concerning Eternal and Immutable Morality* (1731) and *A Treatise on Free Will*. Cudworth argues (echoing Plato) that the objects of true knowledge must have natures or essences that are fixed and unchanging, and this requirement applies no less to moral natures than to physical or mathematical natures. Some of Cudworth's arguments anticipate certain features of G. E. Moore's discussion of the so-called naturalistic fallacy (*see* IS/OUGHT). The goodness of an act depends neither on the conventions of society (contra **Thomas Hobbes**, for example) nor on the commands of God (contra **Samuel Pufendorf** and the Calvinists, for example). Acts of a certain sort are good (or not) in themselves. For Cudworth, this means that we have innate notions of morality—right, justice, virtue, etc.—just as we have innate notions of God, substance, truth, etc. We could not acquire any of those notions from the constantly changing welter of **perceptions** that come to us by way of the senses.

Hume mentions Cudworth, **Nicolas Malebranche**, **Samuel Clarke**, and Montesqieu as espousing an "abstract theory of morals"—a theory that "excludes all sentiment, and pretends to found everything on reason" (EPM, 197n1; 93n12). Of course, Hume regards the theory as wrong-headed (*see* MORAL SENSE). In EHU, Hume notes with approval that Cudworth attributes "a real, though subordinate and derived power" to material objects. This sets him in opposition to the doctrine of **occasionalism**, which restricts the exercise of causal efficacy to God (EHU, 73n1; 143n16). Cudworth's doctrine of free will anticipates certain features of Hume's treatment of **liberty and necessity** (or *freedom and determinism*, as we would say). For example, Cudworth and Hume agree that freedom does not mean indifference, or the absence of motivation; and they agree that it is properly the person or agent, and not the will itself, that is free (or not).

– D –

DESCARTES, RENÉ (1596–1650). In Latin, the name is *Renatus Cartesius*, from which the adjectival form *Cartesian* is derived. Sometimes referred to as "the father of modern philosophy," Descartes did much to define the character and to mark out the path of philosophy for the next three centuries. His work in mathematics (to which he made important contributions) convinced him that the only **knowledge** worthy of the name had to be clear and certain, like mathematics. That level of knowledge is accessible only to **reason**, not to the senses; hence the label *rationalist* (versus *empiricist*, the tag applied to Hume). The correctness of the Cartesian *paradigm* of knowledge is accepted (in practice, if not always in theory) even by philosophers who deny that human beings are capable of certainty about matters of fact (such as Hume and, with qualifications, **John Locke**). In other words, these philosophers accept the Cartesian *conception* of knowledge—the criteria that must be satisfied—even if they disagree about whether some particular proposition satisfies those criteria.

Hume rarely mentions Descartes by name, but he accepts some of the fundamental assumptions of the Cartesian philosophy (in addition to the definition of *knowledge* just mentioned). Three instances of those assumptions may be noted. In the first place, Hume follows Descartes' example in stressing the importance of *method* (as do many modern philosophers). Without a clear notion of how to think systematically (e.g., by dividing complex problems into simpler ones), philosophers are doomed to confusion and failure. Second, he concurs in Descartes' assumption that the direct, or immediate, objects of consciousness are mental entities (whether they be called **perceptions** or *impressions* or *ideas*). This doctrine has been called "the theory of ideas" (by **Thomas Reid**) or "the way of ideas," and its influence is virtually incalculable. According to that theory, we are not directly aware of physical objects, or of anything else outside the mind. Third—and this is a consequence of the second—true knowledge is about ideas. Hume also typically follows this usage, restricting knowledge in the full, unqualified sense to what he calls **relations of ideas**. (It should be noted in passing that some scholars deny that Descartes is committed to "the theory of ideas," but he has been widely interpreted as embracing that theory.)

Hume rejects certain important parts of the Cartesian system. Indeed, some of Hume's most distinctive epistemological doctrines may be seen as reactions to Descartes (even if Hume did not have Descartes specifically in mind). For one absolutely basic example, Descartes holds that we know with a priori certainty that every object or event that begins to exist must have a cause of existence (expressed in the Latin phrase *ex nihilo nihil fit*). This is a truth that we know by the light of reason—so Descartes insists. Hume argues at length and with great ingenuity that we have no such knowledge, either by direct intuition or by demonstration. Note well, however, that Hume does not *deny* the causal principle; he denies only that we have any purely rational basis for the **belief** (*see* CAUSE). It is interesting that the English *empiricist* John Locke agrees with Descartes on this issue. As noted above, Hume agrees with Descartes on the importance of method, but he rejects the first maxim in Descartes' own method; namely, that we should not accept anything as true unless it is certainly and evidently so. Hume has two objections to this piece of advice, either of which is sufficient to scuttle it. First, we cannot consciously control what we believe or do not believe; so the maxim is impossible to follow. Second, we cannot know any matter of fact with the degree of certainty that Descartes demands. We have indubitable knowledge only of factually empty propositions (e.g., "every square has four sides" and "no bachelor is married"), and these cannot be what Descartes has in mind. If Hume is right, the news for Descartes is as bad as it could possibly be: We cannot help believing a lot of propositions that have no rational support.

More generally, Hume rejects Descartes' estimate of the role that reason plays in our knowledge of matters of fact. Whereas Descartes holds that reason (or the intellect) is at work even in what appears to be simple sense perception (see, for example, *Meditation II*),

Hume argues, at the other extreme, that "all probable reasoning is nothing but a species of sensation" (THN, 103; 1.3.8.12). Against Descartes (and other rationalists), who sharply separate the intellect (or reason) from the imagination and the senses, Hume contends that "reason is nothing but a wonderful and unintelligible instinct in our souls" (THN, 179; 1.3.16.9). A parallel passage in EHU makes the same point more forcefully: " . . . the experimental reasoning itself, which we possess in common with beasts, and on which the whole conduct of life depends, is nothing but a species of instinct or mechanical power, that acts in us unknown to ourselves" (108; 168.6). Both quotations are from sections titled "Of the Reason of Animals," which appear in both THN and EHU. (Hume no doubt had in mind Descartes' well-known theory that non-human animals are automata that have neither reason nor even sentience.)

Hume also rejects what he takes to be the Cartesian use of **skepticism**—"antecedent skepticism," as Hume calls it. In the *Meditations* (Descartes' best-known and most widely read work), Descartes *begins* his quest for an unshakable foundation of knowledge by systematically doubting not only particular beliefs but also (on Hume's reading of Descartes, at any rate) the very faculties by which we reach any beliefs—sense perception, memory, etc. Hume observes that such a universal doubt is impossible and would be radically incurable if it were possible: Once we question the reliability of our cognitive faculties, we have divested ourselves of the only means of overcoming the initial doubts. Nevertheless, Descartes proceeds in the *Meditations* to try to establish the existence of his own self (epitomized by the phrase *cogito, ergo sum* [I think; therefore, I am], which does not literally occur in the *Meditations*) and the existence of an omnipotent God, whose benevolence guarantees the trustworthiness of our clear and distinct perceptions. Hume's wry comment on Descartes' appeal to divine goodness is worth quoting: "To have recourse to the veracity of the Supreme Being, in order to prove the veracity of our senses, is surely making a very unexpected circuit" (EHU, 153; 202.13). (Historians of philosophy may argue that Hume misinterprets Descartes, but that is a different issue.)

Although Hume rejects Descartes' antecedent skepticism as self-stultifying, he accepts a version of what he calls *consequent* (or *academical*) skepticism—a salutary skepticism that emerges from a careful examination of human mental faculties and helps to keep our speculations within modest limits. (The final section of EHU—"Of the Academical or Sceptical Philosophy"—is an excellent source for Hume's "mitigated" skepticism.)

Descartes is the first and most famous of modern rationalist philosophers, but Hume was also familiar with some home-grown (i.e., British) philosophers who fall under that label—e.g., **Samuel Clarke** and **Ralph Cudworth**, who are rationalists in both epistemology and ethics.

DESIGN, ARGUMENT FROM/TO. This argument for the existence of God is also called the *teleological* argument (from the Greek word τέλος [*telos*], which means purpose, goal, or aim). The main sources for Hume's discussion of this argument are *Dialogues Concerning Natural Religion* and section 11 of EHU ("Of a Particular Providence and of a Future State").

Hume is willing to take the design argument seriously because it is a posteriori; i.e., it is based on experience, not on merely abstract reasoning. It yields, at best, a probable conclusion. This means that Hume rejects the standard a priori demonstrations of the **existence** of God—the *ontological* and the *cosmological* (the latter based on the putative necessity of an eternal, underived cause of all finite existents). Hume holds that anything that exists, might not exist. It is impossible to demonstrate the existence of any matter of fact. "The non-existence of any being, without exception, is as clear and distinct an idea as its existence" (EHU, 164; 209.28). We can argue for the existence of a being only by considering its **causes** or effects.

At least so far as Hume is concerned, the inference in the design argument is *to* design, rather than *from* design—a fact that will become apparent in due course. The argument is based on analogy—i.e., on the supposition that if two or more entities or events are similar in certain respects, they will probably be alike in at least one additional respect. For example, human beings and chimpanzees are analogous in being mammalian vertebrates, in having a heart, two lungs, a fairly big brain, a complicated nervous system, etc., etc. Based on these analogies, we infer that if chimps react in certain ways to an experimental drug, human beings will probably react in similar ways. The inference is only probable, not demonstrative. But we would have very little basis for even a probable conclusion if we administered the drug to *beetles*, which have few relevant anatomical and physiological similarities to human beings.

The design argument trades on similarities between nature and certain human artifacts. We observe that nature exhibits all manner of orderly processes and means-to-ends adaptations: the seasons come and go with such predictable regularity that we can plant and harvest at propitious times, prepare for cold weather, predict lunar and solar eclipses with great accuracy, etc.; and birds and beavers build homes for their future young. These natural arrangements invite—or perhaps even compel—comparison with the kind of order that undeniably depends on intelligent design and foresight: houses, clocks, highways, boats, etc. On the principle that like effects require like causes, we infer by analogy that the cause of natural order must be an intelligent deity. Notice that the premises do not beg the question by *assuming* that nature exhibits design. That is a conclusion inferred from the similarity of natural phenomena to objects *known* to be the products of design. That is, the argument proceeds *to* design as the best explanation of certain observable facts about nature—what Hume calls "the religious hypothesis" (EHU, 139; 192.18).

Hume does not reject the design argument out of hand. Indeed, he seems (at least) to accept a scaled-down version of the argument, but he points out weaknesses that significantly diminish its force. A few such flaws may be mentioned. First, intelligent design is not the only possible explanation of the order we find in the world. Perhaps the world is more like an animal or a vegetable (which grow and propagate without obvious intelligent design) than it is like a machine (which does require intelligence). In jargon that was (fortunately?) not available to Hume, we might say that facts underdetermine theory; i.e., facts are always compatible with more than one theory. Hume warns in particular against endowing the cause (the intelligent designer/deity in this case) with more and greater attributes than are strictly required by the effects (i.e., the observed phenomena). While it is *possible* that the deity may have attributes that we have not seen manifested, we cannot reliably *infer* such attributes from the evidence we have.

The problems just noted are of a very general epistemic sort (e.g., going beyond the evidence in making inferences). Hume also raises questions more specifically about the strength of the *analogy* on which the argument turns. For convenience, we may simplify Hume's misgivings as posing a dilemma for proponents of the design argument: The analogy is either too weak or too strong to yield the desired conclusion. We will consider the two horns of the dilemma in turn.

The analogy is weak because the two things being compared—the making of human artifacts and the "making" of the world—are so disparate as to make even using the term *analogy* problematic. We can compare chimps and humans because we have empirical knowledge of the physiology and anatomy of the two classes of things being compared. We have no comparable basis for likening the work of a clockmaker to the work of the deity in fashioning the world. One side of the analogy is well known; the other side is almost completely unknown. Any inference resting on that supposed analogy is bound to be incurably dubious.

If, for the sake of argument, we grant the required analogy, we encounter equally unwelcome consequences. For example, building a house normally requires the cooperation of a number of workers— carpenters, bricklayers, plumbers, et al. Do we conclude that the universe had multiple designers/creators? The proponents of the design argument did not have polytheism in mind. Likewise, human craftsmen, both individually and collectively, get better with practice. Is this true of the deity? Human artisans die. Does the deity also die? And so on.

Hume also raises the age-old problem of evil. If the deity is omnipotent, omniscient, and perfectly good, as monotheistic religions commonly hold, why is there evil in the world? Hume does not suppose that this is a logically insuperable difficulty, but he does think that it poses a nagging problem for traditional theists.

What is Hume's own last word about the design argument? Hume scholars have debated, and continue to debate, the answer to that question. At the end of the *Dialogues*, Hume has Philo (one of the principals) endorse what has been described as an "attenuated deism" (or, sometimes, as an "attenuated theism"); namely, *that the cause or causes of order in the universe probably bear some remote analogy to human intelligence"* (*Dialogues*, 227; italics are in Hume's text). Whether this represents Hume's own view is a point of contention. What is clear is that Hume's deity (if any) is profoundly unlike the God of the Apostles' Creed—"the Father Almighty, Creator of heaven and earth." It is also clear that Hume adamantly rejects any tie between the deity and morality. We have no obligation to do or forbear doing anything because the deity has commanded or forbidden it. Indeed, the deity has no moral nature at all and so would have no disposition to enjoin or proscribe anything.

DIALOGUES CONCERNING NATURAL RELIGION. Writing the *Dialogues* was Hume's frequently interrupted occupation for more than 20 years; but it was not published until 1779, three years after Hume died, thanks to the courage and persistence of his nephew, also named David. Hume was proud of this work, and with reason. Good philosophical dialogues are extremely rare, and many critics rank Hume's next only to those of Plato, which are obviously in a class by themselves. After mentioning Plato's, Hume's, and **George Berkeley**'s *Three Dialogues between Hylas and Philonous*, one is hard pressed to think of any other philosophical dialogues that are worth much attention.

First, a word about the title. The issues raised in the *Dialogues* are about *natural* religion, i.e., religion based on reason. The implied contrast is with *revealed* religion, i.e., religion based on divinely inspired truths—those in the Bible or the Koran, for example. Toward the very end of the *Dialogues*, Hume has Philo, one of the principals in the debate, declare that any person who understands the limitations and imperfections of natural reason "will fly to revealed truth with the greatest avidity" (227). We are entitled to suppose that Hume is here indulging in irony, but it really does not matter. Whatever we may think about divine revelation, Hume's *Dialogues* is about something else.

Besides Philo, whose opinions most closely resemble Hume's own, there are two other characters in the *Dialogues* proper: Demea, a rationalist who champions a priori arguments, and Cleanthes, an empiricist who advocates the analogical reasoning found in the argument from/to design. Because Philo and Cleanthes agree in rejecting Demea's a priori approach, Demea functions mainly as a foil for the other two (though he does occasionally have some interesting and curious things to say).

The primary question the *Dialogues* sets out to answer is whether we have reasonable grounds for believing in a deity that is endowed with intelligence, purposes, and moral character. Note carefully that "reasonable grounds" does not mean demonstrative certainty. In Hume's view, we cannot demonstrate the existence of *any* being, including God. Accordingly, Hume rules out the so-called ontological and cosmological arguments, which purport to do what Hume says is impossible: Offer a rationally compelling argument for the existence of God. Given that limitation, do we have good empirical, inductive reasons for concluding that the existence of God is probable? This means that the argument from (or to) design (also called the *teleological argument*) is our only hope. *See* DESIGN, ARGUMENT FROM/TO.

The *Dialogues* is the best single source for Hume's views on the reasonableness of religious belief. (*See* RELIGION for a discussion of other sources.) It is a richly detailed examination of many issues and problems associated with the most intuitively compelling of all the arguments for the existence of an intelligent deity; namely, the argument from/to design. If Hume did not completely explode that argument, he certainly changed the whole tenor of discussion about it. It is virtually unthinkable that a philosopher or theologian after Hume would venture an opinion on the topic without taking account of the *Dialogues*.

– E –

ECONOMICS. David Hume the economist is overshadowed by his good friend Adam Smith, one of the most famous and influential economists who ever lived, who acknowledged a large debt to Hume. Nevertheless, Hume's writings about economics are valuable both for their shrewd observations on a number of subjects (commerce, money, the balance of trade, interest, taxes, etc.) and as illustrating certain features of his science of human nature. That science is based on "a cautious observation" of the behavior of human beings in a wide range of circumstances—"in company, in affairs, and in their pleasures" (THN, xix; 5–6.10). To make the point explicit: Economic phenomena are part of the observational base of Hume's science of human nature. Something like the opposite is also true: Once the general laws of human nature have been discovered, they can be used to throw light on economic phenomena and to criticize certain theories within economics. In this entry we will look briefly at a couple of Hume's essays about economic subjects, concluding with a few comments about the relation between his economic doctrine and his science of human nature.

The chief target of several of Hume's essays is mercantilism, which comprises a few basic assumptions without being a single unified theory. It tends to identify wealth with money, and that means, among other things, trying to maintain a favorable balance of trade with other nations. If a nation sells more than it buys, it will acquire precious metals (especially gold), which can pay for just about anything the nation may need, or think it needs (e.g., a large army or navy). A mercantilist nation may discourage imports (e.g., by tariffs or restrictions on the circulation of money) in the hope of acquiring more specie than foreign nations. But that is a forlorn hope, Hume argues in "Of the Balance of Trade," because it is self-defeating. Money behaves like water in two connected bodies: If the level drops on one side, water from the other side will flow in to make up the loss. Likewise, the ebb and flow of specie exchange between nations is governed by causal laws. The increase of money in one nation (with an attendant rise in prices) will be matched by a corresponding decrease of money in its trading partner (with lower prices).

A prudent government will "preserve with care its people and its manufactures. Its money, it may safely trust to the course of human affairs, without fear or jealousy" (*Essays*, 326). If Britain were to lose four-fifths of all its money overnight, Hume contends, the effect would be dramatic and quick—but not lasting. The resulting abundance of cheap labor and commodities would make it virtually impossible for other nations to compete with Britain in the world marketplace. Before long, the lost money would have been recouped. (*Mutatis mutandis*, the same reasoning would apply if the supply of money in Britain were *increased* fivefold—with the opposite result. Before long, the surfeit of money would be gone, and things would be back to normal.)

Having subverted one species of "ill-founded jealousy"—i.e., that fair and open foreign trade will rob a nation of its money—Hume fingers a second variety in "Of the Jealousy of Trade." It is a "narrow and malignant opinion" that one nation cannot flourish commercially except at the expense of other nations. For Hume, that view is exactly wrong: " . . . the encrease of riches and commerce in any one nation, instead of hurting, commonly promotes the riches and commerce of all its neighbours; and . . . a state can scarcely carry its trade and industry very far, where all the surrounding states are buried in ignorance, sloth, and barbarism" (*Essays*, 328). Such benighted states could neither sell us anything nor buy anything from us. For that reason, Hume says, he prays for the commercial success of Germany, Spain, Italy, "and even FRANCE itself" (ibid., 331).

Hume's essays on economic subjects are liberally sprinkled with historical references to other times and places, as well as to writings from both ancient and modern authors. This will not be surprising to readers familiar with Hume's more narrowly philosophical works (e.g., THN, EHU, and EPM), which also abound with direct references and allusions to many writers. The study of history provides a wide range of "experiments" to be used for the development of the science of human nature. Studying what actually happened in history and how people actually behaved is incomparably preferable to trying to deduce factual conclusions from abstract premises. These economic essays of Hume are also laced with psychological insights about what moves us to do, or refrain from doing, certain things. He does not hesitate to invoke facts about the individual psyche to explain economic facts. Hume makes proper allowance for individual differences, but he still insists that most of us fit a standard emotional and social profile: We like to acquire things, but also to use them; we love activity, but we need respite from activity (short of idleness, which is a monstrous curse); we are motivated most strongly by our own interest, but we are capable of some measure of altruism. Indeed, helping others often redounds to our own benefit (as in the case of foreign trade). Hume is more interested in psychological explanations of economic phenomena than many later economists, but that is part of their value. His essays on economics also bear on the nature of knowledge in general. They embody what Annette Baier calls "cultural epistemology," which takes account of the influence various communities (family, economic, religious, legal, etc.) exert on what we count as knowledge.

EGOISM. *Egoism* (not a term that Hume uses) as a philosophical theory takes two forms: *psychological* egoism, which holds that all voluntary human actions are selfish; and *ethical* egoism, which holds that people *ought* always to act from self-interest. Hume's comments on the subject are mainly about the first sort of egoism—the factual claim that human beings are always motivated by self-interest and nothing else—but what he says has obvious consequences for the second variety (ethical egoism). In Hume's view, egoism is "utterly incompatible with all virtue or moral sentiment" (EPM, 295; 164.1). That is because morality presupposes the human capacity for making disinterested judgments—judgments that go beyond self-interest and reflect a general point of view.

The extreme egoist (exemplified, perhaps, by **Bernard de Mandeville**) would have us believe that "all *benevolence* is mere hypocrisy, friendship a cheat, public spirit a farce, fidelity a snare to procure trust and confidence"—all such "virtues" being, at bottom, ploys to throw others off their guard and "expose them the more to our wiles and machinations" (EPM, 295; 164.1; italics are in Hume's text). Hume describes a related, but less cynical, version of egoism, which holds that benevolence need not be hypocritical but is, often unknown even to ourselves, always an expression of self-love. Hume mentions **Thomas Hobbes** and **John Locke** as modern philosophers who espouse this modified version of egoism.

For all its appearance of being a simple, realistic, unflinching explanation of (ostensibly) moral behavior, egoism runs counter to experience and nature. Hume concedes—or, rather, insists—that human beings often act selfishly; but it is thoroughly implausible to try to reduce all generosity, self-sacrifice, sympathy, and disinterested goodwill to disguised self-interest. A philosophy that denies the reality of human affection and friendship "is more like a satire than a true delineation or description of human nature; and may be a good foundation for paradoxical wit and raillery, but is a very bad one for any serious argument or reasoning" (EPM, 302; 168–69.13). *See also* HOBBES, MANDEVILLE.

EMPIRICISM AND RATIONALISM. The terms *empiricism* (from the Greek word for experience—*empeiria* [ἐμπειρία]) and *rationalism* (from the Latin word for reason—*ratio*) mark a fundamental divide between theories of **knowledge**; namely, those that take **experience** as primary (the empiricists) and those that take **reason** as primary (the rationalists). (It should be noted that Hume himself does not use these terms.) Like most labels, the terms *empiricism* and *rationalism* can be useful in a rough-and-ready way, but they may be misleading in one or both of two ways: They may cover up similarities between the empiricists and the rationalists, and they may disguise internal differences within the two groups. Because David Hume is an empiricist, we will focus on certain features of empiricism, using rationalism as a foil. To make a large subject manageable in limited space, we will confine our attention primarily to the 17th and 18th centuries, the era of British Empiricism (exemplified by **John Locke**, **George Berkeley**, and David Hume) and Continental Rationalism (exemplified by **René Descartes**, Benedict Spinoza, and Gottfried Wilhelm Leibniz). We will mention other empiricists or rationalists only in passing.

After a brief look at what empiricists typically mean by *experience*, we will consider two distinct ways in which philosophers can be empiricists, and, finally, show how the general philosophical method and outlook of the empiricists differ from those of the rationalists.

One

Empiricists hold that experience, not reason, is the primary source of knowledge. But what does that mean? After all, experience comes in many varieties or modes—a fact that empiricists need not, and do not, deny. However, when they appeal to experience, they mean *sense experience* (i.e., experience that comes by way of sight, hearing, etc.), which they construe to include memory and the products of certain natural associative principles (resemblance, for example) and mental operations (combining, for example). It is sense experience—and not reveries or mystical visions or purely cerebral speculations—that provides empiricists the explanatory power and the justificatory norms they seek. (For a more detailed account of the sorts of phenomena covered by the term *experience*, as well as a fuller discussion of Hume's notion of experience, *see* EXPERIENCE.)

Two

As intimated above in the caveat about labels, empiricism and rationalism are not unitary schools of thought. In particular, scholars have proposed numerous distinctions among philosophies that fall under the general rubric *empiricist*. Two common and useful sub-varieties are *content-empiricism* (or *conceptual empiricism*) as against *knowledge-empiricism*, *belief-empiricism*, or *justification-empiricism*. The last three terms are not strictly synonymous, but they are alike in denoting something different from content-empiricism. According to *content*-empiricism, all our ideas (or concepts) come from experience, either directly or indirectly. According to *knowledge*-empiricism, all our legitimate claims to know something must be justified by experience.

To see why these two sorts of empiricism are distinct, we need to remember that all the philosophers we are discussing (empiricists and rationalists alike) agree that an idea by itself is neither true nor false, i.e., does not constitute a knowledge-claim. Only *judgments* can be true or false. If I have an idea of a centaur, I have made no mistake: I really have the idea. However, if I judge that there is a centaur in my backyard, then I have asserted something true or false. Since experience affords no evidence that centaurs actually exist, the knowledge-empiricist (and just about everybody else) would say that my judgment is false in this case. (We may note in passing that writers in the 17th and 18th centuries do not use the term *judgment* in a consistently univocal sense. However, they agree that an idea per se must be distinguished from a judgment, which always involves something more than an idea as such.)

Content-empiricism and knowledge-empiricism are logically independent; i.e., they are mutually compatible, but neither entails the other. As we shall see, Locke, Berkeley, and Hume all espouse content-empiricism but (with a qualification in Hume's case) reject knowledge-empiricism. The rationalists reject both kinds of empiricism.

Content-empiricists accept the medieval dictum *nihil in intellectu nisi prius in sensu*: there is nothing in the intellect (or mind) that was not first in the senses. Locke devotes more than 50 pages of his *Essay* to refuting the most prominent contrary view, the doctrine of **innate**

ideas. (It is logically possible to reject both content-empiricism and the doctrine of innate ideas [**Nicolas Malebranche** seems to hold this position], but rationalists typically accept the doctrine of innate ideas.) *Idea* is the term widely used by Locke and others to denote what Locke calls "the immediate object of Perception, Thought, or Understanding" (*Essay*, 134.§8). (Hume uses *perception* to mean what Locke means by *idea*, but this does not signify a substantive difference in doctrine.)

If we are not born with any ideas, Locke argues, then we must get all of them from experience, which comprises Sensation (from which we get ideas of color, sound, odor, etc.) and Reflection (from which we get ideas of mental operations such as thinking, willing, believing, etc.). Locke observes that although Reflection has nothing directly to do with external objects, it is sufficiently like Sensation to be properly called the Internal Sense. From these two "fountains"—Sensation and Reflection (the External Sense and the Internal Sense)—come all our simple ideas. The mind can form complex ideas by combining, separating, comparing, etc., the elements supplied by experience; but it is utterly unable to create even one simple idea by its own power. So far as simple ideas are concerned, either we acquire them by experience or we do not have them. (For an explanation of *simple*, *see* PERCEPTIONS.)

Although Berkeley and Hume (especially Berkeley) pursue philosophical projects significantly different from Locke's, they still embrace content-empiricism. For our present purposes, their versions of content-empiricism are close enough to Locke's to obviate the need for a separate discussion. (For *other* purposes, the differences may be interesting and important.)

The rationalists paint a very different picture of how we get our ideas. Indeed, rationalists uniformly reject the claim of content-empiricism, for (at least) two related reasons. First, we have ideas (or concepts) that experience (in the empiricist sense) allegedly could not have produced—e.g., ideas of God, infinity, substance, identity, etc. Whether such ideas are literally innate in the way Locke construes that term, they are functionally or practically innate. They are, the rationalists contend, clearly beyond the reach of the senses or the imagination (the faculty that works with images); they can be known only by the mind or intellect. Second, as Descartes tries to show in

Meditation II, even ideas that seem to issue directly from sense experience (or sense experience plus the imagination)—e.g., the ideas of extension and flexibility—are in fact discerned by the mind or intellect. The senses and the imagination afford only a fuzzy, inchoate notion of the essential properties of bodies (or physical objects). Spinoza and Leibniz likewise make frequent invidious comparisons between the products of the intellect and those of the senses or the imagination. Leibniz adds a phrase to the medieval principle quoted above: *nihil in intellectu nisi prius in sensu—nisi intellectus ipse [except the intellect itself]*. This insistence on a sharp separation between the intellect and the imagination/sensation is a hallmark of rationalist doctrine. Rejection of any such clear boundary is, on the other hand, a hallmark of empiricist doctrine.

As noted above, content-empiricism and knowledge-empiricism are logically independent. This means that a philosopher could consistently reject the doctrine that all our ideas/concepts come from experience (*content*-empiricism) and yet accept the doctrine that any claim to knowledge of matters of fact can be justified only by experience (*knowledge*-empiricism). However, we expect that those who deny content-empiricism will deny knowledge-empiricism as well, and the three rationalists we have mentioned do not surprise us on this score. Indeed, their rejection of knowledge-empiricism is too obvious to require anything beyond a reminder. Consider, as a single example, Leibniz's doctrine that, from the infinitely many logically possible worlds available, God chose to actualize the best one; i.e., the actual world is the best possible world. To what experience should we appeal to justify that claim? (We could just as easily have taken examples from Descartes or Spinoza, but the one from Leibniz is telling and also famous as the butt of Voltaire's raillery in *Candide*.)

The rationalists are predictable in repudiating knowledge-empiricism; the empiricists are less so. Locke, Berkeley, and Hume agree with the rationalists that our knowledge of mathematics (and, more generally, of what Hume calls **relations of ideas**) is independent of experience. On this point, the Big Three empiricists are unanimously and straightforwardly *opposed* to knowledge-empiricism. Surprisingly, however, Locke and Berkeley (but not Hume) profess to know propositions about the world ("matters of fact and real existence," in Hume's language) that, at least prima facie, cannot be justified by appealing to experience in the empiricist sense. For example, Locke declares the causal principle (that nothing produces nothing) to be intuitively certain, and both Locke and Berkeley offer demonstrations of the existence of God. Their departure from knowledge-empiricism goes beyond mathematics and extends to metaphysics. (Whether Locke's and Berkeley's departures are justifiable or even regarded *as* departures by the principals are separate questions, which we need not go into.)

Unlike Locke and Berkeley, Hume holds fast to a version of knowledge-empiricism that exempts only our knowledge of relations of ideas from the requirement of experiential confirmation. All our knowledge of matters of fact beyond immediate perception and memory rests on the relation of cause and effect, which we discover by experience, never a priori. This means, contrary to Locke, that we have no intuitive assurance of the universality of causation; and it means, contrary to both Locke and Berkeley, that we cannot demonstrate the existence of any being, including God.

A note on terminology: In THN (especially book 1), Hume contrasts knowledge with probability, reserving *knowledge* for propositions that we can know with intuitive or demonstrative certainty (*see* RELATIONS). In EHU he seems to be less concerned to maintain the sharp distinction between knowledge and probability, but he always adamantly insists on a sharp dichotomous division between what we can know a priori and what we can know only by experience. If we want a term to mark the distinction Hume draws between knowledge in the strict sense and probability, we can call Hume a *belief*-empiricist but not a *knowledge*-empiricist. Whatever terms we use, the substantive difference is clear enough. (*See* KNOWLEDGE.)

Three

In this section, we will take a broad look at how empiricism and rationalism seek to answer the questions raised by philosophical reflection. Their assumptions about method and the reach of the human mind are of central importance, and the two approaches diverge pretty sharply.

Both the empiricists and the rationalists take the problem of *method* seriously. Indeed, Descartes published two works explicitly about method—*Rules for the Direction of the Mind* and *Discourse on Method*—but the empiricists (especially Locke and Hume) also take pains to say how they intend to proceed. If the empiricists take natural sciences (e.g., physics, chemistry, biology, medicine) as models for their own philosophies, the rationalists expressly take mathematics as embodying their ideal of knowledge. In their view, any knowledge worthy of the name must be clear and certain, with mathematics as the paradigm. Descartes and Leibniz were important mathematicians in their own right, but Spinoza (who had no special gifts as a mathematician) gives us the supreme example of rationalism in full flower. In his *Ethics*, he takes Euclidean geometry as the archetype for his philosophical system, using definitions, axioms, and postulates to deduce hundreds of propositions (or theorems) that purportedly cover the whole of reality. He regularly depreciates the senses as providing very little beyond random, confused, disorderly perceptions. To *know* anything, we must rely on reason. How else could we know that God is an absolutely infinite being, or substance, consisting of infinitely many attributes, each one of which expresses an infinite and eternal essence (definition 6 of part 1 of *Ethics*)?

The empiricists see method as no less important than the rationalists do. In "The Epistle to the Reader" of his *Essay*, for example, Locke recounts a discussion among himself and several friends that produced much puzzlement but no progress toward a satisfactory answer to the questions they had raised. Upon reflection, he decided that before he began the investigation of particular subjects, he must first undertake a careful examination of the powers and limitations of the human mind. Without such a foundation, philosophers often succumb to the blandishments of high-flown (but illusory) metaphysical speculation while despising the useful knowledge that lies within their reach. For his part, Locke is content to work at the humble task of clearing the ground of rubbish by following what he calls a "Historical, Plain Method" (*Essay*, 44.§2). Using this modest approach, Locke seeks to ascertain the source(s) and extent of human knowledge, as well as the essential features of "Belief, Opinion, and Assent" (*Essay*, 43.§2)—a pretty ambitious project after all, but one that he attempts to tie to actual human experience.

Berkeley criticizes Locke (sometimes by name, sometimes by clear implication) for, in effect, not being a consistent empiricist in clearing the rubbish that stands in the way of genuine knowledge. In particular, Berkeley faults Locke for holding on to notions that have no warrant in experience—notably, **abstract ideas** and material **substance** (with the related doctrine of **primary and secondary qualities**). Locke repeatedly admits that we have only the barest, foggiest idea of any kind of substance, but he will not give it up. In Berkeley's opinion, the case is radically worse than Locke supposes: the idea of material substance—a putative entity that we can neither perceive nor conceive—is incoherent and, fortunately, plays absolutely no role in science or common sense. By getting rid of such delusive, confusion-producing concepts, Berkeley seeks to fulfill the negative purpose stated in the subtitle of his *Principles of Human Knowledge*; namely, to remove the causes of error and difficulty in the sciences and to refute skepticism and atheism. His own positive philosophy—a version of immaterialism that recognizes only minds (including God's) and their objects (i.e., ideas) as real—is more openly metaphysical and religious than Locke's.

Hume is generally regarded as a more thoroughgoing empiricist than either Locke or Berkeley. His overall project is obviously much closer to Locke's than to Berkeley's, but he lays out his empiricist orientation more clearly and fully than Locke does. Hume's avowed purpose in THN is to produce a science of human nature, and his method is announced in the subtitle of that work: *Being an attempt to introduce the experimental method of reasoning into moral subjects*. Although Hume seems to have in mind such experimental scientists as Robert Boyle and **Isaac Newton**, he understands that his science of human nature is "experimental" in being based on experience, not as involving laboratory experiments. Like experimental science in the strict sense, Hume's project rejects authority and a priori speculation as sources of knowledge, admitting only what passes the test of experience. Hume's wry comment on the metaphysical doctrine of **Occasionalism** epitomizes his empiricist attitude toward gossamer theories about subjects lying outside the sphere of experience: "We are got into fairy land, long ere we have reached the last steps of our theory; and *there* we have no reason to trust our common methods of argument, or to think that our usual analogies and probabilities have any authority. Our line is too short to fathom such immense abysses" (EHU, 72; 142.24; italics are in Hume's text). By contrast, Hume seeks to use the empiricist method to explore subjects that lie within experience, specifically those that have to do with human nature.

To avoid confusion, readers should note that for Hume and many other 18th-century writers, *ethical* rationalism (not their term) is contrasted with *sentimentalism*, which grounds morals in sentiment or feeling. The customary contrast between empiricism and rationalism is mainly about knowledge, not about ethics. The purveyors of ethical rationalism are **Samuel Clarke**, **Ralph Cudworth**, et al., not Descartes and Leibniz. (*See* ETHICAL RATIONALISM.) Spinoza is not an ethical rationalist either, since he does not hold that reason discerns moral truths in the way it discerns mathematical or metaphysical truths. But he ties his moral theory to his metaphysics, which *is* rationalistic (with elements of mysticism worked in). He argues that we cannot know how to live well unless we know the true nature of reality. Part 4 of his *Ethics*—"Of Human Bondage"—explains how we live in a kind of slavery so long as we do not understand the causes of our affects (desires, passions, emotions). Part 5—"Of Human Freedom"—shows how reason can enable us to live a life of freedom, blessedness, and happiness (granting that it is not easy: "All things excellent are as difficult as they are rare"). Once we have the metaphysical theory right (including, of course, the correct account of knowledge), we find that ethics is a particular application of that overarching theory. Hume's take on the relation between reason and feeling is very nearly the polar opposite of Spinoza's: "Reason is, and ought only to be the slave of the passions, and can never pretend to any other office than to serve and obey them" (THN, 415; 2.3.3.4). Even if we allow for some measure of Humean hyperbole, the contrast is dramatic.

Without going into detail—and certainly without suggesting any significant affinities between Locke and Spinoza—we may note that Locke holds that "*Morality is capable of Demonstration*, as well as Mathematicks" (*Essay*, 516.§16; italics, capitalization, and spelling are in Locke's text). That is because our ideas (or concepts) of morality and mathematics are about *modes* and are, consequently, susceptible of being known fully and perfectly—unlike our ideas of *substances* such as gold and lead, whose real essences are hidden from our understanding. Locke concedes that we are very far from developing a science of morality, in part because the ideas involved are more complicated than those of mathematics.

To repeat what we said at the beginning of this entry, *empiricism* and *rationalism* are convenient labels that should be used carefully. Empiricist philosophers do not differ from rationalist philosophers on every important epistemological doctrine, any more than empiricist philosophers agree with one another on every such subject. For one important example, empiricists and rationalists (at least the six we are considering) agree that our knowledge of mathematical truths is a priori; i.e., it is independent of—does not depend on—experience. In other words, they all reject knowledge-empiricism for mathematical (and certain other non-empirical) truths. They do differ about where ideas come from (content-empiricism) and about how we know matters of fact (the boundaries of knowledge-empiricism). Hume is the purest and the most consistent of the empiricists in drawing clear lines of demarcation between the a priori and the a posteriori.

A historical note: The German philosopher **Immanuel Kant** assigns mirror-image strengths and weaknesses to empiricism and rationalism. The empiricists are right, he says, in emphasizing the importance of sense experience in knowledge; they are wrong in underestimating the importance of reason. The rationalists are right in recognizing the indispensable function of reason in knowledge; they are wrong in not recognizing the indispensable role of sense experience. Kant uses Locke and Leibniz to illustrate the opposite errors of the two schools. Locke *sensualizes* the concepts of the understanding (or intellect) by making them no more than ideas of reflection, which are like sensations. At the other extreme, Leibniz *intellectualizes* appearances (the products of sensation) by making them confused or incipient thoughts. In fact, Kant argues strenuously, reason and experience are both necessary for knowledge, and neither is reducible to the other. Without sensibility (i.e., sense experience), we would have no objects to think about; without understanding, we would not be able to make the objects intelligible. Kant summarizes his views in a well-known passage: "Thoughts [or concepts] without content are empty; intuitions [i.e., sense perceptions] without concepts are blind" (*Critique of Pure Reason*, A 51/B 75).

AN ENQUIRY CONCERNING HUMAN UNDERSTANDING. Note: The first paragraph of this entry introduces the immediately following entry as well.

Disappointed by the ill-success of his *Treatise*, which he attributed more to its style than its content, Hume decided to recast each of its three books into separate, more readable works. Book 1 ("Of the Understanding") reappeared as *An Enquiry Concerning Human Understanding* (1748); book 2 ("Of the Passions"), as *A Dissertation on the Passions* (1757); and book 3 ("Of Morals"), as *An Enquiry Concerning the Principles of Morals* (1751). The two *Enquiries* have long been part of the canon of Hume's major philosophical writings; the *Dissertation* (which is described by Terence Penelhum as "a spiritless summary of book II of the *Treatise*") attracts little attention from Hume scholars.

Sometimes called the "first *Enquiry*," EHU appeared in 1748 under the title *Philosophical Essays Concerning Human Understanding*, the current title dating from 1756. This new version of book 1 of THN ("Of the Understanding") amounts more nearly to a fresh work than merely a recasting of the earlier in less forbidding form—which is not to deny a substantial area of overlap (for example, the analysis of causation, necessary connection, and the role of nature in securing us against any dangerous consequences of skepticism). As to content, EHU differs from book 1 of THN both by subtraction and addition. First, a few of the important subtractions. Hume simplifies his treatment of **perceptions** in EHU by omitting some distinctions drawn in THN (e.g., simple vs. complex ideas, and impressions of sensation vs. impressions of reflexion). Part 2 of book 1 of THN ("Of the ideas of space and time") is entirely missing from EHU—a lacuna that many readers of THN welcome. On the other hand, part 4 ("Of the sceptical and other systems of philosophy") includes some of Hume's most distinctive and brilliant pieces—e.g., "Of scepticism with regard to reason," "Of scepticism with regard to the senses," and "Personal identity." It has no real counterpart in EHU. The last section of EHU ("Of the Academical or Sceptical Philosophy") covers some of the same topics as THN but much more briefly and in a strikingly different manner.

One very useful simplification of material in THN is effected in EHU, and it involves both subtraction and addition. In the earlier work, Hume divides seven **relations** into two categories—four that can be "the objects of knowledge and certainty" and three that cannot (THN, 70; 1.3.1.2). This somewhat confusing taxonomy is replaced in EHU by the comparatively simple dichotomy **relations of ideas and matters of fact** (EHU, 25; 108.1). In EHU the treatment of **causation** and the idea of necessary connection is doctrinally of a piece with the account in THN, but briefer and simpler.

As for additions, two sections of EHU—"Of Miracles" and "Of a Particular Providence and of a Future State"—do not occur in THN. Not surprisingly, the two essays—especially "Of Miracles"—provoked lively controversies, which continue unabated to this day. "Of the Reason of Animals" appears both in book 1 of THN and in EHU. "Of Liberty and Necessity" is section 8 of EHU, but its counterpart in THN appears in book 2 ("Of the Passions").

In EHU, Hume realized his goal of rewriting book 1 of THN in a more engaging and felicitous style. No one doubts that. Whether the recasting rises to the level of philosophic genius evident in the original is a different question. L. A. Selby-Bigge, one of Hume's 19th-century editors and a sometimes unsparing critic of Hume, offers this estimate: "Bk. I of the Treatise is beyond doubt a work of first-rate philosophic importance, and in some ways the most important work of philosophy in the English language. It would be impossible to say the same of the Enquiries . . ." ("Introduction" to EHU, x). Selby-Bigge's invidious comparison of the two *Enquiries* with THN has been vigorously contested, particularly as it applies to EHU. Some commentators argue that EHU not only deserves careful study for its own merits, but is in fact a more faithful account of Hume's considered opinions than is THN. In any case, EHU remains a splendid piece of philosophical writing and perhaps the best way for a new reader to make the acquaintance of David Hume the philosopher. Indeed, it would not be a bad introduction to the study of philosophy itself. *See also* KNOWLEDGE.

AN ENQUIRY CONCERNING THE PRINCIPLES OF MORALS.
Note: The first paragraph of the immediately preceding entry serves to introduce this entry as well.

Sometimes called the "second Enquiry," EPM (first published in 1751) consists of nine sections plus four appendices and a dialogue.

The sections cover the general principles of morals, the virtues benevolence and justice, political society, why utility (or usefulness) pleases, qualities useful or agreeable to ourselves or to others, and a conclusion. The appendices are about moral sentiment, self-love, justice, and verbal disputes. The dialogue is set in a fictitious nation (Fourli) whose inhabitants espouse moral principles diametrically opposite our own. It addresses the problem of reconciling Hume's commitment to universal moral principles with the obvious differences in moral judgments found in societies separated by time and geography.

Hume himself says that EPM is "incomparably the best" of all his writings, though he concedes that he is probably not the best judge of such matters. It represents his recasting of book 3 ("Of Morals") of THN. Whether one agrees with Hume's high estimate of the work, no one who compares it with its THN counterpart can doubt that it is clearly superior as a piece of writing. In THN, Hume repeatedly ties his moral theory to the impressions-ideas distinction, a practice that sometimes seems to complicate his exposition needlessly. In EPM, he states his theory without recourse to the impressions-ideas scheme—a change that makes both for better writing and simpler explanations.

A second substantive difference is the role assigned to **sympathy**, which in THN is not a specific sentiment or feeling or passion but a fundamental feature of human nature that Hume invokes to explain a variety of phenomena. The case is very different in EPM. Hume still speaks of sympathy, but he equates it with "general benevolence, or humanity" (298n1; 166n60); i.e., he makes sympathy one sentiment or feeling among others (albeit an important one).

Hume never tires of reminding his readers of the limitations of **reason**, whether to discover cause-effect relations or to motivate us to do something or to discern moral distinctions. In THN he relentlessly pushes the case against **rationalism** in moral theory, adducing several arguments to show that reason is impotent in this area. He is still anti-rationalist in EPM, and he still has arguments (mainly in appendix 1—"Concerning Moral Sentiment"); but he is less obsessive about it, and he more clearly and explicitly concedes the indispensable role of reason in morality. Just as we may correct a particular sense perception (of distance, for example) by reference to other perceptions and the laws of physics, so we may correct a particular sentiment of moral approval or blame by a fuller knowledge of the circumstances or by reference to (the right kind of) general rules. The very idea of *correcting* a particular perception or sentiment would be impossible apart from reason. In most cases, Hume says, reason and sentiment concur in "moral determinations and conclusions" (EPM, 172; 75.9). For more details about the role of reason in morals, *see* PASSIONS; REASON.

In a linguistic departure from THN, Hume concludes in EPM that the contrast between *natural* and *artificial* virtues is "merely verbal" (307–8n2; 173.9n64). This does not signify any substantive change in Hume's views: Notions such as *property*, *justice*, and *promise-keeping* make sense only within the conventions, or *artifices*, established by a society. He is simply unwilling to wrangle over the application of a word. (For more on these topics, *see* NATURAL; JUSTICE; VIRTUE.) In THN, Hume argues that *self-love* is not a proper term, inasmuch as the object of love is always some other person (329; 2.2.1.2); but in appendix 2 of EPM ("Of Self-Love") he discusses the substantive question whether we are always motivated by self-interest. *See* EGOISM.

Hume develops his own positive account of "personal merit," which includes but is not limited to virtue, by appealing to four sorts of qualities or traits: those that are *useful* either to ourselves or to others, and those that are *agreeable* either to ourselves or others. EPM is organized around the discussion of these qualities—e.g., discretion, frugality, prudence; benevolence, justice, gratitude; cheerfulness, dignity, courage; and politeness, wit, modesty. Of course, some qualities may fall under more than one classification. Benevolence, for example, might reasonably be listed under all four categories. *See also* ETHICAL RATIONALISM; ETHICS; MORAL SENSE; SENSIBLE KNAVE.

ENTHUSIASM. *See* SUPERSTITION AND ENTHUSIASM.

EPISTEMOLOGY. *See* KNOWLEDGE.

ETHICAL RATIONALISM. Although Hume does not use the term *ethical rationalism*, he consistently inveighs against the doctrine referred to by the term; namely, that moral distinctions—between virtue and vice, good and evil, right and wrong—are derived solely (or primarily) from **reason**. Hume also denies the closely associated claim that reason by itself can motivate us to act or to refrain from acting. Indeed, Hume invokes the motivational impotence of reason as evidence that moral distinctions must have some other source, inasmuch as moral distinctions (or our discernment of them) are powerful motivators. Ethical rationalists (Hume mentions **Samuel Clarke**, **William Wollaston**, **Ralph Cudworth**, and **Nicolas Malebranche** as examples) do not agree on details, but they all concur in locating the origin of morals in reason—either causal reason or abstract reason. Wollaston, for example, argues that an act is immoral because it gives rise to (i.e., causes) a false judgment. Clarke, on the other hand, seeks to base moral obligations on relations of "fitness" or "unfitness" that obtain among acts and persons. These relations mirror the necessary connections we find in logic and mathematics.

Hume carefully examines the ways reason functions in making causal inferences and in tracing relations among ideas (or concepts), and concludes that in neither capacity could reason by itself generate any notion of good or evil or prompt us to do anything. For that, we must look to *sentiment* or *feeling*, i.e., to some sort of *passion*. For a sustained and thorough account of Hume's anti-rationalism in ethics, see THN, book 3, part 1, which comprises two sections: "Moral distinctions not deriv'd from reason" and "Moral distinctions deriv'd from a moral sense." See also appendix 1 ("Concerning Moral Sentiment") of EPM, which is simpler and briefer.

Because Hume does not always state his thesis precisely or fully, it is important to remember that he recognizes the indispensable role that reason plays in ethical or moral judgments. Reason alone cannot discern moral distinctions, but sentiment alone is dumb. Adapting **Immanuel Kant**'s language about concepts and percepts, we might say that, so far as morals are concerned, reason without sentiment is empty, and sentiment without reason is blind.

A note on terminology: ***Rationalism*** is usually contrasted with ***empiricism*** when the subject is epistemology, or theory of knowledge. However, in the context of Hume's *moral* philosophy, *rationalism* is contrasted with what may be called (misleadingly perhaps) *sentimentalism*—the theory that moral distinctions are derived ultimately from sentiment or feeling or passion, and not from reason, either in the narrow sense of a priori analysis or in the broader sense that includes causal inferences. The "cut" between *ethical* rationalism and its opposite is not at all the same as the "cut" between *epistemological* rationalism and empiricism.

ETHICS. Ethics is usually ranked with metaphysics and epistemology as a major branch of philosophy. Ethics considers questions about right, good, duty, obligation, and the like, i.e., questions about what we *ought* or *ought not* to do or be. It also considers questions about the first set of questions, though in most cases the two sorts of questions are not neatly separated. Thus, for example, the German philosopher **Immanuel Kant** not only tells us *that* we ought to keep our promises, but also tells us *why* we ought to keep our promises. The first part of Kant's doctrine illustrates what is often called *normative ethics*—theories about what we should or should not do, what is good or right, etc. The second part falls under *meta-ethics*, which addresses what may be called second-order questions about the meaning or basis or presuppositions of first-order ethical concepts or assertions. To take just one example, *freedom* (or *freedom of the will*, as it is sometimes called) is a meta-ethical issue of great importance. That is because almost everyone agrees that freedom is a necessary condition of moral responsibility: A person is not morally responsible for an act if he did not perform the act freely. But what does it mean to perform an act freely? Is freedom really possible in a world governed by physical and psychological laws? For Hume's answer, *see* LIBERTY AND NECESSITY.

Ethics is sometimes described as *moral* philosophy, or as being about *moral* problems or *moral* judgments. In fact, the terms *ethics/ ethical* and *morality/moral* are often used as more or less equivalent, though not always. Lawyers and physicians have codes of ethics peculiar to their professions, but presumably have no comparably circumscribed codes of morality. Some philosophers distinguish systems of ethics from systems of morality, but that distinction is not important for our purposes (and it is not one that Hume draws). A further note about terminology: Terms such as *good* and *right* are often used in a non-moral sense. A good (i.e., skilled, accomplished) violinist may or may not be a morally good person. The right (i.e., correct) answer to a problem in mathematics has nothing to do with what is morally right. We will not be concerned with non-moral uses of words such as the two just mentioned.

Normative Ethics

Normative ethical theories may be classified in more than one way, depending upon which feature(s) we take as a basis for classifying. We will briefly describe three such principles of division: *teleology* (goals, ends, purposes), *deontology* (duties or obligations), and *virtue* (character traits). An ethical theory may (and usually does) incorporate elements from all three types, but it cannot make them all equally basic.

According to one common dichotomy, ethical theories are either *teleological* (also called *consequentialist*) or *deontological* (also called *formalist*) in the answer they give to the question, "How should we judge the goodness or rightness of an action (or a *rule* or *principle* implied by or exemplified by the action)?" As the labels suggest, the teleologist/consequentialist deems an action or a rule of action to be good if it leads (or typically leads) to good consequences, and to be bad if it leads to bad consequences. Accordingly, teleological theories may be described as *forward-looking*. Giving to charity, for example, is morally good because it produces the desirable result of meeting human needs. *Utilitarianism*, the best-known species of consequentialism, holds that we should seek to maximize utility or happiness (which is often identified with pleasure). John Stuart Mill, probably the most famous proponent of utilitarianism, gives a succinct distillation of what he calls the "greatest happiness" principle: "Actions are right in proportion as they tend to promote happiness; wrong as they tend to promote the reverse of happiness."

At the other extreme, deontological (or formalist) ethics sets duty or obligation above good-producing consequences as the touchstone of moral action (or the principle thereby exemplified). To "sloganize" the point, *right* takes moral precedence over *good* in deontological ethical theory. This means that an action (or the principle it exemplifies) may be morally praiseworthy even if it does not lead to desirable consequences—or, indeed, even if it leads to undesirable consequences; and it may be morally blameworthy even if it leads to good consequences. Robbing a bank at gunpoint would be morally bad even if the robber gave half his loot to a worthy charity. For a deontologist/formalist, the consequences of an action may be of great importance, but its morality is determined by the principle that motivated the action. Deontological theories are, as it were, *backward-looking*. Kant argues, for example, that lying is wrong by its very form, quite apart from any harm (or good) it may do to other people. His injunction is simple and uncompromising: "Let justice be done [and this includes telling the truth] though the heavens fall."

Some ethical theories do not fit neatly under either half of the *teleological-deontological* division. *Virtue* ethics, for example, emphasizes the centrality of virtues and character in making moral evaluations, and that feature is not usefully or unambiguously classified as either forward-looking or backward-looking. Aristotle is the obvious example of this sort of theorist, but Hume also sees the doctrine of virtues as being at the core of moral philosophy.

Meta-ethics

Moral philosophers from the time of Plato do more than advance ethical theories; they offer reasons or grounds in support of those theories. In other words, they do *meta-ethics*, too. For a couple of decades in the middle of the 20th century, many Anglo-American philosophers shy away from doing normative ethics. They see their enterprise as wholly meta-ethical, i.e., analyzing such first-order ethical notions as *good*, *right*, *ought*, etc., without putting forward any theory of their own. Some critics argue that so clean-cut a distinction is illusory—a dispute we will not get into. Instead, we will look at a few meta-ethical questions that we may conveniently (but perhaps misleadingly) lump under the umbrella term *moral epistemology*. Given Hume's concern with motivation and the variety of things that influence our will, the compound term *moral epistemology-psychology* would be more accurate. (A note, which probably labors the obvious: Below, we call attention to a few meta-ethical questions or issues, but do not try to answer or settle them. That would be impossible in the space available—if at all.)

The simple non-moral proposition "Abraham Lincoln, the 16th president of the U.S.A., was assassinated in April 1865" is true because it correctly reports a fact about the world; and we *know* that the proposition is true because we have compelling evidence of its truth. Are *moral* or *ethical* propositions (or judgments)—e.g., "The assassination of Abraham Lincoln was a morally detestable act," or general principles such as "We ought to keep our promises"—also true or false; and if they are, what makes them true or false? A related but logically distinct question: Is it possible for us to *know* whether moral propositions are true or false? (The two questions are logically distinct because moral propositions might be true or false even if we could never know which.) These questions have stirred controversy for more than two millennia; answers go off in all directions.

Non-cognitivists hold that moral judgments are neither true nor false, but rather express feelings, attitudes, etc. Hume says that morality is "more properly felt than judg'd of" (THN, 470; 3.1.2.1), though this is only half of Hume's theory. Such feelings and attitudes do not correspond—or fail to correspond—to anything and, consequently, cannot be true or false. The label *non-cognitivism* covers a wide and diverse range of positions, which reflect different interests and approaches and may or may not be mutually compatible: relativism, nihilism, emotivism, skepticism, and prescriptivism. Some of these (e.g., nihilism) deny that there are any objective moral principles, while others (e.g., skepticism) hold that we cannot know whether such moral principles exist. Hume's moral philosophy exhibits some affinities with non-cognitivism, but it has deeper ties with certain kinds of **naturalism**. Let us assume (for the sake of argument at least) that non-cognitivism is mistaken, or to put it positively, that moral knowledge is possible. How can we cash out that assumption?

Ethical rationalists contend that moral principles are discerned by reason, either intuitively or through logical inference. One type of ethical rationalist—the Intuitionists—claim that basic moral truths are self-evident, standing in no need of further justification. For example, that gratuitous cruelty is morally repugnant is no less indubitable than that a triangle has three sides. On the other hand, some moral principles may not compel our acceptance upon first sight but quickly do so if we think about them. **John Locke** quotes the English natural-law theologian Richard Hooker ("the judicious Hooker," Locke calls him) on the obligation to mutual love and respect among humans: " . . . for seeing those things which are equal, must needs all have one measure; if I cannot but wish to receive good, even as much at every man's hands, as any man can wish unto his own soul, how should I look to have any part of my desire herein satisfied, unless myself be careful to satisfy the like desire, which is undoubtedly in other men, being of one and the same nature?" (quoted in Locke's *Second Treatise of Government*, chapter 2, §5). In the same vein, Kant argues that we act morally only when we can consistently endorse the maxim (or principle) of the action as universal, i.e., when we can will that everyone be free to act on the same principle. This line of reasoning—Kant's Categorical Imperative—prohibits us (for example) from making promises with the intention of breaking them if we find it convenient: If everyone acted on that maxim, promises would not exist at all. It would be self-contradictory to make or accept promises on the understanding that they could be broken at will. The very institution of promise-making would be destroyed.

According to **ethical rationalism**, the moral principles mentioned in the preceding paragraph (and other moral principles as well) are sui generis, i.e., not reducible to any non-moral categories (religious or metaphysical, for example). This means that ethics is *autonomous*. For examples of ethical rationalists, *see* CLARKE, SAMUEL; CUDWORTH, RALPH; WOLLASTON, WILLIAM.

Two other types of ethical theory allow the possibility of some sort of moral knowledge but deny the autonomy of ethics (either directly or by implication): divine-command theories and naturalism.

According to divine-command ethical theory, our knowledge of things moral (principles, duties, rights, etc.) comes from God's commands. But how do we know what God's commands are? We could demonstrate God's existence and infer from his character how we ought to act—or so a proponent might argue. Or we could accept some set of writings as revealing God's will, and act in accordance with that revelation. Apart from the obvious problem of making sure that God's will is indeed revealed in the writings we accept, there is a vexatious question as old as Plato's *Euthyphro*: Is an action good because God commands it, or does God command the action because it is good? Divine-command theorists take the first option, which makes moral principles dependent on a non-moral fact—namely, the will of God. This means that ethics is not autonomous. Many theists (Leibniz, for example) reject the divine-command theory on the grounds that it makes morality quite arbitrary: God wills *A* because . . . God wills *A*. Such theists would still agree that God's will is an infallible guide to what is good or right, but would deny that good or right is *constituted* by an act of God's will. God wills what is good or right precisely because it *is* good or right. It does not work the other way around. *See* IS/OUGHT.

Divine-command ethics may be regarded as a species of naturalism—*supernatural* naturalism, if we want to make it look paradoxical. As noted above, this type of ethical theory denies that moral principles are sui generis. They are rooted in a non-moral fact about the world, and this qualifies the theory as naturalistic. However, naturalist ethical theories are usually associated with philosophers such as John Dewey, John Stuart Mill, and, of course, Hume. While they reject God's will as the basis of ethics, they hold that moral judgments are not—or need not be—merely subjective expressions of liking or disliking or preferences; they may be about real characteristics of real people in the world. They may be appropriate or inappropriate, and they are revisable in the light of more extensive knowledge. Dewey emphasizes the experimental nature of our moral standards. We adopt them because they have proved to be useful in helping us to achieve our personal and social goals. If we are at all prudent, we will not confuse our momentary desires with what would be desirable in the long run. We know the difference between what is temporarily *valued* and what is more durably *valuable*—for example, playing video games all night instead of preparing for a semester final exam the next morning. But notice that, according to Dewey and other ethical naturalists, there are no free-standing moral imperatives apart from human needs and desires.

If there are no irreducibly moral facts, and we do not appeal to the will of God, how can we make objective, non-arbitrary moral judgments? When we say, for example, that a person has some moral virtue or other, what are we referring to? For Hume, the sense of morality (and, with it, the possibility of moral judgments) arises in certain circumstances. He likens our sense of morality to our perception of the so-called secondary qualities (color, sound, odor, etc.), which are relegated by some theories to a parasitic status. A physical object is really round in a sense that it is not really red, so we are told. It is red only in the derivative sense that the primary qualities of the object (shape, solidity, motion or rest, etc.) normally cause us to have a sensation of red. Nevertheless, there are objective, non-arbitrary standards of color perception, and some people are really color-blind. Colors may not enjoy the same metaphysical status as shapes and sizes, but they are not merely figments of the imagination; they are rooted in reality. *See* PRIMARY AND SECONDARY QUALITIES.

In an analogous way, we have standards of morality, and most people concur in approving or disapproving certain character traits. Suppose we notice that Sturdley helps his invalid neighbor every day, and we know that Sturdley gives 50% of his income to charity. According to Hume's lights, these are simply facts about Sturdley; they have no moral significance when taken by themselves. We do not literally perceive anything that we can identify as the virtues of benevolence and generosity, nor can we infer those virtues by way of logical or causal reasoning. However, we may *feel* a disinterested sentiment of approval toward Sturdley (disinterested, or general, because our personal concerns are not involved), and that sentiment invests the situation with a moral quality. Without the feeling, there would be no sense of morality, and no basis for a moral or ethical judgment. But the feeling is not free-floating or created *ex nihilo*; it is elicited by objective facts about Sturdley, just as the sensation of red arises from objective facts about a red ball. We would regard a person as insensitive or cloddish who knew the facts about Sturdley but felt no sentiment of approval toward him.

The kind of ethical theory we are describing denies that ethics is autonomous, in that ethical judgments are not about anything uniquely and irreducibly moral; but it affirms that ethical judgments may be about real properties of human beings. Of course, a feeling or sentiment per se cannot be true or false, but it may be appropriate or inappropriate; and judgments or propositions about feelings or sentiments may be straightforwardly true or false. Hume speaks of *correcting* our sentiments (or at least our language) by divorcing our judgments from our own narrow interests and adopting a more general view (which is an essential component of the *moral* point of view). For a more detailed answer, see the account of Hume's ethics in the sketch of his philosophy before the dictionary proper; *see also* MORAL SENSE.

EXCESSIVE SKEPTICISM. *See* PYRRHONISM.

EXISTENCE, THE IDEA OF. Readers of Hume might expect him to treat the idea of existence (THN, book 1, part 2, section 6) as either an ***abstract idea*** or a *distinction of **reason***. He does not do that (at least not in any straightforward way), and it is instructive to understand why he does not. Whatever the **idea** of existence may be, it is not like garden-variety abstract ideas or distinctions of reason. We get the abstract idea *white* by observing that snow, chalk, milk, and so on, all exemplify that color. On the contrary, we do *not* get the idea of existence by noting that Rover and Fluffy and Dobbin all exemplify the property *existence* (and perhaps negatively by noting that Pegasus and Cerberus and Hercules lack that property).

Nor do we get the idea of existence by way of a *distinction of reason*, which enables us to separate in our minds features of an object that are not in fact separable. Thus, for example, we are able to distinguish in our mind the color of a globe of white marble from its shape, though we perceive only a color "dispos'd in a certain form, nor are we able to separate and distinguish the colour from the form" (THN, 25; 1.1.7.18). If we later observe a globe of black marble and a cube of white marble, we are able to compare the objects in respect of color *or* shape, while effectively relegating the other property to the background. Even though we cannot literally perceive or imagine a color apart from some shape or other, we can focus our attention on one property (the color or the shape) and see how it invites comparison with other objects of the same sort (white or black or globose or cubic). This is *not* how we get the idea of existence. As Hume points out, "no object can be presented resembling some object with respect to its existence, and different from others in the same particular; since every object, that is presented, must necessarily be existent" (THN, 67; 1.2.6.6).

We do have an idea of existence, but it is not derived from a particular impression—unlike, say, the idea of *red*, which *is* derived from a particular impression. (The ideas of **space and time** are like that of existence in this respect.) If the idea of existence is not derived from a particular impression, still less is it derived from a single distinct, separate impression that is conjoined with "every perception or object of our thought" (THN, 66; 1.2.6.2). Hume makes essentially the same point in his discussion of the nature of **belief**: "We have no abstract idea of existence, distinguishable and separable from the idea of particular objects" (THN, 623; 396.2). To put it another way, we do not add a discriminable *property* or *quality* or *characteristic* to X when we assert that X exists. The idea of existence is, rather, identical with the idea of whatever is before our mind. "To reflect on any thing simply, and to reflect on it as existent, are nothing different from each other. That idea, when conjoin'd with the idea of any object, makes no addition to it. Whatever we conceive, we conceive to be existent" (THN, 66–67; 1.2.6.4).

To clarify Hume's point, here is a simple example. Suppose that I am at the airport to pick up a person whom I have never met. I am told that he is about six feet tall and of medium build—a description that is probably going to fit several persons getting off the plane. But suppose I also know that he has a full beard and a shaved head. The additional characteristics narrow the set of candidates radically— very likely to just one. At the other extreme, consider how helpful (!) it would be for me to be told that the person I am to meet is *existent* (and how puzzled—or, possibly, amused—I would be at being *told* that my "quarry" actually exists).

Hume's account of the idea of existence is anticipated by **René Descartes** and Pierre Gassendi (1592–1655)—a contemporary critic of Descartes. Descartes holds that existence is contained in the idea or concept of every single thing; we cannot conceive of anything except as existing. Notice two things: (a) Neither Descartes nor Hume suggests that we *believe* that everything we think of actually exists. (b) Nor do they mean that there is no difference between an *imaginary* (or *non-existent) X* and a *real* (or *existent) X.* (A. N. Whitehead reminds us that an imaginary terrier cannot kill a real rat.) What, then, do they mean when they say that conceiving a flying horse and conceiving a flying horse as existing are one and the same thing? Certainly *not* that they believe a flying horse *actually exists.* They mean that when they conceive a flying horse, they conceive it as it *would be* if it existed.

Gassendi criticizes Descartes' so-called *ontological argument* for the existence of God (i.e., that God, as the *ens realissimum*, possesses all perfections, including existence) by arguing that existence is not a perfection at all, either in God or anything else. Rather, existence is a necessary condition of the reality of whatever perfections a thing may have. If a thing does not exist, we do not say that it is lacking a perfection, but rather that it is nothing at all. It is something of a historical injustice that Gassendi is seldom given credit for anticipating (by almost a century and a half) **Immanuel Kant**'s famous dictum "*Existence* (or *being*) is not a real predicate." Descartes answers Gassendi's objection by noting that to exist *necessarily*, as God does, *is* a perfection, even if existence as such is not. In Hume's view, the only necessary truths are about **relations of ideas** (e.g., those in mathematics), never about matters of fact. Nothing *exists* necessarily: "Whatever *is* may *not be*" (EHU, 164; 209.28; italics are in Hume's text).

Hume treats the idea of *external* existence in the same section of THN that he treats the idea of existence per se. Since he holds that **perceptions** (impressions and ideas) are the only entities ever present to the mind, he argues that it is "impossible for us so much as to conceive or form an idea of any thing specifically different from ideas and impressions" (THN, 67; 1.2.6.8). To be *specifically* different, an object would have to be of a different species from our perceptions; would have to be qualitatively different from our perceptions. We have no clue what such an object would be. The best we can do, Hume says, is to form a *relative idea* of external objects that are supposed to be *specifically* different from our perceptions, "without pretending to comprehend the related objects" (THN, 68; 1.2.6.9). This means that such objects would be unknown Xs that presumably satisfy some description; e.g., *the cause of my perception of red*. We have no positive idea of such objects but suppose them to be in some relation to our experience.

A historical note: **John Locke** says that God could make a creature endowed with a sixth—or seventh or eighth or *nth*—sense beyond the five that we have; for we have no reason to suppose that the omniscient, omnipotent creator would be limited to the compass of our little world. However, we have no idea whatsoever of a sensible quality that would not be conveyed to us by seeing, hearing, smelling, tasting, or touching. In the same way, Locke argues, a congenitally blind person would have no idea of color. On Hume's account, we are all in the same boat as the congenitally blind person, so far as our knowledge of the external world goes. What objects are like apart from our perceptions is an impenetrable mystery. Perhaps inconsistently with his own principles, Locke disagrees with Hume on this point. For Locke, external objects literally have the so-called primary qualities (extension, shape, solidity, motion or rest, number), but do not literally have the so-called secondary qualities (color, sound, odor, taste) except as causal powers. Hume's agnosticism about external objects seems to be more self-consistent than Locke's realism, inasmuch as Locke agrees with Hume that we are aware only of our perceptions. This means that an additional sense—or any number of additional senses—would furnish us with novel perceptions but would get us no closer to the world that exists independently of perception. *See* PRIMARY AND SECONDARY QUALITIES.

EXPERIENCE. This entry addresses three main topics: (1) the extremely wide range of phenomena covered by the term *experience*; (2) some general philosophical or theoretical questions about experience; and (3) Hume's use of experience (with some references to other philosophers). In the first section we will do an informal (and admittedly incomplete) survey of various sorts of experience. One important purpose of this survey is to show that when empiricists such as Hume and **John Locke** make experience the cornerstone of their philosophical method, they have in mind certain kinds of experience and not others. Not just any experience will do. Fortunately, both Hume and Locke are pretty clear about the sorts of experience they mean to invoke in defense of their theories.

One

According to Hume (and empiricists generally), the final appeal on matters of fact is to *experience*. All our knowledge comes, directly or indirectly, by way of experience. This dictum holds both for particular matters of fact (e.g., that bread will nourish humans but not tigers) and for scientific/philosophical principles of the highest generality (e.g., that every event has a cause). In setting out the fundamental method and assumptions of his science of human nature, Hume observes that it is impossible to go beyond experience. It follows, he says, that "we can give no reason for our most general and most refin'd principles, beside our experience of their reality" (THN, xviii; 5.9).

What does "our experience of their reality" mean? Before we consider Hume's answer to this question, we will see that his answer—or *any* answer—is not going to be self-evident. The English word *experience* (as either noun or verb) is extraordinarily capacious, covering every imaginable state of consciousness or awareness. Consider the following cases, which give some indication of the range and variety of experiences:

1. Seeing a flower; also remembering or imagining the flower (the latter two being experiences that Hume calls *ideas*).
2. Thinking about thinking (or willing or desiring or perceiving or . . .)
3. "Seeing" (i.e., understanding) that $(a + b) = (b + a)$.
4. The (putative) rational intuition (endorsed, for example, by both **René Descartes** and John Locke) that nothing comes out of nothing.
5. The visions of mystics.
6. A whole catalogue of feelings and emotions (fear, elation, depression, grief, love, anger, satisfaction, frustration, joy, sorrow, etc., etc.).
7. Optical illusions (e.g., "seeing" water on a dry highway in summer).
8. Full-fledged hallucinations (e.g., the powerful visual or tactile illusions associated with episodes of delirium tremens).
9. "Going blank" on an exam.
10. Reflecting on how much better one reads German after two years of practice.

We might classify these ten examples by what the experiences are *about* (the kinds of objects involved—real, imaginary, conceptual, hallucinatory, etc.), or by *the "organ" of experience* (the senses, the imagination, the rational intellect, etc.), or by what we might call *"the mode of reception"* (how the mind reacts to what it experiences—with belief, skepticism, fear, relief, etc.). Certain kinds of experience—e.g., an itch, ennui, melancholy, elation—often have no obvious objects. Whatever their taxonomy (which we shall not pursue any further at this point), all these cases may be described as experiences, but not all of them will do the work Hume has in mind.

The examples above (including, especially, the 10th) illustrate another feature of experiences: their widely varying temporal durations. We may apply the term *experience* to something as transient and particular as hearing a clap of thunder, or to a deposit of skill or knowledge (e.g., in medicine or woodworking) built up over many years. (*Experience* is also used to refer to facts or events that have nothing to do with human consciousness; e.g., in the statement "Several western states have experienced [i.e., undergone] three years of drought." We will not consider that sort of experience.)

As with many other notions, we can understand *experience* better by considering what it may be *contrasted* with. Significantly, in most cases, the items contrasted with experience are themselves experiences, but of a different sort. The invidious comparisons suggest that some kinds of experience are *better*—more to be trusted or relied upon—than other kinds, at least as a general rule. Some sorts of experience, that is, have a *normative* or *probative* function: They may provide evidence or warrant for claims. We will look at three types of contrast, which comprise numerous subtypes. These contrasts will help us to see what sorts of experience Hume appeals to and why he does so.

1. Experience is often contrasted with *secondhand* or *indirect* or *notional* knowledge. It is one thing to read or hear about the severe pain caused by kidney stones; it is a very different thing to experience that pain oneself, to know it firsthand. To use the language (but not the associated theory) of Bertrand Russell, one person knows *by acquaintance*; the other knows *by description*. A small child learns more from a painfully burned finger than from parental admonitions to avoid touching hot surfaces. A nephrologist who has never suffered from kidney stones knows more about the etiology and treatment of the condition than people who know the pain from personal experience. This example is an important reminder—namely, that experiencing X directly does not give one discursive knowledge about X—but it has no bearing on the contrast between direct and

indirect knowledge. Notice that secondhand or indirect or notional knowledge is itself a kind of experience.

2. Experience may also be contrasted with *opinion* or *wishful thinking* or *hope* or *fear*. According to a dictum attributed to Daniel Patrick Moynihan, everyone is entitled to his own opinion, but not to his own facts, which are known by experience. In 1775, on the eve of the American Revolution, Patrick Henry of Virginia appealed to experience to rebut those who counseled further peaceful supplications to Britain, in the hope that the British crown and parliament would soften their repressive policies toward the North American colonies. What was the basis of such hopes? Certainly not experience. For 10 years Britain had uniformly treated the colonies' petitions with contumely, neglect, or threats of force. Henry invokes a principle: "I have but one lamp by which my feet are guided, and that is the lamp of experience. I know of no way of judging the future but by the past." Because experience of the sort he is talking about is tied to the real world of fact, it carries an authority and conviction denied to wishful thinking. As Patrick Henry uses the term, *experience* refers to our knowledge of a a set of facts or a portion of history. But let it be noted that wishful thinking is itself a (different) kind of experience. (A fictional example: Readers of the comic strip *Peanuts* will recall that Charlie Brown never learned from many unhappy experiences not to trust Lucy Van Pelt's promises to hold the football properly while Charlie kicked it. Year after year, he defied experience in the hope that Lucy had reformed, with zero positive outcomes.)

3. Experience is often contrasted with *theory*, though experience may verify or confirm a theory. Perhaps the best-known example of a theory refuted by experience is the set of four purported demonstrations by the ancient Greek thinker Zeno of Elea that motion (and, more generally, all change) is impossible. The first two arguments turn on the impossibility of completing an infinite series of journeys (half of a half of a half of a half ad infinitum) in a finite time. (The details of all four arguments are available to interested readers in numerous books and web-sites—e.g., the on-line *Stanford Encyclopedia of Philosophy*.) Even if Zeno's "demonstrations" were theoretically impeccable (aside from the false conclusions), they would be decisively exploded by experience. Achilles will overtake the tortoise (in

the most famous of the arguments), and we do go from one place to another. Zeno argues that our experiences of change are illusory, but we do not—cannot—believe that either. There are untold numbers of less dramatic hypotheses or conjectures that may work "on paper" but fail the test of experience, ranging from sophisticated theories in physics, to algorithms for predicting the bullish or bearish behavior of the stock market, to advertising schemes designed to sell beer or automobiles. A common phrase aptly states the relation between experience and a failed or defective theory: "Back to the drawing board!" In most cases, we adjust the theory to fit experience, not the other way around. As the old adage has it, "experience [as opposed to abstract theory] is the best teacher." Most of us would choose an experienced cardiovascular surgeon over a neophyte with a higher IQ.

On a perennially controversial subject, Samuel Johnson asserts that all theory is against free will but all experience for it. The point of the illustration is not that Dr. Johnson is right about free will or that he accurately fixes the ratio of evidence-from-theory to evidence-from-experience, but that he unequivocally sides with experience against theory (as he conceives the issue). (It is worth noting parenthetically that the word *theory* does not always carry any suggestion of mere conjecture or surmise, as *the theory of gravity* and *the theory of relativity* show. Such theories may push us to correct experiences that *seem* to be contrary to the theories. But even long-standing and well-confirmed theories—e.g., classical Newtonian physics—are liable to revision in the light of further, more extensive experience. Widespread, insistent, intractable experience is the final test of *any* theory.)

So far, our survey shows that experience is often contrasted favorably with notional or secondhand knowledge, with wishful thinking, or with (mere) theory. In this sense, experience trumps opinion, surmise, conjecture, hope, speculation, book learning, and such like. To put the point another way, experience is often used normatively, as a way of settling (or at least clarifying) disputes. It would be more accurate to say that certain *kinds* of experience (e.g., those tied to fact by sense perception or recollection) carry more weight than other kinds, whose ties to fact are sometimes tenuous or suspect. The Irish philosopher **George Berkeley** points out that what he calls "ideas of sense" (i.e., experiences arising from the senses) are stronger, livelier, more distinct, steadier, more orderly, more coherent, and less subject to our will than ideas of the imagination. Of course, the pale, indistinct, confused ideas of the imagination are just as much a part of experience as the vivid, distinct, orderly ideas of sense; but we instinctively credit the ideas of sense while rejecting those of the imagination, or at least regarding them with suspicion. Note that the *real verus imaginary* distinction is based on properties disclosed in experience. See Berkeley's *Principles* §30.

Two

Whether explicitly or implicitly, philosophers typically answer two related questions about experience: What is the nature of experience? and What is the role of experience in the philosophical system? The answers to these two questions lie at the root of the divergence between **empiricism and rationalism** and do much to shape the character of any philosophy. It was noted in the preceding paragraphs that *experience* is a flexible and comprehensive term, covering the ordinary perception of a flower, the abstract thinking required to demonstrate a theorem in geometry, transcendental meditation, the wildly irrational illusions of a paranoid schizophrenic, and any other state of consciousness that one may care to add. But notice that in listing the various kinds of experience, we have drawn distinctions that arise from reflection on experience (which is, of course, another sort of experience). Experience does not come wearing labels; we have to provide the tags. It is a matter of philosophical dispute (and undoubted importance) just how that "tagging" occurs.

It is often easy enough to describe the objects, events, and processes that we know through experience. Given a modicum of specialized knowledge and the appropriate technical vocabulary, we could, for example, provide a clear account of how an automobile engine operates. Or we could describe the properties of a sunset, if we put ourselves to it. But what about *experience itself*, as distinguished from the things that experience may reveal to us? We cannot get at experience the same way we get at other things. We are always *in* experience; we can never get outside it and view it as an object distinct from us. Describing experience is itself an experience, whereas describing an automobile engine is not itself an automobile engine; describing a sunset is not itself a sunset. The English philosopher G. E. Moore characterizes consciousness or awareness—the "inner" or subjective side of experience—as *diaphanous*: When we try to focus on it, we see *through* it to its object(s). There is no suggestion here that we should be able to describe experience in itself, completely apart from all objects. The problem is to isolate, so far as possible, the act of *experiencing* from whatever it may be about. The French existentialist philosopher Jean-Paul Sartre says that consciousness is nothing, or, rather no-thing (i.e., not a thing). (It should be noted that not all philosophers agree that Moore has put his finger on a genuine problem. Philosophers hold widely divergent views on the best way to describe experience. Most—but not all—of them agree that the problem is fiendishly difficult. For a brief discussion of this question, *see* MIND.)

Historical note: More than two centuries before G. E. Moore, the French philosopher **René Descartes** called attention to the Januslike character of ideas. In his *Meditations* (published in 1641), he notes that *idea* can be taken *materially* (or *formally*) as an operation of the intellect *or* it can be taken *objectively* as *representing* something. The idea of the sun, for example, is both a mental entity—something that exists in the mind—and a representation of the sun itself. It is *about* the sun. To express the same distinction in a different way, ideas are both *acts* and *representations*. These correspond, roughly, to the *subjective-objective* distinction in Moore's analysis, though Descartes uses the distinction in ways that Moore never dreamed of doing.

The American philosopher-psychologist William James warns against committing what he calls *the psychologist's fallacy*, which is the mistake of confusing our own standpoint with that of the mental state we are trying to report. So, for example, James tries to heed his own warning when he describes the experience of a newborn baby as a "blooming, buzzing confusion." So far as we can tell, a neonate does not distinguish *inner* from *outer*, *here* from *there*, *now* from *then*, and so on. But the growing baby learns some things very quickly. He or she gradually acquires a language and a store of remembered experiences and therewith comes to discern spatial and temporal patterns and other kinds of order in what was earlier a welter of discrete, meaningless sensations and feelings. Among other amazing things, a baby learns how to deal with *time*, especially with delayed gratification. At five months, he is enraged if he is not fed immediately when he is hungry; at 18 months, he is (comparatively) patient because he is told (and perhaps can see) that food is on the way.

Precisely *how* human beings do the sorts of thing just described— i.e., acquire the categories and concepts by which experiences are organized—is a point of dispute among philosophers, anthropologists, linguists, and other scholars. Obviously, such categories and concepts are to some extent shaped by our physiology and anatomy, by the language(s) we learn to use, by the culture in which we live, by the larger world beyond our own culture, and by the widely varying demands of everyday life ("Lion ahead!!" would take precedence over "Consider the problem of induction" in most circumstances).

More interesting to philosophers than such (relatively) straightforward influences are questions about how the perceiver/knower contributes to the form and/or the content of experience. Philosophers have long disagreed about whether there is a purely "given" element in experience (often not referred to in precisely that language), i.e., whether some of the items we discriminate in our experience are simply *there*, independent—at least initially—of any interpretation we may put upon them. Is there any such entity as a raw, uninterpreted datum (or given)? Or does even the apparently simple perception of a flower require the cooperation of the cognitive "machinery" of the perceiver? Is there any discernible boundary between the theoretical and the pre-theoretical parts of experience, or is *all* experience, to some extent, *theory-laden* (i.e., shaped by the classifying/sorting activity of the mind)? If there is no such sharp demarcation, would the blooming, buzzing confusion of the newborn qualify as experience? Perhaps. It is a useful (and, therefore, pardonable) oversimplification to say that empiricists tend to hold that some items in experience (typically, those tied to the senses) are just *given* and, because of that status, are foundational to other forms of experience (causal inferences or abstract reasoning, for example).

Some empirically inclined philosophers (e.g., C. I. Lewis) concede that in normal experience we are not aware of two distinct "moments" or parts. Nevertheless, they argue, we can by analysis separate a sheerly given element from whatever meanings or interpretations or inferences we may, more or less automatically, supply. On the contrary, rationalists typically reject the notion of a brute given and insist that the mind or intellect (as distinct from the senses or the **imagination**) is essential to any kind of intelligible experience. Is *intelligible experience* redundant? In the 20th century, the American philosopher Wilfrid Sellars inveighs against several forms of what he calls the "myth of the given," though he has more sympathy with **Kant** than with the rationalist philosophers. *See* EMPIRICISM AND RATIONALISM.

Three

Given the wide and varied uses of the word *experience*, readers must be careful to see how a particular philosopher uses the term. Hume characteristically sets experience in opposition to reason (or the a priori), and often links experience with observation. He uses the phrase *custom and habit* in very much the same way, i.e., to contrast with (a priori) reason. Thus, Hume may assert that we come to believe in causal relations by *experience and observation* or by *custom and habit*, depending on whether he wants to stress the repeated particular experiences/observations or, on the other hand, the disposition (infixed by a series of experiences) to expect the customary effect whenever the customary cause occurs. In either case, Hume means to exclude a priori reasoning as the source of belief in causation. In the broad, comprehensive sense of *experience* as covering any sort of conscious awareness whatever, a priori reasoning is itself a kind of experience. Keep in mind that Hume does *not* ordinarily use *experience* in that all-inclusive way. (This Humean contrast has affinities with the opposition between *experience* and *theory*, discussed above.)

According to Hume, we can know by the mere operation of reason (i.e., we can know a priori) that *three times five equals half of 30*. We do not have to consult experience in such a case. On the other hand, as just noted, we can never discover causal relations by reason (or a priori), but only by observation and experience. Considered abstractly (or a priori), anything may cause anything; it is only by consulting experience that we can determine what *really* causes what. This illustrates what we might call the default meaning of *experience* in Hume. (See, for example, THN, 173; 1.3.15.1 and EHU, 25–29;

108–11.) One can usually tell from context whether Hume means *individual* or *collective* experience, but in any case the *experience vs. reason* contrast is not affected. *See* RELATIONS OF IDEAS AND MATTERS OF FACT; CAUSE.

The mathematical examples just given show that a priori reason operates *independently* of experience, but it is easy to misconstrue what that means. As an empiricist, Hume holds that *all* our perceptions (impressions and ideas) come ultimately from experience. However, once we acquire ideas, concepts, notions—whatever name we may give them—we find that they have a life of their own, so to speak. Once they are born, the manner of their birth becomes irrelevant to the ways they may or may not be combined or compared. We know a priori, without having to appeal to experience for confirmation, that a square is not a circle, that black is not white, that three is greater than two, and so on. We know these things from the intrinsic character of the ideas, whatever their genesis. We cannot know a priori that any object actually exists, but we can know a priori certain things about objects in case they exist. Interestingly, we know a priori that God cannot literally be dead (because the concept of God includes the property of being eternal), even though we cannot know a priori that God exists.

The English philosopher **Thomas Hobbes** draws a distinction that in some ways anticipates Hume's—a distinction between two kinds of knowledge: *knowledge of fact* and *knowledge of the consequence of one affirmation to another*. Knowledge of fact comes from sensation and is absolute (by which Hobbes does not mean *infallible*, but rather *not* merely conditional upon something else). The second kind of knowledge is what Hobbes calls reasoning or science and consists in drawing the consequences of a set of assumptions. *Reasoning* is hypothetical or conditional: If *A* is true, then *B* must also be true; etc. If we ask whether *A* is in fact true, reasoning has no answer. On the other hand, there is nothing *iffy* about sensory experience. It is *categorical*, and that is what gives it authority. In a similar vein, John Locke asserts a causal link between our sensory experience and real objects in the world. Our ideas of yellow, white, cold, heat, soft, hard, bitter, sweet, etc., are conveyed from external objects into the mind by the senses (*Essay*, 105.§3). That sort of experience provides a basis for distinguishing reality from daydreaming or idle speculation. Hume's use of *experience* is in this tradition. We should add that Hume follows Locke in recognizing a second legitimate mode of experience—what Locke calls *Reflection*, or the inner sense, by which we acquire ideas of the operations of our mind (perceiving, willing, etc.).

Given the sharp contrast that Hume often draws between experience and reason, it is important to note that he does not use *reason* with a single, precise meaning. He sometimes speaks of "experimental reasoning" (e.g., EHU, 108; 168.6), as distinguished from a priori or abstract reasoning. In defending his claim that moral distinctions are not derived from reason, he characterizes reason as "the discovery of truth or falshood [*sic*]"; and he proceeds to explain that truth or falsehood "consists in an agreement or disagreement either to the *real* relations of ideas, or to *real* existence and matter of fact" (THN, 458; 3.1.1.9; italics are in Hume's text). As the name suggests, experimental (or causal) reason is answerable to experience in a way that a priori reason is not. *See* REASON; REASON IN ANIMALS.

Hume criticizes writers who profess to discern a difference in kind between reason and experience in morals, politics, physics, and other empirically based subjects. The putative distinction disappears on close examination: The supposed a priori principles governing, for example, the motions of physical bodies or the behavior of human beings turn out to be generalizations based on observation and experience, not genuinely a priori truths. To be sure, an experienced practitioner of a discipline moves more easily and surely through an argument than a beginner; but that has nothing to do with the real distinction between reason and experience.

We often try to summarize the fundamental methodological difference between Hume and a rationalist such as Descartes by saying that Hume bases his philosophy on experience, whereas Descartes bases his on reason. Whatever its merits, that contrast obscures another important difference between the two philosophers; namely, the way they construe experience. (For a survey of the surprisingly frequent and varied appeals to experience by Descartes, see *Descartes' Philosophy of Science*, by Desmond M. Clarke.) We will look briefly at two examples that illustrate Descartes' and Hume's disparate readings of experience: freedom of the will (an interesting and important question for both philosophers) and causation (a bedrock issue for both).

According to Descartes, we know by experience that we can refrain from believing anything that is not certain and clearly understood. He asserts numerous times that we experience our own volitional freedom. Hume takes the contrary view that **belief** is not under our direct conscious control, that belief is more akin to sensation (wherein we are passive) than to "*the cogitative part of our natures*" (THN, 183; 1.4.1.8; italics are in Hume's text). Here we have two philosophers appealing to experience to justify incompatible claims. Without trying to settle this dispute, we may note that Hume claims to show that "freedom" of the sort Descartes describes is an illusion (THN, 408; 2.3.2. 2).

According to Descartes, the natural light of reason teaches us that something cannot arise from nothing; or, as Hume would put it, that whatever begins to exist must have a cause of existence. Descartes contends that we cannot understand that proposition without assenting to it; that we cannot resist believing the causal principle when it is before our mind. And it *is* the *mind* or *intellect*—not sense perception—that finds the principle absolutely compelling. Descartes holds that our idea of causation is **innate**, which is to say that it arises from our own nature and not adventitiously (i.e., from without, by way of the senses). Notice carefully that Descartes does *not* argue that the idea of causation is indubitable because it is innate. Rather, he argues that it is innate because (a) it is indubitable and (b) sense perception could not have produced so compellingly clear and distinct an idea.

Hume's account of the origin and status of our idea of causation goes directly against Descartes'. According to Hume, we get the idea of cause and effect by observing the constant conjunction of two objects or events; we never discern any necessary connection between what we call the cause and what we call the effect. We can always conceive or imagine the cause without the effect, or vice versa, which means that the causal principle is not self-evidently true. Hume does not say that the causal principle is false. In fact, he thinks that it is true. It is just not self-evident, and could not be, given its pedigree.

The impasse between Descartes and Hume stems from their divergent theories of experience; or that is at least one useful way of understanding their disagreement. The rationalist Descartes separates and elevates the intuitions of our minds above the deliverances of our senses. This means that the mind or intellect is an independent—and superior—source of ideas. In direct opposition to Descartes, the empiricist Hume sees no sharp separation between intellect and sense, and he makes the intellect dependent on the senses for its materials. Both intellectual intuitions and sense perceptions fall under *experience* in its broad meaning. Hume opts for the senses as primary because, among other reasons, they act as a check on the ruminations of the mind, which, left to themselves, run very quickly to fantasies. Accordingly, when Hume talks about experience, he means *sense* experience, which includes memory and such closely related phenomena as the **association of ideas**. *See* PERCEPTIONS for Hume's account of the basic elements of experience.

The social character of experience, something Hume never intends to deny, tends to be obscured by the language of THN and EHU—i.e., *impressions* and *ideas*, which are, between them, supposed to name everything the human mind can be conscious of. Especially in book 1 of THN ("Of the Understanding") and in some sections of EHU, impressions and ideas look a lot like (merely) private mental entities; but even in those places, Hume invokes custom and habit and education, which cannot be purely private. And books 2 and 3 of THN are about the passions and morals, which are by nature social, even though Hume continues to use the old taxonomy. Fortunately, Hume wrote most of his works (EPM, the *Essays*, the *Dialogues*, the *History*) without trying to fit everything into the impressions-ideas mold. This made it easier for him to take proper account of the private and public sides of experience.

Historical notes: Many philosophers after Hume continued to be mightily interested in the description of experience, but only two will be mentioned by name here: William James (cited earlier in this entry) and the English-American mathematician-logician-philosopher Alfred North Whitehead. They agree with Hume and his fellow classical empiricists John Locke and George Berkeley that experience is the final appeal on philosophical questions; but they find the traditional empiricist account of experience to be thin, denuded, excessively intellectualized versions of the real thing. They reject any effort to construct ordinary, full-fledged, constantly changing and growing human experience out of atomistic bits of sensation and reflection by a few mechanical operations of the mind. The basic elements of what

James and Whitehead take to be Hume's analysis of experience—i.e., discrete, clear-cut impressions and ideas—are abstractions, not faithful reflections of actual experience. Whitehead labels this sort of error—i.e., substituting abstractions for concrete realities—the "fallacy of misplaced concreteness." James proposes a *radical empiricism*, which recognizes the vague, messy, inchoate character of real experience, as contrasted with the truncated, stick-man picture painted by many philosophers in the empiricist tradition. That emaciated version of experience generates gratuitous problems—e.g., about the way human beings acquire the notion of **cause**—or so James and Whitehead contend.

Defenders of Hume may argue that James and Whitehead exaggerate the differences between their own and earlier accounts of experience. In any event, the question how best—or most helpfully—to describe experience still excites lively debates among philosophers. What is beyond dispute—at least to anyone who has ever tried to do it—is that writing about experience is exceedingly difficult. In some sense, we all know the nature of experience, but "only with exquisite care can we tell the truth about [it]." (The last clause is taken from C. I. Lewis's *Mind and the World-Order*.)

EXPERIMENT. Hume follows 18th-century usage and typically uses the word *experiment* to mean *experience*—a sense that is now obsolete. In "Of Miracles," he describes probable judgments as always involving "an opposition of experiments [i.e., experiences] and observations" (EHU, 111; 170.4). He sometimes uses *experiment* to mean *thought experiment* (in German, *Gedankenexperiment*), as when he is seeking to ascertain the cause(s) of belief: ". . . I make a third set of experiments [in the mind], in order to know, whether any thing be requisite, beside the customary transition, towards the production of this phænomenon of belief" (THN, 103; 1.3.8.11). Nowadays, we ordinarily use *experiment* more narrowly, to refer to a procedure carried out under controlled circumstances, often with sophisticated equipment—e.g., the Michelson-Morley experiments, in which an interferometer was used to measure the expected "ether drag."

Although Hume greatly admired the work of experimental natural scientists such as **Isaac Newton**, he understood that the science of human nature is "experimental" only in the broad sense of being based on experience. When Hume gives *A Treatise of Human Nature* the subtitle *being an attempt to introduce the experimental method of reasoning into moral subjects*, he intends to ally his undertaking with the general methods of natural science, but not with chemistry laboratories, astronomy observatories, or such like. The telescope, the microscope, and (after Hume's time) the Bunsen burner would be of little value in helping one to find the laws that govern human behavior. For Hume's own estimate of the different methods required by *natural philosophy*, on the one hand, and *moral philosophy*, on the other, see THN, xix; 5–6.10.

– F –

FREEDOM AND DETERMINISM. *See* LIBERTY AND NECESSITY.

– G –

GROTIUS, HUGO (1583–1645). (Dutch form Huigh de Groot.) Grotius, a Dutch jurist and political and legal philosopher, is best known for his theory of natural law and international law—expounded, most notably, in *On the Law of War and Peace*, a work that Hume was familiar with. Although Grotius was a Christian theist (and, indeed, a theologian of note), he sought to found morality and law on an accurate description of human nature, without recourse to God. To this extent, at any rate, Grotius and Hume are agreed. Grotius is more inclined than Hume to see the principles of human nature as analogous to the axioms of mathematics and, accordingly, to see moral reasoning as the deducing of necessary consequences from those axioms. (Grotius is often quoted as saying that even God could not change the immutable character of human nature.) In this respect, Grotius anticipates **John Locke**, who holds that "*Morality is capable of Demonstration*, as well as Mathematicks" (*Essay*, 516.§16; italics, capitalization, and spelling are as in Locke's text). All of this sounds very *un*-Humean, and in some important respects, it obviously is; but scholars are divided about the relation of Hume's moral and political philosophy to natural-law theories.

– H –

HISTORY. In his own time, Hume was equally well known as an essayist/historian and as a philosopher. His fame as a philosopher has long since eclipsed his status as a historian, but the British Museum Library still lists him as "HUME, David, the Historian." His six-volume *The History of England from the Invasion of Julius Caesar to the Revolution of 1688* was published in reverse chronological order, beginning with the early Stuarts (James I and Charles I) in 1754 and ending with the final volumes in 1762. After a disappointingly slow start, the *History* sold extremely well, going through several editions before Hume's death in 1776 and helping to make him "opulent" (as he put it). Over the next century, the *History* was reissued literally scores of times. After that period of great popularity, it was out of print for almost 90 years, from 1894 until 1983 (as Nicholas Phillipson points out in his book *Hume*)—a hiatus that would no doubt have distressed Hume. On the other hand, Hume would be pleased by the renewed interest during the past couple of decades or so in his *History* and *Essays*, tardy though it was in following Hume's rehabilitation as a philosopher in the early 20th century.

Although Hume himself suggests a threefold classification of his writings—"historical, philosophical, or literary"—his philosophical temperament and principles are evident in most of what he wrote. The Hume of the *Treatise* and the Hume of the *History* are by no means antagonists, though each has his own distinctive voice. The philosophical Hume regards history as affording materials to most of the sciences and, in particular, to his science of human nature. If we construe *history* broadly, it is *the* most important source of data for that science. "Indeed, if we consider the shortness of human life, and our limited knowledge, even of what passes in our own time, we must be sensible that we should be for ever children in understanding, were it not for [history], which extends our experience to all past ages . . ." (*Essays*, 566).

Recall that Hume proposes to establish the science of human nature "from a cautious observation of human life" (THN, xix; 6.10) rather than from (allegedly) self-evident axioms. History provides a useful and accessible source for cautious observations.

> Mankind are so much the same, in all times and places, that history informs us of nothing new or strange in this particular. Its chief use is only to discover the constant and universal principles of human nature, by showing men in all varieties of circumstances and situations, and furnishing us with materials, from which we may form our observations, and become acquainted with the regular springs of human action and behaviour. (EHU, 83; 150.7)

The politician or philosopher uses records of "wars, intrigues, factions, and revolutions" to fix the principles of his science, just as botanists and chemists use experiments with plants and physical substances to learn their nature. To be sure, the inquirer into the laws of human nature cannot emulate botanists and chemists in using controlled experiments, but the overall methods and aims are similar.

As noted above, Hume rejects any a priori approach to the science of human nature. This means, for practical purposes, that most of what we know about human beings we learn from reflecting on what people have actually done and thought and felt—i.e., on history. But it works the other way around as well. That is, we can use our knowledge of human nature to interpret historical phenomena according to what Hume takes to be sound causal principles. In particular, Hume seeks to provide an account of English history based on empirically plausible assumptions, in sharp contrast to other accounts that invoke divine providence, miracles, prophecies, and biblical authority generally. In Hume's view, the historian, no less than the metaphysician, should respect the boundaries within which human understanding can legitimately work—the boundaries drawn by experience. Outside those limits, there is only "sophistry and illusion" (to use words from the last sentence of EHU).

Hume's *History* has been praised as being on a par with such undoubted masterpieces as Thucydides's *History of the Peloponnesian War* and Edward Gibbon's *The History of the Decline and Fall of the Roman Empire*—the latter of which Hume read (and praised in a note to Gibbon) during the final months of Hume's life. On the other hand, Hume has been faulted for relying on too narrow a range of authorities and of being careless and uncritical with the ones he did use, the penalty being a great many avoidable errors. In spite of making much of his own impartial attitude, Hume was scored for his (at least alleged) Tory prejudices and for his sometimes mindless and ignorant dismissal of certain eras (e.g., the Middle Ages) as utterly barbarous. But even critics who lodge such complaints against the *History* typically concede that it is a historical/philosophical/literary work of genius.

HOBBES, THOMAS (1588–1679). Hobbes is regarded by some as the greatest political philosopher (not the greatest philosopher *tout court*) the English-speaking world has produced, but he was viewed in a very different light by many in the 17th and 18th centuries. To them, he was the "Monster of Malmesbury" (Hobbes's birthplace in Wiltshire, England), the most prominent advocate of what they believed to be a degrading and odious theory of human beings as incorrigibly self-seeking and warlike. This description of Hobbes's picture of the human condition may not be entirely accurate or fair, but it was the prevailing one; and Hobbes's own penchant for dramatic and hyperbolic statement was partly to blame for the misconception (if such it be). Many philosophers—among them, the third Earl of **Shaftesbury**, **Joseph Butler**, **Francis Hutcheson**, and Hume himself—criticize what they take to be the excesses in Hobbes's account of human nature, which is not entirely mistaken but heavily one-sided.

Hobbes's view of human nature and society comes pretty straightforwardly out of his materialistic metaphysics, which holds that reality, including human beings, consists exclusively of bodies governed by mechanistic laws. Hume cites Hobbes the metaphysician as offering a question-begging "demonstration" of the proposition *"whatever begins to exist, must have a cause of existence"* (THN, 80; 1.3.3.4; italics are in Hume's text). However, Hume is much more interested in the moral and political side of Hobbes's philosophy.

Hume names Hobbes and **John Locke** as philosophers who "maintained the selfish system of morals"—but immediately adds that they lived "irreproachable lives" (EPM, 296; 165.3). According to that system (which is often called **egoism**, though not by Hobbes or Hume), we are not capable of disinterested benevolence, friendship, or public service—even though we suppose that we are. Appearances to the contrary notwithstanding, they tell us, all voluntary human acts are selfish. We call something *good* only because it is an object of our appetite or desire; and we call it *evil* only because it is an object of our hate or aversion. Hume indignantly denounces the theory as evincing a "depraved disposition," but his philosophical criticisms are both more measured and more significant. (Hume's strongest language seems to be directed more toward someone like the openly cynical **Bernard de Mandeville,** who is not mentioned by name, than toward Hobbes; but the criticisms apply to any egoistic theory.)

Hume adduces basically two arguments against Hobbesian (or any) egoism; namely, it flies in the face of plain and universal **experience**, and it is incompatible with morality. The most obvious objection to the "selfish hypothesis" is that we regularly observe what we take to be acts of generosity and friendship, as well as acts of selfishness and malice; and the differences between the two kinds of act are embodied in our language and other institutions. This is simply a fact of human experience. To be justified in rejecting such widespread experience as uniformly delusive, we would require a powerful, well-established theory that cast light on the deepest levels of human motivation and revealed them to be contrary to what the common person and most philosophers believe them to be. Egoism is no such theory. It denies the obvious with no compensating gain in understanding. Hume conjectures that an inordinate love of *simplicity* lies at the root of this theory, and generally of "much false reasoning in philosophy" (EPM, 298; 166.6). Whatever its provenance, egoism violates (at least) two requirements of an acceptable theory: it must be compatible with observed facts, and it must have significant explanatory power.

Besides the first objection—that it denies plain facts—Hobbes's doctrine of human motivation lies open to a second, equally damning criticism; namely, that it is "utterly incompatible with all virtue or moral sentiment" (EPM, 295; 164.1). Since it is impossible—practically at any rate—to deny the reality of moral distinctions, this objection is, if sound, fatal to egoism. A *moral* sentiment *essentially, by its very nature*—not accidentally or contingently—transcends personal interest. The logic of moral evaluation requires that I allocate praise and blame impartially. I must recognize courage in my enemy if he performs the same sort of act as my friend, whom I praise as courageous. If Hobbes were right, then morality would be impossible. *See* MORAL SENSE.

In affirming the possibility of disinterested acts, Hume does not deny the reality of selfishness. On the contrary, he understands that we are naturally inclined to exhibit only "confin'd [i.e., limited] generosity," and that unchecked self-love is the source of injustice and violence (THN, 480; 3.2.1.10). Our sympathy with others is typically weaker than our concern for ourselves, and our sympathy with people remote from us in geography or affection is fainter than our sympathy with those close to us. But this psychological and ethical myopia is neither total nor incorrigible; it can be mitigated, just as our perceptual judgments (of distance, for example) may be corrected by further experience and by reflection (THN, 603; 3.3.3.2). Hume makes his point memorably in the conclusion of EPM: "there is some benevolence, however small, infused into our bosom; some spark of friendship for human kind; some particle of the dove kneaded into our frame, along with the elements of the wolf and serpent" (271; 147.4).

Hume agrees with Hobbes that people need a civil society both to curb the destructive effects of selfishness and to channel the energy of self-interest into cooperation that benefits all citizens. However, he rejects as incoherent the Hobbesian doctrine that a society is formed by a contract among its members: The very idea of a contract (and the implied notion of *promising*) *presupposes* the rules and conventions it is invoked to explain. (See THN, book 3, part 2, section 7 ["Of the origin of government"] and section 8 ["Of the source of allegiance"].) In his essay "Of the Original Contract," Hume grants that, *in some weak and loose sense*, all government is at first founded on a contract; but this toothless concession is consistent with his considered rejection of contractarianism.

On one contentious philosophical issue, Hume agrees with Hobbes almost entirely—the reconciliation of **liberty** with **necessity** (or freedom with determinism). The question that generates the (putative) problem is this: How is it possible to believe both that all events (including human choices) are caused *and* that some human actions are free? The correct answer, according to both Hobbes and Hume, is that the supposed incompatibility is a pseudo-problem generated by an equivocation on the word *free*. A person is free if he can do what he chooses to do; otherwise, he is not free. The causal question of *why* he wants to do this or that is completely irrelevant. To say that an action is free is not to say that it is uncaused. It is, rather, to say that it is uncoerced. Hobbes is the first modern philosopher to adopt this *compatibilist* solution to the problem.

HOME, HENRY (LORD KAMES) (1696–1782). Henry Home may have been a relative of David Hume (*Home* and *Hume* are variant spellings of the same surname); and he was certainly an extremely important figure in David's life, especially the middle years—friend, correspondent, adviser, defender, and critic. Henry Home acquired the judicial honorific *Lord* in 1752, when he became a judge in the Court of Session (Scotland's supreme civil court); in 1763 he became a Lord of Justiciary in Scotland's supreme criminal court. *Kames* was the name of his ancestral estate, only a few miles from David's family home, Ninewells, in Berwickshire. It was mainly at Henry Home's urging that David excised the essay on **miracles** from the *Treatise*, and Henry was not a little annoyed when David published the essay eight years later (1748) in *Philosophical Essays Concerning Human Understanding* (later retitled ***An Enquiry Concerning Human Understanding***).

As with a number of other bright young fellows, David's relations with Henry became less intimate and cordial as he (David) asserted his own independent views, though they remained friends as long as David lived. Henry Home was not a likeable man—imperious, irascible, vitriolic, abusive—but he was also (in J. Y. T. Greig's words) "one of the most virile, odd, irritating, versatile and stimulating men in Scotland." He was not a great thinker or a great writer, but he recognized genius when he saw it. David Hume, **Adam Smith**, and **Thomas Reid** are perhaps the greatest of the many young men encouraged and protected by this indefatigable, splenetic Scotsman. He wrote a number of books himself, about a variety of subjects, two of them explicitly about philosophy: *Essays on the Principles of Morality and Natural Religion* (1751) and *Elements of Criticism* (1762), a widely read and frequently reprinted statement of Lord Kames's aesthetic theory.

HUME'S FORK. This term (which is, of course, not Hume's own) refers to Hume's dichotomous division of "all the objects of human reason or inquiry" into those that are intuitively or demonstratively certain and those that are not (EHU, 25; 108.1). To put the distinction in linguistic terms, every proposition is a member of one or the other of the two classes, and no proposition is a member of both classes. This means that the fork has exactly two prongs or tines, as opposed to the three- or four-tined forks seen on dinner tables. A more instructive fork analogy may be the branching of a road into two separate ways—a fork in the road. *See* RELATIONS OF IDEAS AND MATTERS OF FACT for a fuller discussion.

HUME'S LAW. This "law" refers to a thesis attributed to Hume: We cannot validly infer a moral (or a normative) conclusion from non-moral (or non-normative) premises. The term *Hume's Law* (though not the substance of the supposed law) is associated most closely with the English moral philosopher R. M. Hare (1919–2002), who formulates the law as "No *ought* from an *is.*" *See* IS/OUGHT for a fuller discussion.

HUTCHESON, FRANCIS (1694–1746). Hutcheson was born in Ireland but spent much of his life in Scotland. As the professor of moral philosophy in the University of Glasgow from 1730 until his death in 1746, Hutcheson exerted a salutary, humanizing influence on several generations of his students. Against ethical rationalists, who hold that we discern moral truths by our **reason**, Hutcheson argues (*Inquiry into the Original of Our Ideas of Beauty and Virtue*, 1725, and *Essay on the Nature and Conduct of the Passions and Affections, with Illustrations upon the Moral Sense*, 1728) that we discover moral distinctions by a ***moral sense***, which is analogous to ordinary perception. Hutcheson's debt to **Shaftesbury** is obvious and freely acknowledged by Hutcheson, though he thinks that Shaftesbury regrettably strays from orthodox religious doctrine. On the title page of the first edition of his first book (the *Inquiry*), Hutcheson adds the subtitle "In which the principles of the late Earl of Shaftesbury are explain'd and defended, against the author of the *Fable of the Bees* [i.e., **Bernard de Mandeville**]." Specifically, Hutcheson seeks to refute the bald **egoism** of Mandeville—the doctrine that all voluntary human actions are motivated solely by self-interest.

Hume was certainly influenced by Hutcheson's anti-rationalist account of morality (and, more generally, by his placing of feeling or sentiment above reason) and by his rejection of egoism, but scholars disagree about the precise character and degree of that influence. For a discussion of the issue and a canvass of some of the divergent opinions, see James Moore, "Hume and Hutcheson," in *Hume and Hume's Connexions.*

– I –

IDEAS. *See* PERCEPTIONS; IMAGINATION.

IDENTITY. *Identity* is the second of the seven **relations** that Hume introduces very early in THN. It is, he says, the most universal of all relations, "being common to every being, whose existence has any duration" (THN, 14; 1.1.5.4). He is here speaking of identity in its "strictest sense," which applies only to "constant and unchangeable objects." As a kind of negative prelude to his later and fuller treatment of identity, Hume explains why he does not include *difference* among the relations. *Difference* is not a true relation; it is, rather, the negation of a relation. There are two kinds of difference: difference in *number* (which is opposed to *identity*) and difference in *kind* (which is opposed to *resemblance*). This is an anticipation of a distinction that he later makes between two senses of *identity*— numerical and specific (THN, 257; 1.4.6.13). There is nothing in all this to suggest the minefield of difficulties that Hume later finds in the notion of identity.

Hume tackles the problem of identity in earnest, so to speak, in "Of scepticism with regard to the senses" (THN, book 1, part 4, section 2), where he tries to explain how we come to believe in the distinct and continued existence of external objects—i.e., of objects that are distinct from our **perception** of them and that continue to exist when we are not perceiving them. This means that we attribute identity— persistence through time—to such objects. The tree that I saw yesterday is the selfsame tree that I see today, or so I believe. But Hume wonders how that can be. He is puzzled by the very idea of ("strict" or "perfect") identity; for it involves combining two properties—unity and number (or multiplicity)—that seem (at least) not only to be mutually incompatible but also to be very different from identity. When I perceive a single object, I get the **idea** of *unity* (or *oneness*), not that of identity; and when I perceive two or more objects (even if they are very similar), I get the idea of *number* (or *multiplicity*), not that of identity. Identity appears to exclude both unity and number, and to "lie in something that is neither of them" (THN, 200; 1.4.2.28). Yet absolutely *everything* is comprehended under either *unity* or *number*, and nothing is comprehended under both categories. As Hume puts it, there is no medium between unity and number. In logical jargon, *unity* and *number* are mutually exclusive and jointly exhaustive (like *odd* and *even* in the domain of whole numbers). It looks very much as if the very notion of identity is incoherent.

Strictly speaking, the notion of identity *is* incoherent, in Hume's view. We make sense of it by "a fiction of the imagination" (THN, 200–201; 1.4.2.29) that allows us to attribute *invariableness* and *uninterruptedness* to an object "thro' a suppos'd variation of time" (THN, 201; 1.4.2.30). Recall that, for Hume, we cannot get the idea of identity from a single perception of an object. Identity links an object at one time to that object at a different time. Unfortunately, temporal succession would destroy the impression of identity. Thus, paradoxically, the lapse of time is both necessary for and subversive of the notion of identity. So we pretend that the *object* remains the same while our *perceptions* of it change.

Hume draws a **commonsense** distinction between *numerical* identity and *specific* (or *qualitative*) identity, which may help to explain how we sometimes mistake a succession of resembling perceptions for one unchanging perception. The distinction is easy to illustrate. Suppose a robin—the same robin—sings his song—the same song—every morning. It is obvious that the word *same* does not mean precisely the same thing in both occurrences. It is literally, numerically the same robin that sings, but it is not literally, numerically the same song. The song he sings one day is identical with (i.e., qualitatively indistinguishable from) the song he sings the next day, but the two songs are numerically distinct. No one is likely to confound the two senses of identity involved in the example. (The American philosopher Charles Sanders

Peirce suggests a useful terminology for marking the distinction we have just illustrated; namely, *type* and *token*. The robin sings the same song [type] every day but a different song [token] every day. We might say that the robin sings the same song but gives a new performance or rendition of it every day. A slightly different illustration should make the point clear: When I write *and and*, have I written one word or two words? In Peirce's language, I have written one type and two tokens of the same word. Hume would probably accept the recommendation as practically helpful but as not settling the philosophical puzzle about strict or perfect identity.)

It is important to note that *Hume the philosopher* would accept only half of the distinction between the robin and the songs he sings on two different days. The song he sings on Monday may indeed be qualitatively (or specifically) identical with the one he sings on Tuesday; but, in Hume's view, the robin himself cannot be numerically (i.e., perfectly) identical on two successive days. That is because our perception of the robin on Monday is wholly distinct from our perception on Tuesday. To understand Hume's problem with identity (that is, strict or perfect identity), we must remember that, for Hume, we are directly or immediately aware only of images or perceptions; or, to state the point negatively, we are never directly or immediately aware of independent external objects. This means that any change in perception destroys the perfect identity of what is perceived. Indeed, Hume describes it as a "gross illusion" to suppose that our resembling perceptions are numerically the same (THN, 217; 1.4.3.56). But no theory can persuade us to give up our **belief** in the numerical identity of external objects (or some of them at any rate) from one perception to the next. There is, thus, a conflict between what our instincts impel us to believe and what philosophical reflection requires us to doubt. Hume thinks that philosophers try to solve the problem—if "solve" can be applied to so unsatisfactory a remedy—by the theory of "double existence": *Perceptions* change constantly, but *objects* continue uninterrupted (THN, 215; 1.4.2.52). The senses provide no basis for the theory, nor does reason; but the **imagination** provides us with a fiction that we embrace *faute de mieux*. *See* EXISTENCE for a discussion of the idea of *external existence*.

In his account of **personal identity**, Hume calls attention to several sorts of "imperfect identity"; e.g., the identity of plants, animals, ships, houses, and social and political institutions (THN, 259; 1.4.6.15). He offers a number of useful observations about the identity of those kinds of entities (some of which parallel similar observations in **Locke**'s *Essay*).

Hume's interest in identity is mainly *epistemic* (how do we get the idea of identity?) rather than *metaphysical* (what does it mean for objects to be in fact identical?). This explains why he insists that identity is indissolubly bound up with time. Other philosophers interested in identity—most notably, perhaps, the German philosopher-mathematician Wilhelm Gottfried Leibniz—treat the notion more expansively. According to Leibniz (and just about everyone else), if *a* and *b* are identical, then each of them has exactly the same properties as the other (neither more nor fewer). This principle has been called *Leibniz's Law* and also *the indiscernibility of identicals*. The converse of that principle—*the identity of indiscernibles*—is more controversial. It states that if *a* and *b* have exactly the same properties (or, in some formulations, properties of a certain sort), then they are identical. Some philosophers have argued that the second principle seems to be either trivially true (when formulated about *all* properties) or at best contingently true (when formulated more narrowly) and, consequently, not a basic metaphysical principle. *See also* SKEPTICISM; SUBSTANCE.

IMAGINATION. References to the imagination (or *fancy*, as Hume sometimes calls it) crop up repeatedly from the beginning to the end of THN and, less pervasively, in the two *Enquiries*. In the first sentence of book 1 of THN, Hume divides all **perceptions** of the mind into *impressions* and *ideas*, which are distinguished by the superior force and liveliness of impressions. Ideas, which are "the faint images of [impressions] in thinking and reasoning" (1; 1.1.1.1), are subdivided into *memory* and *imagination*, which are themselves distinguished by the superior strength and vivacity of memory-ideas. By comparison, the ideas of the imagination are fainter, more obscure, and more languid. As a matter of **common sense**, we know that *memory* is restricted to what actually happened. We cannot *remember* something that we made up out of whole cloth. *Imagination*, on the contrary, labors under no such limitation. We can imagine events that never occurred (our singing at the Met, for example) and entities that never existed (flying horses and golden mountains, for example). In general, the imagination is able to compound, transpose, augment, or diminish the materials furnished by the senses and **experience** (EHU, 19; 97.4); but it cannot *create* those basic materials. They must be derived from **impressions**. Thus, for all its apparent freedom and creative power, the imagination actually operates within the narrow limits of the outer and inner senses (*sensation* and *reflection*, in the language of **John Locke**). The imagination is active in the ***association of ideas***, whereby the appearance of one **idea** leads naturally to the appearance of others that are related to the original idea by resemblance, spatio-temporal contiguity, or cause and effect.

Hume also contrasts imagination with ***reason***; this infects his use of the term *imagination* with a degree of ambiguity, which he concedes in a footnote: "When I oppose the imagination to the memory, I mean the faculty, by which we form our fainter ideas. When I oppose it to reason, I mean the same faculty, excluding only our demonstrative and probable reasonings" (THN, 117n1; 1.3.9.19n. 22). He seems to compound the equivocation by identifying the *understanding* with "the general and more establish'd properties of the imagination" (THN, 267; 1.4.7.7). To reduce our suspicion of serious equivocation, we should recall that within the capacious bounds of the imagination, Hume separates "the principles which are permanent, irresistable [*sic*], and universal" (e.g., the **cause-effect** relation) from those that are "changeable, weak, and irregular" (THN, 225; 1.4.4.1).

On several occasions, Hume invokes imagination to explain how we come to have ideas that we could not have acquired by sense or by reason. For example, we believe that external objects exist independently of perception and that they continue to exist when we are not perceiving them; but pretty clearly those convictions cannot come from sense-**perception**. Neither can they come from causal reason, since one side of the causal relation—the external objects—lie outside experience. But we do in fact have such **beliefs**, and they are immune to skeptical attack. Hume says that imagination fills the gap, so to speak, and *feigns* the continued independent existence of external objects. He explains our belief in **personal identity** (a self that exists continuously through changing perceptions) in a similar fashion. Although we do not actually perceive an unchanging self that survives the incessant birth and death of perceptions, our imagination supplies us with a fiction that we accept as the real self. Hume also appeals to the work of the imagination in his account of the **passions**. It is imagination, for example, that enables us to feel sympathy with persons who are distant from us both in space and relationship, and even to feel sympathy for future pains and **pleasures** of strangers (THN, 385; 2.2.9.13). We do that, for example, when we decide not to throw garbage on a highway hundreds of miles from our home, even though we could do so with impunity.

For all its resourcefulness, the imagination cannot explain everything. For example, it cannot explain our approbation of the social virtues. "It is not conceivable, how a *real* sentiment or passion can ever arise from a known *imaginary* interest; especially when our *real* interest is still [i.e., constantly] kept in view, and is often acknowledged to be entirely distinct from the imaginary, and even sometimes opposite to it" (EPM, 217; 107.13). Nor can imagination be pressed into the service of the theory of **egoism**, which makes self-love or self-interest the touchstone of all moral evaluations. "No force of imagination can convert us into another person, and make us fancy, that we, being that person, reap benefit from those valuable qualities, which belong to him" (EPM, 234; 119.3).

IMPRESSIONS AND IDEAS. *See* PERCEPTIONS; IMAGINATION.

INDUCTION. The *problem of induction*, as it has come to be called, is that of establishing that the future will resemble the past; or, in Hume's own words, "*that instances, of which we have had no experience, must resemble those, of which we have had experience, and that the course of nature continues always uniformly the same*" (THN, 89; 1.3.6.5; the italics are in Hume's text). It is natural that the problem would also be called that of establishing *the uniformity of nature*. Hume himself uses the word *induction* only a few times in his writings, and never in the sense here explained. By the term he means something like a canvass or survey or list of instances of a certain sort.

Hume's question is whether we can show, either by demonstration or probable reasoning, that our future experiences will be of a piece with our past experiences. His answer is categorical and emphatic:

We cannot. That we can at least conceive a change in the course of nature shows that such a change is not impossible and, consequently, is not a fit subject for demonstration. By contrast, we cannot even conceive that the sum of the angles of a Euclidean triangle is not equal to two right angles.

Probable reasoning about matters of fact rests almost exclusively on the relation of **cause and effect**, which is based on **experience** (or, as Hume is fond of reminding us, on *custom and habit*). The conclusions of probable reasoning, that is, rest on the *assumption* that the future will resemble the past. To try to prove that assumption by probable arguments would be to go in a circle, to take for granted the very thing we set out to prove. (For Hume's arguments on this issue, see THN, 88–89; 1.1.6.4–7, and EHU, 34–38; 114–17.) It is important to note that Hume does *not* say that our **belief** in induction is *mistaken* or that we can avoid having the belief and acting on it. He says only that we cannot make inductive inferences without a premise about induction, and that the premise has no rational foundation.

We must be careful not to confuse the problem of justifying induction *in general* (if it is indeed a problem) with the wholly different problem of justifying particular inductive inferences. As we have seen, the general problem is insoluble—a fact that has led some commentators to deny both that it is a problem at all (real problems, they say, have at least possible solutions) and that Hume considers it a problem. The human practice of making inductive inferences (a practice absolutely essential to survival) rests on an unprovable assumption—the inductive premise. *Given* that premise, our inferences may be more or less rational, i.e., more or less based on the evidence. Hume says that the wise (i.e., reasonable or prudent) man proportions his belief to the evidence. We revise our conclusions as we unearth more evidence. A recent example has to do with the efficacy of Vitamin E in reducing the incidence of cardiovascular disease. Initial studies, based on an impressive body of data, suggested a causal link: People who took Vitamin E had a lower incidence of heart trouble than people who did not take Vitamin E. Later studies showed convincingly that, despite very high correlations, Vitamin E had nothing to do with the lower risk of heart disease. As it turned out, people who take Vitamin E tend to do lots of other things that really *are* good for the health of the heart (exercising, not eating junk food, etc.). This is a good example of inductive reasoning at work. It does nothing to establish the general proposition that the future will resemble the past, but it does increase our store of knowledge of human physiology.

The problem of induction—or the *so-called* problem of induction—arises as a natural corollary of Hume's analysis of causation, specifically his analysis of *necessary connexion*. If we knew that a cause is *necessarily* connected with its effect, so that it would be impossible for the cause to occur without the effect, then the problem of induction would be essentially solved. But we do not know any such thing.

INNATE IDEAS. This entry is mainly about **John Locke**'s rejection of the doctrine of innate **ideas**, and Hume's comments on how Locke treats the issue.

By the term *idea* Locke means "whatsoever is the Object of the Understanding when a Man thinks"—where *thinks* is taken broadly to include sensing, remembering, and imagining as well as thinking in the narrower sense of *reasoning*. We are aware of ideas whether we are seeing a sunset or smelling a rose or imagining a flying horse or demonstrating a theorem in geometry. An *innate* idea is (or would be if there were any) one that we have from (or before) birth, as against one that we learn or acquire after birth. The doctrine of innate ideas is, in some guise or other, as old as Plato, who argues that the objects of genuine knowledge must be the unchanging Forms, with which we became acquainted in our pre-existent state (the doctrine of Recollection). In modern times, the doctrine is associated with rationalist philosophers such as **René Descartes** and Leibniz. Descartes, for example, argues that our ideas of God, substance, infinity, or even the more mundane ideas of truth and falsity, cannot be derived from **experience** and, consequently, must be innate. For Locke, the doctrine lent itself readily to religious and political intolerance (if a notion is innate, then God must have put it in us, and who are we to challenge it?) and to arrogance and laziness. Little wonder, then, that Locke devotes well over 50 pages of his *Essay Concerning Human Understanding* to the project of refuting Descartes and the other proponents of the theory of innate ideas. His principal arguments may be summarized briefly.

Locke's rejection of the innatist doctrine comprises both *concepts* and *principles*—for example, the concept of God and the speculative principle *whatever is, is* or the practical principle *we should treat other persons as we would want them to treat us.* Note carefully that Locke does not mean that we do not have the concept of God (we do) or that the principles cited are false (they are not). He means only what he says: They are not *innate.* His central argument against the doctrine is straightforward. Ideas, by definition, are objects of consciousness. This means that we cannot have an idea of which we are not aware. Locke says that it is "near a contradiction" to suppose that an idea could fail to exemplify its essence, which is to be an object of consciousness. It follows that if any idea (whether a concept or a principle) were innate in human beings, then everyone would be aware of it. But there is no idea whatsoever—not a single one—that everyone is aware of. Locke cites children and "Ideots" as counterexamples; but he could have used adult persons of normal intelligence, the vast majority of whom pass their entire lives without ever once entertaining the proposition *whatever is, is.* Such ignorance would be impossible if the principle were innate—or so Locke argues. Here is Locke's argument stated explicitly and simply:

> If any idea were innate, then every person would be conscious of it.
> There is no idea of which every person is conscious.
> Therefore, there is no innate idea.

Locke's argument is an instance of the form called *modus tollens*: "If p, then q. Not q. Therefore, not p." Any argument having this form is *valid*; that is, it is impossible for all the premises to be true and the conclusion false. A valid argument may have a false conclusion if at least one premise is false. This means that one could challenge the strength of Locke's argument by denying that the premises are true or that they are sufficiently clear even to qualify as true or false. An argument is *sound* if, and only if, it is valid and all its premises are true.

If Locke's central negative argument is sound, then there are no innate ideas, and there's an end of the matter. But Locke tries to show positively that the facts innate ideas are invoked to explain can be explained without innate ideas. He does not deny, for example, that there are propositions that we cannot understand without knowing immediately that they are true. We cannot understand what "Every triangle has three sides" means and also be in doubt whether it is true. Such propositions are self-evident, but they do not force us to accept innate ideas. We learn to recognize them as a natural part of learning a language. Locke considers several putative reasons for accepting innate ideas, and finds them all wanting.

The German philosopher/mathematician Gottfried Wilhelm Leibniz criticizes Locke's arguments against the theory of innate ideas. To simplify a complicated story, Leibniz alleges that Locke confuses the *genetic-psychological* question how we come to have an idea with the *epistemic-normative* question how we know it to be true. On the face of it, Leibniz's allegation of confusion seems to be false: Locke does not deny that we have the *capacity* to recognize self-evident truths when we meet them. He denies only that we must have been born with those truths imprinted on our minds. This example suggests that disputes about innate ideas may turn on the ambiguous use of terms rather than on substantive differences. Locke's own simile for the mind—white paper or a blank tablet—is misleading in that it suggests, falsely, that *the mind itself* has no innate form or structure. That is not Locke's position. If we state Locke's and Leibniz's positions clearly and carefully, we find fewer real differences than we first suppose—which is not to say that we find no real differences at all. (The issue of innate ideas—or a latter-day descendant of the issue—is still with us. The American linguist-philosopher Noam Chomsky, for example, has argued that the ability of children to acquire a language cannot be satisfactorily explained by an empiricist theory of ideas. But that is another story.)

In view of Locke's near-obsession with the theory of innate ideas, it may be surprising that Hume devotes very little attention to the question. It would be more accurate to say that Hume pays little attention to the question of innate ideas *as Locke poses that question.* By giving the term *idea* a different meaning from Locke's usage, Hume raises and answers a different question. In a footnote to the very first paragraph of THN (after the introduction), Hume complains that Locke conflates two fundamentally different kinds of **perceptions** under the single term *idea.* When we divide perceptions into **impressions** (our stronger, more vivid perceptions) and *ideas* (our weaker, fainter perceptions)—as Hume does—we see quickly that impressions are innate in the sense that they are not copied from antecedent perceptions, and that ideas are not innate in that they *are* copied from antecedent perceptions. What sense does it make, Hume asks, to deny that sensations, self-love, resentment of injuries, and love between the sexes are innate—i.e., arise from the original constitution of human nature itself? Hume obviously thinks that Locke would agree with the implied answer to that question (i.e., it makes no sense).

Hume thus manages to dispatch the question of innateness (to his own satisfaction, at any rate) in a few sentences, concluding that if *innate* means *original* or *copied from no earlier perception*, then impressions are innate and ideas are not innate. (For Hume's observations about innateness, see THN, 7 & 647–48; 1.1.1.12 & 408.6; and EHU, 22n1; 99n1.)

Hume dismisses as frivolous the dispute about the exact time thinking begins—whether before, at, or after birth—a problem that Locke exploits to discredit the doctrine of innate ideas. Hume conjectures that Locke was drawn into a pointless and confused dispute about innateness by using the undefined terms of medieval scholasticism. Hume adds the following acidulous comment about Locke: "A like ambiguity and circumlocution seem to run through that philosopher's reasonings on this as well as most other subjects" (EHU, 22n1; 99.9n1).

IS/OUGHT. The *is/ought* distinction (not Hume's phrase) refers to a paragraph in THN (469–70; 3.1.1.27) about inferring an *ought* (or normative) conclusion from *is* (or factual) premises. It has generated a sizeable secondary literature. Some commentators seek only to clarify or analyze what Hume actually says, while others use the passage as a point of departure for stating their own views. This entry concentrates almost entirely on the passage itself, with only a glance at the use others have made of it. It is important to keep in mind just where the passage occurs and to see whether it adds anything substantive to the section in which it appears.

The very first task Hume sets for himself in book 3 of THN ("Of Morals") is to prove that moral distinctions (*virtuous* vs. *vicious*, *praiseworthy* vs. *blameworthy*, for example) are not derived from reason. Having done this to his satisfaction by a series of arguments, he concludes the section with a kind of coda—the famous *is/ought* passage. He complains that many purveyors of moral systems shift imperceptibly from "the usual copulations of propositions, *is*, and *is not*" to frequent occurrences of *ought* and *ought not*—without a syllable of explanation or justification. And some explanation or justification is called for, since *ought/ought not* differs from *is/is not* in expressing some new relation or assertion. Hume adds that it "seems altogether inconceivable, how this new relation can be a deduction from others, which are entirely different from it" (THN, 469; 3.1.1.27). This "inconceivable deduction" is often described as the impossibility of inferring a normative (e.g., a moral or ethical) conclusion from wholly factual premises. It is not necessary that the words *is* and *ought* or their negatives literally occur in the argument. Thus, the following argument illustrates the sort of inference that Hume is taken to proscribe: "Stalin was responsible for the deaths of millions of persons who had committed no serious crime or no crime at all, and certainly no capital crime. Further, Stalin knew that these people were innocent. Therefore, Stalin was an evil man."

First, a point about terminology. When Hume speaks of a *deduction*, he means any sort of ratiocinative inference, whether it be *deductive* (in the contemporary sense of *logically necessary*) or *inductive* (= probabilistic). It is a mistake to interpret Hume as restricting what he calls deduction to arguments whose conclusions follow (or are claimed to follow) necessarily from their premises by strict entailment. He clearly means to include arguments based on causal reasoning, all of which fall short of demonstration. He first argues at some length that moral distinctions do not consist in **relations** that are "the objects of science" (or, alternatively, "can be the objects of knowledge and certainty"); namely, resemblance, contrariety, degrees in quality, and proportions in quantity or number (THN, 70 and 468; 1.3.1.2 and 3.1.1.26). He goes on to "the *second* part of [his] argument" (THN, 468; 3.1.1.26; italics are in Hume's text), which is to show that morality does not consist in any matter of fact that can be discovered by the understanding (causal reason, in this case). Taken together, the two parts of Hume's argument purport to prove that morality is not an object of reason, either demonstrative reason or (probabilistic) causal reason. Since reason "exerts itself" in only the two ways just mentioned—i.e., from demonstration *or* probability; from the abstract relations of our ideas *or* the relations of objects revealed in experience—it follows that moral distinctions are not based on rational inference at all. *See* MORAL SENSE.

We should note explicitly a couple of things that Hume does *not* say. First, he does not say that reason has no role in moral evaluation. On the contrary, it plays an indispensable role. In EPM, he comes close to making reason an equal partner with sentiment, observing that reason and sentiment "concur in almost all moral determinations and conclusions" (172; 75.9). But he still maintains that moral distinctions originate in the sentiments and that the "final sentence" in morality "depends on some internal sense or feeling, which nature has made universal in the whole species" (ibid.).

Second, Hume does not deny that matters of fact and moral evaluations (whether sentiments or judgments) are closely connected; they are just not connected in the manner of premise(s) and conclusion in a logical inference. He regularly describes how matters of fact give rise to feelings of approval/disapproval or to a feeling of obligation. For example, in the paragraph immediately preceding the *is/ought* paragraph, he tries to prove "that vice and virtue are not matters of fact, whose existence we can infer by [causal] reason" (THN, 468; 3.1.1.26). [It has been pointed out by at least one sharp-eyed commentator—Don Garrett—that the comma after *fact* suggests falsely that the clause *whose existence we can infer by reason* is non-restrictive, or non-essential. Hume's use of commas reflects 18th-century conventions, but not our own. Here, it obscures his own otherwise perfectly clear doctrine that not all matters of fact can be inferred by reason.]

If we consider carefully all the facts about a willful murder, we find nothing in the external circumstances that answers to what we call *vice*. We find vice only when we look into our own heart and find a sentiment or feeling of disapproval toward the perpetrator of the crime. There *is* a matter of fact in the case, but it is the object of feeling, not of reason; it is *in us*, not in the object. Hume follows a similar pattern in explaining the origin of justice and property. *Self-interest*, Hume tells us, is the *original* motive for the establishment of the rules of justice; "but a *sympathy* with *public* interest is the source of the *moral* approbation, which attends that virtue" (THN, 499–500; 3.2.2.24; italics are in Hume's text). In both cases—our disapproval of willful murder and our moral approval of the rules of justice—Hume offers a causal explanation of the provenance of moral sentiments and judgments. To oversimplify just a bit, Hume's explanations are psychological (i.e., based on facts about the human mind) rather than logical (i.e., based on abstract relations or on causal relations among external objects).

Hume's interest in the so-called *is/ought gap* seems to be limited to the one paragraph we have been discussing, and the paragraph itself looks like a by-the-way observation subjoined to a section that was already substantively complete. He shows no inclination to pursue the matter any further, at least not in the same terms. This has not kept a number of commentators from weighing in on the issue. Indeed, the alleged impossibility of deriving an *ought* from an *is* (or a normative conclusion from purely factual premises) is well enough known to have been christened with its own name: "**Hume's Law.**" Some interpretations of Hume's doctrine are inconsistent with other interpretations; so they cannot all be correct (though they might all be incorrect). And some of them seem pretty clearly to be at variance with Hume's text. But some of them make no pretense of getting Hume right; they use the passage (or the slogan allegedly found in it) as a kind of text for laying out their own views on the subject.

Historical note: More than two millennia before Hume, Plato's dialogue *Euthyphro* asks whether something is holy because it is loved by the gods, or is loved by the gods because it is holy. Plato's question may be restated in a generalized, anachronistic form, with a linguistic twist: Can moral terms (or concepts) such as *good* or *right* be replaced, without loss of meaning, by non-moral (or factual or "natural") predicates (e.g., *is commanded by God* or *promotes happiness*); *or*, on the contrary, do such moral terms refer to something sui generis—i.e., irreducibly moral? Philosophers who accept the replaceability of moral predicates (or, negatively, who reject the uniqueness and irreducibility of such predicates) are ethical *naturalists*. Those who subscribe to the unique, irreducible, sui generis status of moral concepts are ethical *non-naturalists* (or *anti-naturalists*). In his *Principia Ethica*, the English philosopher G. E. Moore (1873–1958) contends that those who *identify* good or right with any factual or "natural" property or combination of properties commit the *naturalistic fallacy*. (This is a way of stating "Hume's Law" in terms of definition rather than inference, the basic point remaining the same.)

Moore and others use the so-called *open-question* argument (sometimes called the *trivialization argument*) to show that we may sensibly ask whether *any* natural property or set of properties is *really* good. For simplicity, let us say *good = pleasant*. This means that all good things are pleasant and all pleasant things are good; i.e., *X* is good if and only if *X* is pleasant. The term *good things* and the term *pleasant things* refer to exactly the same set of things. In language suggested by John Stuart Mill, the two terms have identical *denotations* (in later parlance, *extensions*). But we may still sensibly ask—i.e., it is still an open question—whether pleasant things are good, even if the answer seems obvious to most people. We could not sensibly ask that question if *good* literally *meant pleasant*; for in that case we would be asking whether what is pleasant is pleasant—a trivial question. The upshot of Moore's argument is that *good* and *pleasant* (or whatever ethical and non-ethical terms may be involved) cannot *mean* the same thing even if they *apply* to the same things. They have different meanings (or connotations/intensions). An analogy from the language of astronomy: *Morning Star* (*Phosphor*) and *Evening Star* (*Hesperus*) both refer to Venus, but they do not mean the same thing. When we call something good, we are not attributing to it the same quality as when we call it pleasant (or some other factual predicate). That is one way of stating why an ethical conclusion cannot be inferred from factual premises, which takes us back to the *is/ought* passage.

An interesting sidelight of the naturalist/anti-naturalist dispute in ethics is that some metaphysical *super*-naturalists (e.g., orthodox traditional theists) defend the doctrine that good may be identified with what God commands (the divine-command theory), and *that* is a species of ethical naturalism (theological naturalism). Critics of the theory, such as the Earl of **Shaftesbury** and **Francis Hutcheson** (who were themselves traditional theists), point out that if we made good or right to *consist in* being commanded by God, then it would be perfectly idle or trivial to ask whether God commands what is good or right. The answer would be "God commands what God commands." These (and other) philosophers anticipate Moore's open-question argument by nearly two centuries. A distinctly non-trivial but disquieting consequence of the theory, according to its critics, is that God might have commanded that humans treat each other with maximum cruelty (or something equally detestable), inasmuch as there would be nothing beyond God's arbitrary will by which to judge his commands. *See also* CLARKE, SAMUEL; CUDWORTH, RALPH; WOLLASTON, WILLIAM.

– J –

JACOBITES. The Jacobites were supporters of King James II of England (James VII of Scotland) and, later, of his son (James Francis Stuart, the *Old Pretender*) and grandson (Charles Edward Stuart, the *Young Pretender*) in their efforts to retain or regain the English (or, after 1707, the British) crown. The name *Jacobite* comes from *Iacobus,* the Latin equivalent of *James* (the Greek form is ἰάκωβος). Charles II, James's older brother and immediate predecessor on the throne, was sympathetic to Roman Catholicism, but was discreet about it. James, on the other hand, offended many people by his open support of that religion and by his foolishly imperious ways. The English monarch was, after all, the Defender of the Faith, which had been officially Protestant since the reign of Henry VIII, i.e., for about 150 years. In any event, James was deposed by the English Parliament and succeeded by the Protestants William and Mary—a move that galvanized the groups that were to become Jacobites: Roman Catholics, Scots (mainly but not wholly from the Highlands), and English sympathizers, who tended to hold absolutist views about monarchy and the church.

Beginning shortly after the accession of William and Mary (1689), Jacobites mounted several campaigns to restore by force the (rightful, as they believed) Stuart succession. None of these efforts had any realistic chance of success, and some were aborted almost as soon as they began. The *Rising of '45*, led by Bonnie Prince Charlie (the Young Pretender), notched a few tactical victories but in the end was ruthlessly put down by the English army at Culloden, in the Scottish Highlands, in April 1746. In every one of their inchoate rebellions, the Jacobites were egged on by foreign powers, most notably France and Spain, which hoped to weaken Britain's military presence elsewhere. And without exception, the Jacobites were dupes of their European "allies," who uniformly failed to provide the support they had promised. For practical purposes, the tragedy at Culloden Moor put an end to Jacobite military operations against the government in London, though there were Stuart Pretenders into the 19th century.

David Hume had Jacobite friends (and even some relatives), but like most Lowland Scots, he opposed the goals of the Jacobites. See his "Of the Protestant Succession" in *Essays Moral, Political, and Literary.*

JUSTICE. Justice is the most important and the most extensively analyzed of the **virtues** that Hume classifies as "artificial," which comprise also promise-keeping, allegiance, the laws of nations, modesty, and good manners (THN, 577; 3.3.1.9). In calling justice an artificial virtue, Hume does not mean either that its origin is contrary to human nature or that the rules of justice are merely arbitrary. (See, for example, THN, 484; 3.2.2.19.) He means, rather, that the good that comes of justice depends on schemes, conventions, contrivances— i.e., *artifices*—established by human beings. Apart from such social arrangements, an individual act of justice (e.g., requiring a poor citizen to pay a legal debt to a rich one) may provoke indignation rather than approval and, *by itself*, do more harm than good. It is the *whole scheme* of laws and rules that works to the advantage of society (THN, 579; 3.3.1.12). By contrast, the *natural* virtues—beneficence, for example—do not depend on contrivance or artifice (THN, 574; 3.3.1.1). In EPM (307–8; 173.9), Hume concedes that, given the ambiguity of the word *natural*, it is pointless to labor the question whether justice is natural or not. Since there is no issue of substance involved, this dispute is one of several that he labels "merely verbal." *See* VIRTUE for further discussion of natural and artificial virtues. *See also* NATURE/NATURAL.

Hume locates the origin of justice in two general facts—one about the natural world and one about human nature. We would not require rules of justice if nature provided so abundantly for our needs and desires that competition would be wholly unnecessary, or if human nature were so purely benevolent that we would be as careful of others as we are of ourselves. On the other hand, justice would be impossible if we were so unremittingly selfish (and stupid) as never to consider the needs and wishes of others. Justice is *needed* because the goods required by human beings are in limited supply; and it is *possible* because human beings are not unmitigatedly selfish. (See THN, 494–95; 3.2.2.17; and EPM, 183–85; 83–85.)

Although Hume rejects the egoist's claim that all voluntary human acts are motivated solely by self-interest, he recognizes that human beings typically exhibit only a "confin'd generosity," i.e., generosity directed toward family and close friends. Indeed, Hume sounds almost Hobbesian when he describes human greed—the impulse to acquire all the goods and possessions we can for ourselves and those closest to us—as "insatiable, perpetual, universal, and directly destructive of society" (THN, 492; 3.2.2.12). We cannot eradicate or radically alter this propensity in human nature; we can only change its direction by reflecting on how best to satisfy it and thereby bring it under some measure of control. Upon reflection, we see that we would serve our own interests better by cooperation than by unfettered avidity and unrestrained competition.

Having shown that the original motive for establishing rules of justice is self-interest (or, better, *enlightened* self-interest), Hume proceeds to explain how the *moral* approval of justice arises. Very simply, it is *sympathy* with public interest that leads us to regard obeying the rules of justice as *virtuous* and breaking them as *vicious*. Education and nurture, both public and private, are needed to foster, extend, and refine our feelings of approbation or disapprobation about keeping or flouting the rules of justice; but those artificial inducements can only assist what nature herself has provided—namely, a capacity for the sympathy that underlies moral distinctions (see, e.g., THN, 500; 3.2.2.25). "Tho' justice be artificial, the sense of its morality is natural" (THN, 619; 3.3.6.4). We acquire, by degrees, the ability to take a "general" view (as opposed to an "interested" view) of the actions of persons with whom we have no relation of blood or friendship or nationality. We come to detest as iniquitous a flagrant injustice visited upon a complete stranger in a distant land. It is implausible (at best) to claim (as "Hobbists" do) that such apparently disinterested sentiments can be reduced, without remainder, to wholly self-interested impulses (see EPM, 296–98; 165–67). To be sure, it is easier—more automatic, we might say—to condemn injustice done to our limited circle of family and friends; but we learn to correct our sentiments just as we correct our **perceptions** (we learn, for example, that a large object seems small when viewed from a distance). At least, we learn to correct our *language* when our sentiments prove intractable (THN, 582; 3.3.1.16).

Hume's account of the rules of justice centers on the notion of *property*—how it is acquired, held, and transferred—because the fixing of such rules is by far the most important requirement for establishing human society. In the course of his discussion, Hume criticizes the commonly held view of justice as "giving every one his due" (a definition as old as Plato's *Republic*) or some variation of it. This view supposes—fallaciously, as Hume argues—that *right* and *property* (what one is *due* or *owed*) exist antecedent to justice and, indeed, are presupposed by justice. In fact, Hume tries to show, the opposite is true: The very idea of property or right is intelligible only when conventions or social arrangements about justice exist. The relation between a person and his or her property is not natural, but moral and depends on justice. "Our property is nothing but those goods, whose constant possession is establish'd by the laws of society; that is, by the laws of justice" (THN, 491; 3.2.2.11). Hume uses a similar line of reasoning to rebut the "contractarian" theory (not Hume's term)—espoused by **Thomas Hobbes**, **John Locke**, and **Jean-Jacques Rousseau**, for example—that society owes its origin to a contract or covenant entered into by prospective citizens, who mutually promise to obey such laws of justice as may be enacted. This explanation is impossible, Hume contends, because the obligation to keep promises arises only from human conventions, specifically rules of justice. (See THN, 489–90; 3.2.2.9–10.) The contractarian "explanation" is topsy-turvy in that it presupposes the very thing it is supposed to explain.

– K –

KAMES, LORD. *See* HOME, HENRY.

KANT, IMMANUEL (1724–1804). Regarded by some as the greatest philosopher since Aristotle (and, consequently, the greatest philosopher ever to offer an opinion on any aspect of Hume's philosophy), the Prussian Immanuel Kant was both an admirer and a critic of Hume. He defends Hume against critics who, in his opinion, misunderstood Hume's doctrines, especially about **causation** (he singles out **Thomas Reid** and **James Beattie** as deserving a scolding); but he argues that Hume's notion of the cause-effect relation is truncated. "That acute man" (as Kant described Hume) saw clearly that the relation between cause and effect is not *analytic* (Kant's term, not Hume's); i.e., the relation is not purely formal or logical or definitional, as it is, for example, in the statement "All roses are flowers." When we analyze the subject ("roses"), we find the predicate ("flowers"). When Hume realized that we cannot find the effect in the cause merely by analysis, he concluded that the relation between cause and effect must be contingent. For Kant, Hume's account is half-right: the first part is right, the second part is wrong. The causal relation is not analytic, but neither is it contingent.

Kant's own theory of **knowledge** (as set out in his *Critique of Pure Reason*, first published in 1781) gets labyrinthine and difficult in its details, but the general lines of the theory are reasonably straightforward. Against Hume, who allows only two kinds of judgments (or propositions, as we would say)—**relations of ideas and matters of fact**—Kant proposes a third variety, which he calls *synthetic a priori*. These propositions are not purely formal (i.e., they have content), but they are known a priori (i.e., they are not known by experience, and they are necessarily true). They have to do, mainly, with the general conditions of human experience and knowledge—conditions that are not derived from experience but are, rather, presupposed by experience. For our purposes, the most interesting of these a priori pre-conditions (which Kant calls *transcendental*) is the category of cause. Kant argues that our **experience** would be impossible if its raw materials (given by sensation) were not organized according to the law of causation. (This is the nub of Kant's "answer" to Hume, an "answer" that continues to provoke debate.)

In brief, Kant holds that knowledge involves both data given by sensation, on the one hand, and the organizing, classifying activity of the mind, or **reason**, on the other. This means that Kant gives Hume—and the empiricists generally—high marks on the first requirement but low marks on the second. That is, the empiricists recognize the indispensable role of experience but fail to see that *reason* makes experience intelligible. Rationalists have the mirror-image strengths and weaknesses. In Kant's famous slogan, "Concepts without percepts are empty [score one for the empiricists]; percepts without concepts are blind [this one goes to the rationalists]." In this way, Kant claims to incorporate the legitimate insights of both the empiricists and the rationalists, without adopting the mistakes of either. Would Hume have been favorably impressed by Kant's synthesis? We can only conjecture, but it seems likely that he would have regarded Kant's notion of synthetic a priori knowledge as nonsensical—a kind of round square. (One commentator [L. W. Beck] has argued that Hume treats the causal principle—roughly, that every event has a cause—as *functionally* a priori and not as an empirically falsifiable hypothesis. "A priori is as a priori does" is Beck's summary of Hume's actual position.)

KEMP SMITH, NORMAN (1872–1958). Born in Glasgow, Scotland, the subject of this entry was christened Norman Duncan Smith but changed his surname to *Kemp Smith* after his marriage to Amy Kemp in 1910. His early writings (e.g., the two *Mind* pieces on Hume) were published under the name *Norman Smith*. More than any other single scholar, Kemp Smith discredited the picture of Hume as a merely destructive skeptic. On Kemp Smith's reading, Hume is a naturalist who rejects the primacy of **reason** in human **knowledge** and conduct. It is not **skepticism** to find the spring of human activity (including cognition) in custom and habit rather than in reasoning. Reason has an important—but ancillary—role in human life. Other Hume scholars have challenged many of the specific points of Kemp Smith's "naturalistic" Hume, and even the usefulness or accuracy of the term *naturalism* to describe Hume's position; but no one doubts the importance of his contribution to a more balanced picture of Hume.

The details of Kemp Smith's reconstruction of Hume are found mainly in his two *Mind* articles of 1905 and his book *The Philosophy of David Hume: A Critical Study of Its Origins and Central Doctrines*, first published in 1941. Kemp Smith was an indefatigable scholar in the history of philosophy, publishing highly influential works on **René Descartes** and **Immanuel Kant**, and translating Kant's monumental *Kritik der reinen Vernunft* into English (as *Critique of Pure Reason*).

KNAVE, THE SENSIBLE. *See* SENSIBLE KNAVE, THE.

KNOWLEDGE. Philosophers and ordinary people agree that there is a difference between *knowing* something and (merely) *believing* it, but only the philosophers (or some of them) try to say precisely wherein the difference consists. Hume uses the word *knowledge* in a strict sense and a loose sense, but he manages to keep them straight. Strictly speaking, knowledge always involves *certainty* as an essential element. Empiricists and rationalists share this conception of knowledge in the strict sense, although they differ about the sorts of things we can know in the strict sense. They all agree that the propositions of mathematics are certain. For example, to deny that $(3 \times 5) = (30 \div 2)$ would involve one in self-contradiction. The rationalists and the empiricist **John Locke**—*but not Hume*—accord the same status of logical incontrovertibility to the causal principle (*nothing comes out of nothing*). Hume contends that denying a causal connection—or even denying *all* causal connections—never entails self-contradiction (though such denials may be false as a matter of fact). *See* EMPIRICISM AND RATIONALISM; CAUSATION.

The overall title of part 3 of book 1 of THN is "Of Knowledge and Probability," but only one of the 16 sections of this part is devoted explicitly to knowledge. Hume is primarily interested in probability, and more specifically the relation of **cause** and effect and how we come to believe in that relation. He reminds the reader many times that the cause-effect relation is not one of the four **relations** that afford us certain knowledge. "All certainty arises from the comparison of ideas . . ." (THN, 79; 1.3.3.2)—or, in the language of EHU, from the *relations of ideas*. Propositions expressing relations of ideas are certain because they are factually empty; i.e., they assert nothing about the real world beyond ideas. This position echoes Locke's definition of knowledge in the unqualified sense: "*the perception of the connexion and agreement, or disagreement and repugnancy of any of our Ideas*" (*Essay*, 525.§2; italics are in Locke's text).

In the interests of accuracy and completeness, we should note that of the four relations that "can be the objects of knowledge and certainty"—resemblance, contrariety, degrees in quality, and proportions in quantity or number—the first three "fall more properly under the province of intuition than demonstration" (THN, 70; 1.3.1.2). For example, we can see directly that two circular objects resemble each other in shape or that one object is a decidedly deeper shade of blue than a second. This is evidence, if we needed it, that Hume does not restrict certainty to what can be expressed as analytic or formally true propositions. It is true, however, that he is more interested in "proportions in quantity or number"—i.e., in mathematics—than in what we might call perceptual intuitions. (For a fuller discussion, *see* RELATIONS.) In EHU Hume replaces the sevenfold classification of relations in THN with a simpler, less confusing division of "All the objects of human reason or enquiry"—namely, **relations of ideas and matters of fact** (EHU, 25; 108.1).

It is interesting that in THN Hume declines to place geometry with algebra and arithmetic as satisfying the requirement of "perfect exactness and certainty," because geometry is too closely tied to "the general appearance of the objects" with which it deals (THN, 71; 1.3.1.5; cf. 45; 1.2.4.17). However, by the time he wrote EHU, Hume had come to see that geometry is quite as "ideal" as algebra and arithmetic. The Pythagorean theorem expresses a relation between the hypotenuse and the sides of a right triangle and would retain its certainty even if there had never been a triangle in nature (EHU, 25; 108.1). This change of mind reflects Hume's clearer understanding of geometry; it does not signify any change of doctrine about the sharp distinction between relations of ideas and matters of fact. These two classes of propositions are mutually exclusive; i.e., no member of one class is also a member of the other. They are, moreover, jointly exhaustive; i.e., every meaningful proposition is a member of one or the other of these two classes. At the very end of EHU, Hume reaffirms his views about that dichotomy: If a book contains no abstract reasoning about quantity or number and no experiential reasoning about matter of fact and existence, then "it can contain nothing but sophistry and illusion" (165; 211.24).

Having established that knowledge in the strict sense and probability are radically distinct, Hume does not hesitate to speak of our *knowledge* of human nature or of our *knowledge* of the cause-effect relation (which is never discerned by a priori reason and, consequently, is never entirely certain). His frequent use of *knowledge* in a looser sense is a concession to the requirements of style (how awkward it would be to avoid using the word except in its strict sense!) and conforms to ordinary usage. We are intuitively certain that a triangle has three sides, and we are demonstratively certain that the interior angles of a Euclidean triangle are equal to two right angles. But we are also practically certain that a heavy piece of iron will fall if we release it, even though we learn that fact from experience. Hume recognizes distinctions of that sort and proposes terms to mark them.

Hume never denies that we have only two ways of justifying a proposition—by a priori reason or by experience. Thus, the division of human reason into *knowledge and probability* (by Locke, for example) is strictly correct. However, it seems ridiculous to say that it is only probable that the sun will rise tomorrow or that all men must die. Accordingly, Hume suggests a threefold classification that both preserves "the common signification of words" and more faithfully marks the several degrees of evidence we encounter. He distinguishes human reason into three kinds: "*that from knowledge, from proofs, and from probabilities*" (THN, 124; 1.3.11.2; italics are in Hume's text). *Knowledge* arises from the comparison of ideas. **Proofs** are those arguments based on cause and effect that have no negative instances whatever and are, consequently, free from doubt and uncertainty. Our beliefs in human mortality and the rising of the sun are founded on proofs. *Probability* covers those cases in which the positive evidence outweighs the negative but not "infallibly" (i.e., not without exception). When we toss a pair of dice, we reasonably expect to get a number greater than two, but we roll enough snake-eyes to render our confidence considerably less than perfect. Readers may object that *proofs* do not constitute a genuine third category but are only very high probabilities, inasmuch as they do not admit of demonstration. Hume has, in effect, conceded the point in advance; but he still regards the *proof/probability* distinction as useful.

In defending himself against the charge of denying the causal principle (that whatever begins to exist must have a cause of existence), Hume observes that philosophers divide evidence into *four* kinds: *intuitive, demonstrative, sensible, and moral*. He goes on to say that these categories mark differences but do not signify higher and lower levels of certainty. "*Moral Certainty* may reach as *high* a Degree of Assurance as *Mathematical*; and our Senses are surely to be comprised amongst the clearest and most convincing of all Evidences" (*A Letter*, 118; italics are in Hume's text). Whether it is possible to reconcile all the various things Hume says about knowledge is a question we cannot engage here. We suspect that it is possible, if we take proper account of context and add a bit of charity.

A few historical notes: We will take very brief looks backward and forward from Hume's time. It is not possible in a brief entry to do even a cursory sketch of pre- or post-Hume theory of knowledge. We touch on a few items by way of illustration. Readers interested in more details about the topics mentioned should consult an encyclopedia of philosophy.

Philosophers have been keenly interested in the theory of knowledge (or *epistemology*, from the Greek word for *knowledge*, ἐπιστήμη [*epistémē*]) since ancient times. In his dialogue *Theaetetus* (written about 2,400 years ago), Plato examines—and rejects—three candidates for the honorific *knowledge*: (a) perception, (b) true judgment, and (3) true belief accompanied by an account or explanation (a λόγος [*logos*]). The third of these has been resurrected in recent times under the name *justified true belief* (or JTB for short), which purportedly specifies the sufficient and necessary conditions for knowledge: Any state of mind that satisfies these conditions is knowledge, and any state of mind that fails to satisfy one or more of the conditions is not knowledge. As we might suspect, the *justification* condition causes the most trouble. A true unjustified belief is just as true as a true justified belief—a point that Socrates makes in Plato's dialogue *Meno*.

Does a *justified* true belief always count as knowledge? To answer "yes," we must deal with what have come to be known as "Gettier examples" (after the American philosopher Edmund Gettier), which purport to show that a person may have a justified true belief that *p* (some proposition) without thereby knowing that *p*. The following is an adaptation of a familiar example. Consider Sturdley and Hocker, who are competing for the same job. Sturdley has very good reasons for thinking that Hocker—and not he himself—will get the job. He also knows that Hocker has ten coins in his pocket. He concludes, justifiably, that the person who gets the job will have ten coins in his pocket (call this proposition *p*). To his great surprise, Sturdley himself gets the job. Further, without knowing it, Sturdley also has ten coins in his pocket. So, Sturdley is justified in believing *p*, but he does not *know p* because he has no idea that he himself has ten coins in his pocket. His being correct was freakish or a matter of luck. Knowledge requires that the justifying evidence be relevant to the truth of p—or so most philosophers would contend. (Against all odds, I might correctly guess the number of notes in Gustav Mahler's extremely long third symphony [assuming that we had dealt with any uncertainty about what counts as a note], but no one would say that I *knew* the actual number of notes.)

Philosophers have shown great ingenuity in proliferating Gettier-type counterexamples to the JTB definition of knowledge, as well as in suggesting ways to make it Gettier-proof—for example, by adding a *fourth* condition to the standard three. For many philosophers, the search for a unitary conception of knowledge is misguided. They point out that a belief is not a solitary, discrete item that can be assessed independently of other beliefs. Rather, a belief is justified—or not—by the way it fits, or fails to fit, into an immensely large, interconnected network or web of other beliefs, theories, assumptions, presuppositions, etc. These philosophers may be holists or coherentists or pragmatists (classes that overlap but do not coincide). On the other hand, some philosophers still hold to various forms of *foundationalism*, according to which some beliefs must be self-evident or in any case not in need of justification.

Willard Van Orman Quine, one of the best-known Anglo-American philosophers of the last 50 years, proposes that epistemology be "naturalized"—i.e., be turned into an account of how human beings actually learn, with no pretense of establishing an unshakable foundation for knowledge or of disclosing the ultimate nature of reality. This would make epistemology a part of psychology (or perhaps a mix of psychology and anthropology). Quine mentions Hume as a (qualified) earlier practitioner of naturalized epistemology. Hume does in fact see his science of human nature as primarily a descriptive enterprise, which studies (among many other things) how people learn to discriminate good from bad ways of doing things and thinking about things (in politics and morals as well as in farming and carpentry). This means that norms or standards emerge from longer or shorter periods of trial and error—i.e., from experience over the long haul. Nevertheless, Quine's project and Hume's differ in significant ways, as Quine recognizes. (Quine's essay "Epistemology Naturalized" is one of the "other essays" in his book *Ontological Relativity and Other Essays*.)

– L –

LIBERTY AND NECESSITY. In modern terminology, we would speak of *freedom and determinism*. The main source for Hume's view on this topic is "Of Liberty and Necessity," which is the title of similar but not identical sections in both THN and EHU (THN, 399–412; 2.3.1–2; EHU, 80–103; 148–64). His principal objective, which he describes in EHU as a "reconciling project," is to show that human freedom is possible in a world governed strictly by causal laws; that the contrary supposition turns upon a misunderstanding of the terms *liberty* and *necessity*. Because freedom is almost universally taken to be a necessary condition of moral responsibility (i.e., a person is not morally responsible for an act he or she did not perform freely), Hume's project is (by implication) to show that moral responsibility is possible in a deterministic world. Very simply, a person is free if he is able to do what he chooses to do; if he is not able to do what he chooses, then he is not free. The truth or falsity of the theory of determinism has nothing to do with a person's freedom or the lack of it. Hume also wants to show that human volitions and actions are as susceptible of causal explanation as the motions of bodies, but he reminds us of the essentially innocuous character of **causation** (i.e., the "constant union" or constant conjunction of objects or events).

According to the doctrine of necessity, every event is so precisely and fully determined by its causes that it could not have been in any way or to any degree different from what it actually is. Hume takes it for granted that the operations of material bodies are governed by such strict deterministic laws. Whether that assumption is true and whether it is "universally allowed," as he claims, may be doubted; but he is entitled to suppose that *most* of his readers would not object. Human behavior is not so obviously the product of necessity as the motions of physical objects, but that is because the subjects being studied (i.e., human beings) are more complicated than rocks and the like. If we knew the principles of human nature more perfectly, we could discern causal connections between motive and action as surely as those between physical force and motion—or so Hume holds. But even with our imperfect knowledge of the psychological laws of volition and motivation, we still very often have a good idea of what someone is going to do—based on that person's habits and on the uniformity of human actions generally. Even when we are surprised by some unexpected action, it is our ignorance—not the actual absence of causal laws—that accounts for the seeming irregularities in human behavior. If we knew enough, we would see that apparent anomalies are explainable by variations in causes. The word *chance*, when taken to refer to an object or event without any cause, is "a mere negative word" and denotes nothing that actually exists. When we speak of something that happens *by chance*, we mean that it happens without plan or intention, *not* that it has no cause.

Hume points out that the sort of necessity he is talking about is not inimical to morality; it is, rather, presupposed by moral judgments. We judge actions virtuous or vicious only insofar as we take them to proceed from "some *cause* in the character and disposition of the person who performed them" (EHU, 98; 161.29; italics are in Hume's text). Punishments and rewards make no sense apart from the supposition of a causal connection between the person and the blameworthy or praiseworthy act he or she has performed.

To reinforce his claim that necessity applies to the *moral* sphere (i.e., human behavior) no less than to the *natural* sphere (i.e., the operations and motions of physical objects), and to reassure his readers that nothing dire can result from this assimilation, Hume reminds us that *cause* means no more than *regular sequences* and the associated inferences generated in our mind. We never discern, either by the senses or by **reason**, any necessary connection between cause and effect. The necessity that we attribute to the cause-effect relation is "nothing but a determination of the mind to pass from one object to its usual attendant" (THN, 400; 2.3.1.4). (*See* CAUSE and the discussion of *necessary connexion*.) This means that there is but one kind of causation, whether we are dealing with physics or human behavior, and that the specter of some external power forcing us to act against our will should be banished.

The core of Hume's "project" in "Liberty and Necessity" is to demonstrate that human freedom is perfectly compatible with the operation of exceptionless causal laws. This doctrine is referred to (though not by Hume) as *compatibilism*. The American philosopher William James coined the somewhat misleading phrase *soft determinism* to describe this theory—misleading because it may suggest, falsely, that the determinism involved is less than strict. In James's usage, the determinism is *softened* because it (allegedly) does not entail the loss of freedom and responsibility. (*Compatibilism* and *soft determinism* are not strict synonyms. Both the compatibilist and the soft determinist hold that determinism does not exclude human freedom. The soft determinist also holds that the theory of determinism is true; the compatibilist may or may not hold that the theory of determinism is true.) The *hard determinist* bites the bullet, so to speak, and accepts the "hard" consequence that freedom—and, with it, moral responsibility—is largely an illusion. Obviously, Hume is not a hard determinist.

The nub of the compatibilist position is straightforward. A person is free if he is able to do what he wills. If he chooses to move, he may do so; if he chooses not to move, he may refrain from moving. More abstractly, liberty is "*a power of acting or not acting, according to the determinations of the will*" (EHU, 95; 159.23; italics are in Hume's text). According to this theory, the question of liberty or freedom has nothing whatever to do with the question of necessity or determinism, which is about the causes that produce a volition. Whether an act was free depends on whether it was or was not *coerced*, not whether it was *caused*. *All* acts are caused, but only some are coerced (where *coerce* is construed to comprise both *restraint*—preventing a person from doing what he wants to do—and *constraint*—forcing a person to do something he does not want to do.)

Hume describes liberty in the proper sense as *hypothetical*. Compatibilists take this to mean that a person who does, say, A could have done something else—say, *B—IF* she had so chosen. And that is the essence of liberty or freedom. Critics complain that this "solution" is illusory. Assuming that no coercion is involved, a person could have acted differently *if* she had so chosen; but if determinism is true, she could not have *chosen* differently. That is, given precisely the same circumstances, she would have chosen exactly as she did. In other words, the critic concludes, she could have acted differently if she could have satisfied an impossible condition. Some compatibilists, especially more recent ones, reject the hypothetical construal of freedom/liberty and accept the consequence that A could not have acted differently. If A did what she wanted to do, without undue manipulation (overt coercion is ruled out *ex hypothesi*), that is enough to qualify as free.

Most critics of compatibilism are *libertarians* (*not* in the political sense). They argue that persons or agents are able to make decisions that are not fully determined by antecedent conditions. In THN Hume calls this the "liberty of indifference," which he dismisses as chimerical. The only real liberty, Hume argues, is the "liberty of spontaneity," which is the hypothetical freedom already described. (This so-called issue of free will still divides opinion sharply.)

A historical note: Hume's account of liberty and necessity was anticipated by **Thomas Hobbes** and **John Locke**. Hume's discussion, and some of his examples, follow Locke closely. It should be said that at least a few Hume scholars object to assimilating Hume's treatment of liberty and necessity to the standard compatibilist theory. That is not because Hume's account is not compatibilist (in some obvious sense, it is), but because it is significantly richer in exploring some conditions of moral responsibility that cannot be read off the compatibility thesis. This side of Hume's analysis is more apparent in EHU than it is in THN.

LOCKE, JOHN (1632–1704). The English Locke was the first of the "Big Three" of British **empiricism**, the other two being the Irish **George Berkeley** and the Scottish David Hume. It is hard to overstate the depth and range of Locke's influence on subsequent thought. His *Essay Concerning Human Understanding* (first published in December 1689) and his *Two Treatises of Government* (1690)—together with such lesser works as *A Letter Concerning Toleration* (1689) and *The Reasonableness of Christianity* (1695)—have left their mark on philosophy, **religion**, and politics in all of Europe and the New World. Moreover, the *spirit* of Locke's inquiries—a search for the truth unfettered by submission to external authorities and relying only on **experience** and **reason**—was cause to rejoice in the 17th and 18th centuries. Hume celebrates that happy state of affairs by using a phrase from Tacitus as the title-page epigraph of books 1 and 2 of THN: "*Rara temporum felicitas, ubi sentire, quæ velis; & quæ sentias, dicere licet*" [The rare good fortune of an age in which we may feel what we wish and say what we feel].

Although **Thomas Hobbes** (44 years older than Locke) develops his philosophy along broadly empiricist lines, it is Locke who first attempts to provide a detailed and comprehensive empiricist account of the structure and workings of the human mind. He follows the French philosopher-mathematician **René Descartes** in taking *ideas* as the direct or immediate objects of consciousness; but he departs from Descartes in rejecting **innate ideas** and in limiting (without altogether eliminating) the power of reason to find truth a priori (i.e., apart from experience). Locke the Empiricist still retains some distinctively *rationalist* doctrines—e.g., that we know with intuitive certainty that whatever begins to exist must have a **cause** of **existence** (sometimes expressed in the Latin phrase *ex nihilo nihil fit* [out of nothing, nothing comes]). Hume directly challenges the claim that we know the causal principle by intuitive reason, though he does not challenge the truth of the principle. More generally, both Locke and Hume characterize genuine, unqualified *knowledge* in essentially the same way as Descartes, even when they disagree with Descartes (or with each other) about whether some particular proposition actually qualifies as knowledge in the strict sense. They agree, at least in broad terms, about the *definition* of knowledge, but disagree about the sorts of things covered by that definition.

In a preliminary note to readers of the *Essay*, Locke recounts how a fruitless discussion with some friends led him to reflect on the source of the impasse they had reached so quickly. He concluded that they had launched into a substantive enquiry without determining whether the human mind was fitted for such an undertaking. Until we investigate the powers and limits of the understanding, we will always be liable to construct explanations and theories from fantasy rather than fact. Accordingly, Locke's purpose is to inquire into the origin, certainty, and extent of knowledge, as well as the grounds and degrees of **belief**, opinion, and assent (*Essay*, 43.§2). This he does in almost 750 pages of rambling, repetitious, inconsistent—and, withal, amazing and admirable—philosophical reasoning.

Ideas are the fundamental elements—the building blocks—of any form of consciousness, whether knowledge or belief or fantasy or whatever. Where do they come from? Before even starting to give his own answer to the question, Locke carefully considers, and rejects, the only serious competitor; namely, innate ideas. We do not have any innate ideas. This means that all our ideas come from *experience*, specifically from either *sensation* or *reflection*. Our senses provide us with ideas of yellow, white, heat, cold, hard, soft, bitter, sweet, etc.

By reflection we acquire ideas of the operations of our own minds: thinking, doubting, believing, willing, and the like, "which could not be had from things without" (*Essay*, 105.§4). Locke adds that, although reflection has nothing directly to do with external objects, it is sufficiently similar to sensation to be called the *Internal Sense*. From these two "fountains"—sensation and reflection or, alternatively, the external and internal senses—come all the ideas we have or can have.

Locke divides ideas of both types—sensation and reflection—into *simple* and *complex*. A simple idea "contains in it nothing but *one uniform Appearance*, or Conception in the mind, and is not distinguishable into different *Ideas*" (*Essay*, 119.§1; italics are in Locke's text). A complex idea may be defined as one that is not simple. Examples of simple ideas of sensation: a color seen, a sound heard, an odor smelled, etc. Examples of simple ideas of reflection: thinking, willing, perceiving, etc. Some simple ideas come by way of both sensation and reflection: **pleasure**, pain, power, **existence**, and unity. The ideas of ordinary objects of **perception** are complex. An apple is red, round, firm, sweet, etc. Gratitude is an example of a complex idea of reflection. Two things may be noted about Locke's simple-complex dichotomy: All ideas whatsoever, even the most complicated and fantastic, may be resolved into simple ideas; and the human mind, with all its powers of **imagination**, is not capable of inventing even one simple idea from scratch. We get them from sensation or reflection, or we do not have them. (Hume generally agrees with Locke on how we come by simple perceptions, but *see* MISSING SHADE OF BLUE.)

Locke goes into great detail in describing the various kinds of simple ideas and the ways in which the mind combines them into complex ideas, which he classifies under three main heads: Complex ideas of Modes, of Substances, and of Relations. (Hume follows Locke in this classification of complex ideas: THN, 13; 1.1.5.7.) For Locke's influential theory of the so-called primary and secondary qualities of objects, *see* PRIMARY AND SECONDARY QUALITIES.

Although ideas are the ultimate materials of consciousness, they do not, by themselves, constitute *knowledge*. Knowledge always involves a relation between ideas. For Locke, knowledge in the full, unqualified sense is either *intuitive* or *demonstrative*. We know intuitively—immediately and certainly, without having to think about it—that white is not black, that three is greater than two, that a circle is not a triangle, etc. Intuitive knowledge is the indispensable base on which demonstrative knowledge rests. We know that the angles of a Euclidean triangle are equal to two right angles, but not intuitively. We reach that conclusion by a series of steps, which are connected by intuition.

Locke allows a third degree of knowledge—the *sensitive* (i.e., based on sense perception)—but he frets about it because it falls short of the certainty of intuitive and demonstrative knowledge. And that is because sensitive knowledge refers to the properties of independently existing objects; or—to be accurate—purported sensitive knowledge refers to *what we take to be* the properties of independently existing objects. We do not really know what such objects are in themselves; we know only our own ideas. Locke concludes that although sensitive knowledge does not satisfy the criteria for knowledge in the strict sense, it is close enough, and it is all we need. (The Irish philosopher **George Berkeley** argues that any philosophy is doomed to incoherence and self-contradiction if it posits the existence of an unperceivable and unknowable material substance supposedly underlying such ordinary qualities as color and shape.)

Hume's account of "the objects of human reason or enquiry" incorporates the basic divisions of the Lockean version, though not in precisely the same language. According to Hume, every proposition that is either intuitively or demonstratively certain falls under the category **relations of ideas**. Propositions lacking those degrees of certainty fall under the category **matters of fact** (EHU, 25; 108.1).

Although Locke holds that we are directly aware only of our own ideas, he thinks that we have certain knowledge of a few matters that clearly transcend our ideas. Each person knows with intuitive certainty that he or she exists (as **René Descartes** insists in his *Meditations*), and everyone who considers the matter knows with intuitive certainty that bare nothing cannot produce real being (*ex nihilo nihil fit*). Put these two intuitive certainties together and, with a bit of discursive reasoning, we can demonstrate the existence of an eternal, most-powerful, most-knowing, underived being—namely, God. In fact, Locke asserts, we are more rationally certain of God's existence than we are of the existence of other finite persons. Locke's purported demonstration of the existence of God goes dead against Hume's contention that we know about cause and effect only from experience and that no **matter of fact** whatever (including the existence of God) can be demonstrated (see, e.g., EHU, 163–65; 209–11). Since Locke, too, holds that our idea of cause and effect comes from experience, not a few readers have wondered whether Locke can consistently embrace the law of universal causation as intuitively certain.

Descartes raised the so-called mind-body problem about 50 years before Locke's *Essay* was published, but Locke's doctrine of **personal identity** marks the beginning of the modern discussion of that topic. What does it mean for the same person to exist at different times? Note that Locke distinguishes *person* from *man* (or *human being*). A *man* may be characterized as a physiological organism that retains a certain form through time. A *person*, in contrast, is "a thinking intelligent Being, that has reason and reflection, and can consider it self as it self [*sic*], the same thinking thing in different times and places" (*Essay*, 335.9). This account of personal identity has nothing to do with **substance**, either material or immaterial, but with *consciousness* (including memory). Whether consciousness be annexed to any sort of substance is mysterious and, fortunately, irrelevant to the issue. Personal identity depends on being conscious of oneself at different times, and on nothing else. Consider, Locke asks, what would happen if the mind of a prince were to be implanted in the body of a cobbler, and vice versa. Despite the inevitable consternation of the prince's and the cobbler's acquaintances, Locke has no doubt who would be who: The prince would be the person with the *consciousness* of the prince, and the cobbler would be the person with the *consciousness* of the cobbler. One supposes that each of them would be puzzled by his different-looking body and different surroundings.

Locke's theory of personal identity invites comparison with Hume's, which obviously owes something to Locke. While the two accounts agree, for example, in rejecting *substance* as unhelpful or unavailable (for different reasons), they do not represent identical projects. Both philosophers seek to find the essence of personal identity, but they do not start from the same place. Hume devotes most of his efforts to showing how the person or self is constructed out of our experiences—indeed, the self is "a bundle or collection of different perceptions" (THN, 252; 1.4.6.4). On the other hand, Locke shows no interest in providing a genetic account of our idea of a person. In Locke's view, we already know what a person is: a rational, intelligent being (as quoted above). We need only to discover how that gets cashed out. However, the difference just noted may seem less important when the two accounts are set in context. Locke says that *person* is a "Forensick Term" (*Essay*, 346.26); i.e., it has to do with the allocation of responsibility, praise, and blame. Hume stresses the difference between "personal identity, as it regards our thought or imagination, and as it regards our passions or the concern we take in ourselves" (THN, 253; 1.4.6.5). And Hume takes that distinction seriously. When he treats the passions or morals, he takes for granted a more robust, commonsense conception of the self or the person than the narrowly epistemological one we find in "Of Personal Identity."

Hume thinks that his positive theory is, in one respect, more adequate than Locke's—something that Hume claims without mentioning Locke by name. On Locke's view, personal identity is tied exclusively to consciousness, which is, for practical purposes, memory. Hume points out that much of our personal identity lies beyond our actual memories and must be recovered by *causal inferences* from what we do remember or know from other sources (THN, 261–62; 1.4.6.20). For example, we may know from an old photograph that we attended an office party that we had entirely forgotten. The photograph itself may resurrect memories buried over the intervening years. It is not clear from what Locke says that he would object to adding cause and effect to memory as way of establishing personal identity.

Despite his large and obvious debt to Locke, Hume seems eager to point out, and in fact exaggerate, differences, sometimes with gratuitously slighting comments; e.g., about the meaning of the term *idea* and about innate ideas (e.g., EHU, 22n1; 99.9n1). But he shows the gracious side of *le bon David* when he describes Locke as "really a great philosopher and a just and modest reasoner" (in some editions of EHU).

LOGICAL EMPIRICISM. *See* LOGICAL POSITIVISM.

LOGICAL POSITIVISM. Logical positivism (also called *logical empiricism*) was a philosophical movement that arose in western Europe in the 1920s and 1930s, its core being the so-called *Vienna Circle.* Many of the most prominent members of the group emigrated to the United States to escape the murderous depredations of Adolf Hitler's Third Reich (the Nazis). The modifier *logical* serves to distinguish this version of positivism from that of the 19th-century French philosopher-sociologist Auguste Comte (1798–1857), who argues that we should stick to describing observable phenomena and avoid speculation about what is unknowable. This entry focuses mainly on the use that logical positivists make of Hume's philosophy, or a part of that philosophy. Hume is almost unique in being a "traditional" philosopher mentioned favorably by the logical positivists, who dismiss most other such philosophers as fundamentally misguided and bewitched by pseudo-problems.

The phrase *logical empiricism* signifies its historical link to the "classical" empiricism of **George Berkeley** and, especially, David Hume—or, at least, to what its adherents believed to be classical empiricism. Of crucial importance to positivists is Hume's division of "All the objects of human reason or enquiry" into two mutually exclusive and jointly exhaustive categories—**relations of ideas and matters of fact**—sometimes called "**Hume's fork.**" The positivists disembarrass Hume's dichotomy of any suggestion of psychology or introspection (e.g., the derivation of **ideas** from **impressions**), rechristen the "tines" or "prongs" of the fork, and put it to work exposing what they regard as meaningless assertions in metaphysics, **religion**, aesthetics, and (with considerable internal disagreement) **ethics**. They interpret Hume's bifurcation as establishing a criterion of meaning (using the terminology of analytic philosophy in place of Hume's own language): To be cognitively meaningful, a proposition must either be true (or false) as a matter of form (a tautology) or definition (e.g., "a cow is a mammal" or "a triangle has three sides") *or* be empirically verifiable (e.g., "water is heavier than gasoline").

The second half of the criterion—the so-called *verifiability principle*—is the most characteristic doctrine of logical positivism. Positivists use it to brand as meaningless all statements about God or the Absolute or transcendental moral principles or innumerable other matters, inasmuch as statements of this sort cannot be empirically confirmed or disconfirmed. Unfortunately for its defenders, problems about the verifiability principle itself proved to be intractable. In the first place (and this is an obvious if not a fatal objection), the principle itself is neither tautological/analytic nor empirically verifiable, a fact that would seem to make it cognitively meaningless on its own terms. Second, proponents of the principle were never able to formulate the criterion of verifiability so that it would be neither too broad nor too narrow. That is, they could not specify the conditions of verifiability so as to ensure that no "bad" propositions (from metaphysics, for example) were allowed and that no "good" propositions (from science, for example) were excluded. Invariably, the stipulated conditions admitted some supposedly meaningless statements and rejected some plainly good ones. Eventually, the positivists decided that the task was impossible or, at any rate, not worth the cost of continuing the effort.

Besides the Humean "fork" *tautologous* or *empirically verifiable*, positivists find Hume's analysis of **causation** cogent. In particular, they interpret Hume as embracing a *regularity* theory of causation; namely, that causation consists in regular succession of objects or events, and nothing else. That is, they hold that Hume denies any real, objective connection between cause and effect. This reading of Hume is consistent with the positivist creed of sticking to what is observable (a creed, incidentally, that served them very badly in making sense of modern scientific theory). It is still a live issue whether Hume does in fact adopt a regularity theory of causation, with its "thin" relation of mere constant conjunction, or, on the contrary, opts for "thick" objective causal connections.

At the very end of EHU, Hume restates the relations of ideas-matters of fact dichotomy in a more striking and provocative way—one that the polemically inclined positivists would find irresistible. Suppose you open a book ("of divinity or school metaphysics, for instance") and you find that it contains neither abstract reasoning about relations of ideas nor *"experimental reasoning concerning matter of fact and existence. . . . Commit it then to the flames: for it can contain nothing but sophistry and illusion"* (165; 211.34; italics are in Hume's text). It is not surprising that logical positivists would see this passage (and others substantially, if not rhetorically, like it) as an ancestor of their own verifiability principle. However, most scholars find the Hume of the positivists to be a thin, shadowy caricature of the real Hume, who wrote without embarrassment or apology about history, morals, religion, aesthetics, politics, you name it, as well as knowledge, causation, probability, etc. We may suppose that he would be dismayed by the positivists' use of principles they profess to discern in his writings; that he would find their application of the principles narrow, dogmatic, and stifling.

– M –

MALEBRANCHE, NICOLAS (1638–1715). Malebranche is the most famous, the most influential, and the most philosophically gifted of the group of continental thinkers known as *occasionalists*. His influence on Hume in particular is stronger than one might infer from the very few explicit references (ca. half a dozen) to Malebranche in Hume's writings. Hume calls him a Cartesian (i.e., a follower of **René Descartes**); and so he is—with some important differences. Malebranche agrees with Descartes that we perceive and think by means of **ideas**; but, unlike Descartes, he locates these ideas in God. This means that when we perceive physical objects, we are literally aware of ideas in God. This is his doctrine of *vision in God*, which is curious but of no apparent interest to Hume. (It is, on the contrary, of great interest to the Irish empiricist philosopher **George Berkeley**.)

Hume is definitely intrigued (but not persuaded) by Malebranche's occasionalism, which holds that God is the only true **cause** in the universe. This doctrine divests so-called second causes—i.e., natural, finite causes of any sort—of even derivative causal efficacy. Malebranche argues that Cartesian material substance (*res extensa*) is wholly passive, inasmuch as its essence is to be extended, to take up space. It is impossible, therefore, that it could be a cause of anything. Moreover, the mind (or immaterial substance, *res cogitans*) has no intelligible causal connection with either material objects or its own volitions. In other words, neither finite bodies nor minds can function as causes. Since, in Malebranche's view, the causal relation requires a necessary connection between cause and effect, we are driven to the conclusion that God—the omnipotent creator and conserver of all finite beings—is the only true cause. Hume concurs in most of

Malebranche's **skeptical** observations about the impossibility of discerning any causal power connecting objects or events, but he dismisses Malebranche's appeal to God (a *deus ex machina*) as baseless speculation. Indeed, it has been said, no doubt with self-conscious hyperbole, that Hume is Malebranche without God.

MANDEVILLE, BERNARD DE (1670–1733). Mandeville was born in Holland and studied medicine there, but made his name in England writing in English. He is best known for his poem *Fable of the Bees; or, Private Vices, Publick Benefits*, which was initially titled *The Grumbling Hive*. In later editions, Mandeville appended to the poem several essays designed to answer the numerous critics who had attacked him. In the story, all the bees at first pursue their own selfish ends, and the hive prospers; but at the same time they proclaim their commitment to altruism and complain about the immorality of their society. Suddenly, and miraculously, the bees are transformed into true practitioners of what they profess to believe: They become genuinely modest, simple, unpretentious, downright abstemious creatures, whereupon the hive ceases to flourish, loses its vitality, and sinks into insipidity and insignificance.

Moving from the apiary to the human world, Mandeville argues that what we call vices—luxury, avarice, prodigality, vanity, and even theft—actually provide employment for many people and thereby benefit society. Even thieves contribute their bit, spending their purloined booty among any number of merchants and helping to keep locksmiths in business. Our appetite for good food and wine, for luxurious homes, fine clothing, horses, carriages, etc., etc., is essential to the very existence of a prosperous and powerful state. By contrast, the old-fashioned virtues—honesty, self-denial, frugality, discipline—are of scant economic or political value. (It has been noted many times that **Adam Smith** incorporates something like Mandeville's view of the value of selfishness into his own economic theory—though it is purged of Mandeville's thoroughgoing **egoism**.)

Mandeville's economic theory is of a piece with his view of human nature: Human beings are by nature self-seeking, and a good thing, too. But economics apart, it is sheer hypocrisy, Mandeville says, to claim that generosity and benevolence are personal qualities to be admired. In fact, such "virtues" reflect our selfish desire to be thought superior to the common herd. Even so, we need not be stupid. We can realize our own goals better by forming alliances than by going it alone; and so we do. But we never rise above the level of clever self-promotion, which is often best served by tactical concessions to others. The whole business may be greatly facilitated by ingenious politicians who manage to acquire power and push their own schemes by flattering the egos of various groups of citizens.

There is obviously something of **Thomas Hobbes** in Mandeville's story of how societies function, but it is more frankly cynical and demeaning than Hobbes's. Some scholars defend Hobbes against the charge of supposing people to be purely selfish, but there can be no comparable defense of Mandeville. Although Hume includes "Dr. Mandeville" in a short list of philosophers who "have begun to put the science of man on a new footing" (THN, xvii; 5.7), he may have Mandeville in mind when he hotly denounces those who regard benevolence as mere hypocrisy, friendship as a cheat, and in general deny the reality of moral distinctions. When Hume mentions Hobbes and **John Locke** by name a couple of paragraphs later, he adopts a less indignant tone and keeps the discussion at a theoretical level (EPM, 296; 165.3). He is expressly referring to Mandeville in the following passage from "Of Refinement in the Arts": "Is it not very inconsistent for an author to assert in one page, that moral distinctions are inventions of politicians for public interest; and in the next page maintain, that vice is advantageous to the public? And indeed it seems upon any system of morality, little less than a contradiction in terms, to talk of vice, which is in general beneficial to society" (*Essays*, 280).

MATTERS OF FACT. *See* RELATIONS OF IDEAS AND MATTERS OF FACT.

MIND. Hume uses the terms *mind, person, self,* and *soul* more or less interchangeably. They all refer to the faculty (or power or capacity) of human beings to think, feel, and will in a great variety of ways.

In Hume's scheme, the philosophy of mind is practically coextensive with his science of human nature, which includes what we would call epistemology, psychology, ethics, and some parts of anthropology and sociology. It even has an indirect relation to mathematics and the natural sciences, inasmuch as they represent fruits of human understanding. Hume's very wide conception of mind (or human nature) is reflected in the three books of his *Treatise of Human Nature*: "Of the Understanding," "Of the Passions," and "Of Morals." For our purposes, this means that Hume's philosophy of mind pervades this whole dictionary. However, some entries deal with it more directly and specifically than others: *see* PERSONAL IDENTITY; PERCEPTIONS; EXPERIENCE; PASSIONS; MORAL SENSE; CAUSE; BELIEF; LIBERTY AND NECESSITY; VIRTUE.

Today, philosophy of mind still covers a fairly wide range of topics, but it is less comprehensive than it is for Hume. On the other hand, contemporary philosophy of mind deals with issues that Hume either expressly eschews (e.g., the metaphysical status of mind) or, for one reason or another, does not engage. We will take a very brief look at some questions that philosophers of mind continue to debate. *Debate* is an apt term: There are lively, vigorous discussions about virtually *any* topic in the philosophy of mind. To discuss these topics in any detail—or even to *mention* all such topics or subtopics—would obviously be impossible in the space available.

The so-called *mind-body problem* is a legacy of the French philosopher **René Descartes**, who divides reality into two quite disparate kinds of things—minds and bodies. According to Descartes, the essence of mind (*res cogitans*) is thinking, whereas the essence of body (*res extensa*) is extension. (It should be noted that the Latin verb *cogitare* includes all sorts of mental phenomena—believing, doubting, willing, perceiving, imagining, etc., as well as thinking in the narrow sense.) These two substances (as Descartes calls them) seem to have nothing in common. Nevertheless, Descartes insists that they interact. But how? Even friendly readers of Descartes generally agree that he gives no plausible answer to the question but is stuck with an intractable dualism of mind and body. The 17th-century Dutch philosopher Benedict Spinoza holds that thought and extension (which answer to Descartes' mind and body) are not substances at all, but distinct attributes of the one true **substance**—God. Accordingly, mind-body interaction is a pseudo-problem based on a false assumption. The Irish philosopher **George Berkeley** solves (or *dis*solves) the problem by denying the existence of matter (or body), but his immaterialist solution has attracted few other philosophers.

Most contemporary philosophers of mind turn Berkeley on his head. Like Berkeley, they solve the mind-body problem by getting rid of one of the substances, but it is mind rather than body that gets the boot. These philosophers hold (to put it crudely) that the mind can be reduced to the body; hence the term *reductionism* (or *reductivism*). More precisely, this theory holds that any statement about mental phenomena (desires, beliefs, pains, etc.) can be replaced by a statement about something else—i.e., something that makes no reference to anything "mental." "Mental" terms and "physical" terms do not *mean* the same thing, but (according to this theory) they *refer* to the same thing (a state of the brain, for example)—just as "Morning Star" and "Evening Star" have different meanings but refer to the same object, Venus. Reductionism takes a variety of specific forms. According to the *identity theory* (which has many mutations), what may appear to be mental phenomena are in fact identical with physical events or processes (e.g., occurrences in the brain and central nervous system). *Physicalism* has gradually become the preferred name for this species of ontology, since the older term *materialism* may carry some unwanted and misleading connotations. Physicalist theories need not be reductionist, but many are. Reductionist and non-reductionist physicalists agree that only physical entities—e.g., brains and brain states or perhaps their lower-level constituents (molecules, atoms, whatever)—exist; but the non-reductionist holds that the language for mental phenomena cannot be reduced to the language of neurophysiology or, still less, of physics.

Eliminativism, as the name suggests, goes beyond *identifying* mental phenomena with physical events; it denies that such phenomena even exist (it *eliminates* them). We are mistaken, the theory holds, in believing that we believe or desire things. Those categories are vestiges of what is called *folk psychology* and would disappear in a properly regimented scientific theory. Some critics of eliminativism argue that the theory is incoherent, and in any case it seems to fly in the face of common sense. It should be noted that identity theorists do not typically *deny* the existence of mental phenomena; they rather deny that such phenomena are metaphysically distinct from physical states of the body.

Functionalism dates from about 1960 and appears in several guises. It was intended to obviate some of the difficulties in identity theories, among which was a certain parochialism: Why should mental states be *identified* with brain states? Could not the requisite conditions be satisfied in other ways? The most obvious analogy is with a computer: We give the computer a certain "command" (input), and it obliges with a certain result (output), but most of us have only the remotest idea (if that) of how it works. Fortunately, our ignorance of the innards of a computer does not keep us from learning how to use it more or less expertly. Of course, *somebody* must know how to construct such devices; but for almost all computer users, that is somebody *else*. Likewise, the functionalist theory goes, the mind is a causal system in which mental states (beliefs, desires, etc.) supervene upon certain bodily states, of which we have only limited knowledge. Further, the causal system could in principle be something very different from a human body—an arrangement of magnetized coat hangers, for example. An intelligent being from a distant galaxy might be "wired" in ways we can scarcely imagine. (The examples are far-fetched, but they make the relevant point; namely, that it is *function*, not *substance*, that counts.)

A distinct but related question has to do with artificial intelligence (AI): Could a machine be constructed and programmed that would have a mind in (literally) the same way that a human person has a mind? The difficulties in making good on an unqualified "yes" answer have proved to be vastly greater than some early proponents (e.g., the English mathematician Alan Turing) supposed. Many thinkers subscribe to the more modest claim that computers help us to understand certain properties of the human mind, without holding that human minds are literally computers.

Some philosophers argue that mental phenomena are sui generis and, as such, are not susceptible of being reduced to anything else (states of the brain, for example) or, a fortiori, of being eliminated. This means that even an ideally accurate and complete body of objective, third-person observations would fail to explain the subjective side of consciousness. Thomas Nagel's 1974 essay "What Is It Like to Be a Bat?" is perhaps the best-known defense of this position: There is something about being a bat that non-bats cannot know, no matter how rich and detailed their scientific knowledge of bat physiology, anatomy, and behavior may be. The application to human consciousness is obvious. We know from the inside—not from external descriptions of either our behavior or our neurophysiological states—what it means to have a conscious experience. This position is consistent with the causal dependence of consciousness on neurophysiological states of the body.

The German philosopher-psychologist Franz Brentano (1838–1917) points out another bar to any species of reductionism or eliminativism; namely, the *intentionality* or *aboutness* of consciousness, which he takes to be the defining property of the mental. Consciousness is always *about*, or directed toward, something or other (some *object*, which may be real or imaginary or, indeed, anything at all). A physical object—a stone, for example—is not *about* anything and, consequently, is radically different from a mind. (A couple of centuries before Brentano's thesis, Descartes argues that all ideas have an *objective* or *representational* side—i.e., they are always *about* something. However, it was not Descartes but Aristotle and certain medieval exponents of Aristotelianism who inspired Brentano's work.)

Hume is generally skeptical about metaphysical pronouncements, which, he believes, almost always outstrip experienced-based evidence. For example, Descartes tells us that minds and bodies are distinct kinds of substance; but, in Hume's view, the very notion of *substance* as something different from the objects of experience is unintelligible. In any case, we do not know the essence of either the mind or of external bodies; so any theory that claims to reveal the "ultimate original qualities of human nature" should be rejected as "presumptuous and chimerical" (THN, xvii; 5. 8). Neither do we know the ultimate cause of our basic perceptions—impressions of sensation—"whether they arise immediately from the object, or are produc'd by the creative power of the mind, or are deriv'd from the author of our being" (THN, 84; 1.3.5.2). Fortunately, this unbridgeable gap in our knowledge has no bearing on Hume's project. Whatever its ultimate etiology, experience exhibits causal and other patterns that we may discover by wide and careful observations. It seems pretty clear that Hume would have little interest in or patience with disputes about the metaphysics of mind that exercise philosophers in our own time. (Of course, Hume's own theory of mind is a metaphysical doctrine of sorts; but it does not involve appeals to realities inaccessible to experience—or so Hume intends, at any rate.)

Hume is most obviously and directly connected with current philosophy of mind by way of his theory of personal identity. Philosophers still grapple with questions that Hume raises and answers (though not to his own complete satisfaction): What sort of being/ entity is a person or self or mind? What sort of evidence should I look for in answering that question? What kind of identity does a person have at different times? What, for example, makes me the same person today as when I was a 17-year-old high school student? Philosophers today also ask questions that Hume does not ask—e.g., what are we to make of a single person who exhibits multiple personalities, one or more of whom may know nothing of the other(s)? Does Hume's doctrine of the self or person—what it is and how we know it—have any bearing on such questions? Readers may ponder that for themselves.

What of Hume's doctrine of the mind as a bundle of perceptions connected by causal and other relations? Is that of merely antiquarian interest? Not according to Jerry Fodor (a major contributor to the philosophy of mind over the past three or four decades), who argues that Hume's *Treatise* is "the foundational document of cognitive science" because "it made explicit, for the first time, the project of constructing an empirical psychology on the basis of a representational theory of mind; in effect, on the basis of the Theory of Ideas." This means, among other things, that cognitive processes such as thinking "are constituted by causal interactions among mental representations" (*Hume Variations*, 134). In Fodor's opinion, Hume's misguided epistemological empiricism (especially the so-called copy theory, which binds ideas [or concepts] closely to impressions) keeps him from getting even more things right about the workings of the mind. Of course, Hume's philosophy of mind takes in much more than the cognitive part; but that is the part that Fodor finds so remarkably cogent. And Hume himself, in effect, authorizes a separate treatment: "we must distinguish betwixt personal identity, as it regards our thought or imagination, and as it regards our passions or the concern we take in ourselves" (THN, 253; 1.4.6.5).

MIRACLES. Hume's essay "Of Miracles" (section 10 of EHU) has provoked a small library of commentaries, starting shortly after its publication in 1748 and continuing to this day. This essay and the one immediately following it (section 11 of EHU, "Of a Particular Providence and of a Future State") were intended by Hume to be an answer to the common twofold supposition that the argument to (or from) design would convince any rational person of the existence of God and that the miracles described in the New Testament would further convince him or her of the truth of the Christian **religion**. More specifically, Hume may have had **Joseph Butler**'s *The Analogy of Religion* in mind as his target. (Butler's actual position is much more complicated and subtle than that.) If Hume is right, then both parts of the supposition are mistaken about the evidential basis of religious **belief** (even if it should turn out that the beliefs in question are true).

What is a miracle? As an ordinary English word, *miracle* sometimes refers to an extraordinary event effected by the supernatural power of God; or it may refer to any extremely outstanding event or accomplishment. Hume gives a metaphysical definition: "a violation of the laws of nature" (EHU, 114; 173.12). In a footnote, he offers an "accurate" refinement of the general definition: "*a transgression of a law of nature by a particular volition of the Deity, or by the interposition of some invisible agent*" (EHU 115n. 1;173n. 23; italics are in Hume's text). Although laws of **nature** play a central role in his argument against miracles, Hume does not say precisely what a law of nature is; but he provides some clues. Such laws have been established by "a firm and unalterable experience"; that is, there are no exceptions to the laws (at least none that are known). That dead persons do not come back to life, and that heavier-than-air objects fall if they are not supported, are examples of laws of nature.

Hume warns the reader not to confuse what is merely extraordinary or marvelous with what is genuinely miraculous, an actual violation of a law of nature. It would be extraordinary in a very high degree to be dealt precisely the same set of cards in three consecutive games of bridge (assuming that everything is normal, no cheating or monkeying with the cards, etc.), but it would clearly not be miraculous in Hume's sense. Hume provides his own imaginary example of an extraordinary or marvelous—but not miraculous—phenomenon: Total darkness covered the earth for eight days in January 1600—reports of which are supported by a superabundance of varied, high-quality evidence. In that circumstance, we should believe the reports without hesitation. On the other hand, if we have a number of reports that Queen Elizabeth I died (really and truly died) and was buried, and then returned to life after being interred a month, we ought to be skeptical, even if the evidence for the story seems to be strong. That is because such a series of events—a person dead and buried returning to life—would be a violation of a law of nature and, therefore, *practically* beyond belief. (It is obvious that Hume's example is not really about Elizabeth I, but about the central doctrine in Christian theology—the death and resurrection of Jesus of Nazareth; but the contrast between the merely extraordinary or marvelous and the truly miraculous is not affected by Hume's indirection.)

Hume's overall purpose in "Of Miracles" is to lay out a "convenient" and "decisive" argument against the credibility of miracle stories that can serve as "an everlasting check to all kinds of superstitious delusion" (EHU, 110; 169.2). He seeks to establish "as a maxim, that no human testimony can have such force as to prove a miracle, and make it a just foundation for any such system of religion," i.e., *any* "popular" religion (EHU, 127; 184.35). He may think that he has shown that no miracle story ought to command our belief, period, but he thinks it important to add the proviso about miracle-based religions. Although it is *possible* that a person wholly uninterested in religion should believe a miracle story, Hume says that he never heard of a miracle that was not invoked to bolster some religion. Nevertheless, many philosophers have found Hume's arguments about miracles fascinating quite apart from any connection with religion—or, for that matter, any connection with miracles. Their interest lies in the probative force of *testimony*.

It is important to keep in mind that Hume's concern throughout "Of Miracles" is with *testimonial* evidence for miracle stories. From several things he says, we may suppose that he would also be skeptical about miracle stories based on *firsthand* experience; but he does not deal specifically with that issue.

Hume states the nub of his convenient and decisive argument starkly: " . . . the proof against a miracle, from the very nature of the fact, is as entire as any argument from experience can possibly be imagined" (EHU, 114; 173.12). (*Nota bene*: **Proof** does *not* mean *demonstration*.) This means that testimonial evidence for a miracle could establish the miracle only if the falsity of the testimony would be more miraculous than the alleged miracle itself—obviously a very high standard for the credibility of miracle stories. Hume does not—and could not consistently—hold that miracles are literally impossible. Whatever is conceivable is possible, and it is no great feat to conceive a dead person's being brought back to life. Hume makes the same logical point about conceiving an object coming into existence without a cause. Note that we can *conceive* or *imagine* something that we may not be able actually to *believe*. (*See* RELATIONS OF IDEAS.) That interpretation is endorsed by every commentator, and would not be debatable in any case. But some critics argue that Hume's case against believing miracle stories is still a priori, in one of two different ways:

1. By definition, a miracle is a violation of a law of nature, which (on Hume's account) has no exceptions (i.e., violations). Thus, if we ever obtained convincing evidence that a person had been resurrected from the dead, we would conclude that such resurrections were never really miracles in the first place. *Whatever* we may once have believed, we will not *call* an event miraculous if we ever get evidence that it has actually happened. As Hume puts it, such an event "would not merit [the] appellation" *miracle* (EHU, 115; 173.12). Miracles would, then, remind one of Sir John Harrington's take on treason: Treason never prospers; for if it prospers, none dare call it treason. It would be disappointing if Hume's argument should turn out to yield only a trivial linguistic point that begged the substantive question at issue. Fortunately, the preponderance of evidence does not support that reading of Hume as getting at the core of the argument.

2. Hume's a priori argument is *epistemic*, not *metaphysical*. While it is possible that a miraculous event might occur, it is impossible that we could ever have sufficient testimonial evidence to justify our believing it. That is because the experiential evidence supporting a law of nature is "infallible" (i.e., without any exceptions, unfailing). Thus, although Hume allows the (at least) theoretical possibility of testimonial evidence strong enough to balance the presumption against miracle stories, such evidence could never *defeat* the presumption. Even maximally

compelling testimonial evidence for a miracle story could
achieve only a stalemate with the (Humean) *proof* against every
story alleging a violation of a law of nature. A simple analogy:
If a person bowls a 300 game, he or she knows a priori that no
one can top it, but can at best only match it.

Hume seems (at least) to go further than allowing for the (possible)
state of equipoise just described. With the proviso that the alleged
miracles in question are not invoked to support a "popular" religious
system, "there may possibly be miracles, or violations of the usual
course of nature, of such a kind as to admit of proof from human
testimony . . ." (EHU, 127; 184.36). Some commentators—e.g.,
Earman and Howson—agree that Hume's own criteria allow for the
theoretical possibility that a sufficiently large body of independent
testimony could make it more probable than not that the alleged
miracle did in fact occur. This concession seems to make the question of testimony for miracles an *empirical* matter, but it turns out
to be an empty gesture, practically if not theoretically. Never—not
once—has the actual, real-world testimonial evidence for a miracle
come within light years of satisfying Hume's requirement that the
falsity of the testimonial evidence would have to be more miraculous than the event testified to. Real-world testimonial evidence has
never—so Hume asserts—raised a miracle story even to the level
of *probability*, much less to the level of *proof*. Hume cites several
obstacles to the credibility of miracle stories: human mendacity and
gullibility; the love of the marvelous and exotic; the prevalence of
miracle stories among "ignorant and barbarous" nations; and the
existence of miracle stories invoked to support the contrary claims
of competing religions.

What appears to be the main epistemic point of Hume's argument can be stated simply: Given any miracle story, it is always
more likely that the witness(es) is (are) either deceived or lying than
that the miracle actually occurred (while conceding the theoretical
defeasibility of the presumption). It is, therefore, surprising—even
astonishing—that commentators disagree profoundly (and, it seems,
irreconcilably) about what Hume's actual argument is. Some writers
have used **Bayes's Theorem** to try to make the argument precise,
with interesting results. But they have to *assume* that they are work-

ing with Hume's real argument (or at least a significant part of it). It is not obvious that Bayes's Theorem would be of much value in deciding what Hume's argument is, though it might be helpful in evaluating whatever version is settled on.

MISSING SHADE OF BLUE. Hume argues that our weaker, less vivid **perceptions** (which he calls *ideas* or *thoughts*) are derived from, or caused by, our stronger, more vivid perceptions (which he calls *impressions*). More precisely, all our *simple* ideas are in their first appearance derived from simple impressions, "which are correspondent to them, and which they exactly represent" (THN, 4; 1.1.1.7). My actually seeing a blue object is stronger and more vivacious than my remembering or imagining the blue object. For Hume, the impressions-cause-ideas relation is foundational in his system: It is "the first principle I establish in the science of human nature" (THN, 7; 1.1.1.12). Hume challenges his readers to try to find an exception to the principle; that is, to produce a simple idea that was not derived from its corresponding simple impression. The obvious implication is that no such idea will be found. It is, therefore, jarring to find Hume himself posing an exception to the rule—the famous missing shade of blue.

The perception of blue plainly differs from the perception of red. Each is a distinct simple impression. But the perception of cerulean blue is equally distinct from the perception of powder blue. In general, the perception of any hue of a color is a simple impression. Hume asks us to imagine a person who has seen every shade of blue—except one. Upon viewing an array of shades of blue, ranging in equal intervals from the lightest to the darkest—*with that single shade missing*—this person would perceive a blank where the missing shade should go. That is, the gap separating the colors on either side of the missing shade would be greater than the gap between any of the other contiguous pairs. Hume's question: Could this person's **imagination** supply the missing shade, even though he had never seen it? Hume's answer: "Yes." But he goes on immediately to dismiss the exception as "so particular and singular" as not to warrant any change in the general maxim. (Hume gives virtually identical accounts of the missing shade in THN, 5–6; 1.1.1.10; and EHU, 20–21; 98–99.)

If we set aside any reservations we may have about the counter-example itself (for example, how could we tell whether the person had actually supplied the missing shade by his imagination?), what are we to make of Hume's (apparently) offhanded dismissal of it as inconsequential? If we can create ideas of colors we have never seen, why not ideas of sounds we have never heard, ideas of odors we have never smelled, etc.? Indeed, does Hume not effectively scuttle the whole principle of the priority of impressions to ideas? Not surprisingly, the question has provoked a wide range of answers from commentators, some defending Hume vigorously, some attacking him wholesale, and others suggesting ways of modifying the principle so as to preserve its core intact. At one extreme, critics denounce Hume's unperturbed dismissal of the counterexample as "wanton" (A. J. Ayer) and a piece of "effrontery" (H. A. Prichard). A more sympathetic commentator (Robert Fogelin) argues that although there are some exceptions to the empiricist principle, it is still sufficiently general to serve Hume well as he pursues his primary interests—e.g., **causation** and necessary connection, **substance**, **personal identity**, morality, **justice**, and the like, which are radically different from a shade of blue. (One waggishly clever writer asks whether the missing shade of blue is not a red herring.)

Hume may have cited the missing-shade-of-blue exception as a way of beating potential critics to the punch. Whether or not that move was prudent, it implies two things that are congenial to Hume's general outlook. First, the empiricist principle is indeed an empirical generalization, not a factually empty formal truth (e.g., "all triangles have three sides," which admits of no exceptions whatever but tells us nothing about the world). Second, as a consequence of the first, Hume will not discard a generally sound principle merely because it does not cover every possible case. The science of human nature is not mathematics; it can accommodate an (at least apparently) anomalous case from time to time.

MORAL RATIONALISM. *See* ETHICAL RATIONALISM.

MORAL SENSE. Hume uses the term *moral sense* to refer to the human capacity for feeling approval or disapproval of some action or character "upon the general survey" (THN, 499; 3.2.2.24). The last phrase—"upon the general survey"—is of the essence of the peculiarly or uniquely *moral* sense. It means that in feeling *moral* approbation or disapprobation we do not consider our own interest or involvement in the situation, but only the character of the person(s) toward whom the approval or disapproval is directed. This qualification (including the requirement that we are concerned with *character*) serves to distinguish moral sentiments from aesthetic sentiments and from the **pleasure** or pain we feel in our own successes or disappointments. We may feel great pleasure in listening to a Mozart piano concerto, and we would certainly be elated to win millions of dollars in a lottery; but neither of those sentiments would qualify as *moral*. (In EPM, published 11 years after THN, Hume abandons the term *moral sense* in favor of *internal sense* and *moral sentiment*, but this slight change in language does not signal any substantive change in doctrine.) Hume does not pretend that it is easy for us to overcome our propensity to see the world from the narrow perspective of our own interest. He maintains only that we do sometimes make disinterested judgments and that this capacity can be developed. See, for example, THN, 582; 3.3.1.16; and 603; 3.3.3.2.

Hume holds that the sense of morality is part of the fundamental structure of human nature, that it cannot be wholly explained by education or conditioning (what we might call *nurture*). It is obvious, Hume argues, that "a sense of morals is a principle inherent in the soul, and one of the most powerful that enters into the composition" (THN, 619; 3.3.6.3). Education and political artifice may extend and refine our original sentiments, but they cannot be the "sole cause of the distinction we make betwixt vice and virtue." Nature must "furnish the materials, and give us some notion of moral distinctions" (THN, 500; 3.2.2.25). On Hume's view, then, the sense of morality is *innate* in human beings, though Hume himself does not use that term in this context. By contrast, a tiger may be tamed and taught to obey its trainer, but it will never acquire a sense of morality. In this particular, Hume distances himself from "certain writers on morals" who seek "to extirpate all sense of virtue from among mankind" (THN, 500; 3.2.2.25). He does not mention any names, but his readers would have recognized **Thomas Hobbes** and **Bernard de Mandeville** as two principal targets of his criticism.

In discussing the *source* of moral distinctions, Hume (like many writers of the time) sees only two possible candidates—**reason** and sentiment or feeling. He marshals what he regards as a decisive series of arguments against the claims made for reason as that source. Thus, moral sense would be, at worst, the winner *faute de mieux*; but in fact Hume proceeds to offer a detailed and elaborate sentiment-based moral theory—one that nevertheless recognizes the indispensable supporting role played by reason. In EPM, Hume often pictures sentiment and reason as allies rather than competitors. He suspects that "*reason* and *sentiment* concur in almost all moral determinations and conclusions" (EPM, 172; 75.9; italics are in Hume's text). The final verdict of approval or disapproval is pronounced by feeling or sentiment, but reason paves the way by discovering various sorts of facts, comparisons, nice distinctions, and complicated relations.

It is important to understand that, for Hume, the moral sense does not provide a direct rational intuition of moral principles independent of human nature—a meaning that the phrase may misleadingly suggest. It is precisely such an apprehension of moral truths that Hume denies, against the claims of rationalist moral philosophers, such as **Samuel Clarke** and **William Wollaston**. (It should be obvious that the moral sense is not a sixth *physical* sense like seeing or hearing.) The phrase *moral sense* is first used by the Earl of **Shaftesbury** and developed by **Francis Hutcheson**.

– N –

NATURAL BELIEF. Hume himself does not use the phrase *natural belief*; it is due to **Norman Kemp Smith**, who uses it as a term of art. **Beliefs** are natural in this restricted sense if they are acquired without reasoning and cannot be destroyed by any skeptical reasoning. Such beliefs are indispensable for normal functioning in the world and, in some instances, for survival itself. Examples are obvious: belief in the existence of an independent external world, belief in the existence of other persons, belief in the existence of causal relations between objects or events, and the like. A person who seriously doubted such realities would be assured of but one thing—perishing quickly (to use **John Locke**'s phrase). Whatever we may *say* under the spell of theoretical **skepticism**, our actions prove that we do not really doubt that there are physical objects and other people. Hume describes beliefs of this sort as "permanent, irresistible, and universal," which are contrasted with those that are "changeable, weak, and irregular" (THN, 225; 1.4.4.1). It should be noted that Hume does not take the coercive, irresistible character of these beliefs to confer any special rational status on them. To put the matter bluntly but accurately, we have the beliefs because we cannot help having them.

No reader of Hume would dissent from the gist of the paragraph above. The main point of contention is about religious beliefs. Do they qualify as natural in the sense explained? While it seems obvious that a person may lead a normal, prudent life without explicit religious beliefs, some Hume scholars argue that such beliefs *are* natural in the restricted sense under consideration. In another sense of *natural, all* beliefs—even the most bizarre and fanciful—are natural, i.e., they admit of casual explanation.

NATURALISTIC FALLACY. *See* IS/OUGHT.

NATURE/NATURAL. Hume observes that the word *nature* (or, more frequently, the adjectival form *natural*) is "ambiguous and equivocal" (THN, 474; 3.1.2.7). That *natural* is at least usefully elastic may be seen in the following ordinary statements: (a) The sucking instinct in newborn babies is *natural*. (b) It is *natural* for a child to acquire the rudiments of a language by the age of 30 months. (c) It is *natural* for a child to want the approval of his or her parents. Whereas the sucking instinct in newborns is a matter of individual physiology, learning a language and wanting parental approval depend on social interaction; but each of the three cases represents a proper application of the term *natural*. These examples are suggested by Hume's observation (in *A Letter from a Gentleman to His Friend in Edinburgh*) that whereas sucking is a natural human action, speech is in an obvious sense *artificial*, i.e., requires social conventions or artifices. But who can deny that the instinct for speech is as much a part of human nature—that is, as *natural*—as sucking? That is Hume's point.

Hume distinguishes three senses of the term *natural*, each of which evokes a different contrast with nature (THN, 473–75; 3.1.2.7–10):

1. The natural may be contrasted with the *miraculous*. In this sense, *every* event in all of history is natural. (Hume notes an exception, which, given Hume's well-known views, would seem to be ironic or at least not wholly serious; namely, the **miracles** on which Christianity is founded.)

2. The natural may be opposed to what is *rare* or *unusual* (the sense that Hume takes to be the most common). There is no exact boundary between the natural and unnatural in this meaning, inasmuch as what is rare and unusual may increase or decrease as we observe more or fewer instances of some phenomenon. In this sense, the "sentiments of morality" are certainly natural: No person or nation has ever existed that was "utterly depriv'd" of moral distinctions.

3. The natural may be opposed to the *artificial* (or *conventional*, a word that Hume also uses in this context). This is the opposition that Hume has in mind as he develops his ethical theory. On this meaning, we may sensibly raise the question whether our notions of **virtue** are natural. Hume's own view (in THN at any rate) is that some virtues are natural and some are artificial. The most important artificial virtue is **justice**.

Hume sometimes contrasts nature with ***reason***, especially when he is talking about the incompetence of reason to discern causal connections or even to establish the existence of an external world. For example, after showing in section 4 of EHU ("Sceptical Doubts Concerning the Operations of the Understanding") that it is always experience (or, equivalently, custom and habit)—and never "reasonings *a priori*"—that acquaints us with causal relations, Hume proceeds in the next section ("Sceptical Solution of These Doubts") to allay any fear that his brand of **skepticism** might paralyze us and render us incapable of action: "Nature will always maintain her rights, and prevail in the end over any abstract reasoning whatsoever" (EHU, 41; 120.2). Later in EHU, he declares, "Nature is always too strong for principle [i.e., abstract reason]" (160; 207.23). Concerning our belief in external objects, Hume says that nature "has doubtless esteem'd it an affair of too great importance to be trusted to our uncertain reasonings and speculations" (THN, 187; 1.4.2.2). When Hume speaks of nature, in these (and similar) passages, as if it were a superhuman agency, he means only to call attention to certain fundamental and unalterable features of our human constitution.

Some commentators (most notably, **Norman Kemp Smith**) describe Hume's philosophy as a form of *naturalism*—a term that Hume himself does not use and one whose aptness is disputed by some other commentators. Against earlier critics (e.g., **Thomas Reid** and Thomas Hill Green), Kemp Smith argues that Hume is better described as a naturalist than as a thoroughgoing skeptic. As noted in the preceding paragraph, Hume rejects reason as the source of our basic beliefs but does not reject the basic beliefs themselves. He also declines to follow **René Descartes** and Gottfried Leibniz in appealing to a *super*natural guarantor.

The word *natural* is sometimes used normatively. We blame parents for neglecting their children because it shows a lack of the natural affection that parents owe their children. To put it negatively, when we say that it is *un*natural for parents to take no interest in their children's welfare, we mean to condemn their indifference as violating an obligation. (See THN, 478–79; 3.2.1.5–7.)

Hume divides **relations** into *philosophical* and *natural* (THN, 13-15; 1.1.5).

NECESSARY CONNEXION (CONNECTION). *See* CAUSE.

NEWTON, ISAAC. Widely regarded as the greatest natural scientist who ever lived (and indisputably among the greatest), Isaac Newton was born on Christmas Day (O.S.) 1642 and died in 1727. Besides his work in physics (on the composition of light as well as his monumental *Principia*), Newton made mathematical discoveries of the highest order. (He was embroiled in a long-running and acrimonious feud with the German philosopher-mathematician Gottfried Wilhelm Leibniz about who was first to develop the principles of the differential and integral calculus. The truth seems to be that neither stole from the other; they made their discoveries independently.) Newton also wrote extensively about biblical prophecies, theology, and alchemy.

Among a long list of brilliant achievements, Newton's demonstration that terrestrial and celestial motions (the falling apple and the orbiting moon, for example) obey the same laws effected dramatic simplifications. He showed that Johannes Kepler's laws of planetary motion, to take a notable case, could be deduced from a single principle—the inverse-square law. Long before his death, Newton was lionized to the point of apotheosis. The most famous example of such veneration is Alexander Pope's (no doubt partly ironic) epitaph:

> Nature, and Nature's laws lay hid in night:
> God said *Let Newton be!* and all was light.

So far as genius and capacity (Hume's terms) are concerned, Hume puts Newton and Galileo in a class by themselves—a less arresting, but more enlightening, assessment than Pope's. Hume's most famous encomium has Newton alone at the top: "In Newton this island [England] may boast of having produced the greatest and rarest genius that ever arose for the ornament and instruction of the species" (*The History of England*, VI, 542).

The precise extent and character of Newton's influence on Hume is a matter of scholarly dispute (more of this later). In any case, it is clear from Hume's own statements that he drew inspiration from the great success Newton enjoyed in the physical sciences. After noting Newton's genius in discovering the fundamental laws of motion and other natural phenomena, Hume expresses optimism about achieving "equal success in our enquiries concerning the mental powers and economy, if prosecuted with equal capacity and caution" (EHU, 14; 93.15). In Hume's view, all laws are essentially the same (i.e., they point to regular patterns among phenomena), whatever the particular subject matter being investigated. (Hume's doctrine of **cause** differs in important respects from Newton's, but that is another matter.)

The Newtonian atmosphere in which Hume worked is reflected in the subtitle of *A Treatise of Human Nature*: *Being an Attempt to Introduce the Experimental Method of Reasoning into Moral Subjects*. Note that Hume uses the word ***experiment*** as more or less interchangeable with ***experience*** or *observation*—a sense that is now obsolete. Nowadays, we use *experiment* more narrowly, to refer to the sort of controlled operations conducted, for example, in a chemistry laboratory. Hume uses the word *moral* to cover just about anything connected with human capacities or activities—what we would call epistemology or psychology or sociology or politics, etc. *Moral* *philosophy* was contrasted with *natural philosophy*, which comprised physics, chemistry, physiology, etc.

As noted above, scholars do not agree about the precise extent and character of Newton's influence on Hume. It is clear that Hume did not have a detailed knowledge of the technical side of Newtonian mechanics. Like almost everyone else, he lacked the mathematical expertise needed for such knowledge. Beyond that indisputable point, most everything about the Newton-Hume connection is disputed. Was Hume's debt to Newton little more than the adoption of an all-purpose "scientific" method, for which no extensive knowledge of the Newtonian corpus would be required? Or does the debt run deeper than that, and cover more specific and identifiable Newtonian elements? Without being an expert in physics, Hume might still have had a serviceable acquaintance with a reasonably wide range of scientific theories. The title of Nicholas Capaldi's 1975 book— *David Hume: The Newtonian Philosopher*—leaves no doubt where he stands on the question. Peter Jones (in *Hume's Sentiments*) appeals to historical and philosophical considerations to reach the contrary conclusion that Newton's influence on Hume was less than is commonly supposed and, indeed, less than Hume himself originally thought. Other scholars have reckoned the Newtonian influence on Hume as lying somewhere between the polar-opposite views exemplified by Capaldi and Jones.

– O –

OCCASIONALISM. Occasionalism is the doctrine that God is the only active **cause** in the universe; and since a cause is by its very nature active, it follows that God is the only true cause in the universe. What appear to be—and what we ordinarily take to be—causes are in reality only *occasions* for God to act in certain ways (hence the name *occasionalism*). Thus, the collision of a moving billiard ball with a stationary ball is an occasion for God to cause the second ball to move. The occasionalists were also keenly interested in the (apparent) operation of the mind on physical objects and the (apparent) operation of physical objects on the mind. In their view, when I will to raise my arm, my volition is the occasion for God to raise my arm.

And when I touch a hot surface, it is God—and not the hot object—
who causes me to feel pain. This theory is obviously intended to be
(among other things) an answer to the question posed (but not satisfactorily answered) by the French philosopher **René Descartes** about
the relation between the mind and the body (*see* MIND). However,
occasionalism did not arise exclusively—or even primarily—as a
solution to the mind-body problem. It represents an effort to develop
a systematic metaphysics along Cartesian lines, but more thoroughly
and more consistently than Descartes himself manages to do. It is
but a short step from Descartes' doctrine of divine conservation (i.e.,
that God not only created the world but conserves, or sustains, its
existence at every moment) to the full-fledged occasionalist doctrine
that God is the *only* cause in the universe. Descartes does not draw
that radical conclusion, but he is logically committed to it (at least in
the opinion of the occasionalists).

It should be carefully noted that the occasionalists go well beyond
garden-variety theists (e.g., **Samuel Clarke**), who hold both that God
is the *ultimate* cause of finite beings and that such beings exercise
real (though secondary and derived) causal power. Hume notes with
approval that neither Clarke nor **John Locke** nor **Ralph Cudworth**
(all of them English philosophers) subscribes to occasionalism or
even takes any notice of it. (See EHU, 73n1; 143n16.)

The Belgian-born Dutch philosopher Arnold Geulincx (1624–
1669) was the first modern (i.e., Descartes and thereafter) occasionalist, but **Nicolas Malebranche** (1638–1715) was better known and
more influential (and he is explicitly mentioned by Hume several
times). Hume says that Descartes "insinuated that doctrine of the universal and sole efficacy of the Deity, without insisting on it" (EHU,
73n1; 143n16). Gottfried Leibniz's doctrine of pre-established harmony and Baruch Spinoza's doctrine of parallel causation bear some
affinities with occasionalism, but they are sufficiently different to
make a common term unhelpful, if not positively misleading.

Not surprisingly, Hume's interest in the occasionalists focuses
on their theory of causation. He agrees with those philosophers that
neither the senses nor **reason** can discover any necessary connection
between cause and effect, whether we are considering the relation
between two physical objects or the relation between mind and body.
Nor can we discern any real power in the mind's ability to concen-

trate on a particular idea or to call up a particular sentiment or passion. In every case, the cause and the effect are distinct and separable (at least by the mind) and, consequently, are not joined by any necessary connection. It is only a slight exaggeration to say that Hume is content to confess what he takes to be our incurable ignorance of real causal powers, if such there be, and leave the matter at that.

As noted above, the occasionalists seek to avoid a skeptical conclusion by appealing to God as the causal glue that holds things together in lawful ways. As an empiricist, Hume complains that the speculations of the occasionalists about "the universal energy and operation of the Supreme Being" go beyond any possible human experience and, accordingly, lack genuine evidential value. Hume's summary of the methodological case against occasionalism is memorable: "We are got into fairy land, long ere we have reached the last steps of our theory; and *there* we have no reason to trust our common methods of argument, or to think that our usual analogies and probabilities have any authority" (EHU, 72; 142.24; italics are in Hume's text). Besides the discussion in EHU, see THN, 158–60; 1.3.14.7–10.

OUGHT. *See* IS/OUGHT.

– P –

PAIN. *See* PLEASURE/PAIN.

PASSIONS. Hume's theory of the passions is set out in book 2 of THN and, more briefly, as one of the *Four Dissertations*—"Of the Passions" (1757). Many of the details of his account of the passions are of mainly antiquarian interest, but his appeal to the passions (along with the related notions of instinct, sentiment, and feeling) is central to his anti-rationalist stance in epistemology and **ethics**. It is obvious that passions play a large role in his moral philosophy, but less obvious that they are indispensable for understanding his full theory of the self (**personal identity**). Hume says explicitly that we must distinguish personal identity "as it regards our thought or imagination" from personal identity "as it regards our passions or the concern we take in ourselves" (THN, 253; 1.4.6.5). This caveat is not an aside or casual comment. It encapsulates the difference between the thin "bundle of perceptions" of Hume's epistemology and the thick, robust self of his theory of the passions and his moral philosophy.

In Hume's usage, a *passion* is a *secondary* **impression** (which corresponds to an impression of *reflexion* in book 1 of THN). *Original* impressions (a.k.a. impressions of *sensation*) do not depend on any previous perceptions; they comprise such things as sensations of color, sound, touch, etc., as well as directly felt pains and pleasures. The secondary impressions arise from the original impressions, either directly or from ideas generated by the original impressions. This is how we get passions and "other emotions resembling them" (THN, 275; 2.1.1.1). Suppose that I suffer a painful burn. That is an impression of sensation (or an original impression). A month later, I remember the painful burn. That is an *idea* (memory). If my remembering the painful burn produces mental distress, that unpleasant feeling is an impression of reflexion (or a secondary impression).

Secondary (or reflective) impressions are either *calm* or *violent* (*violent* here suggests strength, vigor, or energy, not raving, ranting, cursing, throwing chairs, etc.). Calm impressions (e.g., the moral sense, the sense of beauty, benevolence, and love of life) are sometimes mistakenly confounded with **reason**. Violent impressions comprise the passions, which Hume divides into *direct* and *indirect*. Hume concedes that the *calm-violent* dichotomy is not exact, but it is serviceable for his purposes. (In fact, Hume's taxonomy is worse than "not exact"; it is sometimes downright confusing.) Both the direct and the indirect passions are "founded on pain and pleasure" (THN, 438; 2.3.9.1); but the direct variety spring immediately (i.e., without any intermediary) from an original impression of pleasure or pain, whereas the indirect require "the conjunction of other qualities" (THN, 276; 2.1.1.4), a phrase to be explained presently. As examples of direct passions, Hume lists desire and aversion, grief and joy, hope and despair, and fear and security. Indirect passions, which are Hume's primary interest in book 2 of THN, include ambition, vanity, envy, pity, malice, and generosity; but Hume concentrates on two key antipodal pairs—pride and humility, love and hatred.

The indirect passions are more complicated than the direct ones. Besides a *cause*, they require an *object*. Since the *same person* may feel both pride and shame, we require something else (the *cause*) to explain the difference between the two emotions. Hume's odd terminology is best explained by an example or two. The *object* of pride and its mirror-image passion, humility (*shame* is a more apt term for latter-day readers) is the *self*. If the self (or person) is not involved, pride and humility cannot arise. (In the case of love and hatred, the object is *another* self or person.) The *causes* of pride and humility are various and virtually without number. We may be proud of our quick wit, our memory, our erudition, our good looks, just as we may be ashamed of the opposites of those items. But our pride (or shame) may extend to persons or things that are somehow—even tenuously—connected with us: our children, our country, our houses, our athletic teams, even the weather of our region. Hume draws a substance-property distinction between the *subject* and the *quality* of the cause. Suppose that I am proud of the beauty of my house. The *object* of my pride is my self (I might *admire* my friend's house but would not feel pride in it). The *cause* of my pride is the beauty (quality) of the house (subject).

In the course of book 2, Hume offers many shrewd and interesting observations about the passions and how they are related to one another and to all manner of objects and circumstances. One extension of a doctrine developed in book 1 is worth mentioning—the **association of ideas**. Because the indirect passions are caused (in part) by ideas, they fall under the laws of resemblance, spatio-temporal contiguity, and causation. They are also related qua (secondary) *impressions*, but only by resemblance. This means that feeling one passion leads naturally to feeling a related passion: I move easily from *envying* a person to *hating* him—or, to take a happier case, from *loving* to feeling *benevolence*. More generally, pleasurable passions tend to evoke other pleasurable passions, even when the qualities causing the passions are very different (and the same principle holds for painful passions). Hume ties the two principles of association (i.e., of ideas and of impressions) together in what he calls the "double relation of ideas and impressions." An example (adapted from Capaldi, 1975) should make the notion clear. If one partner in a two-person business absconds with all the company's assets, the aggrieved partner *feels* anger and indignation at the perpetrator. Moreover, he feels uneasy whenever he *thinks* about anything associated with the offending partner.

Hume treats the *will* with the passions, though it is not strictly "comprehended among the passions" (THN, 399; 2.3.1.2), because we cannot understand the passions without understanding the "nature and properties" of the will. He describes the will as one of the most remarkable of the immediate effects of pain and pleasure, conceding that he cannot actually give a *definition* of will. He characterizes the will as "nothing but *the internal impression we feel and are conscious of, when we knowingly give rise to any new motion of our body, or new perception of our mind*" (THN, 399; 2.3.1.2; italics are in Hume's text). How is the will moved, or motivated, to act? Hume examines several sources of influence on the will (e.g., custom, **imagination**, spatial and temporal contiguity or separation), but he is more acutely interested in two disputed issues; namely, *liberty and necessity* (or *freedom and determinism*, to use modern jargon) and *passion and reason*.

From the time of Plato (ca. 427–349 B.C.), philosophers had pictured reason and passion as pitted against one another in a battle for the mind of the person. And these philosophers contended that rational creatures are obligated to conform their actions to the dictates of reason. Hume tries to show that their fundamental doctrine—the primacy of reason over passion—is utterly misguided. In fact, Hume argues, reason by itself can never move us to do, or to forbear doing, anything. According to Hume, reason operates in two, and only two, different ways: as it deals with the abstract **relations of ideas** (e.g., with mathematical demonstrations), *or* as it deals with the causal relations we learn from experience (THN, 413; 2.3.3.2).

It is obvious, Hume continues, that neither of the ways mentioned can, by itself, incline us to do, or refrain from doing, anything. Abstract reasoning affects us only insofar as it can help us attain some goal that we desire to attain; such reasoning is impotent to tell us whether the goal is worth striving for. Given certain causal relations that experience has taught us, we can use mathematics to ensure that the bridge we are building will not collapse under the weight of the traffic passing over it. But neither the mathematical reasoning nor the causal connections can offer the slightest clue about *why* we do not want the bridge to collapse. *That* is the exclusive province of the passions, which arise from the prospect of pleasure or pain.

Hume constructs another argument to show that passions and reason inhabit two different realms and that, therefore, a passion cannot be contrary to reason. Reason deals with truth and falsity, but a passion cannot be either true or false; it is, in Hume's words, "an original existence, or . . . [a] modification of existence" (THN, 415; 2.3.3.5). A passion is not a copy or representation of anything: My anger is no more a copy of something else than is my weighing 140 pounds. But a proposition (as we would say) is true or false as it either does or does not conform to something else—either to real relations of ideas (in the case of purely formal or conceptual propositions) or to real existence and **matter of fact** (in the case of factual propositions). Accordingly, it is quite impossible that a passion should be either reasonable or unreasonable (except in the oblique sense that it may be directed toward a non-existent or unattainable goal). It follows that reason cannot "oppose or retard" the impulse of a passion; only a contrary passion can do that.

The most important application of Hume's doctrine of the passions as non-rational comes in book 3 of THN—his moral philosophy (*see* MORAL SENSE).

Hume introduces and explains the notion of *sympathy* in connection with the passions, but it also plays a fundamental role in his moral theory as that theory is developed in THN. Indeed, Hume declares that "sympathy is the chief source of moral distinctions" (THN, 618; 3.3.6.1). (Sympathy *as such* plays no comparably important role in EPM.)

PERCEPTIONS. Hume's theory of perceptions is at the heart of his basic philosophical project—the construction of a science of human nature. This entry covers several aspects of that theory: his definition of *perception*, his classifications of perceptions, his account of the causal relations among perceptions, his use of the theory to establish a criterion for distinguishing genuine from bogus concepts, and the relation of his theory to those of **John Locke** and **George Berkeley**, two of his most famous empiricist predecessors.

Hume defines *perception* as "whatever can be present to the mind, whether we employ our senses, or are actuated with passion, or exercise our thought and reflection" (THN, 647; 408.5)—a color seen, a sound heard, an odor smelled, a **pleasure** enjoyed, a pain suffered, an emotion felt, and so on (as well as all these things remembered or imagined). Perceptions, then, comprise absolutely every object

that the mind can be aware of. They answer to **John Locke**'s *idea*—
"whatsoever is the Object of the Understanding when a Man thinks"
(*Essay*, 47.§8)—a label that Hume describes as inaccurate in that it
fails to mark the distinction between two fundamental kinds of ideas
(or, accurately, of perceptions).

On Hume's theory, the fundamental distinction within perceptions
is that between *impressions* and *ideas* (or, as Hume also calls the latter, *thoughts*). Impressions are the stronger, livelier, more vivacious
perceptions; ideas are the fainter, weaker images of impressions that
we encounter in thinking and imagining. In Hume's own words, impressions "comprehend all our sensations, passions, and emotions, as
they make their first appearance in the soul" (THN, 1; 1.1.1.1). Con-
cretely, impressions comprise "all our more lively perceptions, when
we hear, or see, or feel, or love, or hate, or desire, or will" (EHU,
18; 97.3). The impressions/ideas dichotomy corresponds roughly to
the **commonsense** distinction between feeling and thinking. There is
an undeniable non-theoretical difference between feeling the pain of
burning one's hand and remembering that pain a month later.

Hume divides ideas into two subclasses: those of *memory* and
those of *imagination*, which are distinguished by the superior liveliness and strength of memory-ideas (THN, 8–9; 1.1.3.1). He also divides impressions into two subclasses: impressions of *sensation* and
impressions of *reflexion* (THN, 7; 1.1.2.1). He later uses the terms
original impressions and *secondary impressions* to mark the same
distinction, noting that "all the impressions of the senses [from seeing, hearing, etc.], and all bodily pains and pleasures" fall under the
first category and that "the passions, and other emotions resembling
them" fall under the second (THN, 275; 2.1.1.1). An illustration will
make clear what Hume means by an impression of reflection (or a
secondary impression). Suppose that I suffer a painful burn. That
is an impression of sensation (or an original impression). When I
recall the pain several months later (by way of an idea of memory),
I may feel a twinge of distress or unease. That twinge of distress is
an impression of reflexion, which follows upon the recollection of
the actual pain.

Another important distinction among perceptions is that between
simple and *complex*. Simple perceptions (either impressions or
ideas) are "such as admit of no distinction nor separation" (THN, 2;

1.1.1.2). By contrast, complex perceptions may be distinguished into parts. Our perception of an apple, for example, is complex, in that it can be analyzed into perceptions of color, shape, taste, etc. On the other hand, if we try to "decompose" our perception of a color (say, red), we find that we get only smaller areas of the same quality, not genuinely different components. Another example should help to make the simple/complex dichotomy clear. Our perception of a musical tune is obviously complex, being analyzable into separate notes, tempo, etc.; but our perception of a single sound (say, middle C) is simple, inasmuch as we are conscious of one homogeneous tone, which may vary in duration without altering its simple qualitative character.

To defend his division of perceptions into two fundamental kinds—impressions and ideas—Hume appeals to the experienced difference between actually tasting a pineapple, for example, and remembering or imagining the taste of a pineapple. It is a matter of direct experience—not mere theory—that the taste itself (the impression of sensation) is more vivid and lively than the same taste recalled or imagined (the idea of the taste). We might describe that side of Hume's doctrine of perceptions as the *phenomenological* (though Hume himself does not use that term). He also provides an *etiological* account of perceptions—that is, how they are caused.

Impressions of sensation—the bedrock of perceptions—"arise in the soul originally [i.e., without any antecedent perception], from unknown causes" (THN, 7; 1.1.2.1). Later, he expands on this agnosticism about ultimate causes, arguing that it is not a barrier to developing a science of human nature. We can never know with certainty the ultimate cause of impressions of sensation, "whether they arise immediately from the object, or are produc'd by the creative power of the mind, or are deriv'd from the author of our being" (THN, 84; 1.3.5.2). Fortunately for Hume's purposes, it does not matter where these impressions come from; we can reason confidently about all our perceptions, since they are by nature objects of consciousness. There is nothing hidden or occult about *them*: "For since all actions and sensations of the mind are known to us by consciousness, they must necessarily appear in every particular what they are, and be what they appear" (THN, 190; 1.4.2.7). In EHU, Hume describes his project as that of sketching a "mental geography" (13; 93.13), which is possible because it deals exclusively with our **experience** and does not speculate about what unknown causes may underlie that experience. Even if we knew those causes, that knowledge would have no effect on the character of our experience or on our description of it.

A historical note: In declining to conjecture about the ultimate causes of our perceptions, Hume follows the lead of John Locke. At the very beginning of *An Essay Concerning Human Understanding*, Locke announces that he will not

> meddle with the Physical Consideration of the Mind; or trouble my self to examine, wherein its Essence consists, or by what Motions of our Spirits, or Alterations of our Bodies, we come to have any Sensation by our Organs, or any *Ideas* in our Understanding; and whether those *Ideas* do in their Formation, any, or all of them, depend on Matter, or no. (43.§2)

Such speculations might prove to be "curious and entertaining," but they have no bearing on what he intends to do.

Hume's skeptical conclusion about knowing the ultimate cause or causes of impressions of sensation does not extend to the causal relations among perceptions themselves. Do impressions cause ideas? Or do ideas cause impressions? Or both? Or neither? We cannot answer those questions by a priori, or purely formal, reasoning. The issue concerns a matter of fact, and must be resolved by appealing to experience. When we consult experience, we find that "our impressions are the causes of our ideas, not our ideas of our impressions" (THN, 5; 1.1.1.8). To be precise, our *simple* ideas are caused by *simple* impressions. Very early in THN, Hume lays down a general empiricist principle (sometimes called the *Copy Principle*, though not by Hume): "*That all our simple ideas in their first appearance are deriv'd from simple impressions, which are correspondent to them, and which they exactly represent*" (4; 1.1.1.7; italics are in Hume's text). Hume adds the qualifying phrase "in their first appearance" to allow for the fact that "we can form secondary ideas, which are images of the primary" (THN, 6; 1.1.1.11). That is, ideas can produce images of themselves in new ideas. We can, for example, remember remembering or imagining a color; we often remember what we thought on certain past occasions. Further, ideas are involved as causes in the production of secondary impressions (or impressions of reflection). But it remains true that "all our simple ideas proceed, either mediately or immediately, from their correspondent impressions" (ibid.).

Since the priority of impressions to ideas is not known a priori, Hume offers factual evidence to support the principle. For example, to give a child the idea of scarlet or orange or sweet or bitter, we show him or her objects that have those properties. That is, we give the child an *impression* of those qualities. We would never even consider trying to produce the impressions by exciting the ideas—for example, by *describing* the color orange to the child, in the expectation that he or she would thereby get the *impression*, or immediate experience, of orange. Further, if a person is congenitally blind or deaf, he or she will be lacking not only the *impressions* of color or sound, but the *ideas* of those qualities as well. (For the arguments, see THN, 3–5; 1.1.1.4–9, and EHU, 19–20; 97–98.) Hume himself calls attention to what seems to be an exception to the causal priority of impressions to ideas—the so-called **missing shade of blue**.

It should be noted that the Copy Principle does *not* apply to complex ideas, at least not in the direct way it applies to simple ideas. We may fabricate ideas of flying pigs and three-headed monsters without ever having seen any (since they do not exist); and we may remember seeing a mountain valley covered with flowers, without recalling all the details of our original experience. However, Hume insists that for all its apparent inventive powers, our imagination is actually limited to working with materials derived from experience. We can combine, compound, augment, or diminish such materials, but we cannot create them from scratch. They are given in experience, or we do not have them.

Having established the *factual* claim that ideas are copies of, or caused by, impressions (and not the other way around), Hume straightaway turns it into a *normative* test of meaning. Ideas— especially abstract ones—"are naturally faint and obscure: the mind has but a slender hold of them" (EHU, 21; 99.9)—a fact that makes it easy for us to conflate resembling ideas. From frequent use of a philosophical term, we may suppose that it has a distinct meaning (i.e., "has a determinate idea annexed to it"), when in fact it has none. By contrast, impressions—whether inward or outward—are strong and vivid and, consequently, not easily mistaken for one another.

Accordingly, when we suspect that a term is being used without any meaning or idea (a depressingly frequent occurrence, Hume thinks), we should pose the following question: *"from what impression is that supposed idea derived?"* (EHU, 22; 99.9; italics are in Hume's text). If we cannot produce the required pedigree, we must renounce the term as vacuous. By using this criterion of meaningfulness, we can distinguish genuine, experience-based ideas from fantasies spawned by an undisciplined imagination. Although Hume does not cite any examples of meaningless terms in the passage just quoted from, we know from his own use of the criterion that he has in mind certain notions that abound in the works of rationalist (and other) philosophers; e.g., an unchanging immaterial self, the general concept of substance, occult (or hidden) qualities, the **occasionalist** doctrine that God is the only real cause in the universe, the infinite divisibility of **space** and **time**, etc.

In THN, Hume uses the impressions/ideas dichotomy to pose the question of the source of moral distinctions: *"Whether 'tis by means of our* ideas *or* impressions *we distinguish betwixt vice and virtue, and pronounce an action blameable or praise-worthy?"* (456; 3.1.1.3; italics are in Hume's text). By seeing the issue in these terms, we can, Hume says, "cut off all loose discourses and declamations, and reduce us to something precise and exact on the present subject" (ibid.). Hume argues that it is sentiment or feeling (an impression of reflection or a secondary impression), and not ideas, that give us the sense of morality. Otherwise stated, it is by passion, not by reason, that we make moral distinctions. Hume concedes that the sentiment or feeling of morality is "commonly so soft and gentle" that we are prone to mistake it for an idea (THN, 470; 3.1.2.1). (In EPM, Hume argues at length that moral distinctions rest on sentiment or feeling, not on reason—just as he does in THN—but he does not use the impressions/ideas language in EPM.)

Hume's account of perceptions is in the empiricist tradition of Locke and Berkeley; that is, it identifies sensation and reflection as supplying the fundamental elements of human experience (including **knowledge**). According to Locke, the mind is originally like white paper (*tabula rasa*, in scholastic terminology), which is supplied with ideas (in Locke's broad sense of the term) by experience. Experience comprises two, and only two, sources (or *Fountains* or *Originals*, as

Locke calls them): Sensation, which gives us ideas of yellow, white, heat, cold, soft, hard, bitter, sweet, etc., and Reflection, which gives us ideas of the operations of the mind—perceiving, thinking, willing, believing, doubting, etc. (*Essay*, 104–5).

At the beginning of his *Principles of Human Knowledge*, Berkeley declares that the objects of human knowledge are of three kinds: ideas actually imprinted on the senses (colors, shapes, tastes, etc.) or ideas "perceived by attending to the passions and operations of the mind" or ideas "formed by help of memory and imagination." Unlike Locke and Hume, Berkeley proceeds immediately to draw a sharp and explicit distinction between ideas of any sort and the mind that perceives them. This move initiates Berkeley's construction of an immaterialist metaphysics—that is, a philosophical system that banishes *matter* in favor of minds (including the Infinite Mind, God) and their ideas. In this respect, Berkeley parts company with Locke and Hume. Indeed, it is important to remember that, despite their common empiricist leanings, Locke, Berkeley, and Hume exhibit numerous substantial differences among themselves, both in doctrines and in the ways they see their own work.

PERSONAL IDENTITY. "Always remember that you are unique—just like everybody else." So goes a piece of sardonic "wisdom." In fact, there is no reason to stop with the uniqueness of human beings: Absolutely every individual being—from electron or dust mite to God—is unique, i.e., is identical with itself and with nothing else. There is nothing special about being unique. **Joseph Butler**, Hume's older contemporary, puts it simply: "Everything is what it is and not another thing." Although Butler's maxim seems to be both true and innocuous, it has proved to be virtually impossible for philosophers to say clearly, precisely, and convincingly what it means for two things to be identical, or for one thing to be identical with itself at different times. For a general account of Hume's theory of identity, *see* IDENTITY. This entry deals with the question of identity as it relates to *persons*. (Hume uses *person*, *self*, *soul*, and *mind* as practically interchangeable.)

Cogito, ergo sum (I think; therefore, I am). That is the formula that encapsulates the **skepticism**-defeating discovery of the French philosopher and mathematician **René Descartes**; namely, that it is quite impossible for him to doubt that he exists so long as he has any kind of **experience**. In the very act of trying to doubt his own **existence**, Descartes proves, past any possible doubting, that he does indeed exist. He then proceeds to ask, "*What* am I—I who know *that* I am?" He argues that he is a *thing that thinks* (*res cogitans*)—a being whose very essence is to think (i.e., to have conscious **experience**). For Descartes, this means that he is a *substance*—an *immaterial* substance, to be precise—a self (or person) that remains unchanged through the constantly changing welter of particular thoughts and experiences.

It is the second part of Descartes' claim—i.e., the positing of a simple, unchanging self—that Hume inveighs against in "Of Personal Identity" (THN, book 1, part 4, section 6; also in the appendix to THN, 633–36; 398–400). In his *Abstract* of THN, Hume mentions Descartes by name as holding that the mind is a substance in which perceptions inhere; but his criticism is intended to apply to *any* doctrine of an unchanging immaterial self—a doctrine usually associated with rationalist philosophers. The empiricist **George Berkeley** regards the mind as an immaterial substance, but his approach is very different from Descartes'.

To understand Hume's objection to the notion of an unchanging self, we must recall that, on his view, all ideas are derived from impressions (*see* PERCEPTIONS). Accordingly, if we are to have an **idea** of such a permanent self, we must first have an **impression** of it. Because the self is supposed to be a simple, unchanging, invariant reality, the impression that gives rise to the idea of the self must likewise be simple, unchanging, and invariant throughout one's life. But impressions are notoriously *in*constant. They are "perpetually perishing" (a striking phrase that Hume borrows from **John Locke**). "Pain and pleasure, grief and joy, passions and sensations succeed each other, and never all exist at the same time" (THN, 251–52; 1.4.6.2). It follows that we have no *idea* of an unchanging self.

Some philosophers invoke *substance* as a way of explaining the "ownership" of properties (of whatever kind). *Blue* and *round* are characteristics of the ball (a material substance); they are not freestanding realities in their own right. In like fashion—so some philosophers contend—perceptions (sensations, thoughts, feelings, etc.) are always "owned" by a substantial self. Properties have only a dependent existence; a substance, by contrast, requires nothing but itself in order to exist. Hume argues that, on this definition of *substance*, every perception is a substance: It is different, distinguishable, and separable from every other perception, and, consequently, may exist separately and independently. How are these quasi-substantival entities connected with the self?

Having shown (as he believes) that we have no idea of a simple, invariant self, Hume turns to the task of explaining the idea of the self that we *do* have—a task that is clearly part of his study of human nature. When he looks within himself, Hume says, he never finds *himself* apart from some particular perception. Rather, he finds "heat or cold, light or shade, love or hatred, pain or pleasure" (THN, 252; 1.4.6.3). And, of course, Hume's experience is not idiosyncratic. Human selves are "nothing but a bundle or collection of different perceptions, which succeed each other with an inconceivable rapidity, and are in a perpetual flux and movement" (THN, 252; 1.4.6.4). Hume suggests an interesting metaphor for our experience: "The mind is a kind of theatre, where several perceptions successively make their appearance; pass, re-pass, glide away, and mingle in an infinite variety of postures and situations. There is properly no *simplicity* in it at one time, nor *identity* in different . . ." (THN, 253; 1.4.6.4; the italics are in Hume's text). He warns us not to be misled by the metaphor. We have no notion at all of the *theater itself.* The mind is wholly constituted by the successive perceptions.

If the self is indeed merely a bundle of diverse perceptions that have no real connection, why do we unfailingly ascribe to the self an unchanging and uninterrupted existence? Hume's answer to this question parallels the one he gives (in "Scepticism with regard to the senses") about our belief in the distinct, continued existence of external objects—a belief that has no foundation in either the senses or (causal) reason but is nevertheless utterly inexpugnable. (*See* IMAGINATION; SKEPTICISM.) To our *feeling*, a succession of closely resembling objects is virtually indistinguishable from a single uninterrupted and invariant object. Even philosophers are bound to yield to this "propension" most of the time. When the interruptions are too obvious to be denied, we feign the existence of some unperceived reality—a soul or self or substance—to connect the perceptions. Such a self is, in Hume's language, a *fiction.*

So far, Hume's explanation of our mistaken ascription of identity to a series of perceptions is pretty general. It is helpful, he says, to consider the sort of identity we attribute to plants, animals, and inanimate objects. There are several features of changes in such objects that serve to mask the changes: When the change in a part is very small in proportion to the whole (as when a mountain loses a boulder); or when the change is very slow or gradual (as when the shape of a rock is altered by the action of water flowing over and around it); or when the parts are related by reference to some end or purpose (as when the sails or timbers of a ship are replaced over the years); or when there is a *sympathy* of parts (as when the organs of an animal work together in preserving its life). These features of changes go some way toward explaining why we overlook the constant fluctuations in our perceptions and suppose them to be identical. The identity—or, rather, the *illusion* of identity—among the different perceptions is "merely a quality, which we attribute to them, because of the union of their ideas in the imagination, when we reflect upon them" (THN, 260; 1.4.6.16).

The union of ideas in the imagination that Hume speaks of is the work of *resemblance* and **causation**, to which must be added the absolutely essential role of *memory*, without which our awareness of both resemblance and causation would be impossible (*see* AS-SOCIATION OF IDEAS). The "bundle" of perceptions that Hume identifies with the self exhibits certain relations that are discovered or produced (or both) by the memory, which is "a faculty, by which we raise up the images of past perceptions" (THN, 260; 1.4.6.18). This chain of *resembling* perceptions is a powerful inducement for the imagination to suppose (falsely) that the chain is actually one continuing object.

In respect of *causation*, Hume says that the true idea of the human mind is to consider it as a "system of different perceptions or different existences, which are link'd together by the relation of cause and effect, and mutually produce, destroy, influence, and modify each other" (THN, 261; 1.4.6.19). This "system" is like a commonwealth or republic, whose inhabitants, laws, and constitutions may vary without destroying its identity. In an analogous way, a person may retain his identity through changes in his character and disposition, as well as in his impressions and ideas. By making causation an essential link in personal identity, Hume shows how we can extend that identity to times, events, and actions that we have entirely forgotten. This aspect of Hume's theory is implicitly a criticism of Locke, who ties personal identity to consciousness (including memory), with no (explicit) reference to causation. (It is not clear that Locke would have objected to the way Hume adds causation to memory as the foundation of personal identity.)

It should be clear from what has been said that Hume does not deny the existence of the self, as some have alleged. To be sure, he does not engage in metaphysical speculation (e.g., about an unchanging immaterial substance), but he appeals to experience to set out a theory of what the self is and how we come to believe in it. Whether his theory is adequate or defensible is a matter of dispute, but not whether he *has* a theory.

Hume's account of personal identity has elicited an enormous secondary literature devoted to clarifying, attacking, and defending it. Critics complain, for example, that Hume's (allegedly) quixotic general concept of identity creates a pseudo-problem; that Hume attributes to the "vulgar" beliefs that they do not in fact hold (e.g., that *perceptions* persist unchanged through time); and that he excludes the person's body from his analysis of the self. Indeed, Hume himself laments that his account is "very defective." This he does in the appendix to THN, which was published as part of book 3 in October 1740, though all the references in the appendix are to book 1. (Books 1 and 2 were published in January 1739.) He says that he cannot reconcile what he takes to be two principles, nor can he reject either of them; namely, that distinct perceptions are distinct existences, and that the mind cannot perceive any real connections among distinct existences. This "confession" has puzzled readers of Hume, inasmuch as there is no logical inconsistency between the two principles considered in themselves. Commentators have engaged in lively debates about the precise character of Hume's problem with his own account of the self—if, indeed, he has a problem at all.

Hume warns, almost in passing, that "we must distinguish betwixt personal identity, as it regards our thought or imagination, and as it regards our passions or the concern we take in ourselves" (THN, 253; 1.4.6.5). This caveat is of fundamental importance in understanding Hume's theory of the passions and of morality. Without a robust, commonsense notion of personal identity, those theories would be radically different from the ones Hume has given us. It is this looser, "thicker" ordinary self that Hume has in mind when he says, in book 2 of THN, that "the idea, or rather impression of ourselves is always intimately present with us" (317; 2.1.11.4). This claim is consistent with his earlier denial (in "Of personal identity") that we have any impression of an invariant substantial self.

Historical note: It is Locke—not Descartes—who is generally regarded as the first modern philosopher to pose the question of personal identity in a concrete way. Descartes says that the self is a substance whose essence is to think (a *res cogitans*) but tells us little about what that means, except in abstract theoretical terms. By contrast, Locke says a great deal about what it means to be a person and about numerous puzzles that hover around the notion. For Locke, a *person* or *self* is "a thinking intelligent Being, that has reason and reflection, and can consider it self as it self [*sic*], the same thinking thing in different times and places; which it does only by that consciousness, which is inseparable from thinking . . ." (*Essay*, 335.§9). It is consciousness (including memory) that makes a person. Substance, whether immaterial or material, has nothing to do with our conception of a person. Though Locke does not categorically deny that a person might *be* a substance, metaphysically considered, he argues that, at best, the notion of substance offers no help whatever in clarifying what it means to be a person and, moreover, introduces gratuitous problems. (Hume's verdict is more radical than Locke's: ". . . the question concerning the substance of the soul [or person or mind] is absolutely unintelligible" [THN, 250; 1.4.5.33].) Locke declares that *person* is a "Forensick Term" (*Essay,* 346.§26); i.e., it has to do with the assessment of legal and moral responsibility, with the allocation of praise and blame. It is this practical concept of person that Hume has in mind when he distinguishes the "fictitious" personal identity discerned by thought and imagination from the self as it is involved in our passions and moral sentiments.

PLEASURE/PAIN. Hume locates the perception of pleasure and pain in the very bedrock of human nature: "The chief spring or actuating principle of the human mind is pleasure or pain" (THN, 574; 3.3.1.2; see also 118; 1.3.10.2). We are immediately attracted to what we find pleasant and repelled by what we find painful. It is in this sense that Hume sometimes speaks of pleasure and pain as identical with good and evil (e.g., THN, 439; 2.3.9.8). He does *not* mean *moral* good and evil, which are linked to a unique kind of pleasure and pain. When pleasure and pain are missing from both thought and feeling, we are not moved to do or desire much of anything.

Garden-variety bodily pleasure and pains are among the most vivid and forceful human experiences—quenching one's thirst with cool water or smashing one's finger with a hammer. These fall under the class of basic perceptions that Hume calls ***impressions*** *of sensation* (along with seeing colors, hearing sounds, etc.). But Hume's main interest in pleasure and pain lies elsewhere—in the more complicated pleasures and pains that arise from the intervention of an ***idea***. Hume calls these perceptions *impressions of reflexion* or *secondary impressions* (*see* PERCEPTIONS).

It is entirely predictable that pleasure and pain would figure prominently in Hume's account of the **passions**: I feel pride (a kind of pleasure) in my successes, but humility/shame (a kind of pain) in my failures. But we may be surprised to find them at the heart of Hume's moral theory, as when he says, ". . . moral distinctions depend entirely on certain peculiar [i.e., distinctive] sentiments of pain and pleasure" (THN, 574; 3.3.1.3). The pleasure and pain inherent in *moral* sentiments or feelings of approval or disapproval are produced by the general (i.e., disinterested) view of someone's *character*.

It should be noted that in spite of the foundational role Hume assigns to pleasure and pain, he is *not* a hedonist. That is, he does not hold either that we do or that we should always act for the sake of realizing pleasure or avoiding pain. We sometimes act from the prompting of our **moral sense**, which necessarily takes the "general view" and not an "interested view."

PRICE, RICHARD (1723–1791). Price was a Welsh non-conformist minister and the son and nephew of non-conformist ministers. He used his exceptional mathematical skills to do pioneering work in the theory of public debt, population, and the actuarial side of insurance. He was a life-long defender of freedom of all sorts and wrote in support of the American Revolution. He completed and published a famous theorem due to Thomas Bayes, known as **Bayes's Theorem**, which has been applied to the question of **miracles** (among many other things). Although Price and Hume became cordial friends, their philosophical views—especially on the nature and foundation of **knowledge** and of morality—represent polar opposites. Price's moral philosophy is most fully presented in his *Review of the Principal Questions of Morals* (first edition 1758), in which he defends a generally rationalist account of moral knowledge. Against Hume, who finds the source of morality in *feeling* or *sentiment*, Price argues that moral discernment is a function of the *understanding*; that the *objective* character of the action being judged, not the *subjective* reaction of the person doing the judging, is the primary concern of moral philosophy.

By far, the most widely studied and discussed of Price's writings is the fourth of his *Four Dissertations* (1767)—the one that undertakes a critical assessment of Hume's arguments in "Of Miracles." Some writers have suggested that Price, in effect if not deliberately, applies Bayes's Theorem to Hume's reasoning about probability. This is especially obvious in Price's objections to the use Hume makes of *prior probabilities*. According to Hume, the presumption against the occurrence of a miracle is so strong that testimonial evidence defeating the presumption would have to be (almost) impossibly strong itself (Hume calls this principle a *general maxim*). Price argues that, with some rare exceptions, we should not consider prior probabilities when we weigh the testimonial evidence in question.

George Campbell makes the same point with a clear example: Suppose that a ferryboat has made 2,000 round-trips across a river, with no mishap. The 2,000 to zero ratio notwithstanding, we would not hesitate to believe the report of an honest, sober, reliable person who tells us that he saw the boat sink just 30 minutes ago. Once the testimony is given, the improbability of the event reported is irrelevant. We are assured that the event actually occurred in the same measure that we are assured that the witness is telling the truth—a platitudinous principle that Hume overlooks, or so critics like Price allege. A defender of Hume might pose something like the following case: Suppose that instead of reporting that he saw the ferryboat sink—an unexpected but perfectly natural event—the witness insists that he saw the ferryboat sprout wings and fly across the river. Would we believe the "honest, sober, reliable" witness in that case, which is, after all, the *sort* of event Hume has in mind when he fixes the prior improbability of a miracle? Quite apart from any question about miracles, scholars have been deeply divided over the issue of prior probabilities.

PRIMARY AND SECONDARY QUALITIES. John Locke describes the *primary* (or *original*) qualities of a material object (a *body*, as he calls it) to be those that are "utterly inseparable from the Body" (*Essay*, 134.§9). These qualities comprise solidity, extension, figure, motion or rest, and number; they exist in the object itself and are the cause of our *ideas* of those qualities. The so-called *secondary* qualities—color, sound, odor, taste; felt heat, cold, and texture— exist in the object only as powers to cause ideas in our minds. Thus, an object really is square, but it is red only in that it produces the idea of red in our minds. *All ideas* are only in the mind; but the ideas of primary qualities *resemble* those qualities in the object, whereas the ideas of secondary qualities *resemble* nothing in the object. This is Locke's theory, which is, with minor variations, the standard view of early modern scientists and many philosophers.

Hume takes the Lockean account as standard, but he rejects the distinction as untenable. In "Of scepticism with regard to the senses" (THN), Hume distinguishes three kinds of impressions produced by the senses: first, "figure, bulk, motion and solidity"; second, "colours, tastes, smells, sounds, heat and cold"; third, "pains and pleasures" (THN, 192; 1.4.2.11). *As perceptions*, these are all on the same footing. The perception of shape (figure) is no more real and no more permanent than the perception of pain. That is, the *senses* afford no basis whatever for the invidious distinction between the so-called primary and secondary qualities. Nor can **reason** justify the distinction by inferring a causal connection between external objects and perceptions, inasmuch as we are acquainted only with our own perceptions. We cannot, that is, establish a causal relation between an entity that is known and one that is unknown. (Hume's concern in this section of THN is to investigate the grounds of our belief in the existence of objects that are independent of our perceptions and continue to exist when they are not perceived.)

Later, in the section entitled "Of the modern philosophy," Hume offers an additional argument against the primary-secondary dichotomy.

(In EHU [154–55; 202–3], he sketches the same argument much more briefly.) He notes that the *"modern philosophy"* holds secondary qualities (colors, odors, tastes, etc.) to be "nothing but impressions in the mind, deriv'd from the operation of external objects, and without any resemblance to the qualities of the objects" (THN, 226; 1.4.4.3). This means that secondary qualities actually have the same status as **pleasures** and pains, which no one supposes to exist in objects. The only unqualifiedly real qualities are the primary—"extension and solidity, with their different mixtures and modifications; figure, motion, gravity, and cohesion" (THN, 227; 1.4.4.5). Unfortunately for the proponents of this theory, we have no idea of the so-called primary qualities apart from the so-called secondary. Hume reaches this conclusion by a careful analysis of motion, extension, and solidity, which turn out to be inconceivable when divorced from colors, sounds, tactile feelings, etc. In excluding "colours, sounds, heat and cold from the rank of external existences" (THN 229; 1.4.4.10), the modern philosophy has unwittingly subverted the idea of external objects entirely. (Before Hume, **George Berkeley** argues for the inconceivability of primary qualities apart from secondary. Before Berkeley, **Pierre Bayle** attacks the primary-secondary distinction.)

Although Hume rejects the primary-secondary quality distinction, he sometimes draws an analogy between secondary qualities and something else; e.g., the notion of necessary connection between causally related objects. The mind has a "great propensity to spread itself on external objects" (THN, 167; 1.3.14.25) and to conjoin them with any internal impressions that are occasioned by the perception of the objects. This happens with colors, sounds, and smells, as we have seen. It also happens when we suppose that causal necessity or power is in the objects we observe rather than in our minds. In his discussion of the source of moral distinctions, Hume likens vice and virtue to the secondary qualities, "which, according to modern philosophy, are not qualities in objects, but perceptions in the mind" (THN, 469; 3.1.1.26). (In assessing the last assertion, we should keep in mind that Hume's opinion of "the modern philosophy" is, at best, mixed.)

PROOF. Hume uses *proof* as a term of convenience for propositions (or arguments) that are *practically*—but not *theoretically*—certain.

Strictly, Hume recognizes two—and *only* two—kinds of propositions (or arguments): those that are either intuitively or demonstratively certain (e.g., "every triangle has three sides" and "the square root of two is irrational") and those that are not certain in that way (e.g., "Abraham Lincoln was assassinated by John Wilkes Booth" and "California has a population of more than 30 million people"). In the language of EHU, propositions express either **relations of ideas** or **matters of fact**. But Hume understands that **common sense** and common language recognize more than two degrees of evidence. Thus, it would be "ridiculous" (Hume's word)—though not self-contradictory—to say that it is only probable that all persons must die or that the sun will rise tomorrow. Hume reserves the term *proof* for "such arguments from experience as leave no room for doubt or opposition" (EHU, 56n1; 131n10). In THN he makes the same trichotomous division in slightly different language: ***knowledge*** [in the full, unqualified sense], *proofs*, and *probabilities* (124; 1.3.11.2). Proofs, then, represent extremely high probabilities, not a genuinely distinct *kind* of knowledge.

Because *proof* is often used by modern writers as more or less interchangeable with *demonstration* (or as a species of demonstration), it is extremely important to remember that Hume does *not* use the term that way. Thus, for example, when he says in "Of Miracles" (section 10 of EHU) that we have a *proof* against the occurrence of **miracles**, he does not—and cannot—mean that miracles are literally impossible. His language in the passage is careful: " . . . the proof against a miracle, from the very nature of the fact, is as entire as any *argument from experience* can possibly be imagined" (EHU, 114; 173.12; italics are not in Hume's text).

PUFENDORF, SAMUEL (1632–1694). Pufendorf was a German historian and political and legal philosopher who exerted considerable influence on 18th-century thinkers. Though Hume rarely refers explicitly to Pufendorf, he certainly read some of Pufendorf's works and may well have had them in mind when he wrote about the foundations of justice and our obligation to obey the laws of society. Hume would concur, for example, in Pufendorf's argument that property (the central topic in Hume's theory of justice) arises from human conventions and does not reside in the essential nature of the things possessed. (See THN, book 3, part 2 ["Of justice and injustice"].) Hume would also agree with Pufendorf that people are neither purely selfish nor purely altruistic; they are capable of disinterested benevolence, but they typically exhibit a more "confin'd generosity." In his best-known work, *Of the Law of Nature and Nations*, Pufendorf tries to develop a theory of natural law that blends **Thomas Hobbes**'s melancholy picture of human nature with **Hugo Grotius**'s more optimistic reading. Human beings tend to be quarrelsome, competitive, and thin-skinned; but they also recognize their need for one another under a system of laws administered by a competent authority. Hume would agree in principle, but he would be unhappy with the theological underpinning Pufendorf supplies for his theory of human nature (and, indirectly, of natural law and morality).

PYRRHONISM. Hume's phrase for *excessive skepticism*, which derives its name from the Greek philosopher Pyrrho of Elis (360?–270? B.C.). Pyrrho left no writings, but he is associated with a kind of **skepticism** that has fascinated philosophers for more than two millennia. He was impressed by arguments that take the (at least apparently) inconsistent reports of our senses as evidence that we do not know what reality is in itself. He seems to have accepted a line of reasoning much like the *antinomies* of the German philosopher **Immanuel Kant**. These are pairs of mutually inconsistent propositions for which we seem to have equally persuasive evidence. Whereas Kant rejects the assumptions that generate the paradoxes (precisely *because* they generate paradoxes), Pyrrho is glad to embrace the results as proving the impotence of human **reason**.

There are incompatible accounts of Pyrrho's own life. One such account pictures him as so imbued with the principles of skepticism as to be incapable of surviving without more or less constant care by his followers. A very different perspective depicts him as a prudent man of sound **common sense**, one whose skepticism extended only to the opinions of "learned" people. In any case, he seems to have been interested principally in living a life free from pointless fears and concerns.

Hume uses Pyrrhonism for his own purposes, embracing its skeptical arguments at an abstract level but rejecting, as inconsistent with human activity, its recommendation to suspend judgment about everything. It is not lost on Hume that using reason to demonstrate the incompetence of reason is self-stultifying, but that is not the main focus of his attack on *excessive skepticism*. He even agrees with the Pyrrhonist that our commonsense beliefs (e.g., in **causation** and the external world itself) have no rational foundation; they rest on custom and habit. But, for all that, we cannot suspend judgment about such things. It is the demands of ordinary human existence—not philosophical rebuttals—that subvert Pyrrhonism (EHU, 158–59; 206.21). No one can actually *live* as a Pyrrhonist. Hume very nicely sums up his attitude in his *Abstract* to THN: ". . . we assent to our faculties, and employ our reason only because we cannot help it. Philosophy wou'd render us entirely *Pyrrhonian*, were not nature too strong for it" (657; 414.27; italics are in Hume's text).

Hume describes his own version of skepticism as *mitigated* or *academical*, in contrast with Pyrrhonism (EHU, 161–65; 207–10). In THN, he attributes *moderate* skepticism to "true philosophers" (224; 1.4.4.10). In his *Dialogues*, Hume says that *reasonable* skeptics reject "abstruse, remote and refined arguments" but "adhere to common sense and the plain instincts of nature" (154). This sort of skepticism has the salutary effect of steering philosophers away from "distant and high enquiries" that the human mind is by no means fitted to pursue (EHU, 162; 208.25). Hume is generous enough to credit the abstract arguments of Pyrrhonism with nudging us in that direction, even while rejecting the possibility of embracing Pyrrhonism as a way of life.

– R –

RATIONALISM. *See* EMPIRICISM AND RATIONALISM.

REASON. Probably the most famous single sentence Hume ever wrote is about reason: "Reason is, and ought only to be the slave of the passions, and can never pretend to any other office than to serve and obey them" (THN, 414; 2.2.3.4). The theme is a familiar one in Hume—the impotence of reason by itself to initiate or to prevent any action or volition—and it is clear what he means by *reason* in this instance. "Reason is the discovery of truth or falsehood", i.e., either the discovery of truths about abstract **relations of ideas** or the discovery of truths about **matters of fact** (THN, 458; 3.1.1.9). Since reason in this sense is perfectly inert, it cannot be the source of moral distinctions. Nevertheless, the *reason-as-slave* metaphor is misleading because it suggests that reason plays no important role in Hume's theory of the **passions** and, even more important, in his moral philosophy. Although reason cannot by itself induce us to do or forbear doing anything, it can indirectly influence the passions (moral or non-moral) by pointing out the best way to satisfy a desire; or, by showing that the desired object (or state of affairs) is either non-existent or unobtainable, reason can actually (though obliquely) extinguish a passion. David Fate Norton suggests that if we keep the slave/master figure, we should think of the arrangement between the Greeks and the Romans. In the end, the Greeks had to obey their Roman masters; but as teachers of the Roman youth, they exercised considerable power over their nominal masters. (*See* MORAL SENSE.)

Hume frequently opposes reason to experience when he is talking about our knowledge of causation: "*causes and effects are discoverable, not by reason but by experience*" (EHU, 28; 110.7; italics are in Hume's text). We never know the **cause**-effect relation by "reasonings *a priori*," but always by experience. This is reason in its a priori mode. On the other hand, "experimental reasoning" (EHU, 108; 168.6) is reasoning from experience. Hume also uses *reason* in other ways, often for the sake of comparing or contrasting it with something else. Sometimes he contrasts reason with *imagination* (e.g., THN, 117n1; 1.3.9.19n22; also the Conclusion of book 1); but sometimes he identifies reason with "the general and more establish'd properties of the imagination" (THN, 267; 1.4.7.7).

In defending his attribution of (causal) reason to animals (i.e., non-human animals), Hume describes reason as "nothing but a wonderful and unintelligible instinct in our souls" (THN, 179; 1.3.16.9). Animals can discern causal connections but cannot reason abstractly—a fact that fits neatly into Hume's account of how human beings acquire the notion of cause (i.e., by custom and habit, not by ratiocination). There is a cautionary note in all this: Do not conflate the *reason* found in dogs and birds with the *reason* found in geometers qua geometers. *See also* REASON IN ANIMALS. For an account of how (in Hume's view) **belief** can survive the skeptical subversion of reason, *see* SKEPTICISM.

REASON IN ANIMALS. Hume argues in both THN (176–79; 1.3.16) and EHU (section 9) that (non-human) animals are endowed with reason—and obviously so. When we (i.e., human beings) accommodate means to ends (e.g., when we prepare food to allay our hunger), we do so by reason and design. By the rules of analogy, we must infer that animals adjust means to ends the same way we do, i.e., by reason and design. And like us, animals never perceive any real connection among objects; they are led by custom and habit to suppose connections between constantly conjoined objects. Given that we share "experimental reasoning" with beasts, Hume concludes that it is "nothing but a species of instinct or mechanical power, that acts in us unknown to ourselves . . ." (EHU, 108; 168.6). He concedes that animals lack the human capacity for abstract or purely formal reasoning, or even slightly abstract practical calculations. A mother cat, for example, knows that she has, say, five kittens in her current litter, but she surely does not know that she has had a total of 16 kittens in her last three litters.

Hume also attributes *passions* to animals (pride and humility, love and hatred, courage, fear, anger), as well as *sympathy*, the communication of passions (THN, 324–28, 397–98; 2.1.12; 2.2.12). It is worth noting that Hume does *not* attribute *moral* sensitivity to animals (they "have little or no sense of virtue or vice"). In one of his arguments against reason as the source of moral distinctions, he assumes, as an obvious fact, that animals are no more capable of moral or immoral acts than a tree (THN, 467–68; 3.1.1.24–25). As a natural corollary, Hume denies that animals have any notion of *right* or *property*.

REID, THOMAS (1710–1796). Reid was born exactly one year (to the day) before Hume and was a philosopher of genius in his own right. He was the first and most distinguished philosopher of what came to be known as the Scottish school of **common sense**. Many regard Reid as second only to Hume among Scottish philosophers. He was born near Aberdeen, Scotland; served as a Presbyterian minister; and held academic appointments in King's College, Aberdeen, and as Professor of Moral Philosophy in the University of Glasgow (the latter with the support of **Henry Home**, Lord Kames).

It would be inaccurate and unjust to describe Reid's own philosophy as merely a response to Hume; but Reid himself confesses that he was wakened from his bewitchment at the hands of **George Berkeley,** only after reading Hume's *Treatise*—long before **Kant** was similarly roused from his dogmatic slumber by the same philosopher. Reid sees Hume's **skepticism** as the inevitable outcome of premises accepted by Berkeley, and this in spite of Berkeley's repeated insistence that his own philosophy is the only proper antidote to skepticism. (The offending premises are found in **John Locke**, though Reid, curiously, says that Locke is not a skeptic.) If a philosopher finds himself in a coal pit, then he may be sure that he has made a wrong turn somewhere—the coal pit in this case being what Reid takes to be Hume's skepticism about our knowledge of ourselves, of the external world, and of moral principles.

Reid locates the germ of Hume's skepticism in the doctrine (inherited, mainly, from Locke) that we are never aware of objects themselves, but only of our own **perceptions**, which Hume classifies as either *impressions* or *ideas*. If that were true, Reid argues, the world of ordinary objects and persons (the perceiver included) would be reduced to a congeries of "perpetually perishing" perceptual bits bound loosely together by certain associational affinities (resemblance, spatio-temporal contiguity, and **causation**). The consequences of this theory ("the ideal system," as Reid calls it) are violently at odds with pervasive human experience—a fact that Hume himself admits in his invocation of *nature, custom, and habit* as the only effective antidotes to his philosophical skepticism.

With so exiguous a supply of basic elements (impressions and ideas), Reid argues, Hume cannot account for even the most elementary sorts of human **experience** (perception, memory, thought). Worse yet, there is no experiential evidence that *ideas* (i.e., Humean *perceptions*)—in the philosophical-theoretical sense—exist at all. All of us see flowers and trees, remember the horse we saw yesterday, and draw conclusions from premises; but none of these activities have any connection with the philosopher's *ideas*. Reid has parallel criticisms of Hume's moral philosophy. Against Hume, Reid argues that morality must rest on something more than feelings or sentiments of approval or disapproval.

Not surprisingly, the secondary literature on Reid's strictures of Hume is sizeable. Some critics claim that Reid simply misreads Hume, supposing Hume to be merely negative, merely skeptical. But whether Reid misconstrues Hume's *intentions* is beside the main substantive point. Reid argues that Hume is bound, by the logic of his commitments (especially the theory of ideas), to end in total skepticism; and further, that Hume's efforts to mitigate the effects of his skeptical premises do not work. The only reasonable response, in Reid's view, is to repudiate the skeptical premises themselves. The issues separating Reid and Hume are complex and fascinating; and they are *philosophical*, not biographical.

So far as one can tell, Hume and Reid never met personally. They exchanged a few letters, which are of scant philosophical value (due mainly to Hume's disinclination to engage Reid in serious discussion). Reid's expressions of respect and admiration for Hume—e.g., "the greatest Metaphysician of the Age"—seem to have been genuine. And Hume has the decency to separate "Dr. Reid" from "that bigoted silly Fellow, Beattie" among his critics. It is regrettable that Hume chose not to respond at greater length to Reid's friendly invitation to comment on an abstract of *An Inquiry into the Human Mind, on the Principles of Common Sense*—a systematic criticism of "the ideal system" by an honest and acute philosopher. In a letter to Hugh Blair, Hume offers a few sketchy comments that beg for amplification. Here is a case where Hume's resolution not to reply to criticism served the world of philosophy badly. Reid's other two books—*Essays on the Intellectual Powers of Man* (1785) and *Essays on the Active Powers of Man* (1788)—were published after Hume died.

RELATIONS. Like **John Locke** in his *Essay Concerning Human Understanding*, Hume reduces the apparently numberless varieties of complex **ideas** to three fundamental kinds: Ideas of Relations, Modes, and **Substances** (THN, 13; 1.1.4.7). He notes that the word *relation* is used in two distinct senses, which he calls the *natural* and the *philosophical*. A relation is *natural* if it connects two ideas in such a way that the one introduces the other automatically, without any conscious effort (i.e., *naturally*). There are three natural relations, which Hume uses to explain the "connexion or **association of ideas**"; namely, resemblance, contiguity or separation in time or place, and **cause and effect**. A *philosophical* relation, on the other hand, does *not* link ideas imperceptibly, without our having to think about it. Philosophical relations are the result of reflection, not of the automatic operation of the **imagination**. We may suppose a philosophical relation between any two ideas we choose to compare, even those that have no natural relation at all. Poets often invoke such relations in their descriptions: "Shall I compare thee to a summer's day? Thou art more lovely and more temperate." Hume himself compares the soul (or self) to a republic or commonwealth (THN, 261; 1.4.6.19).

Hume's division of relations into natural and philosophical arises from a certain ambiguity in the notion of *resemblance*. In one sense, resemblance is a necessary condition of all philosophical relations, inasmuch as all such relations require a *comparison* of objects. In another sense—the more usual one—resemblance holds only between objects that are *alike*, ideas that make us think of the other when we think of the first. Besides the three natural relations mentioned above, Hume lists four additional philosophical relations (seven in all): *identity* (the most universal of relations, since it holds of "every being, whose existence has any duration" [THN, 14; 1.1.5.4]); *quantity* or *number*; *degrees of quality* [e.g., deeper in color, or heavier]; and *contrariety*.

When Hume comes to the subject of **knowledge** and probability (part 3 of book 1 of THN), he divides the seven philosophical relations according to a different principle; namely, those that "depend entirely on the ideas, which we compare together" and those that "may be chang'd without any change in the ideas" (THN, 69; 1.3.1.1). Hume's language here may be puzzling, but his intention becomes clear with a few examples. From the idea of a triangle we discover that its three angles are equal to 180 degrees, and this numerical ratio cannot change so long as we are thinking about a triangle. On the other hand, I may be in my office or 500 miles away from it, without any change in me or my office. I cannot know relations of *distance* merely from the idea. Likewise, I cannot discover a causal relation merely by considering two ideas (*see* CAUSE).

Using this new way of classifying relations, Hume finds that four of the seven relations—those that depend solely on ideas—"can be the objects of knowledge and certainty" (THN, 70; 1.3.1.2): resemblance, contrariety, degrees in quality, and proportions in quantity or number. The first three are known directly, or by intuition, rather than by demonstration. For example, we can normally see (or otherwise discern, by hearing, for example) that two objects resemble each other; and we can see without any reasoning that one object is a much deeper shade of blue than a second object. While the axioms of algebra and arithmetic may be known intuitively, most interesting and useful exercises in mathematics are carried out by demonstration. The other three relations—identity, relations of time and space, and causation—cannot provide certainty but are important as bases for probable **beliefs**. Indeed, Hume is much more interested in them, especially causation, than in the four relations that provide certainty. In EHU, Hume greatly simplifies the distinction between propositions that yield certainty (i.e., **relations of ideas**) and those that yield only probability (i.e., **matters of fact**).

It is worth noting that in THN Hume relegates geometry to a position inferior to that of algebra and arithmetic—a position that he repudiates in EHU. Indeed, in EHU, Hume lists Geometry, Algebra, and Arithmetic (in that order) as sciences that yield intuitive or demonstrative certainty. Compare THN, 71–72; 1.3.1.4–7 with EHU, 25; 108.1.

RELATIONS OF IDEAS AND MATTERS OF FACT. The distinction signified by these terms (sometimes referred to as **Hume's Fork**) is of absolutely fundamental importance in Hume's theory of **knowledge**. Taken together, the two categories exhaust "[a]ll the objects of human reason or enquiry" (EHU, 25; 108.1). This dichotomy is simpler and clearer than the taxonomy of THN, which divides the seven "philosophical **relations**" into two classes: those that "can be the objects of knowledge and certainty" (70; 1.3.1.2) and those that cannot be such objects.

Obvious examples (but not the only ones) of propositions expressing relations of ideas are from mathematics (algebra, arithmetic, and geometry, for example). Such propositions are *necessarily* true or *necessarily* false, and are knowable a priori; or, in Hume's words, by "the mere operation of thought, without dependence on what is anywhere existent in the universe" (EHU, 25; 108.1)—e.g., "3 > 2"; "3 × 5 = 15"; "all the radii of a circle are equal"; "a(b + c) = (ab + ac)"; "the three angles of a triangle are equal to two right angles." These assertions are either *intuitively* or *demonstrably* true, but they tell us nothing about the actual world. As Hume acutely observes, all of Euclid's theorems about triangles and circles would be true even if there had never been a triangle or circle in nature. In THN (82; 1.3.4.8), Hume provides a clear non-mathematical example of an a priori truth (though he does not use the phrase *relations of ideas*): "Every effect must have a cause." This proposition is true by definition, since *cause* and *effect* are correlative terms. It is, therefore, perfectly irrelevant to the factual question whether everything that begins to exist must have a cause of existence (or, more simply, whether every *event* must have a cause). One could just as well infer the false conclusion that all men are married from the indisputable truth that every husband must have a wife.

By contrast, propositions expressing matters of fact are never knowable a priori, are never intuitively or demonstrably true. Examples of propositions expressing matters of fact: "Water freezes at or below 32° F./0° C."; "no human being can swim the Atlantic Ocean non-stop"; "gorillas cannot read English." Whether these three assertions are true or false must be determined by experience, not by merely inspecting the ideas involved.

Hume's *relations of ideas/matters of fact* distinction is anticipated by the famous German philosopher and mathematician Gottfried Wilhelm Leibniz (1646–1716), who distinguishes *truths of **reason*** (or *reasoning*) from *truths of fact*. Truths of reason are *necessary* and their denials *impossible*; truths of fact are *contingent* and their denials *possible*. Hume often uses essentially the same criterion to demarcate relations of ideas from matters of fact. After Hume, philosophers have used a variety of paired terms to capture Hume's bifurcation; e.g., *analytic/synthetic*; *a priori/a posteriori*; *formal/factual*.

Each of the pairs just listed calls attention to a different aspect of the distinction. A proposition is *analytic* if the predicate can be found in the subject merely by analysis ("A rose is a flower"); otherwise, it is *synthetic* ("Some roses grow north of the Arctic Circle"). A proposition is *a priori* if its truth can be determined without any appeal to experience ("A bachelor is unmarried"); otherwise, it is *a posteriori* ("Some bachelors are more than seven feet tall"). A proposition is *formal* if its truth is a consequence of its form ("Either it's raining or it's not raining"); otherwise, it is *factual* ("It rains at least three hundred days a year in Seattle"). It is a matter of dispute whether these pairs refer to strictly coextensive sets of propositions, but it seems clear that Hume regards as certain some propositions that cannot be assimilated to the *analytic* category. For example, the proposition "*Orange* is closer to *yellow* than it is to *blue*" is undeniably true, but surely *not* analytic. This example is adapted from Hume (THN, 637; 1.1.7.7n5). It represents a case of *resemblance*, a relation that affords us intuitive certainty (THN, 70; 1.3.1.2).

If Hume is right about the *relations of ideas/matters of fact* dichotomy, then we cannot demonstrate the **existence** of anything. Anything that exists, might not have existed. "The non-existence of any being, without exception, is as clear and distinct an idea as its existence" (EHU, 164; 209.28). Notice that Hume does *not* deny that we can be (practically) sure of the existence of anything; nor does he say that we can *believe* that certain things do not exist. For example, we cannot believe that no other persons exist. His point is that we can intelligibly conceive the non-existence of any being, and that precludes the possibility of *demonstrating* its existence.

The case is entirely different with relations of ideas. Not only is "3 + 2 = 8" false; it is inconceivable, unintelligible. We know with certainty the truth of "3 + 2 = 5", but that tells us nothing about the real world of **experience**. "Mixed" mathematics (what we call *applied* mathematics) depends on the truth of laws discovered by experience, which are ineluctably tainted with uncertainty (EHU, 31; 112.13). When physicists or engineers apply **Isaac Newton**'s Second Law of Motion (Force = the product of mass times acceleration: $F = m \times a$), they may be quite certain that they have multiplied the two numbers correctly, but they can *never* be certain that the numbers correctly represent the physical facts involved. Empirical measurements are never absolutely precise or absolutely certain.

Armed with his two-pronged weapon, Hume thinks that he can fulfill the promise of section 1 of EHU, to destroy "false and adulterate" metaphysics. In the last paragraph of the last section of that book, he bolts the door (so to speak). If we examine a volume that is devoid of "abstract reasoning concerning quantity or number" (relations of ideas) and also devoid of "experimental reasoning concerning matter of fact and existence" (matters of fact), then we may safely throw it into the fire, "for it can contain nothing but sophistry and illusion" (EHU, 165; 210.34). Hume mentions "divinity" (i.e., theology) and medieval scholastic metaphysics as examples of such worthless speculation; but modern readers may suspect that Hume's targets also include rationalist philosophers (e.g., **René Descartes**, Spinoza, and Leibniz), whose writings abound with alleged demonstrations of matters of fact. But he also has in mind such empiricist philosophers as **John Locke** and **George Berkeley**, who offer demonstrations of the existence of God.

RELIGION. This entry is intended as a brief *précis* of Hume's treatment of religion. For a more detailed exposition, see the section *Philosophy of Religion* in the introduction to this book.

Hume professed no religious beliefs and indeed evinced a pretty uniform hostility to religion, but he still found religion fascinating throughout his life. Perhaps it was, in part, the kind of interest a medical researcher takes in the etiology of a disease, for Hume certainly thought that the influence of religion was generally pernicious. Why, then, have human beings almost universally espoused some religion or other? That is a question of genesis, or origin, which Hume seeks to answer in *The Natural History of Religion*. He takes on certain philosophical questions about religious doctrines in *Dialogues Concerning Natural Religion* and in two sections of EHU: section 10 ("Of Miracles") and section 11 ("Of a Particular Providence and of a Future State"). Several of his essays deal with subjects relevant to religion; e.g., "Of Superstition and Enthusiasm," "Of Suicide," "Of the Immortality of the Soul," and "The Platonist."

Religion arose, Hume argues, not from a contemplation of the works of nature but from the precarious and necessitous condition of humans on the earth. "We hang in perpetual suspense [*sic*] between life and death, health and sickness, plenty and want; which are distributed amongst the human species by secret and unknown causes, whose operation is oft unexpected, and always unaccountable. These *unknown causes*, then, become the constant object of our hope and fear . . ." (NHR, 28–29; italics are in Hume's text). In those circumstances, it was virtually inevitable that our imagination would invest the unknown causes with human qualities of intelligence and will (i.e., turn them into gods), and that humans would devise ways to placate the gods (by sacrifices and rituals, for example). Monotheism (belief in exactly one God) came later, with ostensibly better intellectual credentials but with a greater tendency to intolerance than one finds in polytheism (especially its earlier forms).

The so-called ontological and cosmological arguments purport to demonstrate the **existence** of God. On Hume's view, we cannot demonstrate the existence of *any* being; so he rejects those arguments out of hand. In the *Dialogues* and section 11 of EHU, he examines the argument from/to **design**, since it purports to show only that God's existence is *probable* in the light of the evidence. Although Hume does not unqualifiedly reject that argument, he finds it considerably weaker than its proponents suppose. He seeks also to show that testimonial evidence cannot justify belief in **miracles**, which were regularly invoked to support certain religious claims.

Hume's considered position seems to be that religion is incurably superstitious, which is to say, among other things, that it is not founded on good causal reasoning (not all faulty causal reasoning is superstitious). Because **superstition** is often emotionally powerful, Hume contends that "Generally speaking, the errors in religion are dangerous; those in philosophy only ridiculous" (THN, 272; 1.4.7.13). Consequently, readers must be puzzled to have Hume say, more than once, that religion (or sometimes *true* religion) is a species of philosophy (e.g., EHU, 146; 196.27). But Hume may mean only that true religion is like philosophy in not carrying any emotional charge. This seems to be the burden of Philo's statement at the end of the *Dialogues*; namely, that we may believe that the cause of the universe is probably like the human mind, provided that we do not infer from that conclusion any moral or social obligation or, indeed, anything that affects human life at all. A good religion does not promulgate speculative doctrines, and it does not animate us to do anything. One is reminded of Alfred North Whitehead's *bon mot* about the Unitarian creed: "There is one God at most."

Critics—some of them generally sympathetic—have scored Hume for his relentlessly negative depiction of religion. In particular, such critics complain (among other things) that Hume's analysis of religion is based on a narrow and biased selection of evidence, that it ignores the salutary effects of religion (many of them obvious), that it fails to prove the *inherently* superstitious character of religion, that it often represents little more than armchair theorizing. These strictures point to genuine flaws in Hume's treatment of religion, but they mainly reflect Hume's ignorance of certain facts about religion and his personal animus against religion. They have little to do with the *philosophical* questions Hume raises about the status of certain religious doctrines. On questions of that sort, Hume remains a watershed figure, whatever one may think about Hume's own answers to the questions.

ROUSSEAU, JEAN-JACQUES (1712–1778). Philosopher, essayist, musician, and novelist, Rousseau was born in Geneva but spent most of his life elsewhere, mainly in France. He is undoubtedly one of the most influential thinkers of the 18th century, and his influence extends far beyond philosophy in the narrow academic sense. This entry deals with Rousseau's thought, not his biography (fascinating as that may be). For an account of his ill-fated relationship with Hume, see the sketch of Hume's life in the introduction of this book.

In 1750, Rousseau won the prize offered by the Academy of Dijon for his *Discourse on the Sciences and Arts* (often referred to as the *First Discourse*), which answers the Academy's question "Has the restoration of the sciences and arts tended to purify morals [*épurer les moeurs*]?" Whether we construe *moeurs* as *morals* or as *manners/ customs/culture*, the rise of the sciences and arts has been a corrupter, in Rousseau's opinion. He cites numerous examples of how the dissemination of knowledge enfeebles: ancient Egypt, Greece, Rome, Constantinople, and modern China. They fell to external conquerors as they developed philosophy, the arts, and the sciences. On the contrary, the Persians, Scythians, the early Germans, and the Swiss were virtuous but unenlightened. Sparta was moral, and Athens corrupt. Athens became a model of civility and good taste, the country of orators and philosophers—and also a veritable model of corruption.

In the second part of his *First Discourse* Rousseau explains how and why enlightenment corrupts. In the first place, we are more likely to find dangerous errors than truth when we pursue the sciences. The medieval maxim "Truth is one, error many" is exactly right. Even well-intentioned seekers of truth have no sure criteria to tell them when they have found it. And who seeks truth sincerely? Further, knowledge produces luxury, which breeds wasted time—a serious offence in Rousseau's judgment. The spread of luxury and living conveniences—the fruit of the sciences and arts—saps courage and the military virtues. Equally important, cultivation of the arts and sciences vitiates the moral qualities of citizens. A foolish education fills the minds of children with useless, degrading twaddle, but teaches them nothing about equity, temperance, humanity, courage, or patriotism. This elevation of specious, useless talents and the debasement of virtue leads to a disastrous inequality among people—a topic that Rousseau treats in his *Second Discourse*.

The *First Discourse* shows Rousseau as mordantly anti-enlightenment; it must be balanced by the other side of his political philosophy. Even in that generally iconoclastic work, Rousseau gives occasional hints that his denunciation of the arts and sciences is hyperbolic, that they are not *inherently* mischievous but become so when they are misused. He exempts true geniuses—Verulam (i.e., **Francis Bacon**), **René Descartes**, and **Isaac Newton** are mentioned by name—from his interdiction against studying the sciences and the arts. They needed no teachers but were themselves "preceptors of the human race." The bulk of humankind, however, are well advised to stay away from learned professions and do something suited to their talents. Rousseau reminds us how much better it is to be an excellent cloth maker than a bad poet or a middling geometer.

Rousseau's *Discourse on the Origin and Foundations of Inequality among Men* (a.k.a. the *Second Discourse*), published in 1755, answers the question posed by the Academy of Dijon: "What is the Origin of Inequality among Men and is it Authorized by the Natural Law?" Although the *Second Discourse* did not win a prize, it is much longer than the prize-winning essay of 1750 and is a more accurate harbinger of the comprehensive political philosophy in *The Social Contract* (1762). Despite its title, the question of inequality is not the only—or even the primary—focus of the *Second Discourse*. That question gets answered in the course of Rousseau's discussion of human nature and the rise and corruption of civil government.

Following the lead of **Thomas Hobbes** and **John Locke** in the 17th century, Rousseau uses the *Gedankenexperiment* of a "state of nature" (i.e., the condition of humans without civil government) to discover what we were like before the trammels of society turned us into *citizens*. In this way, he seeks to find the essence of human being in its purity, before it acquires the accidental (i.e., non-essential) characteristics that come with socialization. This sets Rousseau in opposition to Aristotle (to take only the most prominent example of a whole school of thought), who holds both that human beings are by nature political (or social) animals and that the state is a creation of nature (e.g., *Politics*, book 1, chapter 2, 1253).

Rousseau's view of "primitive" or "natural" man is complex and subtle, in contrast to the simplistic picture evoked by the phrase often associated with Rousseau—the "noble savage." Although he endorses Hobbes's method of probing human nature by mentally stripping away the accretions of socialization, Rousseau rejects at least two Hobbesian doctrines about that imaginary state of affairs. First, Hobbes's description of the pre-civil state as a "condition of war"— the war of every man against every man—is actually a description of civilized people who have been divested of all effective restraints and the fruits of cooperation. Genuinely primitive men would lack the concepts, the emotions, the mental facility, and the language required to live in a perpetual state of fear, suspicion, and mistrust. The very idea of a pervasive Hobbesian war—a state of unremitting suspicion and truculence—would have been beyond them.

Second, Rousseau agrees with Hobbes that self-preservation is a fundamental instinct in humans; but unlike Hobbes, he discerns a balancing instinct—pity or compassion—which enables us to enter into the suffering of our fellow creatures and restrains us from inflicting gratuitous pain. The "natural sentiment" of pity lies at the root of all the social virtues—generosity, clemency, benevolence, even friendship. It tempers the natural love of self that each of us embodies; it inclines us to seek our own good with the least possible harm to others. Unfortunately, the products of reasoning—education and philosophy of a destructive sort—tend to make us vain and callous: "I've got mine; the devil take the hindmost." Fortunately, reasoning need not ineluctably turn us into uncaring egoists. Properly used, reason points to a solution to the problem of reconciling the interests of individual citizens with the good of society.

When Rousseau discusses inequality, he is not talking about differences in size, strength, intelligence, dexterity, etc., i.e., natural or physical inequality. He is, rather, concerned with moral or political inequality, which depends on conventions established by human beings and allows some persons to enjoy certain privileges that work to the detriment of others—to be richer, more honored, more powerful, etc. In the "state of nature," people are free and equal, at least to the extent that they are not subject to external coercion (constraint or restraint). In such a state, there is no "mine or thine" (Hobbes's phrase). The first person who declared "this is mine" and persuaded others to accept his claim laid the foundation for civil society. This notion of *property*, which engendered all manner of noxious consequences (war, murder, crime, and other horrors), became thinkable only after eons of time, during which human beings very slowly developed their mental capacities, including the ability to use *language*. A natural (though contingent) corollary of increased sophistication was the division of labor, which fostered inequality. Rousseau mentions the rise of agriculture and metallurgy as being especially important in the emergence of class distinctions. The smelter, the smith, the farmer, the soldier—to say nothing of the owner or master—have different functions and, inevitably, different levels of respectability and wealth.

The first reasonably permanent and stable governments arose after an extremely long period of temporary associations (*herds*, as Rousseau calls them) that were formed for a specific purpose and dissolved as soon as the purpose was achieved; and also after the longer-lived relationships intrinsic to the family and its ramifications. These people did not need an explicit agreement or contract setting out the terms and arrangements for their common good. The contracts that emerged from the stratification of society were fraudulent in that they helped to ensure the continued domination of the wealthy and powerful. In later works—the *Discourse on Political Economy* and, most important, *The Social Contract*—Rousseau explores the possibility of enacting a covenant or contract that would secure justice as well as order.

The Social Contract is the most systematic and complete account of Rousseau's political philosophy. In the "Introductory Note" to that work, he states his aim: To determine "whether, taking men as they are and laws as they can be made, it is possible to establish some just and certain rule of administration in civil affairs." In answering this question, he tries to "reconcile what right permits with what interest prescribes," so that justice and utility will not be sundered. The first sentence of book 1 is probably Rousseau's most famous pronouncement: "Man is born free, and everywhere he is in chains." This striking claim reflects Rousseau's love of paradox; but it also sets a fundamental problem of civil societies in all times and places: how to create and maintain the proper balance between individual liberty and the general interest of the state, which are desiderata that sometimes conflict with one another. Rousseau recognizes that although the general problem is universal, particular solutions (the form of government, for example) may vary widely, depending on such contingent factors as geography, climate, the abundance or scarcity of natural resources, the character of the people, etc., etc. But it is of the highest importance to understand that the overarching problem *is* universal. Since no one has any natural authority over other human beings, and since sheer force (of whatever sort) never makes right, it follows that conventions, or social arrangements, constitute the only basis for lawful authority. The crux of Rousseau's own solution lies in what he calls *the general will.*

It is hard to say precisely what the Rousseauvian general will is, but we can begin by considering a straightforward logical point about the relation between the parts of a whole and the whole itself. It is a fallacy—called the fallacy of *composition*—to suppose that a property of every part of a whole must also be a property of the whole itself. A related but logically independent version of the fallacy may be stated negatively: It is a fallacy to suppose that a whole cannot have a property that the parts taken singly do not have. For example, a paragraph consisting of six well-written sentences will be a thoroughly bad paragraph if the sentences are about six unrelated subjects; and, conversely, a badly written paragraph may consist entirely of well-written sentences. (To avoid misunderstanding, we should note that a whole *may* have a property that each of its parts has.) The general will is not just the sum of the individual wills in the commonwealth; that would be merely an agglomeration of private wills with private interests. In consenting to the creation of a state or commonwealth, a person gives his/her individual rights to the community; or in Rousseau's language, the person *alienates*—conveys or transfers—his/her rights to the whole community. By this "act of association," the people produce what Rousseau calls a "moral and collective body," the body politic, which has a life and will that transcend the lives and wills of individuals or factions. In this way, the citizens of a state or commonwealth are both the *sources* of social and political authority and the *subjects* who must obey laws enacted under that authority. On its metaphysical side, the body politic arises from the free corporate acts of individual persons, and would not exist apart from such acts; but it is not reducible to those acts. It has properties not found in any one of the "contractors" or in the mere juxtaposition of any number of "contractors." To use the philosophical jargon of a later time, we might say that the body politic, or state or republic, is an *emergent* entity, or that it *supervenes* upon the relationships among the contracting people.

According to Rousseau, the Sovereign qua Sovereign (which is never identical with any particular government) is "infallible"; i.e., it has no interests contrary to the people. This relationship is not symmetrical, which is to say that individual citizens or groups of citizens may well have (or suppose that they have) interests contrary to general preservation and welfare of the state (i.e., the whole of all the citizens). Human beings always desire their own good, but they do not always discern what that good really is. They may be deceived even if they are not corrupt. The pursuit of disruptive private interests must be controlled, on pain of injury to the body politic, or even its dissolution. (The phrase *body politic* suggests an analogy with certain features of the human body, which is a complex organism comprising many sub-organisms that work together for the overall health of the whole body. A diseased part of the body—a gangrenous leg, for example—must be amputated for the survival of the "parent" organism. In some conditions [e.g., lupus], the body's immune system mysteriously attacks a part of the body as if it were a foreign invader. Readers will probably think of ways to apply this last example to the body politic.)

It has been suggested that the Rousseauvian general will bears some affinity with aspects of the theory of justice set out by the American philosopher John Rawls. Rawls describes a hypothetical situation that he calls "the original position," in which citizens would adopt laws of justice behind a "veil of ignorance." That is, they would have no way of knowing whether a given proposal would or would not be to their benefit in the nascent state, since they would have no idea what their position in that state would be. They would, consequently, opt for laws that treat citizens fairly and objectively, without regard to such extrinsic, accidental matters as wealth or social status. These laws would redound to the advantage of the whole commonwealth, although they were chosen by rational, self-interested individuals, i.e., persons who were looking out for their own interest, but not blindly or stupidly. In Rousseau's language, Rawlsian citizens choosing behind a veil of ignorance would express the general will.

Even casual readers of Rousseau cannot fail to be struck by his love of paradox: embracing what appear (at least) to be inconsistent positions on any number of issues. He says that he would rather be a man of paradoxes than a man of prejudices, suggesting that a person must be one or the other. Before proceeding further, we should note that the word *paradox* covers a range of cases, from apparent but tractable inconsistencies to genuine conceptual paradoxes, which philosophers have found fascinating since ancient times. So-called *semantic* paradoxes are generated by certain anomalies of self-reference. A very old example is about a Cretan named Epimenides, who proclaims "All Cretans are liars." Should we believe this honest-sounding fellow? If he is telling the truth, then we should not believe him. That is a paradox.

Rousseau's paradoxes are *not* descendants of Epimenides'. They are, rather, exemplified by statements such as "[people] will be forced to be free," which exploits an equivocation on *free*. A person is *naturally* free in the pre-civil condition, inasmuch as he is limited only by his own power and abilities and not by any external authority. That person acquires *civil* freedom or liberty only in a commonwealth or republic, in which his will is limited by the general will. In the state of nature, the individual has *possessions* for so long as he can keep them. In the civil state, he acquires a rightful *title* to his *property*, which is protected by the power of the state. Thus, the prima facie paradox of forcing a person to be free vanishes when we understand that one sort of freedom (the natural but precarious freedom of the solitary individual) is exchanged for another sort (the stable and protected freedom afforded by the state). The same analysis helps to dispel the appearance of inconsistency in Rousseau's pronouncements about *property*; namely, that it is both the root of countless terrible wrongs (e.g., in his *Second Discourse*) and also a cornerstone of the civil state created by the general will (as in *The Social Contract*). Both assertions are true, but not in the same sense. Rousseau should not be taken as repudiating the institution of *property* per se, but only its pernicious misuse to enshrine inequality and injustice. That we can so easily find instances of such misuse is a melancholy but undeniable fact of human history.

In Rousseau's view, the civil state confers on its citizens another fundamentally important dimension of freedom; namely, *moral* freedom. In the state of nature, a person might be *good*, if by *good* is meant only that he follows his natural impulses; but that is actually a kind of slavery. Unlike other animals, human beings are not condemned to obey their impulses without recourse. They may acquiesce in the impulses or resist them; they are free agents. It is this freedom and the consciousness of it, more than understanding or reason, that chiefly distinguishes persons from tigers, badgers, birds, snakes, and the like, and that demonstrates the spirituality of the soul. But this metaphysical seed cannot grow and flourish in solitude. Only in a community can a person become the master of himself by submitting to a self-prescribed law. In this way, a person attains moral freedom and the possibility of being *virtuous*. (For Hume's views on some of the issues Rousseau addresses, *see* JUSTICE.)

Historical note: Rousseau's formula for preserving individual freedom through submission to a kind of self-legislation is an inchoate anticipation of the more fully developed Kantian doctrine of the *categorical imperative*. The categorical imperative provides this fundamental criterion for determining the morality of an act: "Act only according to that maxim by which you can at the same time will that it should become a universal law." This cryptic-sounding statement means that we should always act in accordance with a maxim, or principle, that we would prescribe for all persons. Since we cannot consistently will a universal principle of mendacity, we cannot regard lying as morally permissible. The same reasoning rules out murder, theft, etc. In one of his several re-formulations of the categorical imperative, **Immanuel Kant** describes it as a principle of *autonomy*—the idea that moral agents obligate themselves to obey the law because they helped to establish it. Although Kant rejects important parts of Rousseau's theory, his own doctrine of morality as rooted in self-imposed obligations has a Rousseauvian flavor to it. Kant was much taken by Rousseau's

Émile, or On Education, without accepting all its claims about the proper way to educate children.

Published as part of *Émile* was *The Profession of Faith of a Savoyard Priest*, which is an important source of Rousseau's reflections on religion. We cannot discuss those works (or others, such as the autobiographical *Confessions*) in this entry, but they may be recommended as eminently worth reading.

Rousseau is never mentioned in any of Hume's published works. On the other hand, Hume's letters refer to Rousseau many times (some of the letters are to Rousseau himself) but reveal little of Hume's considered judgment of Rousseau's philosophy. Such judgments as Hume offers about Rousseau the thinker and writer are by the way and very brief, not detailed or carefully laid out. Hume expresses admiration for Rousseau's elegant writing style while describing his thought as undisciplined and fanciful (*extravagant* is Hume's word). Indeed, according to Hume, Rousseau himself feared that his works had no foundation (*ils pechent par le fond*). Interestingly, Hume regarded the fictional work *Heloise* as Rousseau's masterpiece, whereas Rousseau thought most highly of *The Social Contract*—a judgment (Hume implausibly maintained) as preposterous as Milton's preference for *Paradise Regained* over his other writings. Hume criticizes the sort of contractarian theory of the origin of civil society that Rousseau embraces; but, of course, chronology makes it impossible that he should have had Rousseau in mind.

– S –

SCEPTICISM. *See* SKEPTICISM.

SECONDARY QUALITIES. *See* PRIMARY AND SECONDARY QUALITIES.

SELF-LOVE. In THN, Hume objects to the term *self-love* as at least linguistically improper (THN, 329; 2.2.1.2), but he nevertheless asserts that unrestrained self-love is "the source of all injustice and violence" (THN, 480; 3.2.1.10). Strictly speaking, love always has as its object some *other* person, of whose thoughts, actions, and sensations the one who loves is not directly aware. Hume's attitude (toward the term at any rate) is different in EPM, where he discusses self-love at length and attaches an appendix on the topic. Hume rejects the claim that all human actions stem exclusively from self-love, though he concedes that self-love is a powerful motive in shaping our behavior. *See also* EGOISM; HOBBES, THOMAS; MANDEVILLE, BERNARD DE.

THE SENSIBLE KNAVE. Toward the very end of section 12 (conclusion) of EPM, Hume raises the possibility that a "sensible knave" (a "free rider" or clever criminal) might exploit the system of **justice** for his own greedy purposes without ever getting caught—and, we may suppose, without ever even being suspected. The maxim "honesty is the best policy" may be a good general rule, but it admits of many exceptions; and a man might be thought very wise who observed the general rule and cashed in on all the exceptions. Add the proviso (as Hume does) that this canny fellow would never do anything to threaten the system itself (since that would be against his own interests), and you have what appears (at least) to be a difficulty for Hume's account of justice. (We may be inclined initially to think of the sensible knave as a *sociopath* or *psychopath*, but that reading does not fit Hume's description. The knave is not compulsive or self-destructive; he is clever, cunning, and calculating, not obsessive. And we have no reason to think that he would take abnormal pleasure in seeing others suffer. He is selfish and greedy, but not a sadist.)

Hume goes on immediately to declare that anyone who *seriously* required an answer to that reasoning would not understand the answer. "If his heart rebel not against such pernicious maxims, if he feel no reluctance to the thoughts of villainy or baseness, he has indeed lost a considerable motive to virtue; and we may expect that his practice will be answerable to his speculation" (EPM, 283; 155.23). Honest persons—those with "ingenuous natures"—regard treachery and roguery with an antipathy and revulsion too strong to be overcome by the prospect of "profit or pecuniary advantage." On the contrary, "Inward peace of mind, consciousness of integrity, a satisfactory review of our own conduct; these are circumstances very requisite to happiness, and will be cherished and cultivated by every honest man, who feels the importance of them" (EPM, 283; 155–56.23).

Hume's response to the sensible knave is eloquent and moving and seems to strike exactly the right note of indignation. But can it be squared with what Hume says about the provenance (and the continuing status) of justice? According to Hume's doctrine, justice (comprising, e.g., keeping promises and obeying laws) is an "artificial **virtue**," i.e., one that depends on convention or social arrangement, as contrasted with the "natural virtues," which do not depend on convention. (In EPM, Hume scraps the "natural-artificial" distinction as merely verbal, but that does not signal any substantive change in doctrine.) In Hume's account, human beings establish rules of justice out of self-interest, which is better served by cooperation than by unlimited competition. The *moral* approbation of justice arises from **sympathy** with the public interest (THN, 499–500; 3.2.2.24). This is consistent with Hume's general view of virtue as rooted in some nonmoral fact about human beings: " . . . *no action can be virtuous, or morally good, unless there be in human nature some motive to produce it, distinct from the sense of its morality*" (THN, 479; 3.2.1.7; italics are in Hume's text). This means that Hume cannot appeal to some bedrock, irreducible moral obligation in evaluating an action or character.

Hume finds that "Personal Merit" (which includes, but is not limited to, virtue) consists entirely in possessing qualities of mind that fall into one or more of four categories: those that are *useful* or *agreeable* to the *person himself* or to *others* (EPM, 268; 145.1). What basis does Hume's theory provide for condemning the sensible knave? Being shrewd, the knave conceals his wrongdoing, so that he does not occasion disagreeable feelings in others. His actions are certainly useful and agreeable to himself, and they do no real harm to the public welfare. Indeed, we may well imagine that his public persona is that of a philanthropist, a solid citizen full of good works. Perhaps he contributes some of his ill-gotten wealth to charity, clever fellow that he is. (He would certainly not be the first or last to do that.)

It is a fact that we all (including Hume) do still heartily condemn such a swine, but why? Is Hume's instinctive response better than his theory? In the next paragraph, Hume reminds his readers that even the cleverest criminals are almost certain to be nailed sooner or later, with calamitous consequences for their reputations and fortunes. That observation is true—and reassuring—but it is completely irrelevant to the "ingenuous natures" passage. Honest people are certainly not offended by the prospect of exposure and punishment for the sensible knave—just the opposite, in fact.

Thomas Reid, a Scottish contemporary of Hume, argues that Hume's answer to the sensible-knave problem assumes that human beings have an intuitive sense that injustice and chicanery are morally detestable, whether detected or not. Without that assumption, Hume's answer does not work and, indeed, seems to be incoherent—or so Reid contends.

Not surprisingly, Hume scholars continue to engage the issue of the sensible knave. Some commentators maintain that Hume effectively abandons, or severely modifies, the account of justice he gives in THN. Others respond that Hume does no such thing, that the sensible-knave story does not require any significant change in his "standard" account of justice.

Historical note: The sensible knave will remind readers familiar with Plato's *Republic* (book 2/360) of the story of the ring of Gyges, which confers on its wearer the power to become invisible and, therewith, the power to do all sorts of wrong with impunity. Using the mythical amulet (or, actually, two of them) as a starting point, Plato poses the question whether it pays (i.e., is profitable) for a person to be just (or virtuous). The best possible condition would be to reap all the benefits of a thoroughly unjust and vicious life (wealth, power, pleasure) without ever being caught and punished—or so one of the characters in the dialogue argues. Plato takes most of the dialogue to refute that claim and to establish that *justice*—not injustice—is in fact profitable. Despite all the differences between the *Republic* and Hume's EPM, we may still think that the two philosophers are dealing with essentially the same question. Indeed, we may discern a Platonic tinge to Hume's instinctive, indignant verdict on the sensible knave, though his explicit theory seems very different indeed from Plato's.

SHAFTESBURY, THE THIRD EARL OF. Anthony Ashley Cooper (1671–1713), the third Earl of Shaftesbury, was the grandson of the first Earl, a famous Whig politician who became lord chancellor during the reign of Charles II. The first Earl was a friend and benefactor of **John Locke**, who was put in charge of the grandson's education. The grandson (the philosopher) came to disagree with some of Locke's positions (e.g., Locke's strong rejection of the doctrine of innate ideas), but their friendship survived intact until Locke died in 1704.

Shaftesbury's writings on a variety of topics (virtue, art, religious enthusiasm, wit, humor, etc.) were collected, with added notes and commentaries, into one volume—*Characteristics of Men, Manners, Opinions, Times* (1711), a revised edition of which appeared in 1714, the year after his death. Shaftesbury's writings were widely read and exerted an influence on several well-known thinkers, including Hume, who describes him as "the elegant Lord Shaftesbury" (speaking of his literary style, not his manner of dress). **Bernard de Mandeville** wrote *The Fable of the Bees* as an antidote to what he regarded as Shaftesbury's excessively amiable picture of human nature. **Francis Hutcheson** explicitly defends Shaftesbury against Mandeville's raillery.

Though a professed theist himself, Shaftesbury argues that morality can be separated from **religion**. Indeed, the religious conception of God as morally perfect makes sense only if we already have a conception of moral virtue—on pain of being reduced to the tautology "God is whatever God is." Religious teaching may provide an additional inducement to moral virtue, but religion is not necessary for morality. (**Ralph Cudworth** and **Samuel Clarke**—two well-known theistic philosophers of the period—are also keen to make morality independent of God's will, though they differ from Shaftesbury in other important respects; e.g., how we discern moral distinctions.)

A recurring theme in Shaftesbury's writings is the teleological—or goal-oriented—character of human beings and of **nature** itself (finally, the whole universe). We cannot understand an individual person without seeing his/her feelings, passions, sentiments, affections—the "stuff" of his/her conscious life—as constituting an internal system or order or "economy." The parts make no sense divorced from the whole and its purposes (just as the *hands* of a clock are intelligible only in relation to the function of the clock itself). Equally, we cannot understand human beings without seeing them as parts of a teleologically ordered natural world (which is itself part of the larger, teleologically ordered universe). This means that the well-being—the orderly, harmonious condition—of human beings is intimately tied to the well-being of the larger community.

Shaftesbury agrees with **Thomas Hobbes** that other-regarding behavior may be good for all concerned; but Shaftesbury denies the Hobbesian doctrine that all voluntary actions arise from selfish motives, even those actions that benefit others. Shaftesbury holds that a person may be motivated to an action by the prospect that it will be good for others and not merely as serving his or her own private interests. If Hobbes were right about this issue, the moral distinctions we draw (between virtue and vice, good and evil, etc.) would be baseless and illusory; and that is a position that no one seriously and, on sober reflection, can defend. *See* EGOISM.

If human beings are teleological creatures, what is their proper end? Virtue, of course. Human beings are capable of achieving virtue because they are capable of a certain kind of reflection, which may be hinted at by contrast. A mother cat may show courage in rescuing her kittens from a burning house, and a dog may show grief at the death of its owner. But neither the cat nor the dog (nor any other non-human animal) can reflect on the psychological states—the *affections*, as Shaftesbury would say—that motivated their actions. That is, they cannot entertain second-order (or "reflected") sentiments about the first-order sentiments that their courage or grief evince. They cannot feel gratified by their bravery or sorrow, nor could they feel guilty for their cowardice or insensitivity if they had acted in blameworthy ways. *We* (i.e., human beings) can, and regularly do so. We have the capacity to act from pity, kindness, gratitude (or their "Contrarys" [*sic*]); and, unlike non-human animals, we have the capacity to make those very actions and affections themselves "the Subject of a new Liking or Dislike." It is this capacity to feel the worthiness or unworthiness of our actions and sentiments that make us capable of virtue and vice. Shaftesbury suggests a natural affinity between our apprehension of aesthetic beauty (the balance, order, and harmony of light and color or tone and tempo, etc.) and our apprehension of moral beauty (the balance, order, and harmony of the affections, both within the individual person and with the natural and human environment).

Hume agrees with Shaftesbury that we discern moral distinctions by sentiment rather than by reason, but Hume complains that Shaftesbury occasionally yields to the rationalist urge to derive these distinctions "by metaphysical reasonings, and by deductions from the most abstract principles of the understanding" (EPM, 170; 74.4). It was Shaftesbury who first used the phrase *moral sense*, which Hume and other philosophers (such as Francis Hutcheson) adopted. Hume also speaks of *moral taste* (versus *reason*) as the source of our approbation or disapprobation of moral qualities (THN, 581; 3.3.1.15)—a phrase that suggests Shaftesbury's linking of aesthetic and moral discernment. Hume strongly concurs in Shaftesbury's rejection of egoism.

SKEPTICISM. (British spelling is *scepticism.*) It is essential to be clear that *ordinary* skepticism and *philosophical* skepticism are two very different things. The ordinary non-philosophical person is (or should be) skeptical of many claims; e.g., that horoscopes provide reliable advice for planning our activities for the day, that we can eat gluttonously and still lose weight if we take a certain pill, that many people have been abducted by space aliens, etc., etc. This sort of skepticism is directed to specific assertions or to limited classes of assertions (e.g., those based on ESP or Tarot cards). On the other hand, some philosophers claim to be skeptical of the very possibility of human **knowledge** about anything—the real nature of the world, the objective status of values, etc. Sometimes, the skepticism is more restricted. **John Locke**, for example, says that human beings cannot know the "real internal constitution" of physical objects; but he does not extend such doubts to mathematics. We are concerned here with philosophical skepticism only.

Writing in his *Abstract* of the *Treatise*, Hume declares that "the philosophy contained in this book is very sceptical" (THN, 657; 413. 27). Just what this simple statement means and entails has proved to be anything but simple. Indeed, the nature and extent of Hume's skepticism has been debated from his own lifetime to the present (the early years of the 21st century). The German philosopher **Immanuel Kant** accuses Hume's contemporary fellow Scot **Thomas Reid** (and some lesser figures) of misunderstanding *what* Hume is skeptical about. *That* Hume is skeptical in some non-ordinary sense, is beyond dispute; he says as much himself. But it is also beyond dispute that he never recommends that we quit believing in certain things that we cannot demonstrate (e.g., the **existence** of the external world and that the future will resemble the past). In fact, he holds that we could not help believing in those things even if we wanted to doubt them. The targets of Hume's skepticism are often rationalist *theories* of **causation** or morality, for example, rather than causation or morality itself. There is near-universal agreement about Hume's enmity toward rationalism, but scholars are still divided about Hume's own position. That able and responsible philosophers continue to disagree about Hume's skepticism suggests (a) that the issue is not simple, (b) that Hume sometimes states his views loosely, and (c) that we should pay careful attention to the specific contexts in which Hume talks about skepticism.

The sources of Hume's skepticism. Some critics—especially the earlier ones such as Thomas Reid and Thomas Hill Green (1836–1882)—claim that Hume's skepticism merely traces out the logical implications of the empiricist premises of John Locke, in a way and to an extent that Locke himself does not do and does not intend. Whether or not this view of the consequences of Hume's philosophy is defensible, it is not an accurate indicator of the actual sources of his skepticism. (As a matter of historical fact, it is **George Berkeley**, not Hume, who systematically and self-consciously seeks to demonstrate that Locke leads us into a cul-de-sac.) Hume was widely acquainted with the works of ancient and modern philosophers, but it was **Pierre Bayle**, the French author of the *Historical and Critical Dictionary*, who most directly shaped Hume's understanding of classical skepticism.

Hume discusses skepticism in many places. David Fate Norton notes that Hume evinces interest in at least five kinds of skepticism: Ethical or moral, religious, antecedent or Cartesian, Pyrrhonian or excessive, and academic or mitigated. In this entry we will concentrate on three places where Hume treats *epistemic* skepticism—the question whether knowledge is possible. We will list several entries that treat other examples of Humean skepticism.

In part 4, book 1 of THN—"Of the Sceptical and Other Systems of Philosophy"—Hume examines the trustworthiness of both **reason** and the senses, as means to knowledge. (He takes up other topics as well, but these are the relevant ones for our purpose here.)

1. "Of Scepticism with Regard to Reason" purports to show the ultimate futility of pure reason as a source of certain knowledge. (Strictly, the phrase *certain knowledge* is pleonastic, inasmuch as

any level of cognition short of certainty cannot count as knowledge; but Hume often uses *knowledge* in a less strict sense.) Although the rules of all the demonstrative sciences are "certain and infallible" in themselves, the reasoning powers of persons who use the rules are very far from that level of certitude. Indeed, we know from experience that we are liable to fall into error when we work with arithmetic or algebra, especially when the demonstrations are long and complicated. Hume proceeds to try to show that even very simple calculations are unavoidably attended with some degree of uncertainty, such is the inexpugnable weakness of our reasoning powers. This means that even our best efforts at abstract reasoning produce only probable conclusions, i.e., "all knowledge resolves itself into probability" (THN, 181; 1.4.1.4). Because demonstrative reasoning and probable reasoning are mutually exclusive, we cannot hope to find an area of overlap, one that is part demonstrative, part probabilistic. That is as impossible as finding a whole number that is both odd and even; we are stuck with probability.

Unhappily, probable reasoning is beset with the same crippling liability as the demonstrative: Its level of assurance must be adjusted not only by the nature of the subject matter involved, but also by the capacity of the person doing the reasoning, which is always less than ideal. This requirement has the effect of progressively lowering the probability of any judgment to the vanishing point. Here is a way of seeing Hume's point, though he does not use it. Consider any two non-zero numbers, m and n. When $n < 1$, the product of $m \times n$ will be less than m. Perform the multiplication endlessly, and the result will be "a total extinction of belief and evidence" (THN, 183; 1.4.1.6). Hume notes the paradoxical spectacle of reason demonstrating that **reason** is imbecilic, but he fastens on the psychological rather than the logical aspect of the paradox. Reason is successively ascendant and impotent, depending on the disposition of the mind (whether dogmatic or skeptical).

Hume's arguments in this section of THN have been both excoriated (e.g., by D. Stove) and defended (e g., by F. Wilson). Viewed in one way, Hume's argument about diminishing confidence is incurably wrongheaded, and obviously so. On this reasoning, we would be *less* confident of our answer to a problem *after* we had reviewed and carefully checked it, and still less confident after half a dozen other competent persons had found our answer to be correct. But this is nonsense! A more sympathetic reading of the "diminution" argument is suggested by D. Garrett, according to which the "rules of logic" that Hume invokes should be construed as part of cognitive psychology, not as strictly epistemic. Hume himself ascribes that argument to "that fantastic sect"—the Pyrrhonists, or extreme skeptics. His purpose is to show that reason alone—"without any peculiar manner of conception, or the addition of a force and vivacity" (THN, 184; 1.4.1.8)—would ineluctably destroy itself and lead to a total suspense of judgment. But in fact, belief is *"more properly an act of the sensitive, than of the cogitative part of our natures"* (THN, 183; 1.4.1.8; italics are in Hume's text).

2. In the second section of part 4—"Of Scepticism with Regard to the Senses"—Hume seeks to prove that we cannot justify our belief in the external world any more than we can justify our reliance on reason. But he assures us from the start that we cannot actually doubt the existence of "body"; we can only try to locate the **causes** that induce that belief. He examines the roles of the senses and of reason in establishing the *continued* and *distinct* existence of material bodies, and concludes that neither faculty can do the job. In the end, it is **imagination** that affords a plausible explanation, though emphatically *not* a justification, for our belief.

A material object is *continuous* if it exists when it is not present to the senses; it is *distinct* if it does not depend on **perception** or thought, whether perceived or not. Hume says (THN, 188; 1.4.2.2) that if a body is continuous, it must be distinct; and vice versa. In fact, the two properties are related asymmetrically: Continuity implies distinctness, but not the other way around. If an object continues to exist when it is not perceived, then it must be distinct, i.e., not dependent on perception. On the contrary, an object might be distinct and yet, for reasons too profound even to be surmised, just happen to exist at only those times when it was perceived, i.e., might *not* be continuous.

That the senses cannot give us the idea of the *continuous* existence of physical objects (i.e., their existence when *not* perceived) is too obvious to require elaboration. But neither can the senses convey the idea of a *distinct, independent, external* object. They convey a *single* perception, without the slightest intimation of anything beyond the perception. The senses, then, can never, by themselves, produce the idea of a *double existence*—the person's perception + the non-perceptual object. That sort of inference is the province of reason or imagination.

It turns out, however, that *reason* is equally incapable of giving us the idea of continuous, distinct external objects. We often attribute external existence to sounds and colors with no recourse to reason or to any philosophical principles. On the contrary, ordinary people suppose that the very things they perceive have a distinct, continuous existence, whereas philosophers hold that the mind is directly aware only of perceptions, which have an interrupted and dependent existence. It is not at all clear precisely what view Hume intends to impute to the "vulgar," but all he needs at this point is the plain fact that ordinary people do not acquire their belief in external objects by way of reason. But the problem is not merely that we do not, in fact, get our belief in external objects from reason. The problem is that we could not possibly get that belief from reason. Our knowledge of cause-effect relations proceeds from observing constant conjunctions between the things we perceive; so the philosopher certainly cannot *reason* (causally) from the things he perceives (i.e., perceptions) to things he never perceives (i.e., independent external objects). Causal reason cannot bridge that gap.

Since neither the senses nor reason can account for our belief in an independent, continuously existing physical world, *imagination* gets the job by default. Hume says that imagination fastens on a couple of features of experience—*constancy* and *coherence*—and explains them by the fiction of persisting material objects. (*Fiction* here does not mean flat-out false, but not justifiable by appeal to any garden-variety perceptions.) In an effort to accommodate both reason and imagination, philosophers have devised the system of *double existence*—an inherently labile Rube Goldberg invention that concedes to reason the impermanence of *perceptions* but grants to imagination the permanence of *objects*. Hume describes the system as "the monstrous offspring of two principles" (THN, 215; 1.4.2.52) that cannot be reconciled but cannot be eradicated either. He concludes his discussion by noting that there is no lasting cure for the skeptical doubts that inevitably arise when we try to defend either reason or the senses. Our best remedy is "carelessness and in-attention," assured that no one will ever actually doubt the reality of either the internal or external world (THN, 218; 1.4.2.57). This overall conclusion fits perfectly with Hume's repeated insistence that our basic beliefs rest on instinct, custom, and habit and are, consequently, beyond the reach of philosophical criticism.

Hume's first *Enquiry*—EHU—takes its readers on a similar but far less complicated journey. Section 4—"Sceptical Doubts Concerning the Operations of the Understanding"—raises questions about the competence of reason to discern cause-effect relations and, consequently, to know what the world is like. Section 5—"Sceptical Solution of These Doubts"—allays the doubts of section 4 by reminding us that nature pays no attention to skeptical arguments, even though we cannot refute them. But it also changes the focus of the question, from trying to *justify* our beliefs about causation and the existence of the external world to describing how we get the beliefs. This follows the pattern in THN: We cannot ask whether physical objects exist, but only what causes us to believe in them.

3. In the last section of EHU—"Of the Academical or Sceptical Philosophy"—Hume discusses some varieties of skepticism (actually just two species, which are carved up in different ways). In his *Meditations*, **René Descartes** promotes what Hume labels *antecedent* skepticism, which calls for wholesale doubts of our previous opinions and even our faculties of sense and reason. But if we could follow Descartes' injunction to doubt everything (we cannot), we would have no way of recovering any of the tools essential for knowledge or belief. (Hume may have misunderstood Descartes, but that is nothing to the present point.) Descartes invokes the veracity of God to vouchsafe a "limited letter of credit" (A. N. Whitehead's apt phrase) to our cognitive faculties. Hume notes that in appealing to God this way, Descartes travels "a very unexpected circuit" (EHU, 153; 202.13), inasmuch as he has called into doubt the very means by which he might prove the existence of God.

Consequent (versus *antecedent*) skepticism grows out of an examination of the human faculties of sense and reason and of the endless disputes that human beings engage in. In the EHU discussion of this species of his subject, Hume restates some of the lengthy, detailed arguments he had given, several years earlier, in book 1, part 4 of THN, but in briefer and less complicated form. As human organisms living in a causally efficacious world, we come naturally to believe in independently existing material objects, animals, and other people. But philosophy tells us that we never perceive such objects, just our own perceptions. So the feud is on again. We cannot win, it seems, because we cannot either renounce our instinctive belief in an independent physical world or find any rational basis for going from perceptions to objects.

George Berkeley dissolves the dilemma by denying one of its "horns": He tries to prove that *matter* (in the philosopher's sense) does not exist; that the usual distinction between primary and secondary qualities is baseless; and that ordinary material objects are complexes of ideas that exist only in the mind of some perceiver (God's if not ours). Hume maintains that although Berkeley sincerely intends his arguments to be *anti*-skeptical, they turn out to be "merely sceptical"—by which Hume means that "*they admit of no answer and produce no conviction*" (EHU, 155n1; 203.15n32; italics are in Hume's text). Indeed, skeptical arguments generally produce momentary amazement, irresolution, and confusion—but no lasting conviction. This is as true of learned wrangles about the infinite divisibility of extension and time as it is of the mundane perplexities about perception. *See* ABSTRACT IDEAS.

Hume contrasts his own *mitigated, or academical, skepticism* with **Pyhrronism**, or excessive skepticism, which indulges in indiscriminate doubts about the possibility of any knowledge whatever. While excessive skepticism may be proof against intellectual refutation, it is easily brushed aside by human activities. If Pyrrhonian principles were to be universally adopted and acted upon, "all discourse, all action would immediately cease" (EHU, 160; 207.23). But that will not happen: "nature is too strong for principle." But even if we cannot swallow Pyrrhonism whole, we can learn from it to be less dogmatic and less opinionated; and we may be encouraged by studying it to limit our enquiries to subjects suited to the narrow capacities of the human understanding.

In responding to the charge that he denies the causal principle (that whatever begins to exist must have a cause of existence), Hume offers some comments that bear on the more general issue of his skepticism. He points out that philosophers divide *evidence* into four kinds—*intuitive*, *demonstrative*, *sensible*, and *moral*. These four categories mark differences but do not denote a hierarchical ordering of higher and lower. *"Moral Certainty* may reach as *high* a Degree of Assurance as *Mathematical*; and our Senses are surely to be comprised amongst the clearest and most convincing of all Evidences" (*A Letter*, 118; italics are in Hume's text). The lesson (one that Hume repeats in many places) is that we should not repine because our fundamental beliefs about the world cannot be grounded in intuition or demonstration. We should be satisfied with the kinds of assurance available to us in the several areas of our lives.

For further discussion of Hume's skepticism as applied to causation and induction, *see* CAUSE; INDUCTION. For his skepticism as applied to moral rationalism, *see* ETHICAL RATIONALISM; MORAL SENSE.

SMITH, ADAM (1723–1790). Adam Smith was one of Hume's closest friends, perhaps his very closest. It was he who wrote the most eloquent and moving eulogy to Hume (in the form of a letter to the printer William Strahan), for which he was reviled by some religious fanatics. As the author of *An Inquiry into the Nature and Causes of the Wealth of Nations* (published in 1776, just a few months before Hume's death), Smith is probably the most famous political economist who ever lived. It is less well known generally that Smith won recognition for his earlier book *The Theory of Moral Sentiments* (1759), a work in which he treats moral psychology and ethics under the influence of **Francis Hutcheson** and Hume without merely echoing them. His debt to Hume (the Hume of the *Treatise*) is most obvious in the prominent role he assigns to *sympathy* in his theory.

SMITH, NORMAN KEMP. See KEMP SMITH, NORMAN.

SPACE AND TIME, OUR IDEAS OF. Hume's discussion of our **ideas** of space and time in THN (book 1, part 2) does not pique the interest of readers the way his treatment of, say, **cause** does. Indeed, Hume himself drops the subject in EHU, his more modest and accessible reformulation of book 1 of the youthful *Treatise*. Nevertheless, he has some interesting and useful things to say about how we come to have ideas of space and time—ideas that are incontrovertibly a basic ingredient of our **experience**.

Note that Hume's subject is our *ideas* of space and time, not space itself or time itself. He expressly disavows any "intention to penetrate into the nature of bodies, or explain the secret causes of their operations"—an enterprise that lies "beyond the reach of human understanding" (THN, 64; 1.2.5.26). Whatever we know about material objects—or any other real existent—must come by way of experience.

Unlike **John Locke**, who holds that our ideas of time and space are *simple*, Hume argues that they are *complex*, and more specifically that they are **abstract ideas** (THN, 34; 1.2.3.5). According to Hume's empiricist "copy" principle, all ideas come from **impressions**, either directly or indirectly. This priority of impressions to ideas holds for our complex ideas of time and space, but this derivation is more complicated than the garden-variety case of remembering a color after seeing it.

Hume's account of how we get the idea of time is pretty straightforward, and at least slightly easier to follow than the comparable account of our idea of space. Although we have impressions of time and space (but not of time and space as entities in themselves), our ideas of time and space do not copy any of those impressions. We can get the idea of time by hearing five notes played successively on a flute, but the idea is not derived from any particular impression that is distinguishable from the other impressions. It is not, that is, derived from a sixth auditory impression (or any other kind of sense impression). Nor do the five sounds give rise to some distinct secondary impression (also known as an impression of reflexion)—a **passion** or emotion, for example—from which the idea of time might be derived. Rather, the idea of time arises from the *manner* in which the impressions appear to the mind, "without making one of the number" (THN, 36; 1.2.3.10). Since our conception of time is not "any primary distinct impression," it "can plainly be nothing but different ideas, or impressions, or objects dispos'd in a certain manner, that is, succeeding each other" (THN, 37; 1.2.3.10).

Just as our idea of time is not bound to the particular five flute notes, so it is not bound to the sense of hearing at all. Because all our perceptions are "perpetually perishing" (Locke's memorable phrase borrowed by Hume), we get the idea of time from impressions of all the five senses, as well as from any succession of passions or emotions. On the contrary, our idea of space comes by way of two senses only—sight and touch. Nothing ever appears extended to us that is not either visible or tangible (THN, 38; 1.2.4.15). When I see any extended (i.e., spatial) object, "my senses convey to me only the impression of colour'd points, dispos'd in a certain manner" (THN, 34; 1.2.3.4). The points will, of course, always be some definite color; but we can frame an abstract idea that will omit any particular color (insofar as we can do that) and focus on the *disposition* (or configuration) of points, or the *manner* of appearance, in which the concrete instances agree. In this way (i.e., by minimizing the importance of any *particular* color), we can extend the compass of the abstract idea of space to include impressions and ideas conveyed by the sense of touch. We have a sense of extension even in the dark, where the ordered points are discerned by touch, not by sight.

Hume denies that we have an idea of a vacuum or of changeless time (which some philosophers call *duration*). That we can have no idea of a vacuum follows from Hume's conception of space; namely, that the idea of space or extension is "*nothing but the idea of visible or tangible points distributed in a certain order*" (THN, 53; 1.2.5.1; italics are in Hume's text). A vacuum contains nothing visible or tangible. Likewise, we have no idea of changeless time. The idea of time can never be conveyed to the mind by "any thing stedfast [*sic*] and unchangeable" (THN, 37; 1.2.3.11). We may mistakenly attribute a fictitious duration to some object if we forget that the very idea of duration arises from a succession of changeable objects.

Hume also denies that our ideas of space and time are infinitely divisible. There are *minima sensibilia*, i.e., units of space and time that cannot be divided by either our **imagination** or our senses. Hume tells us how to see a *minimum sensibilium* of space. Put a spot of ink on a piece of paper; back away from the spot until you can no longer see it. According to Hume, "the moment before it vanish'd the image or impression was perfectly indivisible" (THN, 27; 1.2.1.4). Hume offers no comparable illustration of a *minimum sensibilium* of time, but he explicitly includes time in his doctrine. Critics have pointed out that Hume's reasoning about infinite divisibility is vitiated by (at least) one straightforward mistake; namely, that infinite divisibility requires infinitely many parts, and that would make extension infinite. That is not true. To say that something is infinitely divisible is to say only that we never come to a subdivision that does not admit of further division. It does not mean that there are literally an infinite number of parts.

SUBSTANCE. To understand what Hume says about substance, we must know something of the history of the notion.

The modern notion of substance as a philosophical category derives mainly from the Greek philosopher Aristotle (384–322 B.C.), who develops a systematic theory based on the **commonsense** distinction between a thing and its "accidents" (its properties, characteristics, qualities, conditions, relations, activities, etc.). For example, Dobbin—a particular individual horse—is brown, weighs 1,000 pounds, eats oats, runs in the field, is healthy, knows the difference between a dog and another horse, etc. Dobbin is an independent being who exists in his own right, whereas his color, state of health, activities, etc., exist only as facts about Dobbin. In linguistic terms, *Dobbin* is always a subject, never a predicate. That is, an indefinitely large number of things can be said about Dobbin, but Dobbin the horse can never be said about (or predicated of) anything else. (Some parts of Aristotle's theory—e.g., secondary substances—are not based on common sense; but that is, for present purposes, an interesting but irrelevant detail. Those who are interested in such details should consult Aristotle's *Categories*.)

Rationalist philosophers—**René Descartes**, Baruch Spinoza, and Gottfried Leibniz, for example—find *substance* a congenial notion. That is mainly because, unlike their empiricist counterparts, they hold that the intellect is capable of generating ideas without any dependence on sensory **experience**. (This does not mean that the rationalists are able to say precisely, clearly, and consistently what substance is.) It is self-evident to them that an attribute or property necessarily depends on, or exists in, a substance. "No property without a substance" might be their slogan. In the make-believe world of Lewis Carroll, the Cheshire cat's grin can survive the disappearance of the cat; but in the real world, a grin cannot exist without a grinner. Descartes defines *substance* as "a thing which exists in such a way as to depend on no other thing for its existence" (*Principles of Philosophy*, part 1, no. 51). Strictly, God is the only absolute substance; but, given the concurrence of God, thinking substances and extended substances (minds and bodies, *res cogitans* and *res extensa*) satisfy the stated criterion. Everything else—thoughts, desires, feelings, etc., on the one hand, and shapes, colors, sounds, etc., on the other hand—are *modes* of substances. Spinoza defines *substance* as "what is in itself and is conceived through itself" (*Ethics*, part 1, definition 3). This means that there is exactly one substance, which Spinoza identifies with God. Everything else is either an attribute (which is a term of art in Spinoza) or a mode of God. (It is obvious that Descartes differs from Spinoza on certain features of substance, but that is not relevant here.)

In varying degrees, the empiricists—**John Locke, George Berkeley**, and Hume—find the notion of substance to be puzzling, unintelligible, or (at best) of scant explanatory value. According to Locke, we suppose that the stable collection of qualities of external objects—for example, the color, shape, texture, taste, and aroma of an apple—requires *something* in which the qualities "subsist." This *something* is a *substratum*, or *substance*, that supports the qualities. When we try to say *what* substance is, we find that we have no idea of it at all beyond a supposition of "something, we know not what." This essentially vacuous description applies to every sort of substance, whether general or particular, material or immaterial. Surprisingly, perhaps, Locke never abandons the notion of substance, but rather shows a great deal of ingenuity in describing what he takes to be the effects of substance(s) in experience. He even tells us that we have ideas of exactly three substances: God (the infinite substance), finite intelligences (or minds), and bodies. Our incurably tenuous grasp of the notion of substance notwithstanding, Locke argues that we are theoretically justified in believing in the **existence** of substances, both material and immaterial.

Berkeley tries to show that, contrary to Locke's claim, we have no reason whatever to believe in the existence of *material* substance. The notion is, at best, utterly vacuous and is, in fact, incoherent. There can be no intelligible relation—either representation or causation—between material substance and our experience. Berkeley does not, however, extend his attack to *immaterial* substance, or mind—something that Hume does. Berkeley asserts the existence of immaterial substance, but he says very little about it and seems to be uncomfortable with the notion. He is more inclined simply to call an immaterial substance a mind or spirit, which we can understand more readily.

Using Locke's division of complex ideas into ideas of *Relations, Modes,* and *Substances,* Hume tells us how we get the idea of substance. We do not get it from any impression, whether of sensation or reflexion (*see* PERCEPTIONS): Substance is not a color or sound, etc., nor is it a **passion** or emotion. The idea of substance is, rather, "nothing but a collection of simple ideas, that are united by the imagination, and have a particular name assigned them"—a name that helps us to recall that collection. Thus, *apple* brings to mind *red, round, firm,* etc. The particular qualities combined in a substance are "commonly refer'd to an unknown *something,* in which they are supposed to inhere" (THN, 16; 1.1.6.2; italics are in Hume's text). The apple itself is supposed to be *something* other than the properties by which we recognize it, even if we cannot say *what* that something is (echoes of Locke). Hume's label for this *unknown something* (i.e., a *fiction*) may suggest that he does not find the notion important for his program in THN (except, perhaps, as a foil for his own views). In calling *substance* a fiction, Hume does not mean that we consciously invent the idea, as Herman Melville invented Moby Dick. In one sense, it is a perfectly natural product of the human way of thinking. He means only that it does not have the proper pedigree to serve as a foundation of strict philosophical reasoning—as it does, for example, in Spinoza's system.

Many philosophers, both ancient and modern, hold that the notion of *substance* is necessary to explain how an object can retain its identity through the lapse of time (the "object" may be an ordinary material object or the human mind). In "Of the antient [*sic*] philosophy" (book 1, part 4, section 3 of THN), Hume examines the Aristotelian and post-Aristotelian theory, which posits an "unintelligible something" called "a *substance, or original and first matter*" (THN 220; 1.4.3.4; italics are in Hume's text), along with *substantial forms, accidents,* and *occult qualities.* "Entirely incomprehensible" is Hume's verdict on a system that bristles with so many mysterious, unknowable entities.

Hume's most striking subversion of all forms of substance—the very notion of substance itself as something distinct from the idea of a collection of particular qualities—occurs in "Of the immateriality of the soul" (section 5, part 4, book 1 of THN). Consider the definition of *substance*, which Hume (following Descartes, Spinoza, and others) paraphrases as *something which may exist by itself.* So far from distinguishing one sort of being from another (substance from accident, for example), Hume contends, this definition applies to absolutely anything that can be conceived. Anything that can be conceived may exist, and may exist by itself. In particular, the definition applies to *perceptions*, each of which is distinguishable, distinct, and separable from every other perception, and from everything else in the universe. This means that perceptions are substances, insofar as the usual definition captures the essence of a substance. But substances are not perceptions, according to the traditional account. Since we are acquainted only with our own perceptions, we have no idea of substance as something distinct from perceptions; and "we can never have reason to believe that any object exists, of which we cannot form an idea" (THN, 172; 1.3.14.36).

Hume obviously relishes the irony of his reflections on substance: As it turns out, perceptions—the very things that are supposed to depend on an underlying unperceived substance (an immaterial soul or self) for their existence—are the most perfect candidates for substantiality. This ironic twist obviates any questions about how our perceptions are related to substance—or so Hume claims. (To avoid misunderstanding here, we must note that Hume does not mean to deny that, as a matter of fact, perceptions have causes—the most obvious and natural being the functioning of our bodies. But that is a matter of speculation, which Hume disavows early in THN [basic perceptions arise in the soul "from unknown causes"]. He means only that, considered in itself, every perception is a distinct entity and is, consequently, capable of existing by itself.) *See* PERSONAL IDENTITY.

From what has been said above, we may see that philosophers have used *substance* in (at least) two related but distinguishable senses. *Substance* may refer to the essence of an individual thing (a particular horse—Dobbin, for example), which is whatever makes it that unique individual. Or it may refer to some general *substratum*, which supports properties but may or may not have any properties itself. Hume rejects both notions as being devoid of any intelligible meaning. *See* PRIMARY AND SECONDARY QUALITIES.

SUICIDE. Hume's essay "Of Suicide" (published posthumously in 1777) is probably the most widely read and the most influential philosophical treatment of suicide written in modern times (perhaps in any time). The purpose of the essay is to show that suicide "may be free from every imputation of guilt or blame" (*Essays*, 580). Hume begins with an encomium on philosophy, which he describes as "the sovereign antidote" to **superstition** and false religion. Because superstitions are based on false belief (plus a shot of emotion), they are susceptible (indirectly) to correction by "just philosophy" (which is, essentially, causal scientific reason). Although reason is finally the slave of the passions (THN, 415; 2.3.3.4), it can help to make our passions more reasonable by revealing the truth. Hume supposes (without any supporting argument) that only superstition could prevent a suicide-prone person from taking his own life, once he had freed himself of the natural fear of death. Accordingly, Hume contends, anyone purged of superstition may consider the arguments against suicide dispassionately.

As Hume views the matter, there are three, and only three, possible grounds for prohibiting suicide; namely, that it is a violation of our duty to God, or to society, or to ourselves. He examines each of the three possibilities (devoting far more attention to our putative duty to God than to the other two putative duties combined) and concludes that suicide violates none of the three duties. It follows that suicide is not "criminal"; or, to put it positively, that suicide is morally permissible. This argument is formally valid: If its premises are true, then its conclusion must also be true. Are the premises in fact true? Is the conclusion true? Some commentators—not all of them—complain that Hume's arguments in support of the premises are weak and that the conclusion is ambiguous (is suicide always permissible? or only sometimes? is it laudable? obligatory?). Ernest Campbell Mossner, Hume's highly sympathetic biographer, poses this question about "Of Suicide": "This is eloquence, no doubt—but is it philosophy?" The essay clearly does not show Hume at his philosophical best, but it does raise some of the right questions, and does so in a provocative way.

SUPERSTITION AND ENTHUSIASM. In his essay "Of Superstition and Enthusiasm" Hume describes superstition and enthusiasm as generally pernicious and as corruptive of true **religion** in particular. (Note that Hume uses *enthusiasm* in the now-archaic sense of being possessed by God and receiving special revelations from God.) Although both aberrations are dangerous, they are very nearly opposite in their provenance and manifestation. Superstition is rooted in the terror some people feel about unknown evils directed against them by unknown—but certainly malevolent and powerful—agents. Such unknown and invisible enemies must be appeased or dealt with in some fashion; for example, by ceremonies, sacrifices, gifts, and the like. The true sources of superstition, then, are "weakness, fear, melancholy, together with ignorance" (*Essays*, 74). Superstition lends itself to the emergence of priests, who intercede with the unknown and invisible powers on behalf of the mass of fearful followers. Hume holds that superstition is "a considerable ingredient in almost all religions."

Whereas superstition arises from an excess of fearful imaginings, enthusiasm springs from unbridled psychological elevation and presumption. The superstitious person is burdened with an exaggerated sense of his own guilt and unworthiness; the enthusiast gives himself to raptures, transports, and flights of fancy—all of which testify to his favored relationship with the Deity (or so he believes). In this state of illusion, the enthusiast readily supposes that his fantasies and whimsies are immediate inspirations from God. The true sources of enthusiasm are "hope, pride, presumption, a warm imagination, together with ignorance" (*Essays*, 74). In Hume's etiology, ignorance is the only cause common to superstition and enthusiasm. Not surprisingly, given its extreme individualism, enthusiasm has been the enemy of ecclesiastical authority. In Hume's opinion, this resistance to external authority has made enthusiasm a friend to civil liberty; and by a mirror-image logic, superstition, with its submission to priestly authority, has been an enemy to civil liberty. Hume generally associates superstition with Roman Catholicism and enthusiasm with Protestantism, but the contrast is far from perfect. Some Catholics have been infused with enthusiasm, and some Protestants have hankered after the "popish" practices so detested by the English Puritans.

Of more direct philosophical interest is the contrast Hume draws between the methods of superstition and true philosophy (or science). In his essay "Of Miracles" Hume says that the wise (i.e., prudent or reasonable) man proportions his belief to the evidence. This is precisely what the superstitious person does *not* do. The wise man follows the principles of probable reasoning in his deliberations; the superstitious person ignores or flouts those principles. A couple of caveats should be noted. First, not all violations of sound reasoning arise from superstition. Normally cautious reasoners occasionally reach false or baseless conclusions through haste or inattention, without thereby becoming superstitious. Second, Hume's definition ties superstition so closely to religion that many straightforwardly superstitious beliefs would be excluded if we followed the definition strictly. Indeed, the examples that come most readily to mind (e.g., that breaking a mirror brings bad luck) have no obvious connection to religion. And Hume himself sometimes uses *superstition* in the broader sense. (For some comments on the war between true philosophy and superstition, see section 1 of EHU.)

SYMPATHY. Hume introduces the notion of sympathy in book 2 of THN, "Of the Passions," but sympathy is itself not a **passion**. It is, rather, part of the mechanism by which Hume explains the way human beings enter into the **pleasure** or pain of others. Sympathy, then, is not to be identified with compassion (or pity), which arises from the operation of sympathy. Malice is "a kind of pity reverst" (THN, 375; 2.2.8.9). Interestingly, Hume first invokes sympathy in THN to explain why the passions of pride and humility are affected by the opinions of others. By the operation of sympathy, the opinions that others have of me (whether of approval or disapproval, praise or blame) are transformed from a mere **idea** (my belief) to an **impression** possessing such force and vivacity "as to become the very passion itself" (THN, 317; 2.1.11.3). The strength required for that conversion from idea to impression comes from the lively impression each of us always has of our self. Any object or event that affects the self gets infused with a portion of the liveliness of the "self-impression."

No person is literally and directly acquainted with the passion of another person. We are "only sensible of its causes or effects"—from which we infer the passion. Tears, laughter, shouting, trembling—all are the effects of passion. The sight of preparations for an 18th-century surgical operation—". . . the laying of the bandages in order, the heating of the irons, with all the signs of anxiety and concern in the patient and assistants" (THN, 576; 3.3.1.7)—would affect us greatly, even before the harrowing business actually began. We observe the effects or **causes**, from which we infer the passion; this is the way sympathy arises. The first intimations of sympathy are mere ideas—the idea, for example, that certain observable actions (weeping, laughing) evince a passion belonging to someone else; but very quickly these lively ideas of the affections of another person "are converted into the very impressions they represent" (THN, 319; 2.1.11.8). Sympathy, then, is the transformation of an idea into an impression, of thinking into feeling. In Hume's own language, sympathy is "*a communication of sentiments*" (THN, 324; 2.1.11.19; italics are in Hume's text).

Hume describes sympathy as exhibiting the "double relation" of impressions and ideas. In the illustrations used above, we have one person who has an emotion of some sort; we have a second person who gets an idea of the first person's emotion; and we have the second person's idea converted into an impression by the efficacy of the second person's impression of his own self. Whereas *ideas* are governed by all three of the principles of association (i.e., resemblance, spatio-temporal contiguity, and causation), *impressions* are associated only by resemblance. Passions and sympathy are subject to *both* sorts of association ("a double relation of ideas and impressions")—a circumstance that explains, in part, the strength of the passions. Whatever their accidental differences of height, weight, social standing, color, etc., people are very much alike: ". . . nature has preserv'd a great resemblance among all human creatures," both of the body and "the fabric of the mind" (THN, 318; 2.1.11.5). The impulse to sympathy is strengthened by *contiguity*; we feel the sentiments of others more easily and readily when they are near. And we are convinced of the reality of another's passion by the relation of cause and effect. So far as this writer knows, Hume gives us the first psychological explanation of sympathy.

Having explained in book 2 of THN how sympathy works, Hume makes extensive use of the notion in developing his theory of morals in book 3. *Sympathy* is, in fact, "the chief source of moral distinctions" (THN, 618; 3.3.6.1). Thus, for example, while self-interest supplies the *original* (or natural) impulse to **justice**, it is sympathy that accounts for the *moral* approbation we confer on justice, i.e., why we regard justice as a *virtue* (THN, 498–500; 3.2.2.24). More generally, it is sympathy that enables us to take the disinterested, or general, point of view required for moral judgments. Without sympathy, we could not understand that a virtue (say, courage) in a stranger (or even an enemy) is as worthy of commendation as the same virtue in a friend.

– T –

TELEOLOGICAL ARGUMENT. *See* DESIGN, ARGUMENT FROM/TO.

TIME, OUR IDEA OF. *See* SPACE AND TIME, OUR IDEAS OF.

A TREATISE OF HUMAN NATURE. Like **George Berkeley**'s *The Principles of Human Knowledge* (1710), David Hume's *A Treatise of Human Nature* (1739–1740) is a philosophical masterpiece written and published while its author was still in his twenties. Although Hume publicly repudiated THN in the year before his death (in favor of his later works covering the same subjects), generations of readers have appreciated it for what it is—a work of unmistakable genius. (For an account of the writing and publication of THN, see the sketch of Hume's life in the introduction to this book.)

The word *treatise* in the title signifies that Hume's undertaking is to be systematic and comprehensive. The subtitle—*Being an Attempt to Introduce the Experimental Method of Reasoning into Moral Subjects*—indicates how it will proceed (by appealing to experience [*experiments*, in 18th-century usage] and what it will cover [*moral* subjects in the broad sense: knowledge, emotions, ethics]). Accordingly, he divides the work into three principal units: book 1 ("Of the Understanding"), book 2 ("Of the Passions"), and book 3 ("Of Morals"). Book 1 is divided into four parts, which cover certain facts about **perceptions** (impressions and ideas), the ideas of **space and time**, **knowledge** and probability, and certain skeptical and other systems of philosophy. Book 2 comprises three parts, which deal with pride and humility, love and hatred, and the will and direct **passions**. Book 3 has three parts, which treat **virtue** and vice in general (and, more specifically, the basis of moral distinctions), **justice** and injustice (which are called *artificial* virtues because they depend on social conventions or *artifices*), and the other virtues and vices (including the **natural** virtues and vices, which do not depend on social conventions).

The three books of THN study people as cognitive, affective, and moral beings—a trichotomy that pretty much covers everything about us. A caveat is in order: It would be a fundamental mistake to think of the three books as self-contained, hermetically sealed studies. In fact, each is intelligible only in its relation to the other two. Although we human beings can be examined from different perspectives—philosophical, psychological, sociological, etc.—each of us is a unitary self, not a laminated construct. Readers of Hume have ignored this fact at the price of misunderstanding both his larger purposes and many details. Fortunately, Hume scholars of the past few decades have been less prone to that failing than many older commentators.

In hopes of generating some favorable notice of books 1 and 2 of THN, Hume published an anonymous *Abstract* of the work in early 1740. The true authorship of the work, though suspected by some, was not definitively established until 1938. Most of the *Abstract* is devoted to clarifying the arguments in book 1, with a brief coda about book 2. As the unnamed author, Hume could indulge in a bit of cheerleading for THN; but self-promotion apart, the *Abstract* provides a clear and compendious restatement of some central doctrines in Hume's epistemology. Readers should not neglect it.

Hume's disappointment with the general lack of interest in THN led him to recast its three books in what he hoped would be a more palatable, accessible form. Book 1 reappeared as ***An Enquiry Concerning Human Understanding***; book 2 as *A Dissertation on the Passions*; and book 3 as ***An Enquiry Concerning the Principles of Morals***. The two *Enquiries* became classics in their own right, whereas the *Dissertation* was not nearly so successful.

– V –

VIRTUE/VICE. Hume offers a succinct definition of *virtue* in the conclusion (section 9) of EPM: "Personal Merit [which includes Virtue] consists altogether in the possession of mental qualities, *useful* or *agreeable* to the *person himself* or to *others*" (268; 145.1; italics are in

Hume's text). In the first appendix to EPM he reminds the reader that "morality is determined by sentiment." He then proceeds to define virtue in a way that emphasizes its *effect*: "*whatever mental action or quality gives to a spectator the pleasing sentiment of approbation*" (289; 160.10; italics are in Hume's text). Vice produces the contrary sentiment. In his earlier treatment of virtue in THN, Hume offers a similar definition: "Every quality of the mind is denominated *virtuous*, which gives pleasure by the mere survey; as every quality, which produces pain, is call'd *vicious*" (591; 3.3.1.30; italics are in Hume's text). And he identifies the same four sources of such **pleasure**: qualities that are either *agreeable* to the person himself or to others, or are *useful* to the person himself or to others. The phrase "by the mere survey" serves to distinguish moral judgments from those based merely on self-interest. (Note: Hume uses *vicious* as simply the adjectival form of *vice*. In contemporary usage, *vicious* is usually a much stronger term, suggesting dangerous aggressiveness or savagery. For Hume, a courteous, thoughtful thief would still be vicious, i.e., the opposite of virtuous. On the other hand, an animal—say, a snarling pit bulldog—could not possibly be vicious in Hume's sense, inasmuch as non-human animals are incapable of morality or immorality.)

From what has been said in the preceding paragraph, it should be clear that Hume's theory of virtue is neither subjectivist nor objectivist in any simple way, but contains both subjectivist and objectivist elements. Virtue is discerned by sentiment or feeling, not by **reason**, whether reason be employed about purely formal **relations of ideas** or about **matters of fact**. To make that point, Hume compares virtue to secondary qualities (color, sound, heat and cold), which, "according to modern philosophy, are not qualities in objects, but perceptions in the mind" (THN, 469; 3.1.1.26). He also draws a parallel between virtue and beauty, as being matters of sentiment or taste. On the other hand, the discrimination of colors and of literary or artistic excellence is not a matter of arbitrary personal opinion. Under normal conditions, most people perceive an object as red or as sweet. Whatever "modern philosophy" may say, some people are color-blind, and we have objective tests for diagnosing the condition. Further, most people who are familiar with the poetry of Shakespeare and Edgar A. Guest would agree that Shakespeare is, by a large margin, the superior poet.

In the same way, most people find a certain distinctive kind of pleasure in considering generous or courageous acts; i.e., they find such acts *virtuous*. (Strictly, it is not the acts themselves, but the durable quality of mind or character evinced by the acts, that is virtuous.) Thus, although sentiments and tastes may not be strictly either right or wrong, they may be more or less appropriate in the light of widespread human practice. Hume observes that we learn to *correct* our sentiments in much the same way we learn to correct our perceptions (of distance, for example). See, e.g., THN, 582; 3.3.1.16. This does not mean that Hume posits some distinctively moral property in things themselves that confers objectivity on our moral judgments. He denies that there is any such property. The only basis that Hume ever proposes for moral objectivity is certain facts about human nature and what human beings actually do or have done.

In THN, Hume distinguishes **natural** virtues from *artificial*. Natural virtues "have no dependance [*sic*] on the artifice and contrivance of men" (574; 3.3.1.1). He further explains natural virtues as producing good from every single act (e.g., a benevolent act), whereas artificial virtues (mainly **justice**) produce good only as they are part of "a general scheme or system of action" (THN, 579; 3.3.1.12). A single act of justice—e.g., requiring a poor person to repay a legal debt to a rich skinflint—may be counterproductive when considered in itself, but is necessary as promoting respect for the general principle of honoring legitimate financial obligations. Hume gives several examples of natural virtues: generosity, humanity, compassion, gratitude, friendship, fidelity, zeal, disinterestedness, and liberality (THN, 603; 3.3.3.4).

Hume concedes that the word *natural* is fraught with ambiguity and, consequently, is liable to be misleading. For example, he does not mean to suggest that justice is *un*natural. He observes (in *A Letter*) that sucking is a natural human action and speech an artificial—artificial in the sense that it requires social artifices or conventions. But surely the impulse to speech is as much a part of human nature—i.e., is as *natural*—as sucking. Justice is like speech in this respect—deeply rooted in human nature but requiring social interaction for its realization. In EPM, he pretty much abandons the terminology of *natural vs. artificial*, but he continues to maintain that justice counts as a virtue only by reason of convention or artifice.

– W –

WOLLASTON, WILLIAM (1659–1724). An English moral and religious philosopher, Wollaston is cited by Hume (THN, 461n1; 3.1.1.15n68) as a proponent of **ethical rationalism** (not Hume's term). Although Hume does not use Wollaston's name (this is supplied by the editors), he plainly has Wollaston in mind. In his only published work, *The Religion of Nature Delineated* (1722), Wollaston argues that an action is immoral (or vicious) because it gives rise to false or mistaken judgments. For example, my stealing an automobile is immoral because I am, in effect, telling other people that the automobile is mine. Stated simply, an act is immoral if it induces observers to draw false inferences. This account of the origin of morality runs directly counter to Hume's own view, which is that "moral distinctions are not deriv'd from reason." Hume argues that Wollaston's position generates absurdities; e.g., that inanimate objects may be vicious and immoral (in that they sometimes induce us to make false judgments [the rotten log over the stream appears to be sound until it breaks under my weight]) and that an illegal and immoral act (e.g., burglary) committed in secret would get a free pass on Wollaston's view, inasmuch as it would not cause any false judgment. Hume also contends that Wollaston's reasoning is circular or question-begging. A man who steals someone else's property is, in effect, claiming that it is his own property. But this assumes that the immorality of theft *has already been established*; the immorality cannot consist in the false judgment produced by the theft.

Because philosophers seldom dispatch serious opponents so easily and decisively as Hume seems to do in this instance, some commentators suggest that Hume is not entirely accurate or fair in his treatment of Wollaston, that he misrepresents or misunderstands some portions of what Wollaston actually says. Other commentators defend Hume against this charge.

WOMEN. Hume's best-known statement about women is probably in his brief autobiography, *My Own Life*: "And as I took a particular Pleasure in the company of modest [= decent, proper, or chaste, not necessarily humble or self-effacing] women, I had no reason to be displeased with the Reception I met with from them." We have ample evidence that Hume also took pleasure in the company of some women who would not have been deemed modest. He was never married but was accused by one Agnes Galbraith of being the father of one of her illegitimate children (a charge that may or may not have been true but was not proved). This entry focuses on Hume's observations about women, not on his personal associations with women. Some of those observations are philosophically significant.

Hume's thinking about women is revealed in many by-the-way obiter dicta and, more important, in a few sustained discussions: "Of Chastity and Modesty" (THN, book 3, part 2, section 12), which is part of Hume's theory of **justice**, which generally has to do with the conventions by which societies govern themselves; "Of Polygamy and Divorces" (*Essays*, 181–90); and "Of Love and Marriage" (*Essays*, 557–62). To these sources can be added four essays whose titles do not suggest the interesting observations on women they contain: "Of the Rise and Progress of the Arts and Sciences" (*Essays*, 111–37); "Of Essay-Writing" (*Essays*, 533–37); "Of Moral Prejudices" (*Essays*, 538–44); and "Of the Study of History" (*Essays*, 563–68).

Hume's views about women are not always clear and straightforward. He sometimes makes what appear (at least) to be inconsistent statements, and it is not always clear whether he is *endorsing* a claim about women or merely *reporting* it. As for inconsistency, he says that nature has made men (i.e., human males) superior to women in both mind and body (*Essays*, 133), but also that nature has established a "nearness of rank, not to say equality" between the sexes (*Essays*, 184). Hume might respond to the charge of inconsistency by noting that men and women may, on balance, be equal or nearly so, but not necessarily in the same respects. They may have mirror-image strengths and weaknesses. Men are distinguished by their "force and maturity" (where *maturity* signifies capacity for sober deliberation, not age), women by their "delicacy and softness" (THN, 401; 2.3.1.6). By these qualities of delicacy and softness, women help to civilize men, to make them less rough and barbaric. Hume contends that women are better judges of polite writing than are men of the same level of sense and education (*Essays*, 536). Since polite writings comprise refined, cultured belletristic works and are contrasted with the weightier, more serious writings in science and philosophy, readers may suspect that Hume's compliment is actually a patronizing bit of faint praise ("you tie your shoes better than anyone else in this room"). In fact, Hume does suppose that women are effectively excluded—whether by nature or nurture—from the study of more difficult ("severer") subjects. Accordingly, he advises his female readers to study history rather than spend all their time reading books of amusement (*Essays*, 563ff.). This last recommendation is not so unrelievedly condescending as it may seem; for Hume contends that no one—male or female—can hope to understand human nature without studying history.

Hume notes the obvious but important fact that education (or the lack or slant of it) and other social conventions go some way toward explaining the difference (or the supposed difference) in intellectual capacity between men and women. But not all the way, one gathers from statements Hume makes about the "tenderness" of women's nature and their tendency to subordinate sound prudential reasoning to passion. Women's education—its character and extent—is tied to the role that nature and society have cut out for them; namely, bearing and raising children. Moreover, that role explains the stringent demand that women be chaste and modest. Whereas maternity is easy to determine (at least when the baby is born), paternity is a different matter. Since a man is normally willing or even eager to care for his own children but not for others, he needs assurance that the children his wife bears are in fact his. And that assurance rests on his confidence in his wife's strict fidelity to him. Hume offers numerous additional comments on this head; e.g., about the slighter (but still not negligible) obligation of men to be chaste and the near-impossibility of a woman's regaining her reputation once it has been compromised. In some of these cases, Hume seems to be only reporting facts about social attitudes and practices, not necessarily endorsing them.

With rare exceptions (a bit less rare over the past decade or so), the canonical works of traditional philosophy—those that get included in texts and anthologies of various sorts—are by male authors. That is a straightforward matter of fact. Of what significance is that fact? Feminist philosophers have been arguing for the past few decades that this (virtual) masculine monopoly has profoundly affected the substance and direction of philosophy, in both pretty obvious and

more subtle ways. We will mention a few such ways and will then
see how Hume fares in this reckoning.

Some great philosophers make explicitly misogynist assertions
(Aristotle, **Immanuel Kant**, and Georg Wilhelm Friedrich Hegel
[1770–1831] are notable examples), claiming that women are intellectually inferior to men or even that they are "deformed men" (Aristotle). Statements of this sort are plainly offensive and foolish and
may be rejected out of hand (even if we concede that the philosophers
who make them may well have other views worthy of serious consideration). More subtle and more interesting is the question whether
the fundamental categories and methods of traditional philosophy are
suffused with an outlook that may be described as *male* or *masculine*.
Note that this outlook need not be conscious. Indeed, it may have
seemed so natural that it was not even noticed. When Aristotle or
René Descartes or Kant or Hegel invoke reason in support of their
views, they do not qualify it as masculine or feminine or Greek or
French or German or anything else. To them, it is just *reason* in its
universal form, though they do not hesitate to criticize other philosophers' understanding of it. (A. N. Whitehead observes that our deepest, most important assumptions—the ones that control our thinking
and our actions—are precisely the ones we never feel the need of
questioning because it never occurs to us that they *are* assumptions.
When philosophy fulfills its proper role, Whitehead contends, it
helps us to unearth and examine those assumptions.)

Far from providing a disinterested, God's-eye view of the human
and non-human world, feminist critics argue, traditional philosophers give us a "genderized," one-eyed version of reality. That version embodies notions of reason, objectivity, and universality that
systematically ignore the **experience** of half the human race. It tends
to identify reason with the masculine, and feeling/emotion/senti-
ment (i.e., non-reason) with the feminine. Further, the reason these
philosophers exalt tends to be abstract, linear, and individualistic.
Descartes, the "father" of modern Western philosophy (who is the
mother?), drives that stark individualism to its logical terminus,
which is solipsism, the view that only I and my experiences are real.
To be accurate, Descartes uses radical doubt as a tool to forward
his prejudice-exorcising skepticism, not as a final position. He intends ultimately to restore everything—God, other people, and the

external physical world. But look at how he proposes to effect that restoration. The protagonist of Descartes' *Meditations* is a disembodied reasoner, cut off from everything except his own ideas, faced with the task of excogitating his way back to the world of **common sense** by the power of his intellect ("the natural light of reason," as Descartes sometimes describes this innate faculty). This way of doing philosophy epitomizes what feminist critics find objectionable about the tradition: the apotheosis of detached, denuded, disconnected "reason" as the revealer of truth, coupled with an explicit or implied derogation of the body and the emotions. (Note: Descartes is, of course, not the only traditional philosopher who exemplifies the perspective deplored by feminists, but he is perhaps the most obvious representative of that tradition.)

How does Hume fit into this picture? No brief answer is possible, but a couple of important considerations bear on the question.

1. Hume would seem to be proof against any charge of exalting reason above emotion, feeling, sentiment, or passion. His famous pronouncement fixes the proper office of reason as being the slave of the passions (THN, 415; 2.3.3.4). He never tires of urging the impotence of reason alone to know any matter of fact or to move us to do or forbear doing anything. Of special importance is his doctrine of causality: Our knowledge of cause and effect comes from experience or custom and habit, never from a priori reason. This is (or would have been) devastating news for Descartes, who depends crucially on what he takes to be the self-evident principle of universal **causation** to rescue him from skepticism. (An important caveat: Hume does not use the word *reason* in a single univocal sense. The sense intended here is *a priori reason vs. experience*.)

2. Implied in the first consideration is the *social* character of knowledge in Hume's thought, which is suggested, for example, by the phrase *custom and habit*. This aspect of Humean epistemology is sometimes obscured in book 1 of THN (as well as in some sections of EHU) by the *impressions-ideas* language, which may suggest that humans construct a common external world out of purely private perceptions. That is not Hume's intention even in book 1 of THN, and any lingering suspicion to the contrary is allayed in books 2 and 3, which are about the passions and morals. The core concepts of

Hume's account of the passions and of morals—love and hatred, pride and humility, virtue and vice—are inconceivable as purely private. Though less obvious, the same is true of his account of knowledge, which is not completely laid out in book 1 of THN. In most of his writings, Hume pretty clearly rejects the Cartesian picture of knowing as the activity of an isolated thinker. Hume scholar Nicholas Capaldi encapsulates the Humean and the Cartesian models of knowledge in the phrases "We do" and "I think" respectively. Hume's theory of knowledge reflects actual human practices and institutions, whereas Descartes' embodies the thought of the egocentric individual thinker. (The contrast between "We do" and "I think" applies also to Hume's moral philosophy, except that Descartes is replaced by some ethical rationalist—**Samuel Clarke** or **William Wollaston**, for example.)

The same point (i.e., the social character of knowledge) can be made in a slightly different way. As an **empiricist**, Hume puts the senses above reason as the source of our knowledge of reality. Our bodily senses point to a world of objects that have colors, shapes, etc., whereas reason deals with abstract concepts, which need not refer to anything beyond themselves. This raises the question whether a solitary Cartesian thinker could know anything about reality—or, indeed, whether such a being is merely an abstraction, no more real than the Cheshire cat's grin.

Any appearances to the contrary notwithstanding, Hume tries to square his philosophical doctrines with common sense, in the long run if not from the outset. He looks to actual human experience as the final arbiter in questions of knowledge and morals. That is, *pro tanto*, good, and it distinguishes him from rationalist philosophers such as Descartes, Baruch Spinoza, and Gottfried Wilhelm Leibniz. But a feminist philosopher may ask whether his understanding of human experience (including emotions and social/legal conventions) is not itself androcentric. That is a subtle question and one to which feminists give no uniform answer. Annette Baier, who identifies herself as a friend to truth as well as to Hume's views, poses two questions as the titles of essays: "Hume, the Reflective Women's Epistemologist?" and "Hume, the Women's Moral Theorist?" Her answer to both questions is affirmative, but with some reservations and qualifications.

Two final points. There is no such thing as *the* feminist perspective. Feminist philosophers disagree among themselves on both substantive issues and details, including the proper estimate of Hume's thought. Hume has attracted less attention from feminist writers than have certain other philosophers (e.g., Nietzsche), but there are a respectable number of essays about him, some of them excellent.

Bibliography

This bibliography is of course not exhaustive, but it is extensive. To make it more usable by readers, it is divided into a baker's dozen sections, three of which have subsections, as shown in the following table of contents.

CONTENTS

INTRODUCTION

The *sortals* (to adapt John Locke's apt coinage) in the bibliography are not mutually exclusive: Philosophical writings inevitably cross taxonomic lines of division. They do, nonetheless, provide a useful and reasonably natural scheme for classifying writings by and about Hume. At a minimum, they will direct readers to the general sort of literature they are interested in finding. Some explanatory or factual (not critical or evaluative) annotations are provided. For example, readers may like to know that the essay "Hume and the Fiery Furnace" is about Hume's theory of inductive inference—a fact to which the title provides no clue.

This bibliography begins with an essay that surveys some of the Hume literature (primarily monographs) of the last three or four decades (or *mainly* of that period). Unfortunately, it is impossible to mention all the books and articles that deserve special notice. The essay is organized very loosely along the lines of the categories enumerated above.

Hume's Works

The most nearly complete edition of Hume's philosophical writings remains the four-volume *The Philosophical Works of David Hume*, edited by T. H. Green and T. H. Grose and published originally in 1874–1875. This edition does not include Hume's own *Abstract* of the *Treatise*—a pardonable omission inasmuch as Hume's authorship of the *Abstract* was not firmly established until 1938. Thomas Hill Green, one of the editors and a well-known Oxford philosopher in his own right, supplied a very long (almost 300 pages) and highly critical introduction to the edition. Green argues that Hume's philosophy amounts to a *reductio ad absurdum* of the empiricist assumptions from which John Locke began. Not a few Hume scholars have rejected Green's criticisms as fundamentally wrongheaded.

Oxford University Press has begun an edition of all of Hume's philosophical, political, and literary works (*not* including *The History of England*): *The Clarendon Edition of the Works of David Hume*. So far (i.e., 2008), three individual works have appeared: *A Treatise of Human Nature* (Hume's youthful masterpiece), *An Enquiry Concerning*

Human Understanding, and *An Enquiry Concerning the Principles of Morals*. Both critical and student editions of all three works have been published. These may all be recommended without reservation. They will, one supposes, eventually supplant the Selby-Bigge/Nidditch editions (also published by Oxford), which have substantial virtues of their own. The recent editions offer many features that will be especially helpful to new readers of Hume: introductions, summaries, glossaries, notes, annotations, and the like. In fairness, it should be noted that the indexes prepared by L. A. Selby-Bigge for the 1888 edition of the *Treatise* and the 1894 edition of the two *Enquiries* are, on balance, more useful than the computer-generated indexes of the recent editions. That is because the older indexes are keyed to phrases or sentences in Hume's text. Several inexpensive reprints of the two *Enquiries* are available from other publishers (e.g., from Hackett Publishing Company and Penguin Books).

Of the half-dozen or so currently available versions of *Dialogues Concerning Natural Religion*, the one edited by Norman Kemp Smith is probably the best bet for most readers. There is nothing wrong with the others (quite the contrary), but the wealth of philosophical and historical material in Kemp Smith's introduction sets it apart. *The Natural History of Religion* is readily available in inexpensive paperback editions. Hume's *Essays Moral, Political, and Literary* and his six-volume *The History of England* are published in inexpensive editions by the Liberty Fund.

Hume's Letters

Upwards of 550 of Hume's letters were published in two volumes in 1932; an additional 98 were published in 1954, and still others have appeared since 1954. A new edition of Hume's letters is in preparation.

J. Y. T. Greig, the editor of the two earlier volumes, observes that Hume himself would probably not have approved of the publication of his letters at all. Hume intended that his letters (along with almost all of his private papers) be burned after his death. That would have been a great loss: The letters help immeasurably in filling out our picture of Hume the thinker, diplomat, epicure, brother, uncle, man about town, etc.

Bibliographies

The bibliographies by T. E. Jessop and Roland Hall, taken together, cover the period from Hume's own time until 1976. Since 1976, *Hume Studies* has published regular surveys of the Hume literature (see a recent November issue for details). Most of the secondary literature covered in this bibliography—books and essays alike—have useful citations to other scholarly work. Some web-sites provide valuable bibliographic materials and links to other sites. A few good ones are the *Leeds ElectronicText Centre* (http://www.etext.leeds.ac.uk/hume/), the *Hume Society* (www.humesociety.org), *The Internet Encyclopedia of Philosophy* (www.iep.utm.edu), and the *Stanford Encyclopedia of Philosophy* (www.plato.stanford.edu/).

Biographies

The best biography of Hume, by virtually unanimous opinion, is Ernest Campbell Mossner's affectionate and erudite *The Life of David Hume*. J. Y. T. Greig's *David Hume* is shorter than Mossner's and is written in a lively style (Greig published four novels under the name John Carruthers). The earliest book-length biography of Hume is Thomas Ritchie's *An Account of the Life and Writings of David Hume*, published in 1807—just over 30 years after Hume's death. John Hill Burton's two-volume *Life and Correspondence of David Hume*, published in 1846, was a distinct improvement on Ritchie's occasionally strange and supercilious account of Hume.

General Studies

More than any other single work, Norman Kemp Smith's 1941 book *The Philosophy of David Hume*, which was partly adumbrated by two articles in the British journal *Mind* 36 years earlier, helped to change the common view of Hume as merely a destructive skeptic. On Kemp Smith's reading, Hume is a *naturalist* who recognizes the primacy of custom and habit over reason in human life. Many of Kemp Smith's specific claims have been challenged, but his book is still recognized as a watershed in Hume scholarship. (This book has been recently reprinted with a new introduction by Don Garrett.)

Hume's Philosophical Development, by James Noxon, and *David Hume: The Newtonian Philosopher*, by Nicholas Capaldi, emphasize the influence of Isaac Newton's experimental method on Hume's thinking (especially in the *Treatise*). Capaldi's book is a sympathetic and accessible survey of the several parts of Hume's philosophy. The interweaving of exposition and criticism makes Terence Penelhum's *Hume* a valuable source for readers who already know something about Hume. Penelhum's *David Hume: An Introduction to His Philosophical System* combines his exposition and commentary with selections from Hume's own works. As the title suggests, this book is suitable as an introduction to Hume. Barry Stroud's *Hume* (another book with that bare one-word title) criticizes Hume on numerous points while defending him against some standard complaints. It would be most useful to readers who have some general knowledge of philosophy and some prior acquaintance with Hume.

In *Cognition and Commitment in Hume's Philosophy*, Don Garrett offers close textual exposition and analysis of Humean texts on perception, imagination, reason, cause, personal identity, miracles, morality, and a good many other topics—often defending Hume against his critics. The title of Claudia M. Schmidt's recent book—*David Hume: Reason in History*—offers virtually no clue that the book includes a systematic and useful survey of many themes, familiar and unfamiliar, in the Humean corpus. It is intended to appeal both to novices and to more seasoned students of Hume. Two general studies (of a sort) undertake to defend Hume's first *Enquiry*—the EHU—against invidious comparisons with part 1 of the earlier and more detailed THN. *Hume's Enlightenment Tract* (by Stephen Buckle) and *Reading Hume on Human Understanding* (edited by Peter Millican) seek to refute the widespread opinion that EHU is, in Buckle's words, "a milk-and-water version of [Hume's] serious philosophy [i.e., THN]." The books are not, however, obsessed with pressing the virtues of EHU; they cover the numerous issues raised by EHU—the varieties of philosophy, causation (including necessary connection), miracles, skepticism, etc. The Millican book has a useful 61-page "Critical Survey of the Literature on Hume and the First *Enquiry*." These two books are suitable for readers with some previous acquaintance with Hume and with modern philosophy, but would be less useful for beginners.

Three other "general studies" may be mentioned that do not fit so comfortably under that rubric as the preceding ones. In *Hume's Philosophy of Common Life*, Donald Livingston contends that Hume takes history—and *not* natural science—as the paradigm of knowledge. He paints Hume's philosophy on a very large canvas and offers many shrewd and unorthodox suggestions for understanding that philosophy. A later book by Livingston—*Philosophical Melancholy and Delirium: Hume's Pathology of Philosophy*—is, if anything, even more wide-ranging than the first one (the title of the second offers little clue as to the actual contents of the study). Annette Baier's *A Progress of Sentiments: Reflections on Hume's 'Treatise'* is less "speculative" than the two books by Livingston, but she offers some original thoughts about the proper way of reading the *Treatise*; i.e., as an organic whole. In particular, she deplores the common practice of taking the parts of the *Treatise* as discrete modules that can be understood independently of one another. Baier argues persuasively against that way of viewing Hume's great work. These three books may be commended to readers who already know something about Hume.

Metaphysics and Epistemology

Because Hume's most notable and influential contributions to philosophy lie in metaphysics and epistemology, most of the general studies just mentioned cover those areas as well as (for example) his ethics and philosophy of religion. Some commentators concentrate exclusively on Hume's doctrines about reality and knowledge. Georges Dicker addresses his *Hume's Epistemology and Metaphysics: An Introduction* to readers who have no familiarity with Hume, but he intends that the book be sophisticated and rigorous enough to interest more advanced students. At very nearly the opposite extreme is Louis Loeb's *Stability and Justification in Hume's 'Treatise'* —a demanding, closely reasoned work that will be of most value to serious students of Hume. Among its virtues is Loeb's practice of referring specifically to interpretations that he differs from or agrees with. His footnotes are an excellent source of secondary literature on the topics he covers—much more valuable, in fact, than the conventional bibliography at the end of the book. As the title of his book—*The Sceptical Realism of David Hume*—suggests, John P. Wright argues that the "skeptical" and "realist" interpretations of Hume are both partly correct and partly wrong; that Hume moves dialectically from skepticism to realism without wholly or unambiguously embracing or repudiating either. Wright's book is valuable both for its direct interpretation of Humean texts and for setting Hume in the philosophical and scientific world of the 17th and 18th centuries.

Causation/Induction

Hume's most distinctive contributions to philosophical thought are about causation and induction; but, as with much of Hume's philosophy, commentators do not agree on just what his position actually is. Tom Beauchamp and Alexander Rosenberg argue in their *Hume and the Problem of Causation* that Hume's theory of causation (which they take to be a version of the regularity theory) can be defended against a wide range of criticisms and is, moreover, surprisingly *au courant*. (According to the regularity theory, causation in the world or nature consists in the regular succession of objects, and nothing else.) John P. Wright (*The Sceptical Realism of David Hume*) and Galen Strawson (*The Secret Connexion: Causation, Realism, and David Hume*) describe Hume as a skeptical realist about causation. This means that there are real objective causal connections in the world, although we have no direct cognitive access to them. Obviously, their view of Hume runs counter to the regularity-theory interpretation of Beauchamp and Rosenberg (and many others). *The New Hume Debate* (edited by Rupert Read and Kenneth Richman) comprises about a dozen articles in which proponents and critics of the "new" Hume—the Hume, that is, who believes in "the existence of something like natural necessity or causal power" (Galen Strawson's phrase)—discuss textual and philosophical issues involved in the dispute.

According to Fred Wilson (*Hume's Defence of Causal Inference*), Hume offers a vindication (a "moral certainty" as opposed to a demonstration or rational proof) of the principle of causation based on the success of the principle in grounding laws in many areas. Wilson rejects the claim, made by some commentators (e. g., Lewis White Beck and Robert Paul Wolff), that Hume is a proto-Kantian about causation and mental activity. Colin Howson does two things in *Hume's Problem: Induction and the Justification of Belief*: He defends Hume's argument about induction against a dozen or so purported answers, and lays out a logic of induction that incorporates Hume's great insight in a formal theory. The book is moderately technical in numerous places, though generally not when Howson is talking about Hume directly. In any case, its clarity about what Hume actually says (and does *not* say) concerning induction will repay whatever work may be required to read it (and the reader interested mainly in Hume may skip some parts without serious loss).

Philosophy of Mind

In some fairly capacious sense of *mind*, Hume's philosophy of mind lies at the foundation of his whole system of human nature. If even the ostensibly bloodless sciences of mathematics and physics rest on "the knowledge of man" (as Hume asserts), then a fortiori such disciplines as morals, criticism, epistemology, etc., must do so. But Hume scholars have been drawn to Hume's philosophy of mind conceived more narrowly as a theory (or cluster of theories) about perception, belief, memory, imagination, personal identity, and the like. John Bricke (*Hume's Philosophy of Mind*) and Daniel Flage (*David Hume's Theory of Mind*) have written book-length accounts of the philosophy of mind in Hume. Wayne Waxman is self-consciously (no pun intended) iconoclastic in his *Hume's Theory of Consciousness*. In particular, he inveighs against the widespread interpretation of Hume as a naturalist and not merely a negative skeptic. In Waxman's opinion, Hume's naturalism leads to "a most extreme skepticism." In almost 60 pages of notes, Waxman measures his position against a large body of secondary literature, much (but by no means all) of which he regards as mistaken on fundamental Humean doctrines.

Hume's Philosophy of the Self, by A. E. Pitson, is divided into two parts—"The mental aspects of personal identity" and "The agency aspects of personal identity"—that reflect Hume's warning not to conflate personal identity "as it regards our thought or imagination" with personal identity "as it regards our passions or the concern we take in ourselves." Pitson argues that we cannot appreciate the complexity and pervasiveness of Hume's theory of the self if we effectively ignore the agency part of the theory. In *Hume Variations*, Jerry Fodor, himself a major figure in philosophy of mind and cognitive science, hails Hume's *Treatise* as "the foundational document of cognitive science," inasmuch as it envisages the project of "constructing an empirical psychology on the basis of a representational theory of mind." Fodor admits—or, rather, insists—that his book is not about Hume, but about some themes in Hume. In Fodor's estimate, Hume gets some important things wrong but is remarkably "modern" in some central things that he gets right—in particular, what Fodor calls the "architecture" of psychological theories of cognition.

Ethics

Hume regarded the *Enquiry Concerning the Principles of Morals* as "incomparably the best" thing he ever wrote in any genre. Whether or not this estimate is sound, Hume's moral philosophy has provoked a large body of commentary—not as large, to be sure, as his epistemology and metaphysics, but quite substantial. *Passion and Value in Hume's Treatise*, by Páll Árdal, shows how Hume's moral theory is intimately related to his account of the passions. Forty years after its publication (in 1966), this book is still unexcelled for its treatment of the passion-morality link in Hume. It is worth noting that the most widely read and discussed book about Hume's ethical theory, over the past 20 years or so, is also about metaphysics; namely, David Fate Norton's *David Hume: Common Sense Moralist, Sceptical Metaphysician*. Among the several virtues of Norton's book is the attention he devotes to setting Hume's moral philosophy and metaphysics in historical perspective. Stanley Tweyman's *Reason and Conduct in Hume and His Predecessors* likewise treats Hume within the context of competing ethical views. Tweyman argues that Hume sometimes misconstrues the theories he attacks (e.g., the rationalism of William Wollaston). Yet a third book may be mentioned that is big on the necessity of tying Hume's moral philosophy to its contemporaries and antecedents—*Hume's Place in Moral Philosophy*, by Nicholas Capaldi. Interestingly, Capaldi criticizes certain aspects of the Norton and Tweyman books. John Bricke's *Mind and Morality: An Examination of Hume's Moral Psychology* sets out a coherent version of Hume's own scattered arguments about the relation between certain sorts of mental phenomena (those with specifically moral content) and action. This book is closely reasoned and demanding—rewarding to the serious Hume student, but not for beginners. On the other hand, James Baillie's *Hume on Morality* should be accessible to most readers but is sophisticated enough to be of interest to those who know Hume well.

Philosophy of Religion

Though Hume was not a believer in any religion, his interest in the topic was lifelong and pervasive. Indeed, he probably wrote more about religion than about any other subject. James Noxon points out that even when Hume is not openly dealing with some religious issue, he is often skirting one. In "Hume's Concern with Religion," Noxon explores several possible roots of this fascination. Two book-length studies— *Hume's Philosophy of Religion* (by J. C. A. Gaskin) and *Hume's "Inexplicable Mystery": His Views on Religion* (by Keith Yandell)—take very different attitudes toward Hume's treatment of religion. Gaskin is generally sympathetic, whereas Yandell is consistently critical; but both books are well done and well worth reading. Terence Penelhum's *Themes in Hume: The Self, the Will, Religion* devotes about one-third of its pages to Hume on religion.

It has been argued (by C. S. Peirce, for example) that the important epistemic doctrines in Hume's essay "Of Miracles"—e.g., how to assess testimonial evidence—have no inherent connection with religion; but that connection surely helps to explain the unending stream of commentary—favorable and unfavorable—from Hume's own time to our own. It is, accordingly, appropriate to include the literature on "Of Miracles" in the section on Hume's philosophy of religion. Three books published in the last eight years (there are others) are illustrative of the mountain of commentary on Hume's famous essay: *Hume, Holism, and Miracles* (by David Johnson); *Hume's Abject Failure: The Argument against Miracles* (by John Earman); and *A Defense of Hume on Miracles* (by Robert Fogelin). Conveniently for the reader, Fogelin's book defends Hume against criticisms made by Johnson and Earman. Earman's book contains a dozen historical documents—some of them not readily available to many readers—that bear on miracles. A slightly earlier book—*Hume and the Problem of Miracles: A Solution* (by Michael Levine)—ranges widely over historical and philosophical issues hovering around the question of miracles. A major point of contention among commentators is the precise character of Hume's argument. For a sample of such disagreement, see the exchange between Robert

Fogelin and Antony Flew plus a couple of interested onlookers (bibliographical details are given below). Several authors (including Earman) have discussed the relevance of Bayes's Theorem to Hume's argument about miracles (see, for example, essays by Earman, Owen, and Sobel). Levine aptly points out that invoking Bayes's theorem (or any comparable formal tool) does nothing to help the reader decide what Hume's argument actually is.

On the other hand, setting Hume's essay in its historical context *does* help us understand what Hume is trying to show about belief in miracles; and *that* has at least an indirect bearing on the arguments themselves. *The Great Debate on Miracles*, by R. M. Burns, is probably the most compendious and useful single study of that historical context. *Hume on Miracles*, edited by Stanley Tweyman, is an anthology of responses to "Of Miracles," the earliest dating from 1751 (just three years after Hume's essay was published). Two essays may be mentioned that focus more narrowly on the (probable) direct influences on Hume's thinking about miracles: "Hume's Historical View of Miracles," by M. A. Stewart, and "Hume's 'Of Miracles': Probability and Irreligion," by David Wootton.

Hume and Other Thinkers

Many books and essays about Hume contain at least passing references to his relation to other philosophers; this section is devoted to works that focus on such relations. *Hume and Hume's Connexions* (edited by M. A. Stewart and John P. Wright) comprises a dozen essays about a variety of Hume's connections—to Butler, Hutcheson, Reid, Locke, Kant, et al., to the natural-law tradition, etc. *Hume's Sentiments: Their Ciceronian and French Context* (by Peter Jones) is, as the subtitle indicates, a study of certain influences on Hume's thinking; but it is also an analytic/historical study of several themes in Hume's philosophy (religion, skepticism, knowledge, testimony, criticism, norms, and the like). In *Essays on Kant and Hume*, the distinguished Kant scholar Lewis White Beck explores some of the issues that unite and separate Hume and Kant. In support of his thesis that Hume is a kind of proto-Kantian about the status of causation, Beck gives us a memorable *bon mot*: "A priori *is* as a priori *does*." In his essay "Is There a Prussian Hume?" Fred Wilson criticizes Beck's position as being un-Humean.

Two books of essays deal with various aspects of the philosophical, religious, scientific, and political life of Hume's homeland during what is called the "Scottish Enlightenment": *The 'Science of Man' in the Scottish Enlightenment: Hume, Reid and Their Contemporaries* (edited by Peter Jones) and *Studies in the Philosophy of the Scottish Enlightenment* (edited by M. A. Stewart). Although *The Mind of God and the Works of Man*, by Edward Craig, devotes only one chapter specially to Hume ("One Way to Read Hume"), it provides a backdrop against which, Craig argues, Hume's philosophy is more fully intelligible. The centerpiece of that backdrop is the "Image-of-God" doctrine — espoused by Descartes, Malebranche, Newton, Leibniz, et al. — that sees humans as God-like in being able to attain certainty in mathematics (and in other ways as well). According to Craig, Hume not only rejects that doctrine; he seeks to destroy it and supplant it with a thoroughgoing naturalism.

Varia

In his own time, Hume was famous as a historian and essayist as well as a philosopher, and was certainly held in higher esteem in the former roles. By the 20th century, he was being forgotten as a historian and essayist while being resuscitated as a philosopher. It is heartening to note that the "non-standard" areas in Hume's writings — history, politics, economics, and the like — have attracted much attention over the past 30 years or so. Indeed, Hume scholars have begun to appreciate the relevance of Hume's historical, political, and literary writings to the "standard" topics in his philosophy (metaphysics, theory of knowledge, ethics): the *standard/non-standard* division is an artificial barrier to understanding Hume.

Hume as Philosopher of Society, Politics and History (edited by Donald Livingston and Marie Martin) ranges over topics such as Hume and Georg Wilhelm Friedrich Hegel on the social contract, Hume as a political philosopher, Hume as a Tory historian, and Hume on the American colonies. In *Hume and Machiavelli: Political Realism and Liberal Thought*, Frederick G. Whelan tries to show that Hume's political theory incorporates more of Machiavellian "realism" than one would expect to find in 18th-century liberalism. John B. Stewart seeks to combat another stereotype of Hume the political philosopher: the Tory-leaning conservative who valued order and continuity above all else. According to Stewart's *Opinion and Reform in Hume's Political Philosophy*, Hume set at least as high a premium on reform as on conservation.

Liberty in Hume's 'History of England' (edited by Nicholas Capaldi and Donald W. Livingston) comprises half a dozen essays about Hume's *History* and especially about the central importance of liberty in that work and beyond. In his book titled simply *Hume* (published in 1989), Nicholas Phillipson describes Hume as "the most genuinely historicist of philosophers and the most subtly and profoundly philosophical of historians." Published originally in 1965, *David Hume: Philosophical Historian* (edited by David Fate Norton and Richard H. Popkin) played a key role in breaching the artificial wall separating Hume the philosopher from Hume the historian. In a couple of introductory essays, Norton and Popkin argue persuasively that it is a serious error to see Hume's philosophy and his historical writings as occupying separate, disconnected spheres. If this insight has become almost a commonplace in Hume scholarship of the last few decades, Norton and Popkin deserve a good share of the credit.

In *Hume's Aesthetic Theory: Taste and Sentiment*, Dabney Townsend makes a similar claim for the importance of Hume's aesthetics in his overall philosophy. It is Hume's "implicit aesthetics," Townsend argues, that unifies his philosophy; without it, we are faced with numerous discrete problems that defy consistent understanding. Townsend provides the historical context for better understanding Hume's forays into "criticism"—a virtue, likewise, of Peter Jones's contribution to *The Cambridge Companion to Hume* ("Hume's Literary and Aesthetic Theory") and his book *Hume's Sentiments*.

Feminist Interpretations of David Hume (edited by Anne Jaap Jacobson) presents a dozen or so essays (by various authors) about Hume, written from a feminist perspective. There are discussions of Hume's metaphysics and epistemology, his "gendered" skepticism, his moral philosophy, his misogyny (or lack thereof), his insistence on the importance of sentiment and passion in human life, etc. The purpose of the book is neither to praise Hume nor to bury him, but to deepen our understanding of his texts by looking at them through new eyes.

HUME'S WRITINGS

Published Works

Philosophical Works, edited by T. H. Green and T. H. Grose, in four volumes. London: Longmans, Green, 1874–1875.

An Enquiry Concerning Human Understanding. Edited by Tom L. Beauchamp. New York: Oxford University Press, 1999. Originally published in 1748 under the title *Philosophical Essays Concerning Human Understanding.*

An Enquiry Concerning the Principles of Morals. Edited by Tom L. Beauchamp. New York: Oxford University Press, 1998. Originally published in 1751.

Note: The two *Enquiries* (listed immediately above) are available in both student and critical editions.

An Inquiry Concerning Human Understanding. Edited by Charles W. Hendel. Indianapolis, Ind.: Bobbs-Merrill, 1955. This book is now (2008) published by Prentice Hall. The Hendel edition is notable for including materials from various editions of EHU that do not appear in the Beauchamp version, cited above.

Essays, Moral, Political, and Literary. Edited by Eugene F. Miller. Indianapolis, Ind.: LibertyClassics, 1987. Some information about the complicated and confusing history of these essay is provided in the editor's foreword.

The History of England from the Invasion of Julius Caesar to The Revolution in 1688. Six volumes. Indianapolis, Ind.: LibertyClassics, 1983. Originally published from 1754 to 1762.

A Letter from a Gentleman to His Friend in Edinburgh. Edinburgh: Edinburgh University Press, 1967. This letter contains Hume's answer to charges leveled against him when he sought an academic appointment in the University of Edinburgh, plus material not written by Hume. It was published originally in 1745.

The Natural History of Religion. Edited by H. E. Root. Stanford, Calif.: Stanford University Press, 1957. Originally published in 1757.

A Treatise of Human Nature. Edited by David Fate Norton and Mary J. Norton. Oxford: Oxford University Press, 2000. A two-volume critical edition, published in 2007, is also available (at a much higher price). Books 1 and 2 were originally published in 1739; book 3, in 1740.

Other Items

Hume's Early Memoranda, 1729–1740: The Complete Text. Edited with a Foreword by Ernest Campbell Mossner. *Journal of the History of Ideas* 9, no. 4 (October 1948), 492–518.

Norton, David Fate. "Hume's *A Letter from a Gentleman*, a Review Note." *Journal of the History of Philosophy* 6, no. 2 (April 1968), 161–68.

Norton, David Fate, and Mary J. Norton. "Substantive Differences between Two Texts of Hume's *Treatise*." *Hume Studies* 26, no. 2 (November 2000), 245–77.

Raphael, D. D., and Tatsuya Sakamoto. "Anonymous Writings of David Hume." *Journal of the History of Philosophy* 28, no. 2 (April 1990), 271–81.

Stewart, M. A. "An Early Fragment on Evil," in *Hume and Hume's Connexions*, edited by M. A. Stewart and John P. Wright. See the section *Collections of Essays about Hume and His World* in this bibliography.

Letters

The Letters of David Hume. Two volumes. Edited by J. Y. T. Greig. Oxford: Clarendon Press, 1932.

New Letters of David Hume. Edited by Raymond Klibansky and Ernest C. Mossner. Oxford: Clarendon Press, 1954.

Letters of Eminent Persons Addressed to David Hume. Edited by J. H. Burton. Edinburgh and London: William Blackwood and Sons, 1849.

BIBLIOGRAPHIES

Fieser, James. "The Eighteenth-Century British Reviews of Hume's Writings." *Journal of the History of Ideas* 57, no. 4 (October 1996), 645–57.

Hall, Roland. *Fifty Years of Hume Scholarship: A Bibliographical Guide*. Edinburgh: Edinburgh University Press, 1978.

Hume and the Enlightenment: Essays Presented to Ernest Campbell Mossner. Edited by William B. Todd. Edinburgh: Edinburgh University Press; Austin: The University of Texas Humanities Research Center, 1975. This book contains "a preliminary bibliography of David Hume."

Ikeda, Sadao. *David Hume and the Eighteenth-Century British Thought: An Annotated Catalogue*. Tokyo: Chuo University Library, 1986.

Ikeda, Sadao, Michihiro Otonashi, and Tamihiro Shigemori. *David Hume and the Eighteenth-Century British Thought: An Annotated Catalogue Supplement*. Tokyo: Chuo University Library, 1988.

Jessop, T. E. *A Bibliography of David Hume and of Scottish Philosophy, from Francis Hutcheson to Lord Balfour*. London: Brown & Son, 1938. Note: Lord Balfour died in 1930.

Tweyman, Stanley. *Secondary Sources on the Philosophy of David Hume: A David Hume Bibliography 1741–2005*, in two volumes. Delmar, N.Y.: Caravan Books, 2006.

BIOGRAPHICAL WRITINGS ABOUT HUME

Brandt, Reinhard. "The Beginnings of Hume's Philosophy," in *David Hume: Bicentenary Papers*, edited by G. P. Morice. See the section *Collections of Essays about Hume and His World* in this bibliography.

Buckle, Stephen. "Hume's Biography and Hume's Philosophy." *Australasian Journal of Philosophy* 77, no. 1 (March 1999), 1–25.

Burton, John Hill. *Life and Correspondence of David Hume*. Two volumes. Edinburgh: William Tait, 1846. A facsimile reprint was issued by Garland Publishing Company in 1983.

Christensen, Jerome. *Practicing Enlightenment: Hume and the Formation of a Literary Career*. Madison: University of Wisconsin Press, 1987.

Emerson, Roger L. "The 'Affair' at Edinburgh and the 'Project' at Glasgow: The Politics of Hume's Attempts to Become a Professor," in *Hume and Hume's Connexions*, edited by M. A. Stewart and John P. Wright. See the section *Collections of Essays about Hume and His World* in this bibliography.

Greig, J. Y. T. *David Hume*. Oxford: Clarendon Press, 1932.

Mossner, Ernest Campbell. *The Forgotten Hume: Le Bon David*. New York: Columbia University Press, 1943.

——. "Philosophy and Biography: The Case of David Hume." *The Philosophical Review* 59, no. 2 (April 1950), 184–201. Reprinted in *Hume*, edited by V. C. Chappell. See the section *Collections of Essays about Hume and His World* in this bibliography.

——. *The Life of David Hume*. 2nd ed. New York: Oxford University Press, 1980.

Price, John Valdimir. *The Ironic Hume*. Austin: University of Texas Press, 1965.

Ritchie, Thomas Edward. *An Account of the Life and Writings of David Hume, Esq*. London: Printed for T. Cadell and W. Davies, 1807.

Stewart, M. A. "The Intellectual Development of Hume, 1711–1752," in *Impressions of Hume*, edited by Marina Frasca-Spada and P. J. E. Kail. See the section *Collections of Essays about Hume and His World* in this bibliography.

GENERAL STUDIES

Ayer, A. J. *Hume*. New York: Hill and Wang, 1980.

Baier, Annette C. *A Progress of Sentiments: Reflections on Hume's Treatise.* Cambridge, Mass.: Harvard University Press, 1991.

Basson, A. H. *David Hume*. Baltimore, Md.: Penguin Books, 1958. Reprinted by Greenwood Press, 1981. This book was reissued by Dover in 1968 as *David Hume* by A. P. Cavendish.

Biro, John. "Hume's New Science of the Mind," in *The Cambridge Companion to Hume*, edited by David Fate Norton. Reprinted in *Hume: General Philosophy*, edited by David W. D. Owen. See the section *Collections of Essays about Hume and His World* in this bibliography.

Botwinick, Aryeh. *Ethics, Politics and Epistemology: A Study in the Unity of Hume's Thought.* Lanham, Md.: University Press of America, 1980.

Box, M. A. *The Suasive Art of David Hume*. Princeton, N.J.: Princeton University Press, 1990.

Broughton, Janet. "What Does the Scientist of Man Observe?" *Hume Studies* 18, no. 2 (November 1992), 155–68.

Capaldi, Nicholas. *David Hume: The Newtonian Philosopher*. Boston: Twayne Publishers, 1975.

———. "Hume as Social Scientist." *Review of Metaphysics* 32, no. 1 (September 1978), 99–123.

Cavendish, A. P. *See* Basson, A. H.

Connon, Robert. "The Naturalism of Hume Revisited," in *McGill Hume Studies*, edited by David Fate Norton, Nicholas Capaldi, and Wade L. Robison. See the section *Collections of Essays about Hume and His World* in this bibliography.

Danford, John W. *David Hume and the Problem of Reason: Recovering the Human Sciences.* New Haven, Conn.: Yale University Press, 1990.

David Hume: Philosophical Historian. Edited, with introductory essays, by David Fate Norton and Richard H. Popkin. Indianapolis, Ind.: Bobbs-Merrill, 1965.

De Dijn, Herman. "Hume's Nonreductionist Philosophical Anthropology." *Review of Metaphysics* 56, no. 3 (March 2003), 587–603.

Deleuze, Gilles. *Empiricism and Subjectivity: An Essay on Hume's Theory of Human Nature.* New York: Columbia University Press, 1991. This is a translation of Deleuze's *Empirisme et Subjectivité; Essai sur la Nature Humaine selon Hume*, which was published in 1953.

Evnine, Simon. "Hume, Conjectural History, and the Uniformity of Human Nature." *Journal of the History of Philosophy* 31, no. 4 (October 1993), 589–606.

Flew, Antony. *David Hume: Philosopher of Moral Science.* Oxford: Basil Blackwell, 1986.

Garrett, Don. *Cognition and Commitment in Hume's Philosophy.* New York: Oxford University Press, 1997.

Hampshire, S. N. "Hume's Place in Philosophy," in *David Hume: A Symposium,* edited by D. F. Pears. See the section *Collections of Essays about Hume and His World* in this bibliography.

Hampton, Jean. "Does Hume Have an Instrumental Conception of Practical Reason?" *Hume Studies* 21, no. 1 (April 1995), 57–74.

Hendel, Charles W. *Studies in the Philosophy of David Hume* (new edition). Indianapolis, Ind.: Bobbs-Merrill, 1963. Published originally by Princeton University Press in 1925.

Huxley, Thomas Henry. *Hume.* New York: Harper & Brothers, 1879. The title page identifies the author as "Professor Huxley."

Jacobson, Anne Jaap. "Reconceptualizing Reason and Writing the Philosophical Canon: The Case of David Hume," in *Feminist Interpretations of David Hume,* edited by Anne Jaap Jacobson. See the section *Collections of Essays about Hume and His World* in this bibliography.

Jenkins, John. *Understanding Hume.* Lanham, Md.: Rowman & Littlefield, 1992.

Jessop, T. E. "Some Misunderstandings of Hume." *Revue Internationale de Philosophie* 6, no. 20 (1952, Fasc. 2), 155–67. Reprinted in *Hume,* edited by V. C. Chappell. See the section *Collections of Essays about Hume and His World* in this bibliography.

Kemp Smith, Norman. *The Philosophy of David Hume: A Critical Study of Its Origins and Central Doctrines.* London: Macmillan, 1941.

———. *The Philosophy of David Hume: A Critical Study of Its Origins and Central Doctrines, with a New Introduction by Don Garrett.* New York: Palgrave Macmillan, 2005.

Knight, William Angus. *Hume.* Edinburgh: William Blackwood and Sons, 1886.

Laing, B. M. *David Hume.* London: Ernest Benn, 1932. Reprinted by Russell & Russell, 1968.

Laird, John. *Hume's Philosophy of Human Nature.* New York: E. P. Dutton, 1932.

Livingston, Donald W. *Hume's Philosophy of Common Life.* Chicago: The University of Chicago Press, 1984.

———. *Philosophical Melancholy and Delirium: Hume's Pathology of Philosophy.* Chicago: University of Chicago Press, 1998.

MacNabb, D. G. C. *David Hume: His Theory of Knowledge and Morality.* 2nd ed. Oxford: Blackwell, 1966. Published originally in 1951.

Millgram, Elijah. "Was Hume a Humean?" *Hume Studies* 21, no. 1 (April 1995), 75–93. Note: This essay is about Hume's view of practical reason.

Moore, James. "The Social Background of Hume's Science of Human Nature," in *McGill Hume Studies*, edited by David Fate Norton, Nicholas Capaldi, and Wade L. Robison. See the section *Collections of Essays about Hume and His World* in this bibliography.

Mounce, H. O. *Hume's Naturalism*. London: Routledge, 1999. The scope of this book is in fact wider than its title suggests.

Nelson, John O. "The Conclusion of Book One, Part Four, of Hume's *Treatise*." *Philosophy and Phenomenological Research* 24, no. 4 (June 1964), 512–21.

Noxon, James. *Hume's Philosophical Development: A Study of His Methods*. Oxford: At the Clarendon Press, 1973.

Passmore, John. *Hume's Intentions*. 3rd ed. London: Duckworth, 1980. Published originally in 1952.

Pears, David. *Hume's System: An Examination of the First Book of His Treatise*. Oxford: Oxford University Press, 1990.

Penelhum, Terence. *Hume*. New York: St. Martin's Press, 1975.

———. *David Hume: An Introduction to His System*. West Lafayette, Ind.: Purdue University Press, 1992.

———. *Themes in Hume: The Self, the Will, Religion*. New York: Oxford University Press, 2000.

Price, H. H. "The Permanent Significance of Hume's Philosophy." *Philosophy* 15, no. 57 (January 1940), 7–37. Reprinted in *Hume*, edited by V. C. Chappell; and in *Human Understanding: Studies in the Philosophy of David Hume*, edited by Alexander Sesonske and Noel Fleming. See the section *Collections of Essays about Hume and His World* in this bibliography.

Price, John Valdimir. *David Hume*. Updated Edition. Boston: Twayne, 1991. Published originally in 1968.

Quinton, Anthony. *Hume*. New York: Routledge, 1999.

Radcliffe, Elizabeth S. *On Hume*. Belmont, Calif.: Wadsworth, 2000.

Robison, Wade L. "Hume and the Experimental Method of Reasoning." *Southwest Philosophy Review* 10, no. 2 (July 1994), 29–37.

Rorty, Amelie Oskenberg. "From Passions to Sentiments: The Structure of Hume's *Treatise*." *History of Philosophy Quarterly* 10, no. 2 (April 1993), 165–79.

Russell, Paul. *The Riddle of Hume's 'Treatise': Skepticism, Naturalism, and Irreligion*. New York: Oxford University Press, 2008.

Sapadin, Eugene. "A Note on Newton, Boyle, and Hume's 'Experimental Method'." *Hume Studies* 23, no. 2 (November 1997), 337–44.

Schmidt, Claudia M. *David Hume: Reason in History*. University Park, Penn.: Pennsylvania State University Press, 2003. Because of the unrevealing title, it is worth noting that this book offers a systematic and comprehensive account of Hume's philosophical theories.

Sisson, C. H. *David Hume.* Edinburgh: The Ramsay Head Press, 1976.

Stroud, Barry. *Hume.* Boston: Routledge & Kegan Paul, 1977.

———. "The Constraints of Hume's Naturalism." *Synthese* 152, no. 3 (October 2006), 339–51.

Williams, Christopher. *A Cultivated Reason: An Essay on Hume and Humeanism.* University Park, Penn.: Pennsylvania State University Press, 1999.

Wilson, Fred. "Hume's Defence of Science." *Dialogue* 25, no. 4 (Winter 1986), 611–28.

COLLECTIONS OF ESSAYS ABOUT HUME AND HIS WORLD

The Blackwell Guide to Hume's 'Treatise'. Edited by Saul Traiger. Malden, Mass.: Blackwell Publishing, 2006.

The Cambridge Companion to Hume. Edited by David Fate Norton. New York: Cambridge University Press, 1993.

The Cambridge Companion to the Scottish Enlightenment. Edited by Alexander Broadie. New York: Cambridge University Press, 2003.

David Hume: Bicentenary Papers. Edited by G. P. Morice. Austin, Tex.: University of Texas Press, 1977.

David Hume: Critical Assessments. Six volumes. Edited by Stanley Tweyman. New York: Routledge, 1995.

David Hume: Many-Sided Genius. Edited by Kenneth R. Merrill and Robert W. Shahan. Norman, Okla.: University of Oklahoma Press, 1976.

David Hume: A Symposium. Edited by D. F. Pears. New York: St. Martin's Press, 1963.

David Hume's Political Economy. Edited by Margaret Schabas and Carl Wennerlind. New York: Routledge, 2007.

The Empiricists: Critical Essays on Locke, Berkeley, and Hume. Edited by Margaret Atherton. Lanham, Md.: Rowman & Littlefield, 1999.

Feminist Interpretations of David Hume. Edited by Anne Jaap Jacobson. University Park, Penn.: Pennsylvania State University Press, 2000.

Human Understanding: Studies in the Philosophy of David Hume. Edited by Alexander Sesonske and Noel Fleming. Belmont, Calif.: Wadsworth, 1965.

Hume. Edited by V. C. Chappell. Garden City, N.Y.: Doubleday, 1966.

Hume and Hume's Connexions. Edited by M. A. Stewart and John P. Wright. University Park, Penn.: Pennsylvania State University Press, 1995.

Hume as Philosopher of Society, Politics and History. Edited by Donald Livingston and Marie Martin. Rochester, N.Y.: University of Rochester Press, 1991.

Hume: General Philosophy. Edited by David W. D. Owen. Burlington, Vt.: Ashgate, 2000.

Hume: Moral and Political Philosophy. Edited by Rachel Cohon. Burlington, Vt.: Ashgate, 2001.

Hume: A Re-evaluation. Edited by Donald W. Livingston and James T. King. New York: Fordham University Press, 1976.

Impressions of Hume. Edited by Marina Frasca-Spada and P. J. E. Kail. Oxford: Clarendon Press, 2005.

Liberty in Hume's 'History of England'. Edited by Nicholas Capaldi and Donald W. Livingston. Boston: Kluwer Academic Publishers, 1990.

McGill Hume Studies. Edited by David Fate Norton, Nicholas Capaldi, and Wade L. Robison. San Diego, Calif.: Austin Hill Press, 1979.

The New Hume Debate. Edited by Rupert Read and Kenneth A. Richman. New York: Routledge, 2000; revised edition, 2007. To avoid ambiguity, the title should have a hyphen between *New* and *Hume*; thus, *The New-Hume Debate*. The debate is about a putative new (or newly rediscovered) Hume, a causal realist.

The Origins and Nature of the Scottish Enlightenment. Edited by R. H. Campbell and Andrew S. Skinner. Edinburgh: John Donald Publishers, 1982.

Philosophers of the Scottish Enlightenment. Edited by V. Hope. Edinburgh: Edinburgh University Press, 1984.

Reading Hume on Human Understanding: Essays on the First 'Enquiry'. Edited by Peter Millican. New York: Oxford University Press, 2002. Besides the 14 essays by various authors about the topics covered in EHU, this volume has a useful 61-page "Critical Survey of the Literature on Hume and the First *Enquiry*."

The 'Science of Man' in the Scottish Enlightenment: Hume, Reid and Their Contemporaries. Edited by Peter Jones. Edinburgh: Edinburgh University Press, 1989.

Studies in the Philosophy of the Scottish Enlightenment. Edited by M. A. Stewart. Oxford: Clarendon Press, 1990. This is volume 1 of Oxford Studies in the History of Philosophy.

METAPHYSICS AND EPISTEMOLOGY

General

Aaron, R. I. "Hume's Theory of Universals." *Proceedings of the Aristotelian Society*, New Series, 42 (1941–1942), 117–40.

Allison, Henry E. "Hume's Philosophical Insouciance: A Reading of *Treatise* 1.4.7." *Hume Studies* 31, no. 2 (November 2005), 317–46.

Anderson, Robert Fendel. *Hume's First Principles*. Lincoln: University of Nebraska Press, 1966.

——. "Hume's Account of Knowledge of External Objects." *Journal of the History of Philosophy* 13, no. 4 (October 1975), 471–80.

——. "The Location, Extension, Shape, and Size of Hume's Perceptions," in *Hume: A Re-evaluation*, edited by Donald W. Livingston and James T. King. See the section *Collections of Essays about Hume and His World* in this bibliography.

Anscombe, G. E. M. "Hume and Julius Caesar." *Analysis* 34, no. 1 (October 1973), 1–7. Cf. Donald W. Livingston's "Anscombe, Hume and Julius Caesar," which is listed below in this section.

Árdal, Páll S. "Some Implications of the Virtue of Reasonableness in Hume's *Treatise*," in *Hume: A Re-evaluation*, edited by Donald W. Livingston and James T. King. See the section *Collections of Essays about Hume and His World* in this bibliography.

——. "Language and Significance in Hume's *Treatise*." *Canadian Journal of Philosophy* 16, no. 4 (December 1986), 779–84.

Aschenbrenner, Karl. "Psychologism in Hume." *The Philosophical Quarterly* 11, no. 42 (January 1961), 28–38.

Atkinson, R. F. "Hume on Mathematics." *The Philosophical Quarterly* 10, no. 39 (April 1960), 127–37.

Baier, Annette. "Hume: The Reflective Women's Epistemologist?," in *Feminist Interpretations of David Hume*, edited by Anne Jaap Jacobson. See the section *Collections of Essays about Hume and His World* in this bibliography.

Banwart, Mary. *Hume's Imagination*. New York: Peter Lang, 1994.

Baxter, Donald L. M. "A Defense of Hume on Identity Through Time." *Hume Studies* 13, no. 2 (November 1987), 323–42.

——. "Hume on Infinite Divisibility." *History of Philosophy Quarterly* 5, no. 2 (April 1988), 133–40.

——. *Hume's Difficulty: Time and Identity in the 'Treatise'*. New York: Routledge, 2007.

Bennett, Jonathan. *Locke, Berkeley, Hume: Central Themes*. Oxford: Clarendon Press, 1971. The central themes are meaning, causality, and objectivity.

Blackburn, Simon. "Hume on the Mezzanine Level." *Hume Studies* 19, no. 2 (November 1993), 273–88. This paper is about the analogy (if any) between secondary qualities and moral qualities.

Broad, C. D. "Hume's Doctrine of Space." *Proceedings of the British Academy* 47 (1961), 161–76.

Bruechner, Anthony L. "Humean Fictions." *Philosophy and Phenomenological Research* 46, no. 4 (June 1986), 655–64.

Buckle, Stephen. *Hume's Enlightenment Tract: The Unity and Purpose of "An Enquiry Concerning Human Understanding."* Oxford: Clarendon Press, 2001. Cf. *Reading Hume on Human Understanding*, edited by Peter Millican. See the section *Collections of Essays about Hume and His World* in this bibliography.

Burke, Michael B. "Hume and Edwards on 'Why Is There Something Rather Than Nothing?'" *Australasian Journal of Philosophy* 62, no. 4 (December 1984), 355–62. See the note following the next entry.

Cain, James. "The Hume-Edwards Principle." *Religious Studies* 31, no. 3 (September 1995), 323–28. Note: The Edwards referred to in the title is the Austrian-born American philosopher Paul Edwards (1923–2004). The "principle" is roughly the claim that if we can explain every member of a causal series, there is nothing additional left to be explained about the series as a whole.

Church, R. W. *Hume's Theory of the Understanding.* Ithaca, N.Y.: Cornell University Press, 1935. Reprinted by Greenwood Press, 1980.

———. "Hume's Theory of Philosophical Relations." *The Philosophical Review* 50, no. 4 (July 1941), 353–67.

Coleman, Dorothy P. "Is Mathematics for Hume Synthetic *A Priori?*" *The Southwestern Journal of Philosophy* 10, no. 2 (Summer 1979), 113–26.

Collier, Mark. "Filling the Gaps: Hume and Connectionism on the Continued Existence of Unperceived Objects." *Hume Studies* 25, nos. 1 and 2 (April/November 1999), 155–70.

Costa, Michael J. "Hume, Strict Identity, and Time's Vacuum." *Hume Studies* 16, no. 1 (April 1990), 1–16.

———. "Hume on the Very Idea of a Relation." *Hume Studies* 24, no. 1 (April 1998), 71–94.

Coventry, Angela Michelle. *Hume: A Guide for the Perplexed.* New York: Continuum, 2007.

Cummins, Phillip D. "Hume on the Idea of Existence." *Hume Studies* 17, no. 1 (April 1991), 61–82. Cf. Fred Wilson's "Hume on the Abstract Idea of Existence . . . ," which is listed below in this section.

———. "Hume on Qualities." *Hume Studies* 22, no. 1 (April 1996), 49–88.

Cummins, Robert. "The Missing Shade of Blue." *The Philosophical Review* 87, no. 4 (October 1978), 548–65.

Dauer, Francis W. "Hume's Scepticism with Regard to Reason: A Reconsideration." *Hume Studies* 22, no. 2 (November 1996), 211–29.

———. "Force and Vivacity in the *Treatise* and the *Enquiry.*" *Hume Studies* 25, nos. 1 and 2 (April/November 1999), 83–99.

Davis, John W. "Hume on Qualitative Content," in *David Hume: Bicentenary Papers*, edited by G. P. Morice. See the section *Collections of Essays about Hume and His World* in this bibliography.

Dicker, Georges. "Hume's Fork Revisited." *History of Philosophy Quarterly* 8, no. 4 (October 1991), 327–42.

———. *Hume's Epistemology and Metaphysics: An Introduction*. New York: Routledge, 1998.

Falkenstein, Lorne. "Naturalism, Normativity, and Scepticism in Hume's Account of Belief." *Hume Studies* 23, no. 1 (April 1997), 29–72. Reprinted in *Hume: General Philosophy*, edited by David W. D. Owen. See the section *Collections of Essays about Hume and His World* in this bibliography.

Faulkner, Paul. "David Hume's Reductionist Epistemology of Testimony." *Pacific Philosophical Quarterly* 79, no. 4 (December 1998), 302–13.

Fogelin, Robert J. "Hume and the Missing Shade of Blue." *Philosophy and Phenomenological Research* 45, no. 2 (December 1984), 263–71.

Flew, Antony. *Hume's Philosophy of Belief: A Study of His First "Inquiry."* London: Routledge & Kegan Paul, 1961.

Frasca-Spada, Marina. *Space and Self in Hume's "Treatise"*. Cambridge: Cambridge University Press, 1998.

Frazer, Catherine S. "Hume's Criticism and Defense of Analogical Argument." *Journal of the History of Philosophy* 8, no. 2 (April 1970), 173–79.

Furlong, E. J. "Imagination in Hume's *Treatise* and *Enquiry Concerning the* [*sic*] *Human Understanding*." *Philosophy* 36, no. 136 (January 1961), 62–70.

Garrett. Don. "Simplicity and Separability in Hume's Empiricism." *Archiv für Geschichte der Philosophie* 67, no. 3 (September 1985), 270–88. Reprinted in *Hume: General Philosophy*, edited by David W. D. Owen. See the section *Collections of Essays about Hume and His World* in this bibliography.

———. "Ideas, Reason, and Skepticism: Replies to My Critics." *Hume Studies* 24, no. 1 (April 1998), 171–94. This essay is, in part, a reply to Peter Millican's "Hume on Reason and Induction," which is listed below in this section.

———. "Hume's Naturalistic Theory of Representation." *Synthese* 152, no. 3 (October 2006), 301–19.

———. "Hume's Conclusions in 'Conclusion of This Book'," in *The Blackwell Guide to Hume's 'Treatise'*, edited by Saul Traiger. See the section *Collections of Essays about Hume and His World* in this bibliography.

Govier, Trudy. "Variations on Force and Vivacity in Hume." *Philosophical Quarterly* 22, no. 86 (January 1972), 44–52.

Harris, James A. "Hume's Reconciling Project and 'The Common Distinction Betwixt *Moral* and *Physical* Necessity'." *British Journal for the History of Philosophy* 11, no. 3 (August 2003), 451–71.

Hausman, Alan. "Hume's Theory of Relations." *Noûs* 1, no. 3 (August 1967), 255–82.

Hawkins, R. J. "Simplicity, Resemblance and Contrariety in Hume's *Treatise*." *The Philosophical Quarterly* 26, no. 102 (January 1976), 24–38.

Hearn, Thomas K. Jr. "Norman Kemp Smith on 'Natural Belief'." *Southern Journal of Philosophy* 7, no. 1 (March 1969), 3–8.

———. "General Rules in Hume's *Treatise*." *Journal of the History of Philosophy* 8, no. 4 (October 1970), 405–22.

Hirsch, Eli. "Hume's Distinction between Genuine and Fictitious Identity." *Midwest Studies in Philosophy* 8 (1983), 321–38.

Jacquette, Dale. *David Hume's Critique of Infinity*. Boston: Brill, 2001.

Johnson, Oliver. *The Mind of David Hume: A Companion to Book I of "A Treatise of Human Nature*." Urbana & Chicago: University of Illinois Press, 1995.

Kail, P. J. E. *Projection and Realism in Hume's Philosophy*. Oxford: Oxford University Press, 2007.

Katzav, Joel. "Humean Metaphysics." *Southern Journal of Philosophy* 40, no. 1 (March 2002), 59–74.

Kemp, Catherine. "Two Meanings of the Term 'Idea': Acts and Contents in Hume's *Treatise*." *Journal of the History of Ideas* 61, no. 4 (October 2000), 675–90.

———. "Our Ideas in Experience: Hume's Examples in 'Of scepticism with regard to the senses'." *British Journal for the History of Philosophy* 12, no. 3 (August 2003), 445–70.

Kuehn, Manfred. "Hume's Antinomies." *Hume Studies* 9, no. 1 (April 1983), 25–45.

Lightner, D. Tycerium. "Hume on Conceivability and Inconceivability." *Hume Studies* 23, no. 1 (April 1997), 113–32.

Livingston, Donald W. "Anscombe, Hume and Julius Caesar." *Analysis* 35, no. 1 (October 1974), 13–19. This is a response to G. E. M. Anscombe's "Hume and Julius Caesar," which is listed above in this section.

———. "Hume's Historical Theory of Meaning," in *Hume: A Re-evaluation*, edited by Donald W. Livingston and James T. King. See the section *Collections of Essays about Hume and His World* in this bibliography.

———. "A Sellarsian Hume?" *Journal of the History of Philosophy* 29, no. 2 (April 1991), 281–90. Cf. Fred Wilson's "Is Hume a Sceptic with Regard to the Senses?" which is listed below in this section.

Lloyd, Genevieve. "Hume on the Passion for Truth," in *Feminist Interpretations of David Hume*, edited by Anne Jaap Jacobson. See the section *Collections of Essays about Hume and His World* in this bibliography.

Loeb, Lewis E. "Integrating Hume's Accounts of Belief and Justification." *Philosophy and Phenomenological Research* 63, no. 2 (September 2001), 279–303.

———. *Stability and Justification in Hume's 'Treatise'*. New York: Oxford University Press, 2002.

Lyons, Jack C. "General Rules and the Justification of Belief in Hume's *Treatise*." *Hume Studies* 27, no. 2 (November 2001), 247–77.

Martin, Marie A. "The Rational Warrant for Hume's General Rules." *Journal of the History of Philosophy* 31, no. 2 (April 1993), 245–57.

Maund, Constance. *Hume's Theory of Knowledge: A Critical Examination*. London: Macmillan, 1937. Reprinted by Russell & Russell, 1972.

McCormick, Miriam. "Hume on Natural Belief and Original Principles." *Hume Studies* 19, no. 1 (April 1993), 103–16.

McRea, Robert. "Hume on Meaning." *Dialogue* 8, no. 3 (December 1969), 486–91.

———. "The Import of Hume's Theory of Time." *Hume Studies* 6, no. 2 (November 1980), 119–32. Cf. George Pappas, "On McRea's Hume," which is listed below in this section.

Meeker, Kevin. "Is Hume's Epistemology Internalist or Externalist?" *Dialogue* 40, no. 1 (January 2001), 125–46.

———. "Hume on Knowledge, Certainty and Probability: Anticipating the Disintegration of the Analytic/Synthetic Divide?" *Pacific Philosophical Quarterly* 88, no. 2 (June 2007), 226–42.

Millican, Peter. "Hume on Reason and Induction: Epistemology or Cognitive Science?" *Hume Studies* 24, no.1 (April 1998), 141–59. For a response, see Don Garrett, "Ideas, Reason, and Skepticism," in this section.

Morreall, John. "Hume's Missing Shade of Blue." *Philosophy and Phenomenological Research* 42, no. 3 (March 1982), 407–15.

Murphy, J. S. "Hume's Analogies in *Treatise I* and the Commentators." *Journal of the History of Philosophy* 4, no. 2 (April 1966), 155–59.

Nathan, George J. "A Humean Pattern of Justification." *Hume Studies* 9, no. 2 (November 1983), 150–70.

Naulty, R. A., and P. J. Sheehan. "Hume, Price, and Testimony." *Philosophy and Phenomenological Research* 35, no. 3 (March 1975), 376–84. Note: The Price referred to in the title is the 20th-century Welsh philosopher H. H. Price (and his book *Belief*), not Hume's 18th-century contemporary Richard Price.

Nelson, John O. "Hume's Missing Shade of Blue Re-viewed." *Hume Studies* 15, no. 2 (November 1989), 353–63.

Neujahr, Philip J. "Hume on Identity." *Hume Studies* 4, no. 1 (April 1978), 18–28.

Noonan, Harold W. *Hume on Knowledge.* New York: Routledge, 1999.

Noxon, James. "Remembering and Imagining the Past," in *Hume: A Re-evaluation,* edited by Donald W. Livingston and James T. King. See the section *Collections of Essays about Hume and His World* in this bibliography.

Owen, David. *Hume's Reason.* New York: Oxford University Press, 1999.

Pappas, George S. "On McRea's Hume." *Hume Studies* 7, no. 2 (November 1981), 167–71. McRea's essay "The Import of Hume's Theory of Time" is listed above in this section.

———. "Abstract General Ideas in Hume." *Hume Studies* 15, no. 2 (November 1989), 339–52.

Pitson, Tony. "Hume on Primary and Secondary Qualities." *Hume Studies* 8, no. 2 (November 1982), 125–38.

———. "Sympathy and Other Selves." *Hume Studies* 22, no. 2 (November 1996), 255–71.

———. "Hume and the Mind/Body Relation." *History of Philosophy Quarterly* 17, no. 3 (July 2000), 277–95.

Price, H. H. *Hume's Theory of the External World.* New York: Oxford University Press, 1940.

Price, Kingsley Blake. "Hume's Analysis of Generality." *The Philosophical Review* 59, no. 1 (January 1950), 58–76.

Prichard, H. A. *Knowledge and Perception: Essays and Lectures.* Oxford: Clarendon Press, 1950.

Robison, Wade L. "Hume's Ontological Commitments." *The Philosophical Quarterly* 26, no. 102 (January 1976), 39–47.

———. "David Hume: Naturalist and Meta-sceptic," in *Hume: A Re-evaluation,* edited by Donald W. Livingston and James T. King. See the section *Collections of Essays about Hume and His World* in this bibliography.

———. "One Consequence of Hume's Nominalism." *Hume Studies* 8, no. 2 (November 1982), 102–18.

Rollin, Bernard E. "Hume's Blue Patch and the Mind's Creativity." *Journal of the History of Ideas* 32, no. 1 (January 1971), 119–28.

Root, Michael. "Hume on the Virtues of Testimony." *American Philosophical Quarterly* 38, no. 1 (January 2001), 19–35.

Rosenberg, Alexander. "Hume and the Philosophy of Science," in *The Cambridge Companion to Hume,* edited by David Fate Norton. See the section *Collections of Essays about Hume and His World* in this bibliography.

Russow, Lilly-Marlene. "Simple Ideas and Resemblance." *The Philosophical Quarterly* 30, no. 121 (October 1980), 342–50.

Sainsbury, R. M. "Meeting the Hare in Her Doubles: Causal Belief and General Belief," in *Impressions of Hume*, edited by Marina Frasca-Spada and P. J. E. Kail. See the section *Collections of Essays about Hume and His World* in this bibliography.

Savage, Reginald O. "Hume's Missing Shade of Blue." *History of Philosophy Quarterly* 9, no. 2 (April 1992), 199–206.

Sedivy, Sonia. "Hume, Images and Abstraction." *Hume Studies* 21, no. 1 (April 1995), 117–33.

Seeman, Howard. "Questioning the Basis of Hume's Empiricism: 'Perceptions,' What Are They?" *Noûs* 20, no. 3 (September 1986), 391–99.

Serjeanston, R. W. "Hume's General Rules and the 'Chief Business of Philosophers'," in *Impressions of Hume*, edited by Marina Frasca-Spada and P. J. E. Kail. See the section *Collections of Essays about Hume and His World* in this bibliography.

Smith, Norman. "The Naturalism of Hume (I)." *Mind*, New Series, 14, no. 54 (April 1905), 149–73. "The Naturalism of Hume (II)" is about Hume's moral philosophy. Note: Norman Smith changed his surname to *Kemp Smith* after his marriage to Amy Kemp in 1910.

Steinberg, Eric. "Hume on Liberty, Necessity and Verbal Disputes." *Hume Studies* 13, no. 2 (November 1987), 113–37.

Stern, George. *A Faculty Theory of Knowledge: The Aim and Scope of Hume's First 'Enquiry'*. Lewisburg, Penn.: Bucknell University Press, 1971.

Stroud, Barry. " 'Gilding or Staining' the World with 'Sentiments' and 'Phantasms'." *Hume Studies* 19, no. 2 (November 1993), 253–72. Reprinted in *Hume: Moral and Political Philosophy*, edited by Rachel Cohon. See the section *Collections of Essays about Hume and His World* in this bibliography.

Tienson, John. "Hume on Universals and General Terms." *Noûs* 18, no. 2 (May 1984), 311–30.

Traiger, Saul. "Impressions, Ideas, and Fictions." *Hume Studies* 13, no. 2 (November 1987), 381–99.

———. "The Ownership of Perceptions." *History of Philosophy Quarterly* 5, no. 1 (January 1988), 41–51.

———. "Humean Testimony." *Pacific Philosophical Quarterly* 74, no. 2 (June 1993), 135–49.

———. "Beyond Our Senses: Recasting Book I, Part 3 of Hume's *Treatise*." *Hume Studies* 20, no. 2 (November 1994), 241–59.

Tweyman, Stanley. "Some Reflections on Hume on Existence." *Hume Studies* 18, no. 2 (November 1992), 137–49.

Ushenko, Andrew. "Hume's Theory of General Ideas." *Review of Metaphysics* 9, no. 2 (December 1955), 236–51.

Van Steenburgh, E. W. "Durationless Moments in Hume's *Treatise*," in *David Hume: Bicentenary Papers*, edited by G. P. Morice. See the section *Collections of Essays about Hume and His World* in this bibliography.

——. "Hume's Geometric 'Objects'." *Hume Studies* 6, no. 1 (April 1980), 61–68.

Vanterpool, Rudolph V. "Hume's Account of General Rules." *Southern Journal of Philosophy* 12, no. 4 (December 1974), 481–92.

Waxman, Wayne. "Impressions and Ideas: Vivacity as Verisimilitude." *Hume Studies* 19, no. 1 (April 1993), 75–88.

Welbourne, Michael. "Is Hume Really a Reductivist?" *Studies in History and Philosophy of Science* 33, no. 2 (June 2002), 407–23. Note: This paper is about Hume's views on testimony.

Wertz, S. K. "Hume and the Historiography of Science." *Journal of the History of Ideas* 54, no. 3 (July 1993), 411–36.

Wilbanks, Jan. *Hume's Theory of Imagination*. The Hague: Martinus Nijhoff, 1968.

Williams, Michael. "Hume's Criterion of Significance." *Canadian Journal of Philosophy* 15, no. 2 (June 1985), 273–304.

——. "The Unity of Hume's Philosophical Project." *Hume Studies* 30, no. 2 (November 2004), 265–96.

Williams, William H. "Is Hume's Shade of Blue a Red Herring?" *Synthese* 92, no. 1 (July 1992), 83–99. Williams proposes that Hume's missing shade be called *Marjorie Grene*.

Wilson, Fred. "Hume's Sceptical Argument against Reason." *Hume Studies* 9, no. 2 (November 1983), 90–129.

——. "Is Hume a Sceptic with Regard to the Senses?" *Journal of the History of Philosophy* 27, no. 1 (January 1989), 49–73. Cf. Donald Livingston's "A Sellarsian Hume?" which is listed above in this section.

——. "Hume's Critical Realism: A Reply to Livingston." *Journal of the History of Philosophy* 29, no. 2 (April 1991), 291–96. Wilson is responding to Livingston's "A Sellarsian Hume?" which is listed above in this section.

——. "Hume on the Abstract Idea of Existence: Comments on Cummins' 'Hume on the Idea of Existence'" *Hume Studies* 17, no. 2 (November 1991), 167–201. Cummins's paper is listed above in this section.

Winters, Barbara. "Hume on Reason." *Hume Studies* 5, no. 1 (April 1979), 20–35. Reprinted in *Hume: General Philosophy*, edited by David W. D. Owen. See the section *Collections of Essays about Hume and His World* in this bibliography.

——. "Hume's Argument for the Superiority of Natural Instinct." *Dialogue* 20 (1981), 635–43.

Wright, John P. *The Sceptical Realism of David Hume.* Minneapolis: University of Minnesota Press, 1983.

——. "Hume's Rejection of the Theory of Ideas." *History of Philosophy Quarterly* 8, no. 2 (April 1991), 149–62.

Yolton, John W. "Hume's Ideas." *Hume Studies* 6, no. 1 (April 1980), 1–25. Immediately following Yolton's essay is a response by Robert F. Anderson, "In Defense of Section V: Reply to Professor Yolton."

Zabeeh, Farhang. *Hume, Precursor of Modern Empiricism: An Analysis of His Opinions on Meaning, Metaphysics, Logic and Mathematics.* 2nd rev. ed. The Hague, Netherlands: Nijhoff, 1973. Published originally in 1960.

Causation/Induction

Anscombe, G. E. M. " 'Whatever Has a Beginning of Existence Must Have a Cause': Hume's Argument Exposed." *Analysis* 34, no. 5 (April 1974), 145–51. Cf. A. C. Genova, "On Anscombe's Exposition of Hume," which is listed below in this section.

Arnold, N. Scott. "Hume's Skepticism about Inductive Inferences." *Journal of the History of Philosophy* 21, no. 1 (January 1983), 31–55.

Aronson, Jerrold. "The Legacy of Hume's Analysis of Causation." *Studies in History and Philosophy of Science* 2, no. 2 (August 1971), 135–56.

Baç, Murat. "Is Causation 'In Here' or 'Out There'?: Hume's Two Definitions of 'Cause'." *History of Philosophy Quarterly* 16, no. 1 (January 1999), 19–35.

Beauchamp, Tom L., and Alexander Rosenberg. *Hume and the Problem of Causation.* New York: Oxford University Press, 1981.

Beauchamp, Tom L., and Thomas A. Mappes. "Is Hume Really a Sceptic about Induction?" *American Philosophical Quarterly* 12, no. 2 (April 1975), 119–29.

Beauchamp, Tom L. "Hume's Two Theories of Causation." *Archiv für Geschichte der Philosophie* 55 (1973), 281–300.

Beebee, Helen. *Hume on Causation.* New York: Routledge, 2006.

Bell, Martin. "Hume and Causal Power: The Influences of Malebranche and Newton." *British Journal for the History of Philosophy* 5, no. 1 (March 1997), 67–86.

Blackburn, Simon. "Hume and Thick Connexions." *Philosophy and Phenomenological Research* 50, Supplement (Autumn 1990), 237–50. Reprinted in *Hume: General Philosophy*, edited by David W. D. Owen; and in *Reading*

Hume on Human Understanding, edited by Peter Millican. See the section *Collections of Essays about Hume and His World* in this bibliography.

Boulter, Stephen J. "Hume on Induction: A Genuine Problem or Theology's Trojan Horse?" *Philosophy* 77, no. 299 (January 2002), 67–86.

Broackes, Justin. "Did Hume Hold a Regularity Theory of Causation?" *British Journal for the History of Philosophy* 1 (1993), 99–114.

Broughton, Janet. "Hume's Skepticism about Causal Inferences." *Pacific Philosophical Quarterly* 64, no. 1 (January 1983), 3–18.

Brown, Thomas. *Observations on the Nature and Tendency of the Doctrine of Mr. Hume, Concerning the Relation of Cause and Effect*. New York: Garland, 1983. This is a facsimile reprint of a book published originally in Edinburgh in 1806.

Collier, Mark. "A New Look at Hume's Theory of Probabilistic Inference." *Hume Studies* 31, no. 1 (April 2005), 21–36.

Costa, Michael J. "Hume and Causal Realism." *Australasian Journal of Philosophy* 67, no. 2 (June 1989), 472–90.

Coventry, Angela Michelle. *Hume's Theory of Causation: A Quasi-Realist Interpretation*. New York: Continuum, 2006.

Dauer, Francis W. "Towards a Copernican Reading of Hume." *Noûs* 9, no. 3 (September 1975), 269–93.

Ducasse, C. J. "Critique of Hume's Conception of Causality." *The Journal of Philosophy* 63, no. 6 (March 1966), 141–48.

Ençç, Berent. "Hume on Causal Necessity: A Study from the Perspective of Hume's Theory of Passions." *History of Philosophy Quarterly* 2, no. 3 (July 1985), 235–56.

Garrett, Don. "The Representation of Causation and Hume's Two Definitions of 'Cause'." *Noûs* 27, no. 2 (June 1993), 167–90. Reprinted in *The Empiricists: Critical Essays on Locke, Berkeley, and Hume*, edited by Margaret Atherton. See the section *Collections of Essays about Hume and His World* in this bibliography.

Genova, A. C. "On Anscombe's Exposition of Hume." *Analysis* 35, no. 2 (December 1974), 57–62. Anscombe's essay is listed above in this section.

Gomberg, Paul. "Coherence and Causal Inference in Hume's *Treatise*." *Canadian Journal of Philosophy* 6, no. 4 (December 1976), 693–704.

Gotterbarn, Donald. "Hume's Two Lights on Cause." *The Philosophical Quarterly* 21, no. 83 (April 1971), 168–71.

Gower, Barry. "Hume on Probability." *British Journal for the Philosophy of Science* 42, no. 1 (March 1991), 1–19.

Hacking, Ian. "Hume's Species of Probability." *Philosophical Studies* 33, no. 1 (January 1978), 21–37.

Harpley, F. N. "Hume's Probabilism." *Australasian Journal of Philosophy* 49, no. 2 (August 1971), 146–51.

Hartshorne, Charles. "Causal Necessities: An Alternative to Hume." *The Philosophical Review* 63, no. 4 (October 1954), 479–99.

Howson, Colin. *Hume's Problem: Induction and the Justification of Belief.* New York: Oxford University Press, 2000.

Jacobson, Anne Jaap. "Causality and the Supposed Counterfactual Conditional in Hume's *Enquiry.*" *Analysis* 46, no. 3 (June 1986), 131–33.

——. "Does Hume Hold a Regularity Theory of Causality?" *History of Philosophy Quarterly* 1, no. 1 (January 1984), 75–91.

Johnstone, Henry W., Jr. "Hume's Arguments Concerning Causal Necessity." *Philosophy and Phenomenological Research* 16, no. 3 (March 1956), 331–40.

Kail, Peter. "Conceivability and Modality in Hume: A Lemma in an Argument in Defense of Skeptical Realism." *Hume Studies* 29, no. 1 (April 2003), 43–61.

Kline, A. David. "Humean Causation and the Necessity of Temporal Discontinuity." *Mind,* New Series, 94, no. 376 (October 1985), 550–56.

Lenz, John W. "Hume's Defense of Causal Inference." *Journal of the History of Ideas* 19, no. 4 (October 1958), 559–67. Reprinted in *Hume,* edited by V. C. Chappell. See the section *Collections of Essays about Hume and His World* in this bibliography.

Levine, Michael Philip. "Hume's Analysis of Causation in Relation to His Analysis of Miracles." *History of Philosophy Quarterly* 1, no. 2 (April 1984), 195–202.

Levy, Ken. "Hume, the New Hume, and Causal Connections." *Hume Studies* 26, no. 1 (April 2000), 41–75.

Lindley, T. Foster. "David Hume and Necessary Connections." *Philosophy* 62, no. 239 (January 1987), 49–58.

Livingston, Donald W. "Hume on Ultimate Causation." *American Philosophical Quarterly* 8, no. 1 (January 1971), 63–70.

Loeb, Louis. "Psychology, Epistemology, and Skepticism in Hume's Argument about Induction." *Synthese* 152, no. 3 (October 2006), 321–38.

LoLordo, Antonia. "Probability and Skepticism about Reason in Hume's *Treatise.*" *British Journal for the History of Philosophy* 8, no. 3 (October 2000), 419–46.

MacNabb, D. G. C. "Hume on Induction." *Revue Internationale de Philosophie* 6, no. 20 (1952, Fasc. 2), 184–98.

Madden, Edward H. "Hume and the Fiery Furnace." *Philosophy of Science* 38, no. 1 (March 1971), 64–78. Note: This essay is about Hume's doctrine of inductive inference.

Mandelbaum, Maurice. "The Distinguishable and the Separable: A Note on Hume and Causation." *Journal of the History of Philosophy* 12, no. 2 (April 1974), 242–47.

Miller, Dickinson S. "Professor Donald Williams versus Hume." *The Journal of Philosophy* 44, no. 25 (December 1947), 673–84. Note: The dispute is about induction. Professor Williams loses.

Millican, P. J. R. "Hume's Argument Concerning Induction: Structure and Interpretation," in *David Hume: Critical Assessments*, Volume 2, edited by Stanley Tweyman. Reprinted in *Hume: General Philosophy*, edited by David W. D. Owen. See the section *Collections of Essays about Hume and His World* in this bibliography.

Monteiro, João-Paulo. "Hume, Induction, and Natural Selection," in *McGill Hume Studies*, edited by David Fate Norton, Nicholas Capaldi, and Wade L. Robison. See the section *Collections of Essays about Hume and His World* in this bibliography.

Mounce, H. O. "The Idea of a Necessary Connection." *Philosophy* 60, no. 233 (July 1985), 381–88.

Mura, Alberto. "Hume's Inductive Logic." *Synthese* 115, no. 3 (June 1998), 303–31.

Murdoch, Dugald. "Induction, Hume, and Probability." *The Journal of Philosophy* 99, no. 4 (April 2002), 185–99.

Osborne, Gregg. "Hume's Argument in *Treatise* 1.3.3.3: An Exposition and Defense." *Hume Studies* 31, no. 2 (November 2005), 225–47. The title of *Treatise* 1.3.3.3 is "Why a cause is always necessary."

Okasha, Samir. "What Did Hume Really Show about Induction?" *The Philosophical Quarterly* 51, no. 204 (July 2001), 307–27.

Parush, Adi. "Is Hume a Sceptic about Causation?" *Hume Studies* 3, no. 1 (April 1977), 3–16.

Richards, Thomas J. "Hume's Two Definitions of 'Cause'." *The Philosophical Quarterly* 15, no. 60 (July 1965), 247–53. Cf. J. A. Robinson's essay with the same title, which is listed below in this section. Reprinted in *Hume*, edited by V. C. Chappell. See the section *Collections of Essays about Hume and His World* in this bibliography.

Robinson, J. A. "Hume's Two Definitions of 'Cause'." *The Philosophical Quarterly* 12, no. 47 (April 1962), 162–71. Reprinted in *Hume*, edited by V. C. Chappell. See the section *Collections of Essays about Hume and His World* in this bibliography.

———. "Hume's Two Definitions of 'Cause' Reconsidered," in *Hume*, edited by V. C. Chappell. See the section *Collections of Essays about Hume and His World* in this bibliography. This is Robinson's rejoinder to Thomas Richards's criticism of the essay listed above.

Robison, Wade. "Hume's Causal Scepticism," in *David Hume: Bicentenary Papers*, edited by G. P. Morice. See the section *Collections of Essays about Hume and His World* in this bibliography.

Russell, Paul. "Hume's 'Two Definitions' of Cause and the Ontology of 'Double Existence'." *Hume Studies* 10, no. 1 (April 1984), 1–25. In the next issue of *Hume Studies* (i.e., 10, no. 2 [November 1984], 165–66), Russell published a list of corrections for this essay that were not incorporated into the original printed version.

Schwerin, Alan. *The Reluctant Revolutionary: An Essay on David Hume's Account of Necessary Connection.* New York: Peter Lang, 1989.

Shanks, David R. "Hume on the Perception of Causality." *Hume Studies* 11, no. 1 (April 1985), 94–108.

Stanford, P. Kyle. "The Manifest Connection: Causation, Meaning, and David Hume." *Journal of the History of Philosophy* 40, no. 3 (July 2002), 339–60.

Stove, D. C. *Probability and Hume's Inductive Scepticism.* Oxford: Clarendon Press, 1973.

———. "Why Should Probability Be the Guide of Life?" in *Hume: A Reevaluation*, edited by Donald W. Livingston and James T. King. See the section *Collections of Essays about Hume and His World* in this bibliography.

Strawson, Galen. *The Secret Connexion: Causation, Realism, and David Hume.* New York: Oxford University Press, 1989.

Stroud, Barry. "Hume on the Idea of Causal Necessity." *Philosophical Studies* 33, no. 1 (January 1978), 39–59.

Temple, Dennis. "Modal Reasoning in Hume's Billiard Ball Argument." *History of Philosophy Quarterly* 1, no. 2 (April 1984), 203–11.

Warnock, G. J. "Hume on Causation," in *David Hume: A Symposium*, edited by D. F. Pears. See the section *Collections of Essays about Hume and His World* in this bibliography.

Weintraub, Ruth. "What Was Hume's Contribution to the Problem of Induction?" *The Philosophical Quarterly* 45, no. 181 (October 1995), 460–70.

Wilson, Fred. *Hume's Defence of Causal Inference.* Toronto: University of Toronto Press, 1997.

Winkler, Kenneth. "Hume's Inductive Scepticism," in *The Empiricists: Critical Essays on Locke, Berkeley, and Hume*, edited by Margaret Atherton. See the section *Collections of Essays about Hume and His World* in this bibliography.

———. "The New Hume." *The Philosophical Review* 100, no. 3 (July 1991), 541–79. Reprinted in *Hume: General Philosophy*, edited by David W. D. Owen. See the section *Collections of Essays about Hume and His World* in this bibliography.

PHILOSOPHY OF MIND

Ainslie, Donald C. "Scepticism about Persons in Book II of Hume's *Treatise.*" *Journal of the History of Philosophy* 37, no. 3 (July 1999), 469–92.

———. "Hume's Reflections on the Identity and Simplicity of Mind." *Philosophy and Phenomenological Research* 62, no. 3 (May 2001), 557–78.

Altmann, R. W. "Hume on Sympathy." *Southern Journal of Philosophy* 18, no. 2 (June 1980), 123–36.

Árdal, Páll S. "Hume and Davidson on Pride." *Hume Studies* 15, no. 2 (November 1989), 387–94. Davidson's essay "Hume's Cognitive Theory of Pride" is listed below in this section.

Ashley, Lawrence, and Michael Stack. "Hume's Theory of the Self and Its Identity." *Dialogue* 13, no. 2 (June 1974), 239–54.

Baier, Annette. "Hume's Analysis of Pride." *The Journal of Philosophy* 75, no. 1 (January 1978), 27–40. Cf. Donald Davidson's "Hume's Cognitive Theory of Pride," which is listed below in this section.

———. "Hume on Heaps and Bundles." *American Philosophical Quarterly* 16, no. 4 (October 1979), 285–95.

———. "Helping Hume to 'Compleat the Union'." *Philosophy and Phenomenological Research* 41, no. 1/2 (September 1980), 167–86.

Baxter, Donald L. M. "Hume's Puzzle about Identity." *Philosophical Studies* 98, no. 2 (March 2000), 187–201.

Biro, John I. "Hume on Self-Identity and Memory." *The Review of Metaphysics* 30, no. 1 (September 1976), 19–38.

———. "Hume's Difficulties with the Self." *Hume Studies* 5, no. 1 (April 1979), 45–54.

———. "Hume and Cognitive Science." *History of Philosophy Quarterly* 2, no. 3 (July 1985), 257–74.

Brett, Nathan. "Substance and Mental Identity in Hume's *Treatise.*" *The Philosophical Quarterly* 22, no. 87 (April 1972), 110–25.

Bricke, John. "Hume on Self-Identity, Memory and Causality," in *David Hume: Bicentenary Papers*, edited by G. P. Morice. See the section *Collections of Essays about Hume and His World* in this bibliography.

———. *Hume's Philosophy of Mind*. Princeton, N.J.: Princeton University Press, 1980.

———. "Hume's Volitions," in *Philosophers of the Scottish Enlightenment*, edited by V. Hope. See the section *Collections of Essays about Hume and His World* in this bibliography.

———. *Mind and Morality: An Examination of Hume's Moral Psychology.* New York: Oxford University Press, 1996 [paperback edition, 2000].

Broackes, Justin. "Hume, Belief, and Personal Identity," in *Reading Hume on Human Understanding*, edited by Peter Millican. See the section *Collections of Essays about Hume and His World* in this bibliography.

Butchvarov, Panayot. "The Self and Perceptions: A Study in Humean Philosophy." *The Philosophical Quarterly* 9, no. 35 (April 1959), 97–115.

Capaldi, Nicholas. "Hume's Theory of the Passions," in *Hume: A Re-evaluation*, edited by Donald W. Livingston and James T. King. See the section *Collections of Essays about Hume and His World* in this bibliography.

Chisholm, Roderick M. "On the Observability of the Self." *Philosophy and Phenomenological Research* 30, no. 1 (September 1969), 7–21. Cf. R. Jerold Clack's essay, which is listed immediately below in this section.

Clack, R. Jerold. "Chisholm and Hume on Observing the Self." *Philosophy and Phenomenological Research* 33, no. 3 (March 1973), 338–48. Cf. Chisholm's essay, which is listed immediately above in this section.

Collier, Mark. "Hume and Cognitive Science: The Current Status of the Controversy over Abstract Ideas." *Phenomenology and the Cognitive Sciences* 4, no. 2 (June 2005), 197–207.

Cummins, Phillip D. "Hume as Dualist and Anti-Dualist." *Hume Studies* 21, no. 1 (April 1995), 47–55.

Davidson, Donald. "Hume's Cognitive Theory of Pride." *The Journal of Philosophy* 73, no. 19 (November 1976), 744–57. Cf. Annette Baier's "Hume's Analysis of Pride" and Páll Árdal's "Hume and Davidson on Pride," which are listed above in this section.

Dye, James. "Hume on Curing Superstition." *Hume Studies* 12, no. 2 (November 1986), 122–40.

Enç, Berent. "Hume's Unreasonable Desires." *History of Philosophy Quarterly* 13, no. 2 (April 1996), 239–54.

Falkenstein, Lorne, and David Welton. "Humean Contiguity." *History of Philosophy Quarterly* 18, no. 3 (July 2001), 279–96.

Flage, Daniel E. "Hume's Dualism." *Noûs* 16, no. 4 (November 1982), 527–41.

———. "Hume on Memory and Causation." *Hume Studies* 10th-Anniversary Issue (1985 Supplement), 168–88. For criticism of Flage's essay, *see* Saul Traiger's "Flage on Hume's Account of Memory," listed in this section.

———. *David Hume's Theory of Mind*. New York: Routledge, 1990.

Fodor, Jerry A. *Hume Variations*. New York: Oxford University Press, 2003.

Gardiner, P. L. "Hume's Theory of the Passions," in *David Hume: A Symposium*, edited by D. F. Pears. See the section *Collections of Essays about Hume and His World* in this bibliography.

Garrett, Don. "Hume's Self-Doubts about Personal Identity." *The Philosophical Review* 90, no. 3 (July 1981), 337–58. Reprinted in *Hume: General Phi-*

losophy, edited by David W. D. Owen. See the section *Collections of Essays about Hume and His World* in this bibliography.

Gorman, Michael M. "Hume's Theory of Belief." *Hume Studies* 19, no. 1 (April 1993), 89–101.

Green, Michael J. "The Idea of a Momentary Self and Hume's Theory of Personal Identity." *British Journal for the History of Philosophy* 7, no. 1 (March 1999), 103–22.

Henderson, Robert S. "David Hume on Personal Identity and the Indirect Passions." *Hume Studies* 16, no. 1 (April 1990), 33–44.

Hodges, Michael, and John Lachs. "Hume on Belief." *Review of Metaphysics* 30, no. 1 (September 1976), 3–18.

James, Susan. "Sympathy and Comparison: Two Principles of Human Nature," in *Impressions of Hume*, edited by Marina Frasca-Spada and P. J. E. Kail. See the section *Collections of Essays about Hume and His World* in this bibliography.

Jenkins, John J. "Hume's Account of Sympathy—Some Difficulties," in *Philosophers of the Scottish Enlightenment*, edited by V. Hope. See the section *Collections of Essays about Hume and His World* in this bibliography.

Kalt, Stefan. "David Hume on the Motivating Effect of Moral Perception." *History of Philosophy Quarterly* 22, no. 2 (April 2005), 143–60.

Kamooneh, Kaveh. "Hume's Beliefs." *British Journal for the History of Philosophy* 11, no. 1 (February 2003), 41–56.

King, James. "Pride and Hume's Sensible Knave." *Hume Studies* 25, nos. 1 and 2 (April/November 1999), 123–37.

Laird, J. "Hume's Account of Sensitive Belief." *Mind* 48, no. 192 (October 1939), 427–45.

Loeb, Louis E. "Causation, Extrinsic Relations, and Hume's Second Thoughts about Personal Identity." *Hume Studies* 18, no. 2 (November 1992), 219–31.

———. "Hume's Explanations of Meaningless Beliefs." *The Philosophical Quarterly* 51, no. 203 (April 2001), 145–64.

McDonough, Jeffrey K. "Hume's Account of Memory." *British Journal for the History of Philosophy* 10, no. 1 (February 2002), 71–87.

McGilvary, Evander Bradley. "Altruism in Hume's *Treatise*." *The Philosophical Review* 12, no. 3 (May 1903), 272–98.

McIntyre, Jane L. "Is Hume's Self Consistent?" in *McGill Hume Studies*, edited by David Fate Norton, Nicholas Capaldi, and Wade L Robison. See the section *Collections of Essays about Hume and His World* in this bibliography.

———. "Further Remarks on the Consistency of Hume's Account of the Self." *Hume Studies* 5, no. 1 (April 1979), 55–61.

———. "Personal Identity and the Passions." *Journal of the History of Philosophy* 27, no. 4 (October 1989), 545–57.

———. "Strength of Mind: Prospects and Problems for a Humean Account." *Synthese* 152, no. 3 (October 2006), 393–401.

Mendus, Susan. "Personal Identity: The Two Analogies in Hume." *The Philosophical Quarterly* 30, no. 118 (January 1980), 61–68.

Nathanson, Stephen. "Hume's Second Thoughts on the Self." *Hume Studies* 2, no. 1 (April 1976), 36–46.

Noxon, James. "Senses of Identity in Hume's *Treatise*." *Dialogue* 8, no. 3 (December 1969), 367–84.

Passmore, J. A. "Hume and the Ethics of Belief," in *David Hume: Bicentenary Papers*, edited by G. P. Morice. See the section *Collections of Essays about Hume and His World* in this bibliography.

Pears, David. "Hume on Personal Identity," in *David Hume: A Symposium*, edited by D. F. Pears. See the section *Collections of Essays about Hume and His World* in this bibliography.

———. "Hume's Recantation of His Theory of Personal Identity." *Hume Studies* 30, no. 2 (November 2004), 257–64.

Penelhum, Terence. "Hume on Personal Identity." *The Philosophical Review* 64, no. 4 (October 1955), 571–89. Reprinted in *Hume*, edited by V. C. Chappell; also in *Human Understanding: Studies in the Philosophy of David Hume*, edited by Alexander Sesonske and Noel Fleming. See the section *Collections of Essays about Hume and His World* in this bibliography.

———. "Hume's Theory of the Self Revisited." *Dialogue* 14, no. 3 (September 1975), 389–409. Reprinted in *Hume: General Philosophy*, edited by David W. D. Owen. See the section *Collections of Essays about Hume and His World* in this bibliography.

———. "The Self in Hume's Philosophy," in *David Hume: Many-Sided Genius*, edited by Kenneth R. Merrill and Robert W. Shahan. See the section *Collections of Essays about Hume and His World* in this bibliography.

———. "Hume's Moral Psychology," in *The Cambridge Companion to Hume*, edited by David Fate Norton. See the section *Collections of Essays about Hume and His World* in this bibliography.

Pike, Nelson. "Hume's Bundle Theory of the Self: A Limited Defense." *American Philosophical Quarterly* 4, no. 2 (April 1967), 159–65.

Pitson, A. E. *Hume's Philosophy of the Self.* New York: Routledge, 2002.

Postema, Gerald J. " 'Cemented with Diseased Qualities': Sympathy and Comparison in Hume's Moral Psychology." *Hume Studies* 31, no. 2 (November 2005), 249–98.

Radcliffe, Elizabeth S. "Hume on Passion, Pleasure, and the Reasonableness of Ends." *Southwest Philosophy Review* 10, no. 2 (July 1994), 1–11.

——. "Hume on the Generation of Motives: Why Beliefs Alone Never Motivate." *Hume Studies* 25, nos. 1 and 2 (April/November 1999), 101–22.

Robison, Wade L. "Hume on Personal Identity." *Journal of the History of Philosophy* 12, no. 2 (April 1974), 181–93.

——. "In Defense of Hume's *Appendix*," in *McGill Hume Studies*, edited by David Fate Norton, Nicholas Capaldi, and Wade L. Robison. See the section *Collections of Essays about Hume and His World* in this bibliography.

Rorty, Amélie Oskenberg. " 'Pride Produces the Idea of Self': Hume on Moral Agency." *Australasian Journal of Philosophy* 68, no. 3 (September 1990), 255–69.

Ross, Don. "Hume, Resemblance and the Foundations of Psychology." *History of Philosophy Quarterly* 8, no. 4 (October 1991), 343–56.

Roth, Abraham Sesshu. "What Was Hume's Problem with Personal Identity?" *Philosophy and Phenomenological Research* 61, no. 1 (July 2000), 91–114.

Scarre, Geoffrey. "What Was Hume's Worry about Personal Identity?" *Analysis* 43, no. 4 (October 1983), 217–21.

Schauber, Nancy. "Hume on Motivation: It's Almost Like Being in Love." *History of Philosophy Quarterly* 16, no. 3 (July 1999), 341–66.

Stalley, R. F. "The Will in Hume's *Treatise*." *Journal of the History of Philosophy* 24, no. 1 (January 1986), 41–53.

Stern, Cindy D. "Hume and the Self at a Moment." *History of Philosophy Quarterly* 4, no. 2 (April 1987), 217–33.

Stevenson, Gordon Park. "Humean Self-Consciousness Explained." *Hume Studies* 24, no. 1 (April 1998), 95–129.

Swain, Corliss Gayda. "Being Sure of One's Self: Hume on Personal Identity." *Hume Studies* 17, no. 2 (November 1991), 107–24.

——. "Personal Identity and the Skeptical System of Philosophy," in *The Blackwell Guide to Hume's 'Treatise'*, edited by Saul Traiger. See the section *Collections of Essays about Hume and His World* in this bibliography.

Swoyer, Chris. "Hume and the Three Views of the Self." *Hume Studies* 8, no. 1 (April 1982), 43–61.

Traiger, Saul. "Hume on Finding an Impression of the Self." *Hume Studies* 11, no. 1 (April 1985), 47–68.

——. "Flage on Hume's Account of Memory." *Hume Studies* 11, no. 2 (November 1985), 166–72. Cf. Flage, "Hume on Memory and Causation," which is listed above in this section. Flage's response—"Perchance to Dream: A Reply to Traiger"—immediately follows Traiger's critical essay.

Vitz, Rico. "Sympathy and Benevolence in Hume's Moral Psychology." *Journal of the History of Philosophy* 42, no. 3 (July 2004), 261–75.

Waxman, Wayne. *Hume's Theory of Consciousness*. New York: Cambridge University Press, 1994.

Wilson, Fred. "Hume's Theory of Mental Activity," in *McGill Hume Studies*, edited by David Fate Norton, Nicholas Capaldi, and Wade L. Robison. See the section *Collections of Essays about Hume and His World* in this bibliography. Cf. Robert Paul Wolff's essay with the same title, which is listed immediately below in this section.

Wolff, Robert Paul. "Hume's Theory of Mental Activity." *The Philosophical Review* 69, no. 3 (July 1960), 289–310. Reprinted in *Hume*, edited by V. C. Chappell. See the section *Collections of Essays about Hume and His World* in this bibliography.

Wolfram, Sybil. "Hume on Personal Identity." *Mind*, New Series, 83, no. 332 (October 1974), 586–93.

Yandell, Keith E. "Continuity, Consciousness, and Identity in Hume's Philosophy." *Hume Studies* 18, no. 2 (November 1992), 255–74.

SKEPTICISM

Breazeale, Daniel. "Hume's Impasse." *Journal of the History of Philosophy* 13, no. 3 (July 1975), 311–33.

Broughton, Janet. "Hume's Skepticism about Causal Inferences." *Pacific Philosophical Quarterly* 64, no. 1 (January 1983), 3–18.

Butts, Robert E. "Hume's Scepticism." *Journal of the History of Ideas* 20, no. 3 (June 1959), 413–19.

Coleman, Dorothy P. "Hume's 'Dialectic'." *Hume Studies* 10, no. 2 (November 1984), 139–55.

Cook, J. W. "Hume's Scepticism with Regard to the Senses." *American Philosophical Quarterly* 5, no. 1 (January 1968), 1–17.

Cummins, Phillip D. "Hume's Diffident Skepticism." *Hume Studies* 25, nos. 1 and 2 (April/November 1999), 43–65.

Dauer, Francis W. "Hume's Skeptical Solution and the Causal Theory of Knowledge." *The Philosophical Review* 89, no. 3 (July 1980), 357–78.

De Pierris, Graciela. "Hume's Pyrrhonian Skepticism and the Belief in Causal Laws." *Journal of the History of Philosophy* 39, no. 3 (July 2001), 351–83.

Ferreira, M. Jamie. "Hume's Naturalism—'Proof' and Practice." *The Philosophical Quarterly* 35, no. 138 (January 1985), 45–57.

Fogelin, Robert J. *Hume's Skepticism in the "Treatise of Human Nature."* Boston: Routledge & Kegan Paul, 1985.

Hobart, R. E. "Hume without Scepticism (I)." *Mind*, New Series, 39, no. 155 (July 1930), 273–301.

———. "Hume without Scepticism (II)." *Mind*, New Series, 39, no. 156 (October 1930), 409–25. Note: *R. E. Hobart* is the pseudonym of the American philosopher Dickinson S. Miller (1868–1963).

Immerwahr, John. "A Skeptic's Progress: Hume's Preference for the First *Enquiry*," in *McGill Hume Studies*, edited by David Fate Norton, Nicholas Capaldi, and Wade L. Robison. See the section *Collections of Essays about Hume and His World* in this bibliography.

Maund, Constance. "On the Nature and Significance of Hume's Scepticism." *Revue Internationale de Philosophie* 6, no. 20 (1952, Fasc. 2), 168–83.

McCormick, Miriam. "A Change in Manner: Hume's Scepticism in the *Treatise* and First *Enquiry*." *Canadian Journal of Philosophy* 29, no. 3 (September 1999), 431–37.

Meeker, Kevin. "Hume's Iterative Probability Argument: A Pernicious *Reductio*." *Journal of the History of Philosophy* 38, no. 2 (April 2000), 221–38.

Morris, William Edward. "Hume's Scepticism about Reason." *Hume Studies* 15, no. 1 (April 1989), 39–60. Reprinted in *Hume: General Philosophy*, edited by David W. D. Owen. See the section *Collections of Essays about Hume and His World* in this bibliography.

Penelhum, Terence. "Hume's Skepticism and the *Dialogues*," in *McGill Hume Studies*, edited by David Fate Norton, Nicholas Capaldi, and Wade L. Robison. See the section *Collections of Essays about Hume and His World* in this bibliography.

Popkin, Richard. "David Hume: His Pyrrhonism and His Critique of Pyrrhonism." *The Philosophical Quarterly* 1, no. 5 (October 1951), 385–407. Reprinted in *Hume*, edited by V. C. Chappell. See the section *Collections of Essays about Hume and His World* in this bibliography.

Schlagel, Richard H. "A Reasonable Reply to Hume's Scepticism." *The British Journal for the Philosophy of Science* 35, no. 4 (December 1984), 359–74.

Stanistreet, Paul. *Hume's Scepticism and the Science of Human Nature*. Burlington, Vt.: Ashgate, 2002.

Stove, D. C. "The Nature of Hume's Skepticism," in *McGill Hume Studies*, edited by David Fate Norton, Nicholas Capaldi, and Wade L. Robison. See the section *Collections of Essays about Hume and His World* in this bibliography.

Stroud, Barry. "Hume's Scepticism: Natural Instincts and Philosophical Reflection." *Philosophical Topics* 19, no. 1 (Spring 1991), 271–91. Reprinted in *The Empiricists: Critical Essays on Locke, Berkeley, and Hume*, edited by Margaret Atherton; also in *Hume: General Philosophy*, edited by David W. D. Owen. See the section *Collections of Essays about Hume and His World* in this bibliography.

Wright, John P. "Hume's Academic Scepticism: A Reappraisal of His Philosophy of Human Understanding." *Canadian Journal of Philosophy* 16, no. 3 (September 1986), 407–36. Reprinted in *Hume: General Philosophy*, edited by David W. D. Owen. See the section *Collections of Essays about Hume and His World* in this bibliography.

ETHICS/MORAL PHILOSOPHY

Abramson, Kate. "Two Portraits of the Humean Moral Agent." *Pacific Philosophical Quarterly* 83, no. 4 (December 2002), 301–34.

Aiken, Henry David. "An Interpretation of Hume's Theory of the Place of Reason in Ethics and Politics." *Ethics* 90, no. 1 (October 1979), 66–80.

———. "The Originality of Hume's Theory of Obligation." *Philosophy and Phenomenological Research* 42, no. 3 (March 1982), 374–83.

Árdal, Páll S. *Passion and Value in Hume's 'Treatise'*. Edinburgh: Edinburgh University Press, 1966, 1989. The 1989 reprinting contains an introduction to the second edition, which runs to 30 pages.

———. "Convention and Value," in *David Hume: Bicentenary Papers*, edited by G. P. Morice. See the section *Collections of Essays about Hume and His World* in this bibliography.

———. "Another Look at Hume's Account of Moral Evaluation." *Journal of the History of Philosophy* 15, no. 4 (October 1977), 408–21.

Ashford, Elizabeth. "Utilitarianism with a Humean Face." *Hume Studies* 31, no. 1 (April 2005), 63–92.

Atkinson, R. F. "Hume on 'Is' and 'Ought': A Reply to Mr. MacIntyre." *The Philosophical Review* 70, no. 2 (April 1961), 231–38. (MacIntyre's essay is listed below in this section.) Reprinted in *Hume*, edited by V. C. Chappell. See the section *Collections of Essays about Hume and His World* in this bibliography.

———. "Hume on the Standard of Morals," in *David Hume: Many-Sided Genius*, edited by Kenneth R. Merrill and Robert W. Shahan. See the section *Collections of Essays about Hume and His World* in this bibliography.

Baier, Annette C. "Artificial Virtues and the Equally Sensible Non-Knaves: A Response to Gauthier." *Hume Studies* 18, no. 2 (November 1992), 429–39. Gauthier's essay is listed below in this section.

Baillie, James. *Hume on Morality*. New York: Routledge, 2000.

Baldwin, Jason. "Hume's Knave and the Interests of Justice." *Journal of the History of Philosophy* 42, no. 3 (July 2004), 277–96.

Baron, Marcia. "Hume's Noble Lie: An Account of His Artificial Virtues." *Canadian Journal of Philosophy* 12, no. 3 (September 1982), 539–55. Reprinted in *Hume: Moral and Political Philosophy*, edited by Rachel Cohon. See the section *Collections of Essays about Hume and His World* in this bibliography.

———. "Morality as a Back-up System: Hume's View?" *Hume Studies* 14, no. 1 (April 1988), 25–52.

Botros, Sophie. *Hume, Reason and Morality: A Legacy of Contradiction.* New York: Routledge, 2006.

Brand, Walter. *Hume's Theory of Moral Judgment: A Study in the Unity of "A Treatise of Human Nature"*: Boston: Kluwer, 1992.

Bricke, John. "Hume, Freedom to Act, and Personal Evaluation." *History of Philosophy Quarterly* 5, no. 2 (April 1988), 141–56.

Broiles, R. David. *The Moral Philosophy of David Hume.* The Hague, Netherlands: Martinus Nijhoff, 1964.

Brown, Charlotte. "Is Hume an Internalist?" *Journal of the History of Philosophy* 26, no. 1 (January 1988), 69–87.

———. "Is the General Point of View the Moral Point of View?" *Philosophy and Phenomenological Research* 62, no. 1 (January 2001), 197–203.

Capaldi, Nicholas. "Hume's Rejection of 'Ought' as Moral Category." *The Journal of Philosophy* 63, no. 5 (March 1966), 126–37. Cf. Ronald J. Glossop's essay "Hume's Rejection . . . ," which is listed below in this section.

———. "Some Misconceptions about Hume's Moral Theory." *Ethics* 76, no. 3 (April 1966), 208–11.

———. *Hume's Place in Moral Philosophy.* New York: Peter Lang, 1989.

Clark, Stephen R. L. "Hume, Animals and the Objectivity of Morals." *The Philosophical Quarterly* 35, no. 139 (April 1985), 117–33.

Cohen, Mendel F. "Obligation and Human Nature in Hume's Philosophy." *The Philosophical Quarterly* 40, no. 160 (July 1990), 316–41.

Cohon, Rachel. "Hume and Humeanism in Ethics." *Pacific Philosophical Quarterly* 69, no. 2 (June 1988), 99–116.

———. "Is Hume a Noncognitivist in the Motivation Argument?" *Philosophical Studies* 85, nos. 2–3 (March 1997), 251–66. Reprinted in *Hume: Moral and Political Philosophy*, edited by Rachel Cohon. See the section *Collections of Essays about Hume and His World* in this bibliography.

———. "The Common Point of View in Hume's Ethics." *Philosophy and Phenomenological Research* 57, no. 4 (December 1997), 827–50. Reprinted in *Hume: Moral and Political Philosophy*, edited by Rachel Cohon. See the section *Collections of Essays about Hume and His World* in this bibliography.

Coleman, Dorothy. "Hume's Internalism." *Hume Studies* 18, no. 2 (November 1992), 331–47.

Costelloe, Timothy M. *Aesthetics and Morals in the Philosophy of David Hume.* New York: Routledge, 2007.

Darwall, Stephen. "Motive and Obligation in Hume's Ethics." *Noûs* 27, no. 4 (December 1993), 415–48. Reprinted in *Hume: Moral and Political Philosophy*, edited by Rachel Cohon. See the section *Collections of Essays about Hume and His World* in this bibliography.

Davie, William. "Hume's Catalog of Virtue and Vice," in *David Hume: Many-Sided Genius*, edited by Kenneth R. Merrill and Robert W. Shahan. See the section *Collections of Essays about Hume and His World* in this bibliography.

———. "Hume on Morality, Action, and Character." *History of Philosophy Quarterly* 2, no. 3 (July 1985), 337–48.

———. "Hume on Monkish Virtues." *Hume Studies* 25, nos. 1 and 2 (April/November 1999), 139–53.

Dees, Richard H. "Hume on the Characters of Virtue." *Journal of the History of Philosophy* 35, no. 1 (January 1997), 45–64.

Falk, W. D. "Hume on Is and Ought." *Canadian Journal of Philosophy* 6, no. 3 (September 1976), 359–78.

Fieser, James. "Is Hume a Moral Skeptic?" *Philosophy and Phenomenological Research* 50, no. 1 (September 1989), 89–105.

Flage, Daniel E. "Hume's Deontology." *International Studies in Philosophy* 26, no. 4 (1994), 29–46.

Flew, Antony. "On the Interpretation of Hume." *Philosophy* 38, no. 144 (April 1963), 178–82. This is a criticism of Geoffrey Hunter's essay "Hume on *Is* and *Ought*," which is listed below in this section. Reprinted in *Hume*, edited by V. C. Chappell. See the section *Collections of Essays about Hume and His World* in this bibliography.

Foot, Philippa R. "Hume on Moral Judgement," in *David Hume: A Symposium*, edited by D. F. Pears. Reprinted in *Hume: Moral and Political Philosophy*, edited by Rachel Cohon. See the section *Collections of Essays about Hume and His World* in this bibliography for both collections of essays.

Gaskin, J. C. A. "Hume, Atheism, and the 'Interested Obligation' of Morality," in *McGill Hume Studies*, edited by David Fate Norton, Nicholas Capaldi, and Wade L. Robison. See the section *Collections of Essays about Hume and His World* in this bibliography.

Gauthier, David. "Artificial Virtues and the Sensible Knave." *Hume Studies* 18, no. 2 (November 1992), 401–27. Reprinted in *Hume: Moral and Political Philosophy*, edited by Rachel Cohon. See the section *Collections of Essays about Hume and His World* in this bibliography. Cf. Annette C. Baier's "Artificial Virtues and the Equally Sensible Non-Knaves: A Response to Gauthier," which is listed above in this section.

Glathe, Alfred B. *Hume's Theory of the Passions and of Morals: A Study of Books II and III of the "Treatise"*. Berkeley: University of California Press, 1950.

Glossop, Ronald J. "The Nature of Hume's Ethics." *Philosophy and Phenomenological Research* 27, no. 4 (June 1967), 527–36.

———. "Hume's Rejection of 'Ought'." *The Journal of Philosophy* 64, no. 14 (July 1967), 451–53. Cf. Nicholas Capaldi's essay "Hume's Rejection . . . ," which is listed above in this section.

———. "Hume, Stevenson, and Hare on Moral Language," in *Hume: A Reevaluation*, edited by Donald W. Livingston and James T. King. See the section *Collections of Essays about Hume and His World* in this bibliography.

Harrison, Jonathan. *Hume's Moral Epistemology*. New York: Oxford University Press, 1977.

Hearn, Thomas K. Jr. "Árdal on the Moral Sentiments in Hume's *Treatise*." *Philosophy* 48, no. 185 (July 1973), 288–92.

———. "General Rules and the Moral Sentiments in Hume's *Treatise*." *Review of Metaphysics* 30, no. 1 (September 1976), 57–72.

Henze, Donald F. "Hume, *Treatise*, III, i, 1." *Philosophy* 48, no. 185 (July 1973), 277–83.

Herdt, Jennifer A. *Religion and Faction in Hume's Moral Philosophy*. New York: Cambridge University Press, 1997.

Hudson, W. D. "Hume on *Is* and *Ought*." *The Philosophical Quarterly* 14, no. 56 (July 1964), 246–52. Reprinted in *Hume*, edited by V. C. Chappell. See the section *Collections of Essays about Hume and His World* in this bibliography.

Huff, Thomas. "Self-Interest and Benevolence in Hume's Account of Moral Obligation." *Ethics* 83, no. 1 (October 1972), 58–70.

Hughes, R. I. G. "Hume's Second *Enquiry*: Ethics as Natural Science." *History of Philosophy Quarterly* 2, no. 3 (July 1985), 291–307.

Hunter, Geoffrey. "Hume on *Is* and *Ought*." *Philosophy* 37, no. 140 (April 1962), 148–52. Antony Flew's "On the Interpretation of Hume," listed above in this section, criticizes Hunter's essay.

———. "Reply to Professor Flew." *Philosophy* 38, no. 144 (April 1963), 182–84. This is Hunter's response to Antony Flew's criticism in "On the Interpretation of Hume," listed above. Reprinted in *Hume*, edited by V. C. Chappell. See the section *Collections of Essays about Hume and His World* in this bibliography.

Jensen, Henning. "Hume on Moral Agreement." *Mind*, New Series, 86, no. 344 (October 1977), 497–513.

Jones, Peter. "Another Look at Hume's Views of Aesthetic and Moral Judgments." *The Philosophical Quarterly* 20, no. 78 (January 1970), 53–59.

Kail, P. J. E. "Hume's Ethical Conclusion," in *Impressions of Hume*, edited by Marina Frasca-Spada and P. J. E. Kail. See the section *Collections of Essays about Hume and His World* in this bibliography.

King, James T. "The Place of the Language of Morals in Hume's Second *Enquiry*," in *Hume: A Re-evaluation*, edited by Donald W. Livingston and

James T. King. See the section *Collections of Essays about Hume and His World* in this bibliography.

———. "Hume and Ethical Monism." *History of Philosophy Quarterly* 5, no. 2 (April 1988), 157–71.

Korsgaard, Christine M. "The General Point of View: Love and Moral Approval in Hume's Ethics." *Hume Studies* 25, nos. 1 and 2 (April/November 1999), 3–41. Reprinted in *Hume: Moral and Political Philosophy*, edited by Rachel Cohon. See the section *Collections of Essays about Hume and His World* in this bibliography.

Kydd, Rachel M. *Reason and Conduct in Hume's "Treatise."* New York: Oxford University Press, 1946. Reprinted by Russell and Russell in 1964.

Loeb, Louis. "Hume's Moral Sentiments and the Structure of the *Treatise*." *Journal of the History of Philosophy* 15, no. 4 (October 1977), 395–403.

MacIntyre, A. C. "Hume on 'Is' and 'Ought'." *The Philosophical Review* 68, no. 4 (October 1959), 451–68. Reprinted in *Hume*, edited by V. C. Chappell. See the section *Collections of Essays about Hume and His World* in this bibliography.

Mackie, J. L. *Hume's Moral Theory.* Boston: Routledge and Kegan Paul, 1980.

MacKinnon, Barbara A. "Hare's Use of Hume's Fork." *Ethics* 84, no. 4 (July 1974), 332–38.

Magri, Tito. "Natural Obligation and Normative Motivation in Hume's *Treatise*." *Hume Studies* 22, no. 2 (November 1996), 231–53. Reprinted in *Hume: Moral and Political Philosophy*, edited by Rachel Cohon. See the section *Collections of Essays about Hume and His World* in this bibliography.

Markus, R. I. "Hume: Reason and Moral Sense." *Philosophy and Phenomenological Research* 13, no. 2 (December 1952), 139–58.

Mason, Michelle. "Hume and Humeans on Practical Reason." *Hume Studies* 31, no. 2 (November 2005), 347–78.

McIntyre, Jane L. "Character: A Humean Account." *History of Philosophy Quarterly* 7, no. 2 (April 1990), 193–206.

Moonan, Lawrence. "Hume on Is and Ought." *Journal of the History of Philosophy* 13, no. 1 (Janaury 1975), 83–98.

Norton, David Fate. *David Hume: Common Sense Moralist, Sceptical Metaphysician.* Princeton, N.J.: Princeton University Press, 1982; revised edition, 1984.

———. "Hume's Moral Ontology." *Hume Studies* 10th-Anniversary Issue (1985 Supplement), 189–214.

———. "Hume, Human Nature, and the Foundations of Morality," in *The Cambridge Companion to Hume*, edited by David Fate Norton. See the section *Collections of Essays about Hume and His World* in this bibliography.

Phillips, David. "Hume on Practical Reason: Normativity and Psychology in *Treatise* 2.3.3." *Hume Studies* 31, no. 2 (November 2005), 299–316. The title of *Treatise* 2.3.3 is "Of the influencing motives of the will."

Pitson, A. E. "Projectionism, Realism, and Hume's Moral Sense Theory." *Hume Studies* 15, no. 1 (April 1989), 61–92.

———. "Hume on Morals and Animals." *British Journal for the History of Philosophy* 11, no. 4 (November 2003), 639–55.

Platts, Mark. "Hume and Morality as a Matter of Fact." *Mind*, New Series, 97, no. 386 (April 1988), 189–204.

Postema, Gerald J. "Hume's Reply to the Sensible Knave." *History of Philosophy Quarterly* 5, no. 1 (January 1988), 23–40.

Price, Kingsley Blake. "Does Hume's Theory of Knowledge Determine his Ethical Theory?" *The Journal of Philosophy* 47, no. 15 (July 1950), 425–34.

Prior, Arthur N. *Logic and the Basis of Ethics*. Oxford: At the Clarendon Press, 1949. This book traces what Prior calls the *logic* of the refutation of the so-called naturalistic fallacy (i.e., inferring an *ought* conclusion from exclusively *is* premises) and the *history* of its refutation, from Thomas Hobbes and Ralph Cudworth in the 17th century to G. E. Moore in the 20th.

Radcliffe, Elizabeth S. "How Does the Humean Sense of Duty Motivate?" *Journal of the History of Philosophy* 34, no. 3 (July 1996), 383–407. Reprinted in *Hume: Moral and Political Philosophy*, edited by Rachel Cohon. See the section *Collections of Essays about Hume and His World* in this bibliography.

———. "Moral Internalism and Moral Cognitivism in Hume's Metaethics." *Synthese* 152, no. 3 (October 2006), 353–70.

Russell, Paul. *Freedom and Moral Sentiment: Hume's Way of Naturalizing Responsibility*. New York: Oxford University Press, 1995.

Sapadin, Eugene. "Hume's Law, *Hume's* Way," in *David Hume: Bicentenary Papers*, edited by G. P. Morice. See the section *Collections of Essays about Hume and His World* in this bibliography.

Sayre-McCord, Geoffrey. "On Why Hume's Observer Isn't Ideal—and Shouldn't Be." *Social Philosophy and Policy* 11, no. 1 (Winter 1994), 202–28.

———. "Hume and the Bauhaus Theory of Ethics." *Midwest Studies in Philosophy* 20 (1996), 280–98.

Sen, Amartya K. "Hume's Law and Hare's Rule." *Philosophy* 41, no. 155 (Janaury 1966), 75–79.

Sharp, Frank Chapman. "Hume's Ethical Theory and Its Critics (I.)." *Mind*, New Series, 30, no. 117 (January 1921), 40–56.

———. "Hume's Ethical Theory and Its Critics (II.)." *Mind*, New Series, 30, no. 118 (April 1921), 151–71.

Shaw, Daniel J. *Reason and Feeling in Hume's Action Theory and Moral Philosophy: Hume's Reasonable Passion.* Lewiston, N.Y.: Mellen Press, 1998.

Smith, Norman. "The Naturalism of Hume (II)." *Mind,* New Series, 14, no. 55 (July 1905), 335–47. Note: Norman Smith changed his surname to *Kemp Smith* after his marriage to Amy Kemp in 1910.

Snare, Francis. *Morals, Motivation and Convention: Hume's Influential Doctrines.* New York: Cambridge University Press, 1991.

Sobel, Howard Jordan. "Hume's Utilitarian Theory of Right Action." *The Philosophical Quarterly* 47, no. 186 (January 1997), 55–72.

Spector, Jessica. "Value in Fact: Naturalism and Normativity in Hume's Moral Psychology." *Journal of the History of Philosophy* 41, no. 2 (April 2003), 145–63.

Sturgeon, Nicholas L. "Moral Skepticism and Moral Naturalism in Hume's *Treatise.*" *Hume Studies* 27, no. 1 (April 2001), 3–83.

Sutherland, Stewart R. "Hume and the Concept of Pleasure," in *David Hume: Bicentenary Papers,* edited by G. P. Morice. See the section *Collections of Essays about Hume and His World* in this bibliography.

———. "Hume on Morality and the Emotions." *The Philosophical Quarterly* 26, no. 102 (January 1976), 14–23.

Swain, Corliss G. "Passionate Objectivity." *Noûs* 26, no. 4 (December 1992), 465–90.

Swanton, Christine. "Compassion as a Virtue in Hume," in *Feminist Interpretations of David Hume,* edited by Anne Jaap Jacobson. See the section *Collections of Essays about Hume and His World* in this bibliography.

Sweigart, John. "The Distance Between Hume and Emotivism." *The Philosophical Quarterly* 14, no. 56 (July 1964), 229–36.

Taylor, Gabriele. "Hume's Views of Moral Judgments." *The Philosophical Quarterly* 21, no. 82 (January 1971), 64–68.

Taylor, Jacqueline. "Hume and the Reality of Value," in *Feminist Interpretations of David Hume,* edited by Anne Jaap Jacobson. See the section *Collections of Essays about Hume and His World* in this bibliography.

———. "Hume on the Standard of Virtue." *The Journal of Ethics* 6, no. 1 (March 2002), 43–62.

Tranoy, Knut Erik. "Hume on Morals, Animals, and Men." *The Journal of Philosophy* 56, no. 3 (January 1959), 94–103.

Tweyman, Stanley. *Reason and Conduct in Hume and His Predecessors.* The Hague, Netherlands: Nijhoff, 1974.

Walton, Craig. "Hume's *England* as a Natural History of Morals," in *Liberty in Hume's 'History of England',* edited by Nicholas Capaldi and Donald W.

Livingston. See the section *Collections of Essays about Hume and His World* in this bibliography.

Wand, Bernard. "A Note on Sympathy in Hume's Moral Theory." *The Philosophical Review* 64, no. 2 (April 1955), 275–79.

———. "Hume's Account of Obligation." *The Philosophical Quarterly* 6, no. 23 (April 1956), 155–68. Reprinted in *Hume*, edited by V. C. Chappell. See the section *Collections of Essays about Hume and His World* in this bibliography.

Yalden-Thomson, D. C. "Hume's View of 'Is-Ought'." *Philosophy* 53, no. 203 (January 1978), 89–93.

SOCIAL AND POLITICAL PHILOSOPHY

Baier, Annette. "Hume's Account of Social Artifice—Its Origins and Originality." *Ethics* 98, no. 4 (July 1988), 757–78. Reprinted in *Hume: Moral and Political Philosophy*, edited by Rachel Cohon. See the section *Collections of Essays about Hume and His World* in this bibliography.

Berry, Christopher J. "Hume on Rationality in History and Social Life." *History and Theory* 21, no. 2 (May 1982), 234–47.

Bongie, Laurence L. *David Hume, Prophet of the Counter-revolution.* 2nd ed. With a foreword by Donald Livingston. Indianapolis, Ind.: Liberty Fund, 1999. The first edition, without Livingston's foreword, was published in 1965 by Oxford University Press.

Brownsey, P. F. "Hume and the Social Contract." *The Philosophical Quarterly* 28, no. 111 (April 1978), 132–48.

Buckle, Stephen, and Dario Castiglione. "Hume's Critique of the Contract Theory." *History of Political Thought* 12, no. 3 (Autumn 1991), 457–80.

Cohon, Rachel. "The Shackles of Virtue: Hume on Allegiance to Government." *History of Philosophy Quarterly* 18, no. 4 (October 2001), 393–413.

———. "Hume on Promises and the Peculiar Act of the Mind." *Journal of the History of Philosophy* 44, no. 1 (January 2006), 25–45.

Conniff, James. "Hume on Political Parties: The Case for Hume as a Whig." *Eighteenth-Century Studies* 12, no. 2 (Winter 1978), 150–73.

———. "Hume's Political Methodology: A Reconsideration of 'That Politics May Be Reduced to a Science'." *The Review of Politics* 38, no. 1 (January 1976), 88–108.

Cottle, Charles E. "Justice as Artificial Virtue in Hume's *Treatise.*" *Journal of the History of Ideas* 40, no. 3 (July 1979), 457–66. Reprinted in *Hume as Philosopher of Society, Politics and History*, edited by Donald Livingston and Marie Martin. See the section *Collections of Essays about Hume and His World* in this bibliography.

Day, John. "Hume on Justice and Allegiance." *Philosophy* 40, no. 151 (January 1965), 35–56.

Finlay, Christopher. *Hume's Social Philosophy: Human Nature and Commercial Sociability in 'A Treatise of Human Nature'*. New York: Continuum, 2007.

Flew, Antony. "Three Questions about Justice in Hume's *Treatise*. *The Philosophical Quarterly* 26, no. 102 (January 1976), 1–13.

Forbes, Duncan. *Hume's Philosophical Politics*. New York: Cambridge University Press, 1975.

Gautier, David. "David Hume, Contractarian." *The Philosophical Review* 88, no. 1 (January 1979), 3–38.

Grene, Marjorie, "Hume: Sceptic and Tory?" *Journal of the History of Ideas* 4, no. 3 (June 1943), 333–48. Reprinted in *Hume as Philosopher of Society, Politics and History*, edited by Donald Livingston and Marie Martin. See the section *Collections of Essays about Hume and His World* in this bibliography.

Haakonssen, Knud. "The Structure of Hume's Political Theory," in *The Cambridge Companion to Hume*, edited by David Fate Norton. See the section *Collections of Essays about Hume and His World* in this bibliography.

Hardin, Russell. *David Hume: Moral and Political Theorist*. New York: Oxford University Press, 2007.

Harrison, Jonathan. *Hume's Theory of Justice*. New York: Oxford University Press, 1981.

Hayek, F. A. "The Legal and Political Philosophy of David Hume," in *Hume*, edited by V. C. Chappell. See the section *Collections of Essays about Hume and His World* in this bibliography.

Kalinowski, Franklin A. "David Hume on the Philosophic Underpinnings of Interest Group Politics." *Polity* 25, no. 3 (Spring 1993), 355–74.

Kolin, Andrew. *The Ethical Foundations of Hume's Theory of Politics*. New York: Peter Lang, 1992.

Livingston, Donald W. "Time and Value in Hume's Social and Political Philosophy," in *McGill Hume Studies*, edited by David Fate Norton, Nicholas Capaldi, and Wade L. Robison. See the section *Collections of Essays about Hume and His World* in this bibliography.

———. "Hume's Historical Conception of Liberty," in *Liberty in Hume's 'History of England'*, edited by Nicholas Capaldi and Donald W. Livingston. See the section *Collections of Essays about Hume and His World* in this bibliography.

Marshall, Geoffrey. "David Hume and Political Scepticism." *The Philosophical Quarterly* 4, no. 16 (July 1954), 247–57.

McArthur, Neil. *David Hume's Political Theory: Law, Commerce, and the Constitution of Government*. Toronto: University of Toronto Press, 2007.

McRae, Robert. "Hume as a Political Philosopher." *Journal of the History of Ideas* 12, no. 2 (April 1951), 285–90. Reprinted in *Hume as Philosopher of Society, Politics and History*, edited by Donald Livingston and Marie Martin. See the section *Collections of Essays about Hume and His World* in this bibliography.

Miller, David. *Philosophy and Ideology in Hume's Political Thought*. New York: Oxford University Press, 1981.

Miller, Eugene F. "Hume on Liberty in the Successive English Constitutions," in *Liberty in Hume's 'History of England'*, edited by Nicholas Capaldi and Donald W. Livingston. See the section *Collections of Essays about Hume and His World* in this bibliography.

Miller, J. Joseph. "Neither Whig nor Tory: A Philosophical Examination of Hume's Views on the Stuarts." *History of Philosophy Quarterly* 19, no. 3 (July 2002), 275–308.

Moore, James. "Hume's Political Science and the Classical Republican Tradition." *Canadian Journal of Political Science* 10, no. 4 (December 1977), 809–39.

Postema, Gerald. "Whence Avidity? Hume's Psychology and the Origins of Justice." *Synthese* 152, no. 3 (October 2006), 371–91.

Skinner, Andrew S. "David Hume: Principles of Political Economy," in *The Cambridge Companion to Hume*, edited by David Fate Norton. See the section *Collections of Essays about Hume and His World* in this bibliography.

Stewart, John B. *The Moral and Political Philosophy of David Hume*. New York: Columbia University Press, 1963.

———. *Opinion and Reform in Hume's Political Philosophy*. Princeton, N.J.: Princeton University Press, 1992.

Watkins, Frederick. *Hume: Theory of Politics*. Austin: University of Texas Press, 1953.

Werner, John M. "David Hume and America." *Journal of the History of Ideas* 33, no. 3 (July 1972), 439–56. Reprinted in *Hume as Philosopher of Society, Politics and History*, edited by Donald Livingston and Marie Martin. See the section *Collections of Essays about Hume and His World* in this bibliography.

Whelan, Frederick. *Order and Artifice in Hume's Political Philosophy*. Princeton, N.J.: Princeton University Press, 1985.

———. "Hume and Contractarianism." *Polity* 27, no. 2 (Winter 1994), 201–24.

Wolin, Sheldon S. "Hume and Conservatism." *The American Political Science Review* 48, no. 4 (December 1954), 999–1016. Reprinted in *Hume: A Reevaluation*, edited by Donald W. Livingston and James T. King. See the section *Collections of Essays about Hume and His World* in this bibliography.

PHILOSOPHY OF RELIGION

General

Andre, Shane. "Was Hume an Atheist?" *Hume Studies* 19, no. 1 (April 1993), 141–66.

Bernard, Christopher. "Hume and the Madness of Religion," in *Hume and Hume's Connexions*, edited by M. A. Stewart and John P. Wright. See the section *Collections of Essays about Hume and His World* in this bibliography.

Bricke, John. "On the Interpretation of Hume's *Dialogues*." *Religious Studies* 11, no. 1 (March 1975), 1–18.

Burch, Robert. "Bayesianism and Analogy in Hume's *Dialogues*." *Hume Studies* 6, no. 1 (April 1980), 32–44.

Capitan, William H. "Part X of Hume's *Dialogues*." *American Philosophical Quarterly* 3, no. 1 (January 1966), 82–85. Reprinted in *Hume*, edited by V. C. Chappell. See the section *Collections of Essays about Hume and His World* in this bibliography.

Dean, Eric. "Hume on Religious Language." *The Journal of Religion* 42, no. 1 (January 1962), 44–51.

Dye, James. "Superhuman Speech and Biological Books." *History of Philosophy Quarterly* 5, no. 3 (July 1988), 257–72.

———. "Demea's Departure." *Hume Studies* 18, no. 2 (November 1992), 467–81.

Ferreira, M. Jamie. "Hume's *Natural History*: Religion and 'Explanation'." *Journal of the History of Philosophy* 33, no. 4 (October 1995), 593–611.

Fieser, James. "Hume's Concealed Attack on Religion and His Early Critics." *Journal of Philosophical Research* 20 (1995), 83–101.

Gaskin, J. C. A. "God, Hume and Natural Belief." *Philosophy* 49, no. 189 (July 1974), 281–94.

———. *Hume's Philosophy of Religion*. 2nd edition. Atlantic Highlands, N.J.: Humanities Press, 1988.

———. "Hume on Religion," in *The Cambridge Companion to Hume*, edited by David Fate Norton. See the section *Collections of Essays about Hume and His World* in this bibliography.

Hume on Natural Religion. Edited by Stanley Tweyman. Bristol, England: Thoemmes, 1996. This volume consists mainly of responses to Hume's *Dialogues Concerning Natural Religion, The Natural History of Religion,* and a couple of essays, plus two or three reviews of other writings. The earliest dates from 1757; the latest, from 1907.

Hurlbutt III, Robert H. "David Hume and Scientific Theism." *Journal of the History of Ideas* 17, no. 4 (October 1956), 486–97.

———. *Hume, Newton and the Design Argument.* Lincoln: University of Nebraska Press, 1965. Revised edition, 1985.

Immerwahr, John. "Hume's Aesthetic Theism." *Hume Studies* 22, no. 2 (November 1996), 325–37.

Jones, Peter. "Hume's Two Concepts of God." *Philosophy* 47, no. 182 (October 1972), 322–33.

Logan, Beryl. *A Religion without Talking: Religious Belief and Natural Belief in Hume's Philosophy of Religion.* New York: Peter Lang, 1993.

Merrill, Kenneth R., and Donald G. Wester. "Hume on the Relation of Religion to Morality." *The Journal of Religion* 60, no. 3 (July 1980), 272–84.

Mossner, Ernest C. "Hume and the Legacy of the *Dialogues,*" in *David Hume: Bicentenary Papers,* edited by G. P. Morice. See the section *Collections of Essays about Hume and His World* in this bibliography.

———. "The Enigma of Hume." *Mind,* New Series, 45, no. 179 (July 1936), 334–49.

———. "The Religion of David Hume." *Journal of the History of Ideas* 39, no. 4 (October 1978), 653–63.

Nathan, George J. "Hume's Immanent God," in *Hume,* edited by V. C. Chappell. See the section *Collections of Essays about Hume and His World* in this bibliography.

———. "The Existence and Nature of God in Hume's Theism," in *Hume: A Reevaluation,* edited by Donald W. Livingston and James T. King. See the section *Collections of Essays about Hume and His World* in this bibliography.

Noxon, James. "Hume's Agnosticism." *The Philosophical Review* 73, no. 2 (April 1964), 248–61. Reprinted in *Hume,* edited by V. C. Chappell. See the section *Collections of Essays about Hume and His World* in this bibliography.

———. "Hume's Concern with Religion," in *David Hume: Many-Sided Genius,* edited by Kenneth R. Merrill and Robert W. Shahan. See the section *Collections of Essays about Hume and His World* in this bibliography.

———. "In Defence of 'Hume's Agnosticism'." *Journal of the History of Philosophy* 14, no. 4 (October 1976), 469–73.

O'Connor, David. *Hume on Religion.* New York: Routledge, 2001.

Olshewsky, Thomas M. "Demea's Dilemmas." *British Journal for the History of Philosophy* 11, no. 3 (August 2003), 473–92.

Pakaluk, Michael. "Philosophical Types in Hume's *Dialogues*," in *Philosophers of the Scottish Enlightenment*, edited by V. Hope. See the section *Collections of Essays about Hume and His World* in this bibliography.

Passmore, John Arthur. "Enthusiasm, Fanaticism and David Hume," in *The 'Science of Man' in the Scottish Enlightenment*, edited by Peter Jones. See the section *Collections of Essays about Hume and His World* in this bibliography.

Penelhum, Terence. "Natural Belief and Religious Belief in Hume's Philosophy." *The Philosophical Quarterly* 33, no. 131 (April 1983), 166–81.

Pike, Nelson. "Hume on Evil." *The Philosophical Review* 72, no. 2 (April 1963), 180–97.

Religion and Hume's Legacy. Edited by D. Z. Phillips and Timothy Tessin. New York: St. Martin's Press, 1999.

Russell, Paul. "Epigram, Pantheists, and Freethought in Hume's *Treatise*: A Study in Esoteric Communication." *Journal of the History of Ideas* 54, no. 4 (October 1993), 659–73.

———. "Skepticism and Natural Religion in Hume's *Treatise*." *Journal of the History of Ideas* 49, no. 2 (April 1988), 247–65.

Salmon, W. C. "Religion and Science: A New Look at Hume's Dialogues." *Philosophical Studies* 33, no. 2 (February 1978), 143–76.

Sessions, William Lad. *Reading Hume's Dialogues: A Veneration for True Religion*. Bloomington: Indiana University Press, 2002.

Shelley, Cameron. "The First Inconvenience of Anthropomorphism: The Disanalogy in Part IV of Hume's *Dialogues*." *History of Philosophy Quarterly* 19, no. 2 (April 2002), 171–89. Cf. Stanley Tweyman's "An 'Inconvenience' . . . ," which is listed below in this section.

Siebert, Donald T. "Hume on Idolatry and Incarnation." *Journal of the History of Ideas* 45, no. 3 (July 1984), 379–96. Reprinted in *Hume as Philosopher of Society, Politics and History*, edited by Donald Livingston and Marie Martin. See the section *Collections of Essays about Hume and His World* in this bibliography.

Stahl, Donald E. "Hume's Dialogue IX Defended." *The Philosophical Quarterly* 34, no. 137 (October 1984), 505–7.

Tweyman, Stanley. "An 'Inconvenience' of Anthropomorphism." *Hume Studies* 8, no. 1 (April 1982), 19–42. Cf. Cameron Shelley's "The First Inconvenience of Anthropomorphism . . . ," which is listed above in this section.

———. *Scepticism and Belief in Hume's "Dialogues Concerning Natural Religion."* Boston: Martinus Nijhoff, 1986.

Wadia, P. S. "Philo Confounded," in *McGill Hume Studies*, edited by David Fate Norton, Nicholas Capaldi, and Wade L. Robison. See the section *Collections of Essays about Hume and His World* in this bibliography.

Wieand, Jeffrey. "Pamphilus in Hume's *Dialogues*." *The Journal of Religion* 65, no. 1 (January 1985), 33–45.

Williams, B. A. O. "Hume on Religion," in *David Hume: A Symposium*, edited by D. F. Pears. See the section *Collections of Essays about Hume and His World* in this bibliography.

Yandell, Keith E. "Hume on Religious Belief.," in *Hume: A Re-evaluation*, edited by Donald W. Livingston and James T. King. See the section *Collections of Essays about Hume and His World* in this bibliography.

———. *Hume's "Inexplicable Mystery": His Views on Religion*. Philadelphia: Temple University Press, 1990.

Miracles

Armstrong, Benjamin F. "Hume on Miracles: Begging-the-Question Against Believers." *History of Philosophy Quarterly* 9, no. 3 (July 1992), 319–28.

———. "Hume's Actual Argument against Believing in Miracles." *History of Philosophy Quarterly* 12, no. 1 (January 1995), 65–76.

Bagger, Matthew C. "Hume and Miracles." *Journal of the History of Philosophy* 35, no. 2 (April 1997), 237–51.

Beckwith, Francis J. *David Hume's Argument Against Miracles: A Critical Analysis*. Lanham, Md.: University Press of America, 1989.

Broad, C. D. "Hume's Theory of the Credibility of Miracles." *Proceedings of the Aristotelian Society*, New Series, 17 (1916–17), 77–94. Reprinted in *Human Understanding*, edited by Alexander Sesonske and Noel Fleming. See the section *Collections of Essays about Hume and His World* in this bibliography.

Buckle, Stephen. "Marvels, Miracles, and Mundane Order: Hume's Critique of Religion in *An Enquiry Concerning Human Understanding*." *Australasian Journal of Philosophy* 79, no. 1 (March 2001), 1–31.

Burns, R. M. *The Great Debate on Miracles: From Joseph Glanvill to David Hume*. Lewisburg, Penn.: Bucknell University Press, 1981.

Campbell, George. *A Dissertation on Miracles Containing an Examination of the Principles Advanced by David Hume, Esq; in an Essay on Miracles*. Edinburgh: A. Kincaid & J. Bell, 1762. A second edition of this early systematic criticism of Hume's views on miracles appeared in 1766, and a third in 1796, the year of Campbell's death. The *Dissertation* had made its way to North America by 1790, the year it was published in Philadelphia by Thomas Dobson. It was reprinted by Garland in 1983.

Coleman, Dorothy P. "Hume, Miracles, and Lotteries." *Hume Studies* 14, no. 2 (November 1988), 328–46. Cf. the essays by Hambourger and Sorensen, which are listed below in this section. For a response to Coleman, see Bruce Langtry's essay, which is listed below in this section.

———. "Baconian Probability and Hume's Theory of Testimony." *Hume Studies* 27, no. 2 (November 2001), 195–226.

Dawid, Philip, and Donald Gillies. "A Bayesian Analysis of Hume's Argument Concerning Miracles." *The Philosophical Quarterly* 39, no. 154 (January 1989), 57–65.

Earman, John. "Bayes, Hume, and Miracles." *Faith and Philosophy* 10, no. 3 (July 1993), 293–310.

———. *Hume's Abject Failure: The Argument against Miracles.* New York: Oxford University Press, 2000. Cf. William L. Vanderburgh's essay listed below in this section.

Ellin, Joseph. "Again: Hume on Miracles." *Hume Studies* 19, no. 1 (April 1993), 203–12. Cf. the 1990 *Hume Studies* pieces by Fogelin and Flew that are listed below in this section.

Ferguson, Kenneth G. "An Intervention in the Flew/Fogelin Debate." *Hume Studies* 18, no. 1 (April 1992), 105–12. Cf. the 1990 *Hume Studies* essays by Fogelin and Flew, which are listed below in this section.

Flew, Antony. "Fogelin on Hume on Miracles." *Hume Studies* 16, no. 2 (November 1990), 141–44. This is a response to Fogelin's April 1990 paper in *Hume Studies.*

———. "Hume's Check." *The Philosophical Quarterly* 9, no. 34 (January 1959), 1–18.

Fogelin, Robert J. "What Hume Actually Said About Miracles." *Hume Studies* 16, no. 1 (April 1990), 81–86.

———. *A Defense of Hume on Miracles.* Princeton, N. J.: Princeton University Press, 2003.

Gillies, Donald. "A Bayesian Proof of a Humean Principle." *The British Journal for the Philosophy of Science* 42, no. 2 (June 1991), 255–56.

Gower, Barry. "David Hume and the Probability of Miracles." *Hume Studies* 16, no. 1 (April 1990), 17–31.

Hájek, Alan. "In Defense of Hume's Balancing of Probabilities in the Miracle Argument." *Southwest Philosophy Review* 11, no. 1 (January 1995), 111–18.

Hambourger, Robert. "Belief in Miracles and Hume's Essay." *Noûs* 14, no. 4 (November 1980), 587–604.

———. "Need Miracles Be Extraordinary?" *Philosophy and Phenomenological Research* 47, no. 3 (March 1987), 435–49.

Holder, Rodney D. "Hume on Miracles: Bayesian Interpretation, Multiple Testimony, and the Existence of God." *The British Journal for the Philosophy of Science* 49, no. 1 (March 1998), 49–65.

Houston, Joseph. *Reported Miracles.* Cambridge: Cambridge University Press, 1994.

Hume on Miracles. Edited by Stanley Tweyman. Bristol, England: Thoemmes Press, 1996. This book contains responses to Hume's essay "Of Miracles," the earliest dated 1751 (only three years after the essay was published) and the latest, 1882. "Of Miracles" itself is also included.

Johnson, David. *Hume, Holism, and Miracles*. Ithaca, N.Y.: Cornell University Press, 1999.

Langtry, Bruce. "Hume, Probability, Lotteries and Miracles." *Hume Studies* 16, no. 1 (April 1990), 67–74. Cf. Dorothy Coleman's "Hume, Miracles and Lotteries," which is listed above in this section.

Levine, Michael P. *Hume and the Problem of Miracles: A Solution*. Boston: Kluwer, 1989.

Mavrodes, George I. "David Hume and the Probability of Miracles." *International Journal for the Philosophy of Religion* 43, no. 3 (June 1998), 167–82.

Millican, Peter. " 'Hume's Theorem' Concerning Miracles." *The Philosophical Quarterly* 43, no. 173 (October 1993), 489–95.

Peach, Bernard. "Hume's Mistake." *Journal of the History of Ideas* 41, no. 2 (April 1980), 331–34.

Schlesinger, George N. "Miracles and Probabilities." *Noûs* 21, no. 2 (June 1987), 219–32. Reprinted in *Hume: General Philosophy*, edited by David W. D. Owen. See the section *Collections of Essays about Hume and His World* in this bibliography.

Sobel, Jordan Howard. "On the Evidence of Testimony for Miracles: A Bayesian Interpretation of David Hume's Analysis." *The Philosophical Quarterly* 37, no. 147 (April 1987), 166–86.

———. "Hume's Theorem on Testimony Sufficient to Establish a Miracle." *The Philosophical Quarterly* 41, no. 163 (April 1991), 229–37.

Sorensen, Roy. "Hume's Skepticism Concerning Reports of Miracles." *Analysis* 43, no. 1 (January 1983), 60.

Stewart, M. A. "Hume's Historical View of Miracles," in *Hume and Hume's Connexions*, edited by M. A. Stewart and John P. Wright. See the section *Collections of Essays about Hume and His World* in this bibliography.

Swinburne, Richard. *The Concept of Miracle*. London: Macmillan, 1970.

Taylor, A. E. *David Hume and the Miraculous*. Cambridge: Cambridge University Press, 1927.

Vanderburgh, William L. "Of Miracles and Evidential Probability: Hume's 'Abject Failure' Vindicated." *Hume Studies* 31, no. 1 (April 2005), 37–61. Note: The allusion in the title is to John Earman's book *Hume's Abject Failure: The Argument Against Miracles*, which is listed above in this section.

Wadia, P. S. "Miracles and Common Understanding." *The Philosophical Quarterly* 26, no. 102 (January 1976), 69–81.

Wallace, R. C. "Hume, Flew, and the Miraculous." *The Philosophical Quarterly* 20, no. 80 (July 1970), 230–43.

Weintraub, Ruth. "The Credibility of Miracles." *Philosophical Studies* 82, no. 3 (June 1996), 359–75.

Wilson, Fred. "The Logic of Probabilities in Hume's Argument against Miracles." *Hume Studies* 15, no. 2 (November 1989), 255–75. Reprinted in *Hume: General Philosophy*, edited by David W. D. Owen, See the section *Collections of Essays about Hume and His World* in this bibliography.

Wootton, David. "Hume's 'Of Miracles': Probability and Irreligion," in *Studies in the Philosophy of the Scottish Enlightenment*, edited by M. A. Stewart. See the section *Collections of Essays about Hume and His World* in this bibliography.

Yandell, Keith E. "Miracles, Epistemology and Hume's Barrier." *International Journal for Philosophy of Religion* 7, no. 3 (September 1976), 391–455.

HUME AND OTHER THINKERS

Adair, Douglas. " 'That Politics May Be Reduced to a Science': David Hume, James Madison, and the Tenth *Federalist*." *Huntington Library Quarterly* 20, no. 4 (August 1957), 343–60. Reprinted in *Hume: A Re-evaluation*, edited by Donald W. Livingston and James T. King. See the section *Collections of Essays about Hume and His World* in this bibliography.

Aquila, Richard E. "Brentano, Descartes, and Hume on Awareness." *Philosophy and Phenomenological Research* 35, no. 2 (December 1974), 223–39.

Árdal, Páll S. "Hume and Reid on Promise, Intention and Obligation," in *Philosophers of the Scottish Enlightenment*, edited by V. Hope. See the section *Collections of Essays about Hume and His World* in this bibliography.

Baier, Annette. "Moralism and Cruelty: Reflections on Hume and Kant." *Ethics* 103, no. 3 (April 1993), 436–57.

Barfield, Michael. "Hume and the Culture of Science in the Early Eighteenth Century," in *Studies in the Philosophy of the Scottish Enlightenment*, edited by M. A. Stewart. See the section *Collections of Essays about Hume and His World* in this bibliography.

Battersby, Christine. "The *Dialogues* as Original Imitation: Cicero and the Nature of Hume's Skepticism," in *McGill Hume Studies*, edited by David Fate Norton, Nicholas Capaldi, and Wade L. Robison. See the section *Collections of Essays about Hume and His World* in this bibliography.

Beck, Lewis White. "Once More Unto the Breach: Kant's Answer to Hume, Again." *Ratio* 9, no. 1 (June 1967), 33–37. Reprinted in Beck's book *Essays on Kant and Hume*, which is listed below.

———. "A Prussian Hume and a Scottish Kant," in *McGill Hume Studies*, edited by David Fate Norton, Nicholas Capaldi, and Wade L. Robison. See the section *Collections of Essays about Hume and His World* in this bibliography. Reprinted in Beck's book *Essays on Kant and Hume*, which is listed immediately below. Cf. Fred Wilson's essay "A Prussian Hume? . . . ," which is listed below in this section.

———. *Essays on Kant and Hume*. New Haven, Conn.: Yale University Press, 1978.

Bell, Martin. "Hume and Causal Power: The Influences of Malebranche and Newton." *British Journal for the History of Philosophy* 5, no. 1 (1997), 67–86.

———. "Transcendental Empiricism? Deleuze's Reading of Hume," in *Impressions of Hume*, edited by Marina Frasca-Spada and P. J. E. Kail. See the section *Collections of Essays about Hume and His World* in this bibliography.

Berlin, Isaiah. "Hume and the Sources of German Anti-Rationalism," in *David Hume: Bicentenary Papers*, edited by G. P. Morice. See the section *Collections of Essays about Hume and His World* in this bibliography.

Berry, Christopher J. *Hume, Hegel, and Human Nature*. Boston: Martinus Nijhoff, 1982.

Bosley, Richard. "Do Mencius and Hume Make the Same Ethical Mistake?" *Philosophy East and West* 38, no. 1 (January 1988), 3–18.

Bracken, Harry M. "On Some Points in Bayle, Berkeley, and Hume." *History of Philosophy Quarterly* 4, no. 4 (October 1987), 435–46.

Bradshaw, D. E. "Berkeley and Hume on Abstraction and Generalization." *History of Philosophy Quarterly* 5, no. 1 (January 1988), 11–22.

Brett, Nathan. "Hume's Debt to Kant." *Hume Studies* 9, no. 1 (April 1983), 59–73. Note: There is no glitch in the title; the reversed chronology is intentional.

Butts, Robert E. "Husserl's Critique of Hume's Notion of Distinctions of Reason." *Philosophy and Phenomenological Research* 20, no. 2 (December 1959), 213–21.

Casullo, Albert. "Reid and Mill on Hume's Maxim of Conceivability." *Analysis* 39, no. 4 (October 1979), 212–19.

Conroy, Graham P. "Did Hume Really Follow Berkeley?" *Philosophy* 44, no. 169 (July 1969), 238–42.

Corcoran, Clive M. "Do We Have a Shaftesburean Self in the *Treatise*?" *The Philosophical Quarterly* 23, no. 90 (January 1973), 67–72. Cf. Ben Mijuskovic's essay "Hume and Shaftesbury on the Self," which is listed below in this section.

Costelloe, Timothy M. "Hume, Kant, and the 'Antinomy of Taste'." *Journal of the History of Philosophy* 41, no. 2 (April 2003), 165–85.

Craig, Edward. *The Mind of God and the Works of Man.* New York: Oxford University Press, 1987.

Darwall, Stephen. "Hume and the Invention of Utilitarianism," in *Hume and Hume's Connexions,* edited by M. A. Stewart and John P. Wright. Reprinted in *Hume: Moral and Political Philosophy,* edited by Rachel Cohon. See the section *Collections of Essays about Hume and His World* in this bibliography for both references.

Davie, G. E. [George Elder]. "Hume and the Origins of the Common Sense School." *Revue Internationale de Philosophie* 6, no. 20 (1952, Fasc. 2), 213–21.

——. "Edmund Husserl and 'the as yet, in its most important respect, unrecognised greatness of Hume'," in *David Hume: Bicentenary Papers,* edited by G. P. Morice. See the section *Collections of Essays about Hume and His World* in this bibliography.

——. "Berkeley, Hume, and the Central Problem of Scottish Philosophy," in *McGill Hume Studies,* edited by David Fate Norton, Nicholas Capaldi, and Wade L. Robison. See the section *Collections of Essays about Hume and His World* in this bibliography.

DesJardins, Gregory. "Terms of *De Officiis* in Hume and Kant." *Journal of the History of Ideas* 28, no. 2 (April 1967), 237–42. Note: *De Officiis* refers to Cicero's work on duties.

Doxsee, Carll [*sic*] Whitman. "Hume's Relation to Malebranche." *The Philosophical Review* 25, no. 5 (September 1916), 692–710.

Drever, James. "A Note on Hume's Pyrrhonism." *The Philosophical Quarterly* 3, no. 10 (January 1953), 40–50.

Ertl, Wolfgang. "Hume's Antinomy and Kant's Critical Turn." *British Journal for the History of Philosophy* 10, no. 4 (November 2002), 617–40.

Falkenstein, Lorne. "Hume and Reid on the Simplicity of the Soul." *Hume Studies* 21, no. 1 (April 1995), 24–45.

——. "Hume's Answer to Kant." *Noûs* 32, no. 3 (September 1998), 331–60. Note: The title is correctly given; it has Hume (proleptically?) answering Kant.

Ferreira, M. Jamie. *Scepticism and Reasonable Doubt: The British Naturalist Tradition in Wilkins, Hume, Reid, and Newman.* New York: Oxford University Press, 1986.

Flage, Daniel E. "Hume's Hobbism and His Anti-Hobbism." *Hume Studies* 18, no. 2 (November 1992), 369–82.

Flage, Daniel E., and Ronald J. Glass. "Hume on the Cartesian Theory of Substance." *Southern Journal of Philosophy* 22, no. 4 (December 1984), 497–508.

Flew, Antony. "Did Hume Ever Read Berkeley?" *The Journal of Philosophy* 58, no. 2 (January 1961), 50–51. Cf. essays on this topic by Popkin, Mossner, Morrisroe, and Wiener, which are all listed in this section.

———. "Social Justice: From Rawls to Hume." *Hume Studies* 12, no. 2 (November 1986), 177–91.

Fogelin, Robert. "Hume and Berkeley on the Proofs of Infinite Divisibility." *The Philosophical Review* 97, no. 1 (January 1988), 47–69.

Force, James E. "Hume and Johnson on Prophecy and Miracles: Historical Context." *Journal of the History of Ideas* 43, no. 3 (July 1982), 463–75. Reprinted in *Hume as Philosopher of Society, Politics and History*, edited by Donald Livingston and Marie Martin. See the section *Collections of Essays about Hume and His World* in this bibliography.

———. "Hume's Interest in Newton and Science." *Hume Studies* 13, no. 2 (November 1987), 166–216.

Foster, Stephen. *Melancholy Duty: The Hume-Gibbon Attack on Christianity.* Boston: Kluwer, 1997.

Fraser, Alexander. "Visualization as a Chief Source of the Psychology of Hobbes, Locke, Berkeley and Hume." *The American Journal of Psychology* 4, no. 2 (December 1891), 230–47.

Gawlick, Günter. "Hume and the Deists: A Reconsideration," in *David Hume: Bicentenary Papers*, edited by G. P. Morice. See the section *Collections of Essays about Hume and His World* in this bibliography.

Giles, James. "The No-Self Theory: Hume, Buddhism, and Personal Identity." *Philosophy East and West* 43, no. 2 (April 1993), 175–200.

Greco, John. "Reid's Critique of Berkeley and Hume: What's the Big Idea?" *Philosophy and Phenomenological Research* 55, no. 2 (June 1995), 279–96.

Green, Thomas Hill. *Hume and Locke* [with an introduction by Ramon M. Lemos]. New York: Crowell, 1968. This book comprises the introductions to Hume's *Treatise* in the Green and Grose edition of Hume's philosophical works (first published in 1874–1875); namely, I. General Introduction to Volume I. II. Introduction to the Moral Part of Hume's 'Treatise'. Green devotes almost as many pages to Locke as he does to Hume.

Groarke, Leo, and Graham Solomon. "Some Sources for Hume's Account of Cause." *Journal of the History of Ideas* 52, no. 4 (October 1991), 645–63.

Gross, Mason W. "Whitehead's Answer to Hume." *The Journal of Philosophy* 38, no. 4 (February 1941), 95–102. Cf. essays on this subject by J. W. Robson and Harold Taylor, listed below in this section.

Guttenplan, S. D. "Hume and Contemporary Ethical Naturalism." *Midwest Studies in Philosophy* 8 (1983), 309–20.

Haakonssen, Knud. *The Science of a Legislator: The Natural Jurisprudence of David Hume and Adam Smith.* Cambridge: Cambridge University Press, 1989.

Hallie, Philip P. "Hume, Biran and the *Méditatifs Intérieurs.*" *Journal of the History of Ideas* 18, no. 3 (June 1957), 295–312.

Harrison, Peter. "Prophecy, Early Modern Apologetics, and Hume's Argument Against Miracles." *Journal of the History of Ideas* 60, no. 2 (April 1999), 241–56.

Hope, V. M. *Virtue by Consensus: The Moral Philosophy of Hutcheson, Hume and Adam Smith.* Oxford: Clarendon Press, 1989.

Hume's Reception in Early America. Two volumes. Edited by Mark G. Spencer. Bristol, England: Thoemmes Press, 2002.

Huntley, W. B. "David Hume and Charles Darwin." *Journal of the History of Ideas* 33, no. 3 (July–September 1972), 457–70.

Jacobson, Nolan Pliny. "The Possibility of Oriental Influence in Hume's Philosophy." *Philosophy East and West* 19, no. 1 (January 1969), 17–37.

Jeffner, Anders. *Butler and Hume on Religion: A Comparative Analysis.* Stockholm: Diakonistyrelsens Bokförlag, 1966.

Johnson, Oliver A. "Hume's Refutation of—Wollaston?" *Hume Studies* 12, no. 2 (November 1986), 192–200.

Jones, Peter. "Strains in Hume and Wittgenstein," in *Hume: A Re-evaluation*, edited by Donald W. Livingston and James T. King. See the section *Collections of Essays about Hume and His World* in this bibliography.

———. *Hume's Sentiments: Their Ciceronian and French Context.* Edinburgh: Edinburgh University Press, 1982.

Kemp Smith, Norman. "Kant's Relation to Hume and to Leibnitz." *The Philosophical Review* 24, no. 3 (May 1915), 288–96.

Khamara, Edward J. "Hume Versus Clarke on the Cosmological Argument." *The Philosophical Quarterly* 42, no. 166 (January 1992), 34–55.

Khamara, E. J., and D. G. C. MacNabb. "Hume and His Predecessors on the Causal Maxim," in *David Hume: Bicentenary Papers*, edited by G. P. Morice. See the section *Collections of Essays about Hume and His World* in this bibliography.

King, James. "The Moral Theories of Kant and Hume: Comparisons and Polemics." *Hume Studies* 18, no. 2 (November 1992), 441–65.

Klever, Wim. "Hume Contra Spinoza?" *Hume Studies* 16, no. 2 (November 1990), 89–105.

———. "A Vindication." *Hume Studies* 17, no. 2 (November 1991), 209–12. Cf. Frank J. Leavitt's essay "Hume Against Spinoza and Aristotle," which is listed below in this section.

———. "More About Hume's Debt to Spinoza." *Hume Studies* 19, no. 1 (April 1993), 55–74.

Kuehn, Manfred. "Reid's Contribution to 'Hume's Problem'," in *The 'Science of Man' in the Scottish Enlightenment*, edited by Peter Jones. See the section *Collections of Essays about Hume and His World* in this bibliography.

——. "Kant's Critique of Hume's Theory of Faith," in *Hume and Hume's Connexions*, edited by M. A. Stewart and John P. Wright. See the section *Collections of Essays about Hume and His World* in this bibliography.

Kulenkampff, Jens. "The Objectivity of Taste: Hume and Kant." *Noûs* 24, no. 1 (March 1990), 93–110.

Kuypers, Mary Shaw. *Studies in the Eighteenth-Century Background of Hume's Empiricism*. Minneapolis: University of Minnesota Press, 1930.

Langsam, Harold. "Kant, Hume, and Our Ordinary Concept of Causation." *Philosophy and Phenomenological Research* 54, no. 3 (September 1994), 625–47.

Leavitt, Frank J. "Hume Against Spinoza and Aristotle." *Hume Studies* 17, no. 2 (November 1991), 203–8. Cf. Wim Klever's "Hume Contra Spinoza?" which is listed above in this section.

Legg, Cathy. "Naturalism and Wonder: Peirce on the Logic of Hume's Argument against Miracles." *Philosophia* 28, nos. 1–4 (June 2001), 297–318.

Lehrer, Keith. "Beyond Impressions and Ideas: Hume *vs*. Reid." *The Monist* 70, no. 4 (October 1987), 383–97. Reprinted in *The 'Science of Man' in the Scottish Enlightenment*, edited by Peter Jones. See the section *Collections of Essays about Hume and His World* in this bibliography.

Lesser, Harry. "Reid's Criticism of Hume's Theory of Personal Identity." *Hume Studies* 4, no. 2 (November 1978), 41–63.

Liu, Xiusheng. *Mencius, Hume and the Foundations of Ethics*. Burlington, Vt.: Ashgate, 2003.

Lüthe, Rudolf. "Misunderstanding Hume: Remarks on German Ways of Interpreting His Philosophy," in *Philosophers of the Scottish Enlightenment*, edited by V. Hope. See the section *Collections of Essays about Hume and His World* in this bibliography.

Martin, Marie A. "Hutcheson and Hume on Explaining the Nature of Morality: Why It Is Mistaken to Suppose Hume Ever Raised the 'Is-Ought' Question." *History of Philosophy Quarterly* 8, no. 3 (July 1991), 277–89.

Mathur, D. C. "The Historical Buddha (Gotama), Hume, and James on the Self: Comparisons and Evaluations." *Philosophy East and West* 28, no. 3 (July 1978), 253–69.

Mathur, G. B. "Hume and Kant in Their Relation to the Pragmatic Movement." *Journal of the History of Ideas* 16, no. 2 (April 1955), 198–208.

McCormick, Miriam. "Hume, Wittgenstein, and the Impact of Skepticism." *History of Philosophy Quarterly* 21, no. 4 (October 2004), 417–34.

McGee, Robert W. "The Economic Thought of David Hume." *Hume Studies* 15, no. 1 (April 1989), 184–204.

McLendon, Hiram J. "Has Russell Answered Hume?" *The Journal of Philosophy* 49, no. 5 (February 1952), 145–59.

Merrill, Kenneth R. "Hume, Whitehead, and Philosophic Method," in *David Hume: Many-Sided Genius*, edited by Kenneth R. Merrill and Robert W. Shahan. See the section *Collections of Essays about Hume and His World* in this bibliography.

———. "Hume's 'Of Miracles', Peirce, and the Balancing of Likelihoods." *Journal of the History of Philosophy* 29, no. 1 (January 1991), 85–113.

Meyer, Paul H. "Voltaire and Hume as Historians: A Comparative Study of the *Essai sur les moeurs* and the *History of England*." *PMLA* [*Publications of the Modern Language Association*] 73, no. 1 (March 1958), 51–68.

Mijuskovic, Ben. "Hume and Shaftesbury on the Self." *The Philosophical Quarterly* 21, no. 85 (October 1971), 324–36. Cf. Clive M. Corcoran's essay "Do We Have a Shaftesburean Self in the *Treatise*?" which is listed above in this section.

Milton, J. R. "Induction Before Hume." *The British Journal for the Philosophy of Science* 38, no. 1 (March 1987), 49–74.

Moore, James. "Hume and Hutcheson," in *Hume and Hume's Connexions*, edited by M. A. Stewart and John P. Wright. See the section *Collections of Essays about Hume and His World* in this bibliography.

Morris, C. R. *Locke, Berkeley, Hume*. New York: Oxford University Press, 1931. Reprinted by Greenwood Press in 1980.

Morrisroe, Michael, Jr. "Did Hume Read Berkeley? A Conclusive Answer." *Philological Quarterly* 52 (1973), 310–15. Cf. essays on this topic by Mossner, Popkin, Flew, and Wiener.

Morrow, Glenn R. "The Significance of the Doctrine of Sympathy in Hume and Adam Smith." *The Philosophical Review* 32, no. 1 (January 1923), 60–78.

Mossner, Ernest Campbell. "Did Hume Ever Read Berkeley? A Rejoinder to Professor Popkin." *The Journal of Philosophy* 56, no. 25 (December 1959), 992–95. The essay by Popkin is listed below in this section.

Mouton, David. "Hume and Descartes on Self-Acquaintance." *Dialogue* 13, no. 2 (June 1974), 255–69.

Murphy, Richard Timothy. *Hume and Husserl: Towards Radical Subjectivism*. Boston: Martinus Nijhoff, 1980.

Nadler, Steven. "No Necessary Connection: The Medieval Roots of the Occasionalist Roots of Hume." *The Monist* 79, no. 3 (July 1996), 448–66.

Norton, David Fate. "Hume and His Scottish Critics," in *McGill Hume Studies*, edited by David Fate Norton, Nicholas Capaldi, and Wade L. Robison. See the section *Collections of Essays about Hume and His World* in this bibliography.

Olshewsky, Thomas M. "The Classical Roots of Hume's Skepticism." *Journal of the History of Ideas* 52, no. 2 (April 1991), 269–87.

Owen, David. "Hume Versus Price on Miracles and Prior Probabilities: Testimony and the Bayesian Calculation." *The Philosophical Quarterly* 37, no. 147 (April 1987), 187–202. Note: The Price referred to in the title is Hume's contemporary Richard Price.

———. "Hume and the Lockean Background: Induction and the Uniformity Principle." *Hume Studies* 18, no. 2 (November 1992), 179–207.

Pack, Spencer J., and Eric Schliesser. "Smith's Humean Criticism of Hume's Account of the Origin of Justice." *Journal of the History of Philosophy* 44, no. 1 (January 2006), 47–63.

Pakaluk, Michael. "Quine's 1946 Lectures on Hume." *Journal of the History of Philosophy* 27, no. 3 (July 1989), 445–59.

Pears. D. F. "Hume's Empiricism and Modern Empiricism," in *David Hume: A Symposium*, edited by D. F. Pears. See the section *Collections of Essays about Hume and His World* in this bibliography.

"The Peirce-Langley Correspondence and Peirce's Manuscript on Hume and the Laws of Nature (at the Smithsonian Institution)." *Proceedings of the American Philosophical Society* 91, no. 2 (April 1947), 201–28. Reprinted in *Charles S. Peirce: Selected Writings (Values in a Universe of Chance)*. Edited by Philip P. Wiener. New York: Dover Publications, 1958.

Penelhum, Terence. "Butler and Hume." *Hume Studies* 14, no. 2 (November 1988), 251–76.

Pinch, Adela. *Strange Fits of Passion: Epistemologies of Emotion, Hume to Austen*. Stanford, Calif.: Stanford University Press, 1996.

Pitson, Tony. "George Campbell's Critique of Hume on Testimony." *The Journal of Scottish Philosophy* 4, no. 1 (Spring 2006), 1–15.

Pompa, Leon. *Human Nature and Historical Knowledge: Hume, Hegel and Vico*. New York: Cambridge University Press, 1990.

Popkin, Richard H. "Hume and Kierkegaard." *The Journal of Religion* 31, no. 4 (October 1951), 274–81.

———. "The Skeptical Predecessors of David Hume." *Philosophy and Phenomenological Research* 16, no. 1 (September 1955).

———. "Did Hume Ever Read Berkeley?" *The Journal of Philosophy* 56, no. 12 (June 1959), 535–45. In this essay, Popkin asserts that Hume probably never read Berkeley or got any views from him. For responses, *see* essays (listed in this section) by Flew, Mossner, Morrisroe, and Wiener. For Popkin's own disavowal of his earlier claim, *see* the next entry.

———. "So, Hume Did Read Berkeley." *The Journal of Philosophy* 61, no. 24 (December 1964), 773–78.

Potkay, Adam. *The Passion for Happiness: Samuel Johnson and David Hume*. Ithaca, N.Y.: Cornell University Press, 2000.

Price, John Valdimir. "Sceptics in Cicero and Hume." *Journal of the History of Ideas* 25, no. 1 (January 1964), 97–106.

Radcliffe, Elizabeth. "Kantian Tunes on a Humean Instrument: Why Hume Is Not *Really* a Skeptic about Practical Reasoning." *The Canadian Journal of Philosophy* 27, no. 2 (June 1997), 247–69. Reprinted in *Hume: Moral and Political Philosophy*, edited by Rachel Cohon. See the section *Collections of Essays about Hume and His World* in this bibliography.

———. "Love and Benevolence in Hutcheson's and Hume's Theories of the Passions." *British Journal for the History of Philosophy* 12, no. 4 (November 2004), 631–53.

Raphael, D. D. " 'The true old Humean philosophy' and Its Influence on Adam Smith," in *David Hume: Bicentenary Papers*, edited by G. P. Morice. See the section *Collections of Essays about Hume and His World* in this bibliography.

Raynor, David. "Hume and Berkeley's *Three Dialogues*," in *Studies in the Philosophy of the Scottish Enlightenment*, edited by M. A. Stewart. See the section *Collections of Essays about Hume and His World* in this bibliography.

The Reception of David Hume in Europe. Edited by Peter Jones. New York: Continuum, 2006.

Reichenbach, Hans. "A Conversation Between Bertrand Russell and David Hume." *The Journal of Philosophy* 46, no. 17 (August 1949), 545–49.

Reid, Jasper. "The Metaphysics of Jonathan Edwards and David Hume." *Hume Studies* 32, no. 1 (April 2006), 53–82.

Reinach, Adolf. "Kant's Interpretation of Hume's Problem,' in *David Hume: Many-Sided Genius*, edited by Kenneth R. Merrill and Robert W. Shahan. See the section *Collections of Essays about Hume and His World* in this bibliography. Note: This is a translation of Reinach's essay "Kants Auffassung des Humeschen Problems," which first appeared in *Zeitschrift für Philosophie und philosophische Kritik* in 1908.

Richmond, Samuel A. "Newton and Hume on Causation: Alternative Strategies of Simplification." *History of Philosophy Quarterly* 11, no. 1 (January 1994), 37–52.

Rivers, Isabel. " 'Galen's Muscles': Wilkins, Hume, and the Educational Use of the Argument from Design." *The Historical Journal* 36, no. 3 (September 1993), 577–97.

———. "Responses to Hume on Religion by Anglicans and Dissenters." *Journal of Ecclesiastical History* 52, no. 4 (October 2001), 675–95.

Robison, Wade. "On the Consequential Claim That Hume is a Pragmatist." *The Journal of Critical Analysis* 4, no. 4 (January/April 1973), 141–53.

Robson, J. W. "Whitehead's Answer to Hume." *The Journal of Philosophy* 38, no. 4 (February 1941), 85–95. See related essays by Mason W. Gross (listed above in this section) and Harold Taylor (listed below).

Russell, Paul. "Hume's *Treatise* and Hobbes's *The Elements of Law*." *Journal of the History of Ideas* 46, no. 1 (January 1985), 51–63.

Seth, Andrew. *Scottish Philosophy: A Comparison of the Scottish and German Answers to Hume*. Edinburgh: W. Blackwood & Sons, 1885. Note: At age 42, Andrew Seth (1856–1931) added the surname *Pringle-Pattison* as a condition of inheriting an estate in Scotland. From that time, he used the name *Andrew Seth Pringle-Pattison*.

Shouse, J. B. "David Hume and William James: A Comparison." *Journal of the History of Ideas* 13, no. 4 (October 1952), 514–27.

Siebert, Donald T., Jr. "Johnson and Hume on Miracles." *Journal of the History of Ideas* 36, no. 3 (July 1975), 543–47.

Spencer, Mark G. *David Hume and Eighteenth-Century America*. Rochester, N.Y.: University of Rochester Press, 2005.

Stirling, J. Hutchison. "Kant Has Not Answered Hume." *Mind* 9, no. 36 (October 1884), 531–47.

Sutherland, Stewart R. "The Presbyterian Inheritance of Hume and Reid," in *The Origins and Nature of the Scottish Enlightenment*, edited by R. H. Campbell and Andrew S. Skinner. See the section *Collections of Essays about Hume and His World* in this bibliography.

Talmor, Ezra. *Descartes and Hume*. New York: Pergamon Press, 1980.

Taylor, Harold. "Hume's Answer to Whitehead." *The Journal of Philosophy* 38, no. 15 (July 1941), 409–16. See related essays by Mason W. Gross and J. W. Robson, listed above in this section.

Taylor, W. L. *Francis Hutcheson and David Hume as Predecessors of Adam Smith*. Durham, N.C.: Duke University Press, 1965.

Turbayne, C. M. "Hume's Influence on Berkeley." *Revue Internationale de Philosophie* 39, no. 154 (1985), 259–69. Note: The unexpected chronology in the title is not a slip; it is intentional.

Walton, Craig. "Hume and Jefferson on the Uses of History," in *Hume: A Reevaluation*, edited by Donald W. Livingston and James T. King. See the section *Collections of Essays about Hume and His World* in this bibliography.

Wertz, S. K. "Collingwood's Understanding of Hume." *Hume Studies* 20, no. 2 (November 1994), 261–87.

Westerman, Pauline C. "Hume and the Natural Lawyers: A Change of Landscape," in *Hume and Hume's Connexions*, edited by M. A. Stewart and John P. Wright. See the section *Collections of Essays about Hume and His World* in this bibliography.

Westphal, Kenneth R. "Hegel and Hume on Perception and Concept-Empiricism." *Journal of the History of Philosophy* 36, no. 1 (January 1998), 99–123.

Whelan, Frederick G. *Hume and Machiavelli: Political Realism and Liberal Thought.* Lanham, Md.: Lexington Books, 2004.

Wiener, Philip P. "Did Hume Ever Read Berkeley?" *The Journal of Philosophy* 56, no. 12 (June 1959), 533–35. Cf. essays on this topic by Popkin, Flew, Mossner, Morrisroe, and Wiener, which are all listed in this section.

———. "Did Hume Ever Read Berkeley?" *The Journal of Philosophy* 58, no. 8 (April 1961), 207–9.

Wilson, Douglas L. "Jefferson vs. Hume." *The William and Mary Quarterly*, 3rd Series, 46, no. 1 (January 1989), 49–70.

Wilson, Fred. "Is There a Prussian Hume? or How Far Is It from Königsberg to Edinburgh?" *Hume Studies* 8, no. 1 (April 1982), 1–18. Note: This is a response to Lewis White Beck's essay "A Prussian Hume and a Scottish Kant," which is listed above in this section.

———. "Hume's Cognitive Stoicism." *Hume Studies* 10th-Anniversary Issue (1985 Supplement), 52–65.

Winkler, Kenneth. "Hutcheson and Hume on the Color of Virtue." *Hume Studies* 22, no. 1 (April 1996), 3–22.

———. " 'All is Revolution in Us': Personal Identity in Shaftesbury and Hume." *Hume Studies* 26, no. 1 (April 2000), 3–40.

Wolff, Robert P. "Kant's Debt to Hume via Beattie." *Journal of the History of Ideas* 21, no. 1 (January 1960), 117–23.

Wolterstorff, Nicholas. "Hume and Reid." *The Monist* 70, no. 4 (October 1987), 398–417.

Wood, P. B. "Hume, Reid and the Science of the Mind," in *Hume and Hume's Connexions*, edited by M. A. Stewart and John P. Wright. See the section *Collections of Essays about Hume and His World* in this bibliography.

Wright, John P. "Butler and Hume on Habit and Moral Character," in *Hume and Hume's Connexions*, edited by M. A. Stewart and John P. Wright. See the section *Collections of Essays about Hume and His World* in this bibliography.

———. "Hume vs. Reid on Ideas: The New Hume Letter." *Mind,* New Series, 96, no. 383 (July 1987), 392–98.

Yalden-Thomson, David. "An Index of Hume's References in *A Treatise of Human Nature*." *Hume Studies* 3, no. 1 (April 1977), 53–56.

Yolton, John W. "The Concept of Experience in Locke and Hume." *Journal of the History of Philosophy* 1, no. 1 (October 1963), 53–71.

VARIA

Baier, Annette C. "Hume on Women's Complexion," in *The 'Science of Man' in the Scottish Enlightenment*, edited by Peter Jones. See the section *Collections of Essays about Hume and His World* in this bibliography.

Battersby, Christine. "An Enquiry concerning the Humean Woman." *Philosophy* 56, no. 217 (July 1981), 303–12.

Beauchamp, Tom. "An Analysis of Hume's Essay 'On [*sic*] Suicide'." *The Review of Metaphysics* 30, no. 1 (September 1976), 73–95.

Brunius, Teddy. *David Hume on Criticism*. Stockholm: Almqvist & Wiksell, 1952.

Burns, Steven. "The Humean Female." *Dialogue* 15, no. 3 (September 1976), 415–24.

Cohen, Ralph. "David Hume's Experimental Method and the Theory of Taste." *ELH* [*English Literary History*] 25, no. 4 (December 1958), 270–89.

———. "The Transformation of Passion: A Study of Hume's Theories of Tragedy." *Philological Quarterly* 41, no. 2 (April 1962), 450–64.

———. "The Rationale of Hume's Literary Inquiries," in *David Hume: Many-Sided Genius*, edited by Kenneth R. Merrill and Robert W. Shahan. See the section *Collections of Essays about Hume and His World* in this bibliography.

David Hume: Writings on Economics. Edited with an introduction by Eugene Rotwein. Madison: University of Wisconsin Press, 1970. Originally published in 1955 by University of Wisconsin Press and by Thomas Nelson.

The Dictionary of Eighteenth-Century British Philosophers. 2 volumes. Edited by John W. Yolton, John Valdimir Price, and John Stephens. Bristol, England: Thoemmes Press, 1999.

Early Responses to Hume's Moral, Literary, and Political Writings. Two volumes. Edited by James Fieser. Bristol, England: Thoemmes Press, 1999.

Encyclopedia of Empiricism. Edited by Don Garrett and Edward Barbanell. Westport, Conn.: Greenwood Press, 1997.

Eze, Emmanuel C. "Hume, Race, and Human Nature." *Journal of the History of Ideas* 61, no. 4 (October 2000), 691–98.

Frey, R. G. "Hume on Suicide." *The Journal of Medicine and Philosophy* 24, no. 4 (August 1999), 336–51.

Holden, Thomas. "Religion and Moral Prohibition in Hume's 'Of Suicide'." *Hume Studies* 31, no. 2 (November 2005), 189–210.

A Hotbed of Genius: The Scottish Enlightenment 1730–1790. Edited by David Daiches, Peter Jones, and Jean Jones. Edinburgh: Edinburgh University Press, 1986.

Jones, Peter. "Hume's Aesthetics Reassessed." *The Philosophical Quarterly* 26, no. 102 (January 1976), 48–62.

———. "On Reading Hume's *History of Liberty*," in *Liberty in Hume's 'History of England'*, edited by Nicholas Capaldi and Donald W. Livingston. See the section *Collections of Essays about Hume and His World* in this bibliography.

———. "Hume's Literary and Aesthetic Theory," in *The Cambridge Companion to Hume*, edited by David Fate Norton. See the section *Collections of Essays about Hume and His World* in this bibliogrpahy.

Kivy, Peter. "Hume's Standard of Taste: Breaking the Circle." *British Journal of Aesthetics* 7, no. 1 (January 1967), 57–66.

———. "Hume's Neighbour's Wife: An Essay on the Evolution of Hume's Aesthetics." *British Journal of Aesthetics* 23, no. 3 (July 1983), 195–208.

Lacoste, Louise Marcil. "The Consistency of Hume's Position concerning Women." *Dialogue* 15, no. 3 (September 1976), 425–40.

Lloyd Thomas, D. A. "Hume and Intrinsic Value." *Philosophy* 65, no. 254 (October 1990), 419–37.

Malherbe, Michel. "Hume and the Art of Dialogue," in *Hume and Hume's Connexions*, edited by M. A. Stewart and John P. Wright. See the section *Collections of Essays about Hume and His World* in this bibliography.

Mason, Michelle. "Moral Prejudice and Aesthetic Deformity: Rereading Hume's 'Of the Standard of Taste'." *The Journal of Aesthetics and Art Criticism* 59, no. 1 (Winter 2001), 59–71.

Marshall, David. "Arguing by Analogy: Hume's Standard of Taste." *Eighteenth-Century Studies* 28, no. 3 (Spring 1995), 323–43.

Mayer, Thomas. "David Hume and Monetarism." *The Quarterly Journal of Economics* 95, no. 1 (August 1980), 89–101.

McLean, G. R. "Hume and the Theistic Objection to Suicide." *American Philosophical Quarterly* 38, no. 1 (January 2000), 99–111.

Merrill, Kenneth R. "Hume on Suicide." *History of Philosophy Quarterly* 16, no. 4 (October 1999), 395–412.

Mossner, Ernest Campbell. "Was Hume a Tory Historian? Facts and Reconsiderations." *Journal of the History of Ideas* 2, no. 2 (April 1941), 225–36.

———. "An Apology for David Hume, Historian." *PMLA* [*Publications of the Modern Language Association*] 56, no. 3 (September 1941), 657–90.

Mothersill, Mary. "In Defense of Hume and the Causal Theory of Taste." *The Journal of Aesthetics and Art Criticism* 55, no. 3 (Summer 1997), 312–17.

Noel, Carroll. "Hume's Standard of Taste." *The Journal of Aesthetics and Art Criticism* 43, no. 2 (Winter 1984), 181–94.

Noxon, James. "Hume's Opinion of Critics." *The Journal of Aesthetics and Art Criticism* 20, no. 2 (Winter 1961), 157–62.

Perricone, Christopher. "The Body and Hume's Standard of Taste." *The Journal of Aesthetics and Art Criticism* 53, no. 4 (Fall 1995), 371–78.

Phillipson, Nicholas. *Hume*. New York: St. Martin's Press, 1989. This book is not a general study of Hume, as its one-word title may suggest. It is, rather, a study of Hume the historian-philosopher or the philosophical historian.

Pocock, J. G. A. "Hume and the American Revolution: The Dying Thoughts of a North Briton," in *McGill Hume Studies*, edited by David Fate Norton, Nicholas Capaldi, and Wade L. Robison. See the section *Collections of Essays about Hume and His World* in this bibliography.

Popkin, Richard H. "Hume: Philosophical Versus Prophetic Historian," in *David Hume: Many-Sided Genius*, edited by Kenneth R. Merrill and Robert W. Shahan. See the section *Collections of Essays about Hume and His World* in this bibliography.

Potkay, Adam. *The Fate of Eloquence in the Age of Hume*. Ithaca, N.Y.: Cornell University Press, 1994.

Richetti, John J. *Philosophical Writing: Locke, Berkeley, Hume*. Cambridge, Mass.: Harvard University Press, 1983.

Rotwein, Eugene. "David Hume, Philosopher-Economist," in *David Hume: Many-Sided Genius*, edited by Kenneth R. Merrill and Robert W. Shahan. See the section *Collections of Essays about Hume and His World* in this bibliography.

Sabine, George H. "Hume's Contribution to the Historical Method." *The Philosophical Review* 15, no. 1 (January 1906), 17–38.

Shiner, Roger A. "Hume and the Causal Theory of Taste." *The Journal of Aesthetics and Art Criticism* 54, no. 3 (Summer 1996), 237–49.

Siebert, Donald T. *The Moral Animus of David Hume*. Newark, Del.: University of Delaware Press, 1990. The title of this book offers no clue that it "treats the *History of England* as a primary document" —a focus that distinguishes it from most other studies of Hume's moral philosophy.

Stockton, Constant Noble. "Hume—Historian of the English Constitution." *Eighteenth-Century Studies* 4, no. 3 (Spring 1971), 277–93.

Temple, Kathryn. " 'Manly Composition': Hume and the *History of England*," in *Feminist Interpretations of David Hume*, edited by Anne Jaap Jacobson. See the section *Collections of Essays about Hume and His World* in this bibliography.

Townsend, Dabney. *Hume's Aesthetic Theory: Taste and Sentiment*. New York: Routledge, 2001.

Trevor-Roper, H. R. "Hume as a Historian," in *David Hume: A Symposium*, edited by D. F. Pears. See the section *Collections of Essays about Hume and His World* in this bibliography.

Vickers, Douglas. "Method and Analysis in Hume's Economic Essays." *Economica*, New Series, 24, no. 95 (August 1957), 225–34.

Wertz, Spencer K. *Between Hume's Philosophy and History: Historical Theory and Practice.* Lanham, Md.: University Press of America, 2000.

Wexler, Victor. *David Hume and the 'History of England'.* Philadelphia: American Philosophical Society, 1979.

Wieand, Jeffrey. "Hume's Two Standards of Taste." *The Philosophical Quarterly* 34, no. 135 (April 1984), 129–42.

Wootton, David. "David Hume, 'the Historian'," in *The Cambridge Companion to Hume*, edited by David Fate Norton. See the section *Collections of Essays about Hume and His World* in this bibliography.

About the Author

Kenneth R. Merrill (Ph.D., Northwestern University, Evanston, Illinois) is professor of philosophy emeritus and former department chair at the University of Oklahoma, where he taught for 47 years. His research interests are mainly in 17th- and 18th-century British and continental philosophy and American philosophy. He has published essays and book chapters in those areas and has presented papers in a variety of scholarly venues. He edited and contributed a paper to a book commemorating the 200th anniversary of Hume's death: *David Hume: Many-Sided Genius*. Merrill's interest in Hume was first seriously piqued when he was writing a doctoral dissertation on Alfred North Whitehead, whose attitude toward Hume is curiously ambivalent, ranging from sharp criticism to almost extravagant admiration. Merrill's own admiration for both of these philosophical geniuses continues unabated to this day.